Religion and the Rise of Jim Crow
in New Orleans

Religion and the Rise of Jim Crow in New Orleans

James B. Bennett

PRINCETON UNIVERSITY PRESS

PRINCETON AND OXFORD

Copyright © 2005 by Princeton University Press
Published by Princeton University Press,
41 William Street, Princeton, New Jersey 08540
In the United Kingdom: Princeton University Press,
3 Market Place, Woodstock, Oxfordshire OX20 1SY

Library of Congress Cataloging-in-Publication Data

Bennett, James B., 1969–
Religion and the rise of Jim Crow in New Orleans / James B. Bennett.
p.   cm.
Includes index.
ISBN 0-691-12148-6 (alk. paper)
1. African Americans—Segregation—Louisiana—New Orleans—
History—19th century. 2. Segregation—Religious aspects—Methodist
Church—History—19th century. 3. Segregation—Religious aspects—
Catholic Church—History—19th century. 4. New Orleans (La.)—
Race relations—History—19th century. 5. New Orleans (La.)—Church
history—19th century. I. Title.
F379.N59N4 2005
305.8′009763′3509034—dc22   2004049130

British Library Cataloging-in-Publication Data is available.

This book has been composed in Janson

Printed on acid-free paper. ∞

www.pup.princeton.edu

Printed in the United States of America

10   9   8   7   6   5   4   3   2   1

14140272

For Amy, Megan, & Nicholas

Contents

List of Illustrations

Acknowledgments

THIS WORK HAS BEEN far more perspiration than inspiration, and while I will gladly take credit for the perspiration, I must confess that much of the inspiration has come from others. The support of both individuals and institutions for this project has never ceased to amaze me, making the often lonely task of research and writing less so.

The Center on Religion and Democracy at the University of Virginia provided a post-doctoral fellowship that enabled me to complete the manuscript. That same year I was a fellow of the Center for the Study of Religion and American Life at Yale University. While the financial support and release time the fellowships provided were invaluable, the conversations, both formal and informal, that accompanied the conferences these institutes sponsored were equally important. At Santa Clara University, Catherine Bell, chair of the Department of Religious Studies, and the dean's office of the College of Arts and Sciences graciously allowed me to accept those fellowships despite having just arrived. Santa Clara University provided additional support in the form of a Thomas Terry Research Grant. Previously, a Junior Faculty Fellowship from the University of Oklahoma enabled me to begin research that made its way into this manuscript. A Charlotte W. Newcombe dissertation fellowship and a fellowship from Pew Program in Religion and American History at Yale University supported the research and writing of the dissertation on which this manuscript is based.

Portions drawn from chapters five, six, and seven originally appeared in an essay entitled "Catholics, Creoles and the Redefinition of Race in New Orleans," in *Race, Nation, and Religion in the Americas*, edited by Henry Goldschmidt and Elizabeth A. McAlister (New York: Oxford University Press, 2004). I am grateful to Oxford University Press for permission to reuse much of that material.

I have benefited from the resources of many libraries and archives, and the expert knowledge and generosity of their archivists and staffs, including, the African American Religion Documentary History Project at Amherst University; the General Commission on Archives and History of the United Methodist Church; the Dillard University Archives and Special Collections; the Special Collections Department, Hill Memorial Library, Louisiana State University; the Manuscripts Department and Louisiana Collection, Tulane University; Archives, Manuscripts and Special Collections, Earl K. Long Library, University of New Orleans; the Williams Research Center at the Historic New Orleans Collection; and the Archives of the Sisters of the Blessed Sacrament in Bensalem, Pennsylvania. I am especially grateful to Brenda Square at the Amistad Research Center, Peter Hogan at the Josephite Fathers Archives, and Charles Nolan at the Archives of the Archdiocese of New Orleans, all of whom remained unfailingly helpful and kind during my multiple visits to their archives and unending inquiries as to whether they had anything else related to my topic. During my first research trip to New Orleans, Lester Sullivan at the Xavier University Archives and Special Collections directed my attention to A.E.P. Albert and the untapped potential of the *Southwestern Christian Advocate*. In the final weeks of preparing the manuscript, Mark Shinese at the General Commission on Archives and History of the United Methodist Church proved especially helpful in securing illustrations of leading Methodists in New Orleans.

Many friends and colleagues have been generous with their time in reading and discussing sections of the manuscript with me, answering inquiries large and small, and provoking my thinking on related matters. Thank you, Jon Baer, Lila Corwin Berman, Scott Cormode, Lara Diefenderfer, Julia Erhhardt, Aaron Frith, Paul Fitzgerald, Rich Hamerla, John Giggie, Cathy Gudis, Amy Koehlinger, Kip Kosek, Emily Epstein Landau, Mark Oppenheimer, Jackie Robinson, Jana Riess, Sarah Tracy, Rachel Wheeler, and Diana Williams. Michael Alexander deserves special mention. We first met as teaching assistants, researched at adjoining microfilm machines in the basement of the library, and ended up as colleagues in our first jobs at the University of Oklahoma. He has read the entire manuscript, parts of it several times, and always matched critical insight with graciousness, provided me with good counsel, and taught me the finer points of enjoying good barbecue.

The Honors College at the University of Oklahoma provided the ideal place to begin a scholarly career, and I will remain forever grateful to the faculty, staff and administration of the Honors College for their confidence in me, their unfailing support and generosity, and their camaraderie, both personal and professional.

Several scholars working in similar areas or on related topics provided me with insight and guidance, some in conversations I'm sure they have forgotten they ever had, and others in generous gifts of their time: Caryn Bell, Donald DeVore, Kent Germany, Christine Heyrman, Joseph Logsdon, Anne Loveland, Lawrence Powell, and David Wills. Paul Harvey, John McGreevy, and Judith Weisenfeld all read the manuscript in its entirety, providing encouragement and offering useful suggestions for improvement.

The hardest part of concluding this project is the end of my excuses to travel regularly to New Orleans. Beyond the archivists I have already mentioned, there is also a vibrant community of scholars who not only taught me the history of the city they too were studying, but also introduced me to the city itself. Karen Leathem was the first to welcome me, introducing me to scholars and resources in my field, and continued to point me in the right direction on subsequent visits. Alecia Long was once a host and several times a resource for easing my ignorance of the history of the city, sharing with me her own work in progress. Ros Hinton opened her home on many occasions, enlightened me on aspects of the city's M. E. churches that I did not know, all the while showing me the finer points of Crescent City food and music. Emily Clark was host par excellence, ensuring my comfort on every one of my visits, providing stimulating conversation and useful introductions, and inspiring a passion for good food, good drink, and good scholarship.

Although this study sits well outside their specific areas of research, without the influence and guidance of three teachers I would have long ago apostatized from American religious history. In my final quarter as an undergraduate at UCLA, David Hall introduced me to the joys of research and to the possibility of a career in American religious history. At Princeton Theological Seminary, James Moorhead clarified the path and paved its way, while Ed Gaustad ensured that I could walk along it.

Long before I could articulate the possibility and the promise of this project, my graduate-school advisors saw its potential and skillfully guided me to its completion. Jon Butler, Glenda Gilmore, and Skip Stout have been supportive beyond what words can convey. They are each outstanding teachers, stimulating scholars, and gracious individuals who have continued to be generous with their time and guidance long after I graduated. I was incredibly lucky to have them as advisors—even luckier to count them as friends.

My parents have been unfailing supporters of a project that has seemed endless. Both are teachers, and one a Christian educator, by profession, so it was perhaps inevitable that I ended up teaching and researching religion. From them I learned both the value of education and role of religion in daily living. These gifts are ones that I hope this book and my own teaching career can somehow repay.

This book is dedicated to those closest to me who continually provide me with joy. My children, Megan and Nicholas, arrived while I was working on this book, and every day is better because of them. May they grow into a faith that sustains hope, and a church that confronts injustice wherever it occurs.

My wife, Amy, will deny any contribution to the content of this book. Indeed, her own demanding professional career and role as breadwinner for a graduate student then an academic, not to mention her tireless dedication as a mother, have been contribution enough. Yet this book could not have been written without her. Her support and love have enabled every sentence that follows. This project has been a load we have carried a long way, both figuratively, as a persistent presence in our lives, and more literally, as we have moved the weight of books and papers from one coast to the other. That journey has not only been possible, but also infinitely good, because she has been there every step of the way.

Introduction

"WHERE THE WHITES and colored are both numerous, the Church is exposed to peculiar trials and demands especial sympathy and aid." The warning came in 1873 from the Reverend Erastus Haven, a northern white minister in the racially mixed Methodist Episcopal (M. E.) Church. In New Orleans, the predominantly black membership of the M. E. Church reprinted Haven's admonition in their weekly newspaper, the *Southwestern Christian Advocate*. The Crescent City church members shared Haven's conviction that biracial denominations shouldered a unique burden to prevent segregation. Haven was writing against a proposal to divide black and white M. E. church members into separate jurisdictions. Neither Haven nor his supporters in New Orleans favored division along racial lines. Believing that "the Church is preeminently the fountain and regulator of social life," they recognized that segregation within religious institutions encouraged and justified segregation in every other aspect of American society.[1] Nowhere were these links between church and society more conspicuous than in the racially and religiously complex city of New Orleans. Nor were Haven and his Crescent City compatriots alone in privileging the power of religion to shape the southern racial order. Whether black or white, Catholic or Protestant, late–nineteenth-century church members recognized that patterns of racial inclusion and exclusion within religious institutions would affect the nation's race relations.

During the final quarter of the nineteenth century, church members in New Orleans and the South privileged the importance of their churches in shaping the era's most pressing issue: how black and white residents should interact in a democratic and predominantly Christian society. Many who offered the church as a model for race relations came from racially mixed denominations, especially the Roman Catholic and Methodist Episcopal Churches, whose ongoing racial interaction offered a bulwark against rapidly advancing discrimination. They believed their churches could extend gains made in the secular arena during Reconstruction. Especially in Louisiana, a decade of Reconstruction accomplishments had fostered great hope among African Americans. Black citizens formed a majority of delegates at the state's 1867 constitutional convention, producing a document that guaranteed black political participation and mandated equal accommodations in public spaces. The constitution also prohibited segregated public schools, resulting in New Orleans's unique and brief experiment with integrated education. The Crescent City's black residents had lived the possibility of a better future as they entered the public schools, pursued new business opportunities, and filled a number of elected offices, including the governorship for a brief period in 1872.[2] Interracial opportunities diminished as the federal troops who had enforced civil rights departed when Reconstruction ended in 1877 and Democratic white supremacists, called Redeemers, regained control.[3]

Biracial denominations took on new significance in the uncertain post-Reconstruction racial milieu. Churches in late-nineteenth-century New Orleans fostered important moments of interracial cooperation that ran counter to the predominant separatist tendencies. Catholics of color were leading supporters, both financially and numerically, of many of the city's Catholic parishes. In turn, they received the support of Catholic leaders for inclusion in both the religious and the social orders. At the same time, biracial Protestant denominations, especially the M. E. and Congregational churches, engaged in a variety of explicit and frequently provocative interracial work, from social interaction during denominational meetings and biracial educational institutions, to advocating political, social, and racial reform. These efforts fostered a hope as important as the despair that often countered them. The wide range of biracial religious accomplishments, even when not based on equality, challenged both the prevailing racial order and the example of racially separate denominations that have figured so largely in Americans' historical imagination. Pointing to their accomplishments, church members believed that southern society could likewise retreat from segregation and turn toward the racially inclusive models of mixed-race denominations. Well into the 1890s, most black and a few white members of biracial denominations hoped that a shared religious identity could transcend racial difference as the primary category of identification.

Privileging religious over racial identities would have far-reaching consequences. The struggle for an integrated society remained inextricably intertwined with religious practices. Church members insisted that the examples and efforts of religious institutions could turn back the rising tide of Jim Crow and thereby transform the South's racial future. Resisting racial separation in churches simultaneously bolstered opposition to segregation in the political, economic, and social realms. When churches refused to succumb to separation, they created patterns that politicians, educators, and businesses could follow in their own treatment of African Americans. Throughout the final decades of the nineteenth century, black and white Christians were confident the choices their denominations made would shape the nation's race relations. By 1920 those church members would be proven correct, but with consequences devastatingly contrary to their original hope.

Historians have often overlooked these important links between religion and the rise of Jim Crow. The underlying assumption remains that black and white Christians moved toward racial separation immediately after Emancipation, thereby eliminating religion's engagement with the secular segregation debates that arose in the 1890s. Indeed, many African Americans in the 1860s exercised their newfound freedom by leaving the churches of their masters and forming separate black Baptist or African Methodist congregations. Their exit was a matter of choice, not a result of coercion, since many white congregations preferred to retain their black members as a means of social control. These freely chosen acts of religious self-separation are distant, in form as well as chronology, from the white-imposed and legally mandated political and social Jim Crow practices that became pervasive in the 1890s. If churches settled the question of racial separation by 1870, religion had little or no bearing on the racial struggles that plagued the secular arena almost two generations later. As a result, churches escape direct responsibility for the trajectory of southern race relations at the turn of the twentieth century.

But this prevailing denominational and chronological focus obscures the larger picture. Independent black denominations are not the appropriate comparison, even though whites pointed to them as evidence that black Southerners preferred segregation. Because African Americans formed separate denominations as an assertion of their own free will, their separate churches were qualitatively different from segregated institutions. Unlike the African-American initiative for self-separation in the 1860s, the segregation of biracial denominations between 1890 and 1920 was solely the product of white coercion. The actions of these racially mixed denominations form the more appropriate comparison and entryway into the connections between segregation in church and in society.

The struggles of the nation's two largest racially mixed denominations in the South's largest city illuminate these overlooked connections between religion and the rise of Jim Crow. The religious landscape of New Orleans between 1877 and 1920 challenges the assumption that churches resorted to racial separation immediately after Emancipation. Within the Methodist Episcopal and Roman Catholic Churches, fixed patterns of segregation did not emerge until the second decade of the twentieth century. Well into the 1910s, the city's Catholic parishes served both black and white Catholics, while the M. E. Church in New Orleans continued to be a center of biracial leadership. Crescent City churches interacted with and advocated integration, not just segregation, in the decades after Reconstruction. Religious and racial practices remained intertwined as the move toward church segregation occurred concurrently with efforts to institute Jim Crow in the social and political arenas. Biracial churches adopted the coercive approaches used in secular society, while political leaders defended separatism by pointing to religious examples. By the late nineteenth century, both those who advocated and those who resisted separation insisted that neither the timing nor the methods distinguished debates within the secular and religious arenas. The two were inseparable: one merely reinforced and provided justification for the other. Church members in turn-of-the-century New Orleans recognized that religious segregation was intimately related and ultimately contributed to segregation in southern society at large.

The experiences of Methodist Episcopal and Roman Catholic church members highlight these connections between religion and segregation. For much of the period of this study, Catholics and Methodists were the two largest Christian denominations in the United States. Catholics had become the nation's largest Christian tradition by 1850, a position they have yet to relinquish. Among Protestants, the M. E. Church remained the nation's largest racially mixed Protestant denomination, even when Baptists surpassed Methodists in absolute numbers in the late nineteenth century. In 1920, the M. E. Church claimed three-quarters of all African Americans who belonged to racially mixed denominations.[4] Each of these nationally prominent traditions considered New Orleans the center of its work in the American South. New Orleans was unquestionably the hub of Catholicism in the Deep South. It was the first Catholic see south of Baltimore, and the third in the nation to be elevated to the status of archdiocese. The regions subject to the New Orleans province extended west into Texas and east across the Gulf States. By the mid-nineteenth century, American Catholic leaders regularly looked to New Orleans for guidance on questions of race. The M. E. Church likewise centered much of its southern effort, especially among African Americans, in New Orleans. Only Atlanta approached its importance. As one denominational official explained, "from no point in the South can the Church command so many lines of influence in molding this whole Southern territory for Christ as she can from New Orleans." Other denominations, from Baptists to Congregationalists, also established a range of institutions in New Orleans in recognition of the city's importance for church work in the South. Among the city's black churches, only Baptists could claim more than the M. E. Church. In 1876, the M. E. Church signaled the city's significance by adopting the New Orleans–based *Southwestern Christian Advocate* as the official weekly newspaper for its African-American members. As evidence of New Orleans's ongoing stature, many of the M. E. Church's black leaders between 1880 and 1920 either were from New Orleans and southern Louisiana or had spent time working in the Crescent City in an official denominational capacity.[5]

Catholics and Methodists in New Orleans underwent different, yet strikingly parallel, racial transformations. Different histories led each tradition to contrasting relations to its black members in 1877. The M. E. Church experienced remarkable success in gaining church members during Reconstruction, more than any other northern-based denomination. Although attracted by a rhetoric of equality and inclusion, black and white M. E. church members nearly always worshiped in separate congregations. Racial mixing in the M. E. Church occurred primarily at the regional and national levels. In contrast, Catholics, who lost more black members than they gained between Emancipation and the end of Reconstruction, nonetheless maintained racially mixed parishes in New Orleans. Yet the institutional ranks at the center of Catholic identity, from the priesthood upward, remained closed to Catholics of color. Efforts to resist the spread of segregation thus had different focuses in the two denominations. Ironically, in the hierarchical and institutionally oriented Catholic Church, the struggles took place at the local, parish level. Racial struggles among Methodists, whose American origins emphasized local societies over institutional structures, concentrated first on regional and later on national denominational structures. But different starting points did not result in different outcomes. The two traditions converged in practice, as each moved from resisting to instituting segregation at all levels.

As a history of church segregation, this study focuses on the midpoint between traditional conceptions of religion. It is not primarily about theology or the more broadly construed categories of myth and ritual. Nor is this traditional church history, despite considerable attention to the changing character of denominational institutions. Rather, the focus is on the lived space between these two categories: the intersection and frequent tension between belief and practice. At the center are the experiences of church members and local leaders as they struggled with the meanings of race and the obligations of their churches. For African Americans, segregation was a religious and moral issue wherever it happened. Black church members frequently invoked biblical and theological doctrines to critique segregation both within and beyond their churches. Perhaps aware of the inconsistencies, whites avoided religious language when they used churches to advance their segregationist agenda. White church members defended segregation in light of institutional rather than theological concerns. But segregation became a religious issue when it entered churches, white protests to the contrary. Religious institutions manifest underlying beliefs without having to articulate them. The shape that religious institutions take and the way that people experience them—or are excluded from them—are as much an expression of religious beliefs and values as appeals to theological principles. Action and behavior best illuminate the role of religion in resisting and eventually creating a segregated society. In the highly contested experience of segregation, few could afford the luxury of engaging in extended theological analysis or doctrinal debates. Nonetheless, questions of inclusion and exclusion were central to the way Southerners lived their religion on a daily basis. This study takes these people's experiences as the guiding narrative, pointing to underlying beliefs when possible or evident. Theologies of segregation and integration emerge upon occasion, but this book is not an exploration of these largely hidden aspects. Given the sophistication of biblical defenses of slavery built on presumed racial inferiority, the lack of similar justifications of segregation is striking and ripe for further examination. But it remains largely outside the scope of this study. Rather, people's behavior and the way it shaped churches to include or exclude others remain the focus. This is the place where most Southerners, white no less than black, lived their faith.

NEW ORLEANS MAY APPEAR an unusual choice to study such typically American problems of religion and race, given its reputation as exceptional in both history and the popular imagination. Its French and Spanish colonial history created a cultural and linguistic flavor that distinguished it from the predominantly British-American culture of the rest of the United States. The Catholic majority and influence of Caribbean religious traditions proved an important basis for Anglo-Americans to differentiate and deride New Orleans. The city's racial structure also contrasted with that of most of the nation. From colonial times, the United States advanced a binary racial classification that limited racial categories to black and white. New Orleans and southern Louisiana, on the other hand, embraced a triracial caste system more typical of Caribbean and South American societies. Between white and black stood Creoles of color, who embraced the Latin culture inherited from their mixed parentage or ancestry. Many of these Creoles had descended from antebellum free people of color who had long pursued education and professions in ways not available to most persons of African descent elsewhere in the United States. While Creoles of color were not granted equality with whites, both black and white residents of Louisiana recognized them as a distinct social and racial class.[6]

Yet New Orleans's unique characteristics make it a rich locale for a study of religion and race in the postbellum South. The latter's changing religious attitudes about race coincided with similar transformations in New Orleans society, which moved the city from the periphery to the center of American racial dynamics. As the largest city in the South, New Orleans epitomized the urban context in which racial interaction often took place. The large Catholic presence in New Orleans provides an unparalleled opportunity to compare Catholic and Protestant responses to race. In addition, New Orleans's highly literate black leaders, a legacy of the city's antebellum free black community, produced a body of writings that provide access to the city's postbellum black community. Creoles of color and the triracial social system also complicated race relations in ways that forced the city's residents to express their thinking on racial issues more explicitly than elsewhere in the South. After 1877, Creoles of color lost their distinct status as New Orleans shifted from its triracial order to the biracialism more typical of the United States.[7] This transformation occurred at the same time that churches redefined their racial policies and lowered their tolerance of racial interaction. The changing place of the city's Creoles of color thus serves as a measure of changing conceptions of race and of the shifting relationship between religion and segregation. The hardening of these racial lines in New Orleans coincided with similar processes in cities and churches throughout the American South. As a commentator noted in 1900, given New Orleans's unique history, "it would seem that our city should be extremely liberal on the color question, but to the contrary we dare say there is no city in the South more sensitive in this particular."[8] From its segregation laws to its reconfigured racial order, New Orleans had become a typically southern and American city by the turn of the twentieth century. During these transformations, Catholic and Methodist racial practices in New Orleans affected and were affected by national trends within each denomination, bringing these traditions, their members, and the Crescent City into the larger sweep of American religious history.

THE HISTORY OF RACIALLY mixed denominations in New Orleans opens a window into the complex and highly contested emergence of segregation. Churches in late-nineteenth-century New Orleans facilitated an interracial cooperation that challenged a growing emphasis on separation. When members of biracial churches resisted segregation, they delayed its emergence and preserved moments when alternative possibilities persisted. Attention to these accomplishments in the religious sphere joins with recent analyses of labor, politics, and gender to point to a time when racial practices retained a degree of flexibility that required explicit regulation to eliminate the fluidity that so concerned white segregationists. These often overlooked alternatives explain why African Americans maintained hope in the face of increasing racial hostility. The evidence and later memory of promising alternatives, however unlikely their widespread acceptance, challenged any claim that segregation represented either an unchanging pattern or an instinctive human need. Black church members took hope in churches' ability to outlast many other forms of racial interaction, believing that divine guidance sustained this important example. They hoped God might even expand the church's influence to transform the social order, a faith justified by confidence in God's role in freeing the slaves through the Civil War. In New Orleans, geographic proximity and historical ties to Caribbean and South American societies reinforced the contingent character of segregation. White as well as black residents were aware of more flexible racial patterns that did not resort to strict segregation in a black/white binary, which arbitrarily defined as black anyone with a single drop of African blood. Acceptance of racial mixing in other societies, such as that of Brazil, joined with the example of mixed-race denominations to bolster New Orleanians' hopes that segregation was not the only alternative.[9]

Highlighting racially mixed denominations also brings to light forgotten voices in the struggle against segregation. A few of these voices came from white church members, their cries long lost in the overwhelming roar of those who insisted on segregation. Also overlooked have been African Americans who remained in biracial denominations as an intentional protest against segregation in religious and social spheres alike, and who represent an important but often neglected dimension of black religious experience. These black citizens recognized that church membership was a racial and political statement, not just a religious one. The politics of race and the politics of religion interpenetrated one another. Black members of mixed denominations insisted that both separation by choice, as in the African Methodist traditions, and segregation by force, as in the rise of Jim Crow laws and practices, necessitated resistance if there was to be any hope for integration in either church or society. African-American church members argued that fighting against a segregated social order required, by definition, rejecting racially separate denominations. Their arguments challenged conceptions of the black church as a place of retreat from the racial politics and oppression of the Jim Crow era. Black members of biracial denominations understood their churches as a critical way to engage and transform the larger society that was oppressing them rather than as places of withdrawal or even as safe arenas to practice protest and politics for a later time.

The conflicts that emerged between racially mixed and self-segregated denominations recapitulated similar struggles within the broader African-American community. The debates were especially fierce among Methodists. African Methodists on one side and M. E. church members on the other questioned each other's commitment to the best interests of the race. Those who argued for withdrawing into racially exclusive churches in response to discrimination and segregation did not constitute the only voices concerned with racial advancement. The experiences of black M. E. church members, and Catholics as well, demonstrate that the strategy of withdrawal was highly contested within the black community. Nonetheless, historians have long taken the arguments for separation put forward by racially exclusive denominations, especially the A.M.E. Church, to represent African-American Christians as a whole. Just as there were multiple social and political approaches, most often represented in the debates between Booker T. Washington and W.E.B. Du Bois, so were there multiple religious models for fighting segregation. Those who remained in biracial denominations were confident they represented the best hope for overcoming racial prejudice in church and society alike. They understood their ongoing loyalty as courageous, not as accommodationist, as their critics charged. Black church members remained in biracial denominations to hold their churches accountable to the higher ideals on which they were based, just as African Americans would remain in the United States to hold their nation accountable to its democratic principles. This book privileges these alternative voices in the struggle for equal rights in the late-nine-teenth- and early-twentieth-century South.

This study also complicates assumptions about Methodist and Catholic conceptions of race. White Methodist and white Catholic views on race often stand for the whole. But that is not the entire story. Black M. E. church members and black Catholics brought differing and religiously compelling understandings of Christianity and race to their denominational traditions. Their oft-forgotten arguments challenge the easy tendency to generalize about a particular denomination's racial claims. In the conventional wisdom, neither Catholics nor Methodists considered segregation in religious and moral terms until almost the middle of the twentieth century. But this is only partially true. When we include the black voices in these denominations, a long tradition insisting on theological dimensions of segregation emerges. To claim that biracial denominations did not care about segregation or were unable to speak about it in religious terms is to tell only part of the story. To hear black M. E. and black Catholic voices is to hear differing perspectives that were nonetheless grounded in the particularities of Catholic and Methodist social and theological histories. Though long suppressed, these black voices would emerge in the second half of the twentieth century to shape Methodist and Catholic reflections on the meaning of the church and the inclusion of diverse religious and theological viewpoints.

This emphasis on forgotten possibilities does not point to an unconventional ending. The nearly inexorable force of segregation became pervasive in religion and society alike. But the presence of interracial moments is as important as their collapse. Segregation did not mark a continuation of existing racial practices. The rigid racial structures in Methodism and Catholicism of the 1920s were very different from the flexible relations that lasted from the 1870s into the 1890s. Nor were the highly regulated interactions of 1920 mere codifications of earlier unofficial practices. The change was dramatic: traumatic for blacks, reassuring for whites. Segregated institutions resulted from a long, slow, complicated, and highly contentious journey that extended many decades after Emancipation. This emerging segregation, in churches no less than in other aspects of southern society, represented a reaction against alternate possibilities rather than a perpetuation of existing racial practices. Whites could not point to a continuous line of segregated structures, even if they claimed a continuity of racialist thinking. The recovery of alternative patterns of racial interac-

tion and the voices who advocated them only heightens the tragedy associated with segregation. The triumph of religious segregation resulted from
intentionally foreclosed opportunities, from deliberate and distressing decisions to make abrupt changes in course that disintegrated the hopeful
precedents of previous decades. The role of black church members and
their white allies illuminates how hard fought the battle to retain integration remained. Their struggles also reveal the brutality of white efforts to
close spaces of racial interaction. The need to institute new structures of
racial separation, from streetcars and ballot boxes to Catholic parishes and
Methodist annual conferences, testifies to the ongoing white insecurities
about the perpetuation of racial hierarchies.[10]

The emergence of religious segregation also stands as a reminder that
segregation was not solely a southern problem. The Methodist Episcopal
and Roman Catholic churches' capitulation to segregation was a national
and not merely a regional phenomenon. More than southern counterparts, such as the Southern Baptist or Southern Methodist denominations,
these larger traditions bear much of the burden for segregation in American religion. Most African Americans had left the southern denominations
for either separate black or racially mixed churches. Southern Methodists,
Southern Baptists, and Southern Presbyterians had little power to institute
religious segregation since the mass exodus of black members left them
racially separate by default. The northern or national denominations, in
contrast, faced deliberate choices. At the urging of northern even more
than southern voices, white majorities surrendered to segregation. Assum-
ing segregation to be solely a southern problem and, in the case of religion,
mistakenly associating it only with southern and African-American denominations distract from the crucial contributions of northern and national organizations to the spread of Jim Crow. Just as the national Republican Party, through northern influence, accepted white supremacy, and
the federal government accommodated southern patterns and abandoned
involvement in voting and civil rights, the role of the M. E. and Roman
Catholic churches stands as a sharp reminder of the national culpability
for segregation.

METHODIST AND CATHOLIC CHURCH members who opposed segregation did
not lose all hope, as their ongoing loyalty made clear. Some left, but many
stayed. Those who maintained their membership renegotiated their religious and racial identities within a context increasingly hostile to integration. By 1920, the former standard-bearers of religious biracialism had become segregated from top to bottom. Neither the M. E. nor the Catholic
transformation resulted in a separate denomination for African Americans,
but they might as well have. The Archdiocese of New Orleans instituted a
system of separate black parishes, while the M. E. Church established a

plan to isolate all its black members into a separate national jurisdiction. The same religious traditions that had resisted segregation contributed to Jim Crow's eventual ubiquity in the American South.

The relationship between church and society in New Orleans underwent a dramatic and fateful inversion between 1877 and 1920. In the 1880s, members of mixed denominations believed their churches offered a model that society could follow to integrate black citizens as equals in the nation. By 1920 the relationship had reversed, as African Americans hoped social and political pressures would overturn patterns of religious segregation before the church completely vanished as an alternative to the horrors of racial discrimination. At the same time, New Orleans underwent its own transformation. The city's racial and social structures that had suggested a degree of uniqueness in 1877 had, by 1920, conformed to southern patterns of rigid racial separation. The questions people in New Orleans asked during these transformations—who was black and who was white, and how churches should address the question of race both inside and outside of their institutions—were the same questions being asked throughout the South and the United States. How Americans answered those questions continues to define the shape of religion and race in the twenty-first century.

CHAPTER 1

Interracial Methodism in New Orleans

REFLECTING ON THE STRUGGLE for racial equality in 1877, Methodist Episcopal bishop Gilbert Haven claimed that "nowhere in the land does the battle rage more hotly" than in New Orleans. The city's oppressive summer heat no doubt influenced Haven's choice of metaphor. A leading advocate of racial integration, Haven had spent the previous four years living and traveling throughout the South as the episcopal supervisor of his denomination's southern work. The bishop recognized that New Orleans's complex racial and religious history created a furnace in which "the battle of caste" and the fires of racial prejudice were "already raging . . . hot, hotter, hottest." The political changes marking the end of Reconstruction threatened to fan the flames to new heights. Yet Haven remained optimistic that racial tensions in the Crescent City would not boil over. Surveying the accomplishments of the Methodist Episcopal Church, Haven predicted that in New Orleans "is the battle set" to overcome racial prejudice. M. E. church members in the Crescent City shared Haven's optimism. They believed their racially inclusive denomination would extend its influence to cool the "fires burning in the furnace political" and thereby "mold the State" toward a broad acceptance of racial equality.[1] The M. E. Church in New Orleans would be the soothing salve to heal the nation's racial blisters.

Haven's hope for New Orleans appears striking in hindsight. The M. E. bishop had thrown down the gauntlet for racial reconciliation in a seemingly peculiar place. Would the nation's racial anxieties be resolved in the South's largest, but often marginalized, city? Could the best hope for racial equality come from the city whose Jim Crow laws would lead to the 1896 *Plessy v. Ferguson* ruling that sanctioned segregation for the next half century? Equally perplexing is the centrality Haven assigned to the Methodist Episcopal Church. Could a northern-based, biracial Protestant denomination transform a southern, Catholic, and increasingly segregated city? Haven's optimism seems misplaced, given the course of events that would make New Orleans among the most rigidly segregated cities in the early twentieth century.

But hindsight does not provide twenty-twenty vision, clichés aside. Historical perspective can inspire overconfidence, blurring rather than clarifying our comprehension of the past. What now appears inevitable was only one of several possibilities to those who lived the story. Retrospective emphasis on a steady and inexorable decline into segregation is more prescriptive than descriptive, since it ignores the prevailing hope that sustained much of New Orleans's black population in the face of a worsening racial climate. Like African Americans throughout the postbellum South, black New Orleanians used their churches to assert an alternate vision that challenged white supremacy. For no group was this more true than for the city's M. E. church members. The future was far from certain for these black Christians. M. E. church members believed their city's race relations remained undetermined, even as recent political developments created cause for concern. They also recognized that uncertainty meant the door of possibility remained ajar. The stories of church members in New Orleans open a window into these church-based racial struggles throughout the South, illuminating the extent to which the 1880s were discontinuous with both the antebellum racial order and the imposition of segregation in subsequent decades. During the decade after Reconstruction, black residents found greater affirmation and faced fewer constraints than they would later encounter. Attention to these intervening decades does not change the end result. Nonetheless, recognizing these competing visions reveals the extent to which Jim Crow was contested. Whites had to deliberately impose segregation. It did not emerge smoothly or inevitably as a pattern of religious or racial organization. The experiences of Methodists in New Orleans, like those of their more numerous Catholic counterparts, demonstrate that the question of segregation was neither quickly nor easily resolved in the nation's racially mixed Christian denominations. Our own disappointment with the outcome must not overshadow the very real hope that inspired the city's black church members, despite the nearly overwhelming obstacles they faced.

M. E. church members in New Orleans believed they were best positioned to realize the possibility of a new racial order in the 1880s. They argued that New Orleans offered the most promising locale to advance racial equality, pointing to gains during Reconstruction that included a liberal state constitution and integrated public schools, ongoing black political influence, and only recent "redemption" by white Democrats. The M. E. Church played an important role in fostering this favorable context. The northern-based denomination, with its rhetoric of racial equality, had arrived shortly after New Orleans came under Union control in 1862. While other denominations quickly succumbed to racial separation, the M. E. Church had sustained its biracial membership. Nowhere in the South was its racial commitment more clear than in Louisiana. As M. E. church members recalled these political and religious gains, many believed they had already glimpsed the transformation Bishop Haven had so boldly predicted for New Orleans. M. E. church members in New Orleans continued to fight for a racial equality that was rooted in their churches during the two generations after the end of Reconstruction. Their commitment to racially mixed religious institutions undermines both the contemporary and historical tendencies to associate churches with segregation rather than integration.

These church members privileged the role of the church in social as well as religious transformation. M. E. faithful in New Orleans argued throughout the 1880s that their churches embodied the best hope for building upon the promising foundation the city's religious and racial history provided. They were confident of the church's influence on the political order, believing that efforts to win social, economic, and political equality were inseparable from African-American religious struggles. The fight was the same, whether it concerned racially exclusive denominations or disfranchisement in the political sphere. Church members thus embraced Bishop Haven's contention that "the Church must mold the State." The M. E. Church would continue the project of Reconstruction that the federal government had abandoned. Racial interaction and an acceptance of African Americans as equals would increase as the denomination's biracial example inevitably spilled into the secular arena. Modeling this racial interaction was "alike necessary to the salvation of our Church and nation," and formed "the glorious privilege and duty" of those who lived and worshiped in New Orleans. To M. E. members, the future of the American nation, no less than the church, was at stake.[2]

Black and white M. E. church members offered their own model of a shared religious affiliation that transcended racial differences as the best hope for the uncertainty of the 1880s. Racial inclusion stood at the very center of their M. E. religious identity. In the face of constant criticism and even abuse, theirs was not an easy task. Loyalty to their biracial denomination testified to their confidence in the promise it offered for transforming an increasingly hostile racial order in New Orleans and throughout the South. Black and white members alike defended their church's racial inclusiveness against the exclusionary practices of religious rivals. They believed that by following the M. E. example, black and white Americans could likewise emphasize a new shared identity grounded in religious and national commonalities. This vision of the future motivated those whose stories appear in the following pages to resist both a segregated church and a segregated society. This was the faith that M. E. church members in New Orleans lived and acted during the 1880s.[3]

IN PRIVILEGING THE ROLE of their church, M. E. church members identified denominational affiliation as a critical component of the struggle for racial equality. Following Emancipation, choosing a new church connection marked one of the first assertions of freedom from white control. The choices were numerous. Within Methodism alone, the spectrum ranged from the conservative and mostly white Southern Methodist Church of their masters to the all-black "African" denominations such as the African Methodist Episcopal (A.M.E.), African Methodist Episcopal Zion (A.M.E. Zion), and Colored Methodist Episcopal (C.M.E.) churches.[4] Debates among these Methodist factions concerned far more than contests for members and churches. Each tradition offered competing understandings of freedom and of strategies for advancing racial interests.

This range of denominational choices for black Methodists created a unique pattern in the American religious landscape. Baptists, who claimed the largest number of African-American members, had the widest range of congregations to choose from. But black Baptists were choosing among individual congregations rather than denominations advancing different strategies for racial equality. These independently organized Baptist congregations would not coalesce into formal denominations until the turn of the century. Absent altogether was a racially integrated Baptist association in the South. Within other Protestant denominations, the small number of black church members left them with few choices. Among Congregationalists, Episcopalians, and Presbyterians, only the latter had the occasional option of a racially separate denomination. Unlike Baptists and Methodists, the divisions in most of these and other Protestant traditions were geographic and theological, not racial. None claimed substantial numbers of black churches or clergy. Black Methodists thus faced the unique challenge of contending with rival Methodist organizations as well as with competing Baptist and, especially in New Orleans and Atlanta, Congregationalist churches. Still, no tradition approached the success of the M. E. Church in retaining black and white members in the same denomination. Well into the twentieth century, the M. E. Church was the only substantially biracial Protestant denomination.

Racial inclusiveness was the primary reason African Americans joined or rejoined the M. E. Church after Emancipation. In evaluating religious options, black Christians understood that choosing a religious identity encompassed far more than simply freedom of worship. Religious and racial identities were inextricably intertwined. Choosing a denominational affiliation involved articulating a particular understanding of freedom and racial identity. Debating these differing meanings of freedom and racial priorities stood at the center of denominational rivalries that endured past the turn of the century. Those who joined the M. E. Church emphasized racial equality above all else, pointing to the "anti-caste" appeal that was the centerpiece of M. E. mission work in the South. Black members saw a denomination that strove, albeit imperfectly, to model the racial inclusiveness they envisioned for all of society. White workers no less than black converts recognized that "the equality of relations enjoyed by black and white was the rallying cry which gathered the people to us." Although the recently arrived Congregationalists proclaimed a similarly inclusive message, the large network of existing black Methodist preachers and churches gave the M. E. Church a distinct advantage in building a biracial denomination in the postbellum South.[5]

M. E. church members demonstrated their commitment to a biracial religious identity in their willingness to suffer for their denominational affiliation. Both black and white members endured widespread hostility for their church membership. Remaining in the M. E. Church was not easy in the face of this antagonism. But denominational loyalty testified to church members' confidence that their example offered the best hope for improving the nation's race relations. The suffering of black M. E. church members was by no means unique; it resulted from racial as much as religious identity. Nor was oppression limited to Louisiana. Throughout the South, African Americans of all religious persuasions endured threats and actual harm, as did many with no religious affiliation. Nonetheless, belonging to a biracial denomination only increased vulnerability. M. E. church members experienced their oppression through this dual lens of religious and racial identity, in which one was inseparable from the other. As an M. E. leader in neighboring Mississippi explained, membership in the M. E. Church entailed "repeated efforts all over the land to alienate us from it by force and proscription on the one hand and persuasion on the other."[6]

Efforts to alienate black M. E. church members "by force and proscription" referred primarily to the activities of white antagonists. The religious as well as the racial identity of black members threatened white southerners. Much of the opposition came from Southern Methodists, who had separated from the M. E. Church over the issue of slavery in 1844. Because Southerners considered the division between northern and southern Methodism as much about geography as ideology, they resented the postbellum incursions of the M. E. Church into their territory. Southern Methodists did not oppose a Methodist identity for former slaves. Rather, they argued that Methodism should be racially separated. The southern ideal was two American Methodist denominations, one white and one black. Race would replace geography as the criterion for denominational affiliation. Southern Methodists had already enacted this separation within their own ranks in 1870, creating the Colored Methodist Episcopal (C.M.E.) Church for the few African Americans who had remained in the Southern Methodist Church. The desire for separate denominations was typical of southern white evangelicals; Southern Methodist racial anxieties were hardly distinctive. Presbyterians, both the Southern and Cumberland branches, created separate denominations for their black members, while Baptists segregated almost immediately after Emancipation, if they had not already done so.[7] Nor was opposition to the M. E. Church limited to those concerned about Methodist geography or politics. To southern whites, participation in racially mixed religious institutions formed yet another example of black citizens exceeding acceptable limits. These challenges to white supremacy resulted in assaults to remind black Southerners of their proper place: away from whites.[8]

White hostility took many forms, some disastrous, others deadly. Arson abounded, as report after report filtered into New Orleans that "another of our churches has been burned in the South by some wicked incendiary." More troubling was the risk of death under which black M. E. leaders labored. Two years after the end of Reconstruction, the front page of the M. E. newspaper in New Orleans listed acts of violence carried out against its ministers in the South, noting the murdered clergymen "were all killed because they were laborers in the Methodist Episcopal Church." In Ouchita Parish, Louisiana, two masked men shot Primus Johnson, an M. E. minister, and Eaton Lockwood, a "colored Republican," in October 1876. African Americans in New Orleans knew the murders did not constitute random acts of violence but rather reflected the racial threat that the men's religious and political affiliation represented: "These men were shot because they were leaders among the colored people and because they were Republicans."[9] In this triad of identities—black, Republican, and of a biracial denomination—one characteristic often implied the others. Just one of these traits was enough to provoke whites to hostility.

Other efforts to discourage M. E. loyalty were less deadly but even more widespread. Southern Methodists' tactics reflected not only disgust with M. E. racial policies but also the recognition that black M. E. church members were central to the M. E. establishing a new strength and presence in the postbellum South. This combination of racial and polity concerns led Southern Methodists to agitate for their vision of racially homogenous denominations. Their goal was "the organization of a great Episcopal Methodist Colored Church in the South" along the lines of the C.M.E. they had created in 1870. In the interim, Southern Methodists worked to steer black church members away from the M. E. Church and into any of the racially separate African or Colored Methodist denominations. Church members in New Orleans were well aware of the "constant talk in Southern Methodist papers about the colored people going to themselves, as being the best thing for them and all." The opposition took its toll. In response to a call to build more churches, one black M. E. minister complained of the difficulty, with "Southern Methodists all the time talking to the members and telling them they are in the wrong church."[10]

Southern Methodists tried to discourage M. E. church members by favoring African Americans who belonged to racially separate denominations. In New Orleans, as throughout the South, Southern Methodists refused Methodist fraternity with black M. E. church members, even as they interacted with both African Methodists and white members of the M. E.

Church. African Methodist preachers filled Southern Methodist pulpits during A.M.E. conferences in New Orleans. Black M. E. clergy never received such invitations, in New Orleans or anywhere else. The Southern Methodist General Conference welcomed only white delegates from the M. E. Church, while simultaneously embracing delegates from African Methodist denominations with "an exchange of expressions which indicated a well-defined policy of special interest and cooperation." M. E. congregations also encountered financial intimidation to push them toward separate black denominations. Throughout the South, Southern Methodists used property disputes as leverage against M. E. church members. In New Orleans, Southern Methodists contested the ownership of buildings used by three black M. E. congregations. The southern church promised to release any claim if the congregations would reject their M. E. affiliation and unite with an African Methodist Church instead. Church members rejected the repeated overtures, realizing they risked expulsion should the courts decide against them. For M. E. loyalists, no less than their white antagonists, commitment to their denomination's biracial identity stood at the heart of such disputes. Supporters noted that the black congregants "understood perfectly well the dispute concerning their property titles" and were "ready at any time should it be taken from them, to go out and rebuild the church to which they belonged." In New Orleans, the M. E. church members prevailed and retained possession of their church buildings.[11]

Ironically, belonging to a mixed denomination generated opposition from black Methodists as well as white. Criticizing black M. E. church members was an equal-opportunity activity. When M. E. leaders complained about efforts to alienate their church members, they complained as loudly about the hand of "persuasion" of African Methodist rivals as they did about the hand of "force and proscription" that white opponents used. The rhetoric from African Methodist critics proved louder and more pointed than that of Southern Methodists. The African Methodist antagonists varied by region. In Louisiana and Georgia, the A.M.E. was the prime instigator, while the A.M.E. Zion predominated in North Carolina. By the 1880s, all branches of black Methodism could be found in most parts of the South, and critiques of the M. E. Church tended to be the same regardless of tradition or locale. M. E. church members reported a constant barrage of encounters with African Methodist clergy "whose stock-in-trade is to build up their charges by abusing and misrepresenting the Methodist Episcopal Church."[12] African Methodist arguments and ultimate goals were categorically different than the racist and segregationist aims of Southern Methodists. But the ironic synchronization of the two efforts was not lost on M. E. church members: both black and white opponents agitated to shift M. E. church members into racially separate denominations.

The A.M.E. Church constituted the M. E. Church's primary black antagonist and its biggest competitor for members. The contest remained fierce throughout the 1880s. M. E. publications regularly noted changing affiliations in the final decades of the nineteenth century, challenging long-standing assumptions that African Americans settled questions of denominational identity within a few years of Emancipation.[13] Typical was a report from Louisiana that "about a hundred members of the Union Bethel African M. E. Church, Washington City . . . have organized into a new society of our Church, to be called the Central M.E. Church." The rivalry concerned far more than simply competition for members, ministers, and church buildings. The relationship of religious and racial identity formed a primary concern as African Americans considered and reconsidered their denominational affiliations. Debates centered on the advantages of each to racial advancement and the integration of blacks as equal citizens in American society. Differing perspectives aroused such passion that one M. E. minister charged that "in organizing new works Baptist members very often show us more encouragement than do many Methodists of the colored persuasion."[14]

African Methodists accused M. E. loyalists of betraying the race. M. E. church members reported being confronted with charges that equated membership in their denomination with slavery to white masters. Some opponents suggested a financial slavery, wherein the M. E. Church recruited black members to support white congregations in the North. Church leaders in New Orleans pointed to the impoverishment of most black congregations to refute such charges. "Stop and think," an M. E. minister in New Orleans retorted: "Our people are poor and have little or nothing to give." M. E. churches in Louisiana and the South received far more funding from the North than they raised themselves, a nearly universal situation for black congregations belonging to predominantly northern and white denominations. A more potent charge of subservience came when African Methodists highlighted the limited opportunities for advancement in the M. E. Church. Unfulfilled white promises of leadership opportunities haunted black church members for generations. Church leaders feared the impact of African Methodists who asserted that "young people of color, however pious and well educated, have no rational ground upon which to predicate the hope of being promoted" in the M. E. Church. Culminating these assaults was what members of the M. E. Church considered the most offensive and arrogant step of all: "To assume the right to command our people, particularly the young and promising, to come out of the Old Church, assuring them that their manhood and womanhood would never be acknowledged while they remained in the fellowship of this Church."[15] The cry to abandon imperfect churches has been a repeated theme in American religious history, and the struggles among African-American Christians were no exception.

African Methodist calls to leave the M. E. Church reached their peak over the question of black bishops. The "bishop question" plagued the M. E. Church well into the twentieth century. African Methodists boasted of their own black bishops while pointing to the M. E. Church's failure to elect even one. The dilemma was common to biracial denominations, especially those with an episcopal polity. Like the M. E. Church, the Episcopal Church struggled with unanswered calls for a black bishop until nearly 1920. M. E. church members complained that "our church is confronted everywhere in the South with the fact among the colored people that other churches have Bishops of African descent." With the failure of each General Conference to elect a bishop of African descent, M. E. loyalists were greeted with more taunting. Nor were the charges innocuous. Church members and clergy, black members and white, acknowledged the boost that a black bishop would provide for M. E. work in the South. The biracial New Orleans Preacher's Meeting passed resolutions in favor of a black bishop, while many black clergymen conceded their belief that with the passing of such a milestone, "thousands, yea, tens of thousands, who are this day waiting for our full recognition, will come flocking to our fold." In the meantime, M. E. church members suffered the torment of their foes. Ministers reported "it almost impossible, in some places, to hold our colored members." Those leaving the M. E. Church gave as their reason "Dey hes white bishops."[16]

But most members of the M. E. Church in New Orleans remained loyal, testifying to their confidence in a mixed denomination as the best hope for achieving racial equality. When opponents tried to weaken African-American confidence in the M. E. Church, leaders responded with affirmations of their "implicit and unwavering faith in the Methodist Episcopal Church." African Americans maintained this commitment even as they recognized that their church often marginalized its black members. Church members were optimistic "that the time is not far distant when the last vestige of prejudice on account of color shall be wiped out from among us." Their denominational identity was deliberate, not accidental. "The Negroes are in the Methodist Episcopal Church of choice, not of necessity," explained one of New Orleans's leading black M. E. clergymen. They would remain and work for change from within. "We are in the M. E. Church to stay," affirmed another prominent black clergyman from Kentucky. "We shall wait until the occasion comes, and then as members within the church, under its rules, and by its laws, demand and secure what ever rights we are entitled to by law as members."[17]

Though members endured two decades of antagonism for their religious identity, as the black M. E. leader cited above observed, "There are multiplied thousands of blacks that are as true to the old church as the needle to the pole, notwithstanding the repeated efforts all over the land to alienate us from it by force and proscription on the one hand and persuasion on the other." Membership in a racially mixed denomination was unavoidably risky for African Americans living in the postbellum South. But their willingness to endure both physical and rhetorical opposition demonstrated their commitment to a biracial denomination and their faith that it could create a religious identity that transcended race. They believed the M. E. Church of the 1880s still offered promise in the midst of a worsening racial climate. The tide of Jim Crow was not yet so high that their church could not turn it back. Racially separate denominations made little sense to M. E. members, while the opposition they encountered only confirmed for them that the M. E. Church stood for the racially inclusive principles on which they based their loyalty. Some church members were so confident that they reversed the "come-outism" of their critics, arguing that "any sane person whose heart is clear of prejudice can readily see that the M. E. Church is the church for the colored people," and thus "each and every colored person ought to unite with this grand old mother church of Methodism."[18]

Black church members were not alone in suffering for their loyalty to the biracial M. E. Church. White M. E. church members throughout the South encountered opposition in parallel, though less dangerous, ways. Like their black counterparts, much of the antagonism came from Southern Methodists. Most white Methodists in New Orleans and across the South belonged to the all-white Southern Methodist Church. The few whites belonging to the M. E. Church faced constant criticism and often ostracism. White M. E. church members encountered "a strong spirit of opposition" to their work, discovering that "in many cases these unpleasant incidents would be found to have their inspiration from sources high in authority and influence in sister Churches."[19] Enduring parallel experiences of criticism bound the city's black and white M. E. church members together in a religious identity that transcended race. White faithfulness in the face of hostility also reassured black church members of their denomination's commitment to biracialism. Recognizing the sacrifice of their black counterparts, white church members endured their lesser hardships out of a shared belief in their denomination's promise for improving the nation's race relations.

The experiences of the Reverend Joseph Crane Hartzell (1842–1929) exemplified the challenges facing white M. E. church members in New Orleans and throughout the South. Reared and educated in Illinois, Hartzell arrived in New Orleans in 1870, serving first as pastor of the mostly white Ames M. E. Church and later as a presiding elder in the predominantly black Louisiana Annual Conference.[20] Using his own money, Hart-

Figure 1.1. Joseph C. Hartzell (1842–1929). Courtesy General Commission on Archives and History of the United Methodist Church.

zell founded and served as the first editor of the *Southwestern Christian Advocate*, a weekly newspaper that was a tireless advocate of racial equality and would become New Orleans's largest circulating religious newspaper with a black readership.[21] Hartzell's commitment to African Americans in the M. E. Church never wavered, despite the opposition he encountered during his early years in New Orleans and the occasional spirit of condescension and compromise that characterized even the most sympathetic white workers in the South. During Reconstruction, Hartzell served on the public school board that experimented with integrated schools. Following his work in New Orleans, Hartzell rose through the ranks of the denomination's Freedmen's Aid Society. In 1896 he was elected a missionary bishop to Africa, where he served until retirement in 1916. Upon his return to the United States, Hartzell was an increasingly lonely white voice, even in the North, as he protested his denomination's racism and advocated for the equality of black church members.[22] Like many Northerners who came south to work among African Americans, Hartzell's racial sympathies stemmed from an explicitly religious context and background. Attention to these church workers and the institutions they founded reveals many of the most forceful white advocates for black Southerners in the postbellum South.

The opposition Hartzell and his white colleagues encountered stemmed from three inter-related issues. Sectionalism was one dimension of the antagonism between Hartzell and Southern whites. Most of the members of Ames Chapel, where Hartzell first served as pastor, either hailed from the North or had remained loyal to the Union during the Civil War. Lingering resentments made it difficult for them to penetrate New Orleans's society, where they were derided as carpetbaggers and scalawags. Shortly after his arrival in New Orleans, Hartzell complained of city residents whose sectionalism was so bitter "that they knowingly will not associate with a Northern Family." Compounding the difficulties was the M. E. Church's identity as a northern denomination. In a letter inviting Hartzell to preach in her church, a Southern Methodist woman conceded that "the people here as in other places in the South are considerably prejudiced toward the Northern Methodists." Hartzell's wife fared no better in her work among the city's women, encountering a "most intense opposition . . . among hostile whites" throughout New Orleans. In his work as an editor of the *Southwestern Christian Advocate* and as a traveling M. E. statesman in the South, Hartzell endured much criticism from Southern Methodists who considered the M. E. Church nothing more than another Yankee army invading the South. Hartzell heard often from Southern Methodists who "consider us *intruders* here and throughout the South." As far away as Texas, Southerners alleged that "without doubt Dr. Hartzell and the clan he represents, would gladly rule as conquerors over the South, and compel its people to accept their opinions by all the terrors of the secular arm." Hartzell did little to ease the hostility, suggesting that easing sectional tensions required nothing less than "that the convictions of vast multitudes of white people in the South be remolded."[23]

Political hostility provided a second basis for Southern whites to ostracize white M. E. church members. Like Hartzell, most members of the M. E. Church were Republican as well as Unionist. Hartzell reported that the membership of Ames Chapel was "composed of those who have been loyal enough to their country and God, to 'come up through' the 'great tribulations' of the rebellion and reconstruction." Hartzell bragged of the Republican flavor of his congregation at Ames Chapel during Reconstruction: "the governor and most of the leading state and city officials support us financially—several attend and some are members." None of this endeared him to the antebellum and Confederate Democrats who had been shut out during Reconstruction but returned to prominence with the end of Reconstruction in 1877. Wherever M. E. missionaries entered the southern field, from Tennessee to Atlanta to New Orleans, their Republican politics became a major source of tension with Southern Methodists. Throughout the South, fellow M. E. missionaries joined Hartzell in publishing pro-Republican articles in religious and secular papers alike and in very public support for Republican and northern policies in the South. In Atlanta, Erasmus Q. Fuller used his *Methodist Advocate* to campaign for Republican candidates, while other M. E. clergy advanced their Republican political agenda in secular papers from Knoxville south to Jackson, Mississippi, and from Memphis east to Orangeburg, South Carolina.[24]

But it was a commitment to racial equality that proved the third and greatest source of tension with whites in New Orleans. Hartzell reported that the M. E. Church was "reviled and persecuted by all the aristocratic white Churches of the South because of her work among colored people" and its gospel of racial equality. Ames Chapel, the predominantly white congregation that Hartzell served, struggled to maintain a policy of non-discrimination.[25] When a church member protested Hartzell's invitation to a black colleague to preach at Ames, Hartzell replied, "If I am forbidden to invite a brother minister to preach in my pulpit simply because his color is a shade darker than mine, my pastorate ends in that place." During his tenure at Ames, Hartzell reported that he and his wife also frequently "invited the colored brethren to take tea with us." Later, as a presiding elder visiting area churches, he slept exclusively in the homes of black church members and leaders. As a Southern Methodist woman explained to Hartzell, this sort of behavior was the central cause of animosity that residents of New Orleans felt toward northern Methodists: "They have no objection to your preaching to the colored people but they must not wish them to meet together." Hartzell responded to such complaints by explaining that the M. E. Church was engaged in "the mission of peace and good will to all men, without distinction of race or condition." Ironically, opening a church's doors to all races restricted a congregation such as Ames, which found itself "shut in by barriers of prejudice." Hartzell's commitment to racial equality drew scathing attacks well beyond Southern Methodists, as did many of his northern missionary compatriots. The secular *New Orleans Picayune*, for example, leveled the accusation that Hartzell "has long and actively engaged in misinforming the Northern public in regard to Southern matters, and particularly as to the condition of the colored people of this section. We are not aware that he has any other claim to distinction; but in the department of bloody-shirt and outrage literature he has secured a position of undisputed prominence."[26] While Hartzell and the M. E.

Church hoped to soothe the nation's wounds, many white New Orleanians believed he applied more salt than salve.

Although Hartzell was far from alone in agitating for greater racial equality, he was one of the loudest among M. E. missionaries working in the South. Only Bishop Gilbert Haven, who served in Atlanta between 1872 and 1876, was more vocal, and more reviled. Still, both men were part of a much larger contingent working for the religious and racial transformation of the former Confederacy. Like Haven, many of denomination's most prominent racial activists hailed from New England and could trace their Methodist and ideological roots to the region's abolitionist heritage. The New England Annual Conference was where some of the earliest attempts to integrate M. E. churches and conferences took place, and Boston was home to *Zion's Herald*, the denomination's most vocal advocate of racial equality. The religious and racial commitments of several New England clergymen led them to engage in work for and among African Americans in the South. In New Orleans, Hartzell worked with numerous white M. E. supporters of African-American equality, including ardent integrationist Lucius Matlack, whose "rally cry" was "the equality of relations enjoyed by black and white"; L. P. Cushman, who was, among other responsibilities, Hartzell's successor as editor of the anti-caste *Southwestern Christian Advocate*; and W. D. Godman, one of several M. E. missionaries who served as president of New Orleans University.

Alongside New Orleans, Atlanta formed another center for M. E. work among African Americans. Besides Bishop Haven, Atlanta clergy such as Isaac Lansing, who worked tirelessly in his city and in the Methodist press against segregation in church and society alike, labored. Wilbur Thirkield, Haven's son-in-law and later a bishop himself, was dean of the M. E. Gammon Seminary in Atlanta, where he succeeded in opening "the first Library Building in the South open to all races." Others had carried the call for equality to the large African-American Protestant population in South Carolina. By the end of Reconstruction, the M. E. Church had hundreds of white missionaries, clergy and lay, male and female, who continued working throughout the South. Throughout the 1880s, black church members continued to look to northern strongholds of biracial sympathy. After Haven's death in 1880, several black leaders coordinated their efforts to ensure the episcopal vacancy was filled by another sympathetic New England native, Willard Mallalieu.[27]

Like Hartzell and his colleagues in New Orleans, these white missionaries suffered for their trinity of interrelated identities as Northerners, Republicans, and advocates of racial inclusiveness. The further south they ventured, the greater opposition the missionaries encountered. No less than Hartzell in New Orleans, M. E. missionary families from Memphis to Atlanta, and even as far north as Maryland, faced social and economic ostracism. Social ostracism was the most common response, but some whites also experienced the threats to property and life that routinely terrorized black church members. A black church member in rural Louisiana recalled a white teacher "who was taken out of his schoolhouse, right before his scholars, in broad daytime, and caned half to death by a mob of nearly a hundred." After a ten-day chase with a five-hundred-dollar bounty on his head, the teacher "reached New Orleans in safety, where he could continue in the same line of work with a little more security." A Congressional investigation into violence in the southern states suggested M. E. church members appeared especially vulnerable, although their suffering was far from unique. Northern Presbyterians lost schoolhouses and churches in Tennessee to arson, while their teachers in Mississippi were victims of mob violence.[28]

Opposition to white M. E. missionaries and members left the white portion of the denomination's biracial equation in a precarious position. The struggles of Ames Chapel in New Orleans typified just how unstable the balance remained. Ames, where most white M. E. church members in the Crescent City worshiped, began in 1865 with a sizable loan from the denomination. The church continued to struggle for several decades thereafter. The congregation's sectional, political, and racial views made it difficult to attract enough members to support the church. Adding insult to injury, the church was named after the M. E. bishop who had used Union troops to take possession of Southern Methodist church buildings in New Orleans and Nashville.[29] M. E. loyalists had hoped their church could transform the political order, but they were learning that the opposite could also hold true. Political changes that returned Redeemer Democrats to power in 1877 stifled the effectiveness of M. E. work among whites in New Orleans. Hartzell reported that the end of Reconstruction proved quite a blow for the congregation, for "they have been greatly crippled, owing to the changes which have taken place recently in the political world and the consequent removal from the city of many of its former supporters." But Ames remained important as testimony to the denomination's biracial identity in the Crescent City. Without the predominantly white congregation, the M. E. Church in New Orleans would have had the appearance of another black Methodist denomination. Ames continued to struggle throughout the 1880s. In 1882, the presiding elder in New Orleans responded to the rumors of Ames's closure, saying, "We are not quite prepared to abandon the Ames church as yet."[30] They did not abandon Ames.

Nor did Hartzell and his white colleagues abandon their commitment to bolstering black as well as white membership in the M. E. Church. This small band of whites in New Orleans sustained their commitment to an integrated religious and social world, even in the face of constant harassment and financial difficulties. Their troubles paled in comparison with that of their African-American counterparts, who risked loss of property and life for their denominational loyalty. Nonetheless, white encounters with adversity formed a meaningful complement to the hardship that black members endured for their allegiance to the M. E. Church. Both black and white church members in New Orleans viewed the resistance they encountered through the lens of religious and racial identity. Neither racial nor religious identity alone but the assertion of both combined in an M. E. identity had fostered the opposition that black and white members alike endured. Their parallel experiences strengthened their sense of a shared religious identity that transcended racial differences.

M. E. CHURCH MEMBERS suffered for their religious identity because they believed the stakes were so high. Black members insisted African Methodist rivals offered a far worse alternative to the M. E. Church, even as they were aware of their own denomination's shortcomings. White M. E. church members considered Southern Methodist racial exclusivism equally dangerous. Racially separate denominations, whether the product of self-separation or enforced segregation, fell well short of the society demanded by both the Christian Bible and the recently amended United States Constitution. Accordingly, both black and white M. E. church members went on the offensive against their religious rivals. The shared religious identity of black and white church members was not merely a by-product of similar experiences of oppression. Privileging a common denominational identity over racial distinctions was an intentional activity, not an incidental consequence. Calling attention to their differences from other Methodist traditions enabled black and white M. E. church members to highlight their shared commitment to a biracial denomination, upon which they hoped to build a religious identity that transcended race.

Racial inclusiveness was the most crucial characteristic separating the M. E. church from its rivals. Emphasizing their denomination's biracial membership, M. E. loyalists engaged in parallel processes wherein black members differentiated themselves from African Methodists, while white members distanced themselves from Southern Methodists. Their rhetoric bound them together as they invoked the same critique against racial exclusivism. By accentuating their differences from their respective rivals, black and white church members emphasized a shared space constructed upon a common religious identity that made room for racial differences. The M. E. Church in New Orleans became a middle ground where both races found refuge from the segregation of African Methodism at one extreme and Southern Methodism at the other. This shared middle ground was evidence, especially to black church members, that the M. E. Church could be the catalyst for transforming race relations in church and state alike.

Black M. E. loyalists focused their criticism on the dangers of racially exclusive denominations. They hoped to eliminate caste, a term they used interchangeably with race, as a principle of organization and a measure of worth. Their objection referred as much to the black exclusivism of African Methodists as to the white exclusivism of Southern Methodists. There was no reason to have any more faith in a purely black church than in a purely white one. Black M. E. church members rejected the contention that the immediate leadership opportunities available in a separate denomination necessitated an exodus: "The sentiment that a man to prove his manhood must isolate himself from the bulk of mankind is a mistake." M. E. loyalists believed that in their denomination, a person's skin color would not determine his or her stature. To their rivals touting the advantages of racial homogeneity, M. E. loyalists responded that "color is nothing, character is everything." Black members in other biracial denominations, such as Francis Grimke of the Presbyterian Church, were equally outraged by racial separation among either black or white church members. When invited to join an alliance of black Presbyterians, Grimke responded with a frustration analogous to that of his M. E. counterparts: "It is not true that I am a colored Presbyterian. I did not know that Presbyterianism was any particular color." In a properly constituted Christian church, skin color remained irrelevant, and "as the world learns to more fully appreciate this fact, the use for a purely race church obliterates."[31] For Methodist Episcopalians, churches were central to the struggle to create a color-blind society.

M. E. church members warned that racially homogenous denominations created a greater concession to the color line than any failures within their own denomination. Responding to the "African" in A.M.E. and A.M.E. Zion or the "Colored" in C.M.E., church members lamented the way rival denominations privileged racial over religious identity. These denominations made race intrinsic rather than irrelevant to religion, fusing religious and racial identities into an inseparable whole. The M. E. Church, in contrast, offered a common religious identity regardless of race. M. E. church members believed African Methodist racial separatism represented the very prejudice these rivals decried within the M. E. Church: " 'Caste and race prejudice' is the backbone of their success . . . and they know this." M. E. church members encouraged African Methodists to remove the log from their own eye before attempting to remove the speck from the eye of the M. E. Church. "When the A.M.E. Church works less in the line of race prejudice," challenged one minister, "they can more justly criticise this evil in the M. E. Church." M. E. arguments failed to differentiate between the self-separation that African Methodism was founded upon and the white-imposed limits African Methodists were so critical of in the M. E. Church. For M. E. critics, the contemporary implications were more important than the historical foundations. The first black editor of the New Orleans–

based *Southwestern Christian Advocate* was typical in his analysis of African Methodist influence: "The talk with which their adherents boast of race pride, self-assertion, freedom, manhood, and patriotism is but another form of demanding, asserting and upholding color-caste and the COLOR LINE."[32]

The most stinging criticism against racially exclusive churches charged that separation in the religious sphere supported segregation in other areas of society.[33] M. E. church members believed even the self-separation of African Methodists contributed to the rising tide of Jim Crow. "Those who advocate the color line in churches," one minister charged, "ought not to object to it on railroad cars, steamboats, in hotels, and all other places carried out to its fullest extent." M. E. loyalists worried about the detrimental impact of separate churches on all African Americans, given their belief that churches exerted influence on the larger social order. Black M. E. church leaders warned that black denominations are "full of future mischief to the nation and to the church of Christ." White leaders such as Hartzell concurred, asserting that "the putting of colored people into separate denominational organizations—no matter how much the act may be explained by questions of policy—is an acquiescence in distinctions on account of race and color, which commits those who do it to a defense of those distinctions as being right, and to be perpetuated." When someone tried to downplay the role of the church and blame racial divisions solely on the government, these same Methodists responded, "No, *the pulpit is responsible*. It is the duty of the pulpit to make a public conscience adverse to this state of things. . . . The responsibility remains with the pulpit, and to that responsibility the pulpit must be held." African Methodist preachers looked out upon racially exclusive denominations and thus encouraged rather than opposed the practice of racial segregation. The A.M.E. Church cannot be anything but a perpetuator of racial divisiveness, claimed one M. E. leader, except that it cease "to exist at all as a distinct church for American Africans."[34]

Separate black denominations encouraged the spread of Jim Crow by playing into the hands of conservative southern whites. Southern Methodists had long frustrated black M. E. church members with assertions that "all Methodists should be divided on the color line and one part be united in one great big 'Colored' Methodist Church" and the other in a single white denomination. Southern Methodists interpreted African Methodist growth as evidence that all African Americans shared white segregationist preferences, not only in religion but throughout society. In New Orleans, a leading black clergyman and editor warned that "for the race to isolate itself and wall itself inside of a race church . . . would tend more to continue indefinitely the prejudices of the white people against the colored." M. E. church members stressed that the ramifications extended far beyond denominational organization. They feared that self-segregation in churches provided fodder for whites seeking to enforce separatism outside of the church. A presiding elder in Kentucky cautioned that segregated denominations were "strengthening the hands of our foes by placing arguments in their mouths against interrace mixture for moral and mental development."[35] Whites would argue that in areas where African Americans had the freedom to choose—religion being the most visible—they preferred separation. The imposition of Jim Crow, whites could then claim, merely provided African Americans with the social order they desired.

Black M. E. church members straddled a precarious position in their criticisms of African Methodists. When church members linked African Methodism and segregation, they ironically committed the error of white segregationists whose reasoning failed to differentiate between self-separation and segregation. For this reason, newspapers from rival denominations, such as the A.M.E. Zion *Star of Zion* and the A.M.E. *Christian Recorder*, both of which spoke forcefully to racial concerns, generally refused to engage these particular terms of debate. The self-separation of African Methodists who voluntarily withdrew from biracial communions was qualitatively different from the segregation that white supremacists forced upon black citizens, even when the freely chosen black departure was a direct response to discrimination. Separate railroads and streetcars, separate waiting rooms and drinking fountains, and separate seating in theaters and stadiums were not a matter of choice for African Americans. Even if they might choose to sit apart, segregation denied the opportunity to make such a choice. African Methodists were separate by choice. M. E. critics did not always acknowledge the significance of these differences in their challenges to African Methodists.

Yet white segregationist reasoning also meant that M. E. critics were correct. White supremacists pointed to black organizations and alliances of all types, from labor and professional organizations to social clubs and benevolent organizations, as evidence that African Americans preferred a racially segregated society. Absent was the recognition that discrimination necessitated these separate organizations. Separate churches stood at the forefront of white supremacist arguments for racial segregation. The white Southern Baptist Convention, for example, assumed the explosion of independent black Baptist churches expressed an African-American desire "to have their own organizations" segregated on the basis of race. Yet M. E. church members charged that African Methodist denominations were among the most damaging to the quest for integration. The New Orleans–based *Southwestern Christian Advocate* published testimonies from black church members who, when insisting on equality and integration, were confronted by white separatists who "pointed [to] the African Church for example" of evidence that black Americans preferred separation."[36]

As racial separatism complicated relations with whites, M. E. loyalists also feared it would sow dissension within the black community. In New Orleans, they worried the spread of racially separate denominations would further deteriorate the already racially fragmented society. The diversity of skin color among people of African descent would provide a never-ending opportunity for discrimination. One church leader described the color line in the A.M.E. Church as "a color-caste reaching to the home, taking its grades upwards from deepest black to faintest octoroon; often interfering with the family relations." The danger held especially true in New Orleans, where the range of colors extended from the generally lighter Creoles of color, to Haitian immigrants, to African Americans, most of whom were former slaves and darker-skinned. A hierarchy that placed Creoles and former free persons of color above those who had been slaves had long characterized the Crescent City. St. James A.M.E. Church in New Orleans, an antebellum independent church for free people of color, was already associated with the city's elite, and almost inevitably light-skinned, Protestants. Following Emancipation, many of St. James's members left to form Central Congregational Church, troubled in part by the growing presence of less refined and darker-skinned worshipers who had also been slaves. Commenting on the growing homogenization among different shades of people of color elsewhere in the country, a leading M. E. clergyman in New Orleans observed that as late as 1888, "a notable exception exists in Louisiana where the fusion is not so thorough."[37] The divisions associated with African Methodism contrasted with the ideals of inclusivity and unity that M. E. loyalists in New Orleans believed their denomination upheld and their city needed. Criticisms of African Methodists were therefore more than quibbles within Methodism, or even a mere competition for members and resources. The very future of race relations was at stake.

M. E. church members were defining religion and its influence in the broadest possible terms in their castigations of religious and racial rivals. These Methodists recognized that religion involved a wide range of activity, not merely the realms of formal theology or personal spirituality. Such theoretical or inward religious thoughts had little meaning until they found outward expression. The activities and practices of religious institutions were a far better measure of a church's theology than declarations about a sacred text. A church's acceptance or rejection of racial inclusion not only worked to shape racial attitudes in the society in which it operated, it was itself an expression of religious belief. Proclamations of concern for all souls or statements of inclusion meant little if contradicted by institutional practices and attitudes. Black Christians looked to practical expressions far more than to theological treatises, publications, or even sermons to determine a denomination's beliefs about race. This understanding of religion challenged southern white denominations that asserted churchly concerns were limited solely to the spiritual realm. Neither theology nor practice alone but rather the tension between the two formed the center of religious experience for black Southerners.

Emphasizing this connection between theology and religious institutions, M. E. church members were critical of the theology implied by racially separate denominations. They charged African Methodists with betraying the inclusiveness of their tradition's founder, John Wesley, whose Methodist fellowship was interracial from its inception in America. M. E. church members insisted their denomination maintained Wesley's openness to all people. One minister who transferred from the A.M.E. to the M. E. Church gave as his reason that the only true Methodist church was "the old mother of Methodists—the Methodist Episcopal Church, that knows no North, South, East, nor West, but to preach Christ and him crucified to all the world." The M. E. Church in New Orleans contrasted its own faithfulness with the hypocrisy of opponents who were "tantalizing the Methodist Episcopal Church because it is composed, [as] the Apostolic church was, of men and women 'of every nation under heaven.' " One church member suggested that rivals who criticized the M. E. Church about not having a colored bishop "are not Methodists in heart, but only Methodists in a colored bishop."[38] African Methodist had lost sight of their Methodist lineage in their preference for racial homogeneity.

M. E. church members viewed their concerns through a wider theological lens. They argued that racially separate denominations also fell short of essential tenets of the Christian faith. Such churches did not manifest genuine Christianity. To separate on the basis of race, an M. E. presiding elder challenged, was not only "in violation of the very principle for which we have all along contended," but to "loose the image of Christ and become schismatic beside." Pointing to race as the organizing principle, another minister claimed that "the plan of colored churches is unchristian, because 'color' is the badge of heathenish caste." Likewise, the C.M.E. Church was "an abomination in Christendom" since its constitution excluded whites from membership. "We cannot look upon a mere race church, as the church of the Lord Jesus Christ," another critic charged, because "of all human organizations that take the name of a church, a caste church is the most hateful and harmful." Some claimed the practices of African Methodists were unscriptural, arguing that there is "not a syllable of Bible in favor of such teaching" and that such practices were "not in keeping with the Ten Commandments and the Sermon on the Mount." Congregationalists in Atlanta were equally adamant that the early church described in the book of Acts and the apostle Paul's assertion that "there is neither Jew nor Greek" forbade racial separatism in the church. Others pointed directly to Jesus in supporting their claims: "Jesus came to mix with us. Came all the way from glory. He has no respect for persons; we are to be like Him."

They further reminded both African and Southern Methodists of eternal consequences for falling short of Christ's standards of inclusiveness: "Should we fail, we might miss the crown."[39] As church members emphasized the need to correlate theology and its institutional expression, they were demonstrating to white as well as to black rivals that Christianity in general, and Methodism in particular, were more accurately associated with integration than segregation.

In the end, theological and pragmatic opposition to African Methodist churches merged. African Americans in the M. E. Church asserted that only a mixed denomination could simultaneously remain a faithful church and advance the struggle against race prejudice. They rejected African Methodist arguments that black Christians could only attain the fullest expression in separate churches. While rivals repeatedly issued calls "to come out" and join the African Methodist congregations, M. E. loyalists argued that just the opposite was necessary. M. E. church leaders advised African Methodists that on issues of prejudice, the M. E. Church "was doing away with it more rapidly than any other branch of Methodism." Inverting the language of "come outism," the M. E. Church urged A.M.E. ministers to "come over to our house and take all your folks along," since "no ecclesiastical organization in the land . . . 'is giving caste such deadly blows,' as the Methodist Episcopal."[40] African Americans in the M. E. Church turned the racial criticisms directed at them back on their opponents, remaining convinced that their own denomination was accomplishing more on their behalf than any other organization, religious or secular.

These ongoing debates among Methodist denominations illuminate the fluidity of African-American religious affiliation in the late nineteenth century. Shortly after Emancipation, most black Christians had voluntarily left the ranks of the southern churches that their masters had compelled them to attend. In Georgia and Tennessee, no less than Louisiana and throughout the South, Southern Baptists, Southern Methodists, and Southern Presbyterians witnessed a near total loss of their black members.[41] But that was only the beginning of the journey, not the end. Two decades later, many were still searching for the denominational home that best articulated their understanding of their faith and place in the world. Attention to the resulting denominational competition provides an important window into the unsettled character of segregation and race relations, as debates among black Methodists reveal. African-American understandings of their place in Christianity and in the American nation remained at the center of denominational rivalries, keeping competition alive throughout the decade after Reconstruction. As other avenues of expression were closed to black voices, church debates preserved a space for ongoing discussions about racial organization, segregation, and the nature of black and white relations in the final decades of the nineteenth century. African Americans disagreed about which religious organizations best reflected God's will for their race, just as they differed regarding which political parties and economic strategies best enabled them to claim their constitutional rights. Black citizens, no less than any group in the United States, were far from unified on how best to advance their position in American society. Churches and denominational affiliations would remain at the center of these debates, even as particular loyalties and alliances shifted over time. Most African Americans drifted toward the various Baptist and Methodist bodies—but not all of them did. In New Orleans, in particular, the Congregational Church was another tradition steadfastly committed to biracialism in ways very similar to those of the M. E. Church. The city's black Catholics offered their own challenge to segregation. It thus remains a misnomer to speak of anything approaching a unified "black church" in the decades after Reconstruction.[42]

In carving out their niche in the religious marketplace, black M. E. church members challenged the idea of the church as a place of retreat from racial oppression. Rather, they understood churches as a means to engage and ultimately challenge the prevailing white supremacy in southern society. Like black members of other denominations, they recognized the increasing importance of churches as a locus for debating responses to racial oppression, especially as other avenues for racial protest, from electoral politics to the judicial system, became increasingly closed to African Americans. But the strong link between belief and action meant that the debates could not remain merely in the realm of rhetoric or displaced to the life to come. Black church members understood M. E. churches as places to use otherworldly models to push for this-worldly transformation. As a member from Arkansas explained, "We will have to mix in heaven. Better get acquainted here."[43] The strong legacy of social reform in Methodism, most notably abolition, no doubt influenced M. E. church members' conception of the church and its role in the world. Remaining in a racially mixed denomination formed an important expression of this understanding of the church. As a result, the biracial interactions at the national denominational level was as important a part of the M. E. identity as was the particularity of one's own congregation.

As black M. E. church members differentiated themselves from African Methodists, they also demonstrated their unity with white members of the M. E. Church in New Orleans. Black church members privileged religious unity over racial unity. They were willing to endure intraracial divisions to achieve their goals of racial integration in church and society. In critiquing African Methodists, black M. E. church members assumed an active role in relation to their rivals, refusing to allow their opponents to define them. This critique of African Methodists also enabled black M. E. church members to define their place in their own denomination. They were no more willing to have their position defined by white members of their own denomination than by black members of rival churches. Their membership in the M. E. Church was predicated on equality before God and humanity, and it was on those terms, and those terms alone, that they defended their M. E. membership. Black M. E. church members in New Orleans emphasized racial inclusion as the boundary that separated them from African Methodists and bound them to their own denomination.

Black Methodists found strength in their white counterparts, who were engaged in similar debates with their rivals in the all-white Southern Methodist Church. Race stood at the center of these debates. While Southerners primarily invoked territorial protectiveness, M. E. church members countered that differences between the two denominations centered on morality more than geography. Nor was the divide unique to Methodism. The nation's other major evangelical traditions, Baptists and Presbyterians, also divided over slavery, and none would see their rifts healed in the nineteenth century. In each instance, Southerners resented the postbellum northern incursions into southern territory, the resulting mass exodus of black members, and the efforts to educate freed slaves. Southerners characterized these efforts as propagandizing northern and Republican values, which included notions of racial equality. Episcopalians and Catholics proved an exception to the evangelical tendency. Although northern and southern church members and leaders defended the Union and Confederacy respectively, neither Catholics nor Episcopalians made an official ecclesiastical split. Following the war they therefore continued as unified traditions, aided by the lack of zealous northerners coming south. Episcopalians, for example, sent funds rather than missionaries, leaving the expenditures to the dictates of southern clergymen.[44]

The tensions among divided denominations remained high. White M. E. advocates castigated Southern Methodists for their racial record. Just like northern Presbyterians, M. E. missionaries claimed that these failures, ranging from a pro-slavery stance and Confederate sympathies to a failure to provide for emancipated slaves and the eventual shunting of black members into the C.M.E. Church, justified the northern religious incursion into the southern states. Scanning the ranks of Southern Methodists, Hartzell and his colleagues saw no evidence "which could be interpreted as indicating any change of sentiment in the Church, South, as to the relative positions to be maintained between the white and the colored people." The failure to recognize African Americans as fellow human beings, let alone as brothers and sisters in faith, marked the clearest difference between the M. E. Church and Southern Methodists. While M. E. leaders portrayed Southern Methodist racial views as particularly horrendous, they were in fact representative of the attitudes of most southern denominations. Virginia Baptists, for example, no more equated Emancipation with a changed social status than did Louisiana Methodists.[45]

White M. E. church members challenged the racial exclusivism of Southern Methodism in arguments that paralleled black members' criticism of African Methodism. Southern Methodists were even less welcoming of black members than African Methodists were of white members. M. E. leaders chastised Southern Methodists because "they don't want our colored members. If they should seek a home in the M. E. Church South, the door would be closed against them, and they would be informed that the Church South was for white people." By 1883, the entire Louisiana Conference of the Southern Methodist Church included only 29 black members, constituting two-tenths of one percent of the total membership. Across the whole denomination, African Americans comprised just over one-tenth of one percent of the denomination's members. Hartzell found the Southern Methodist commitment to racial homogeneity so extreme as to be humorous. In 1881, a newspaper mistakenly identified the Southern Methodist Church as the denomination in which a famous black politician had been appointed a newspaper editor and presiding elder. The appointment actually occurred in the M. E. Church. So remote was the likelihood of a black leader in Southern Methodism that when the mistake appeared, Hartzell chided that "neighbors of the Church South, misled by the erroneous paragraph, must have thought the millennium had come!"[46]

Like their black counterparts, white M. E. church members also criticized their Southern Methodist rivals from a theological perspective. Leading white advocates called upon Methodists north and south to "have the illogical, fastidious, unchristian discrimination of the Negro from all other races ... abandoned as unworthy of our religion." The M. E. Church invoked Southern Methodism's failure to uphold the entirety of the Christian faith as justification for sending missionaries and funds within its rival's bounds. "Our work in behalf of the colored people is providentially appointed," proclaimed M. E. missionaries in defense of their decision to enter Southern Methodist territory. M. E. loyalists questioned Southern Methodists' ability to recognize genuine Christian service. One clergyman defended the M. E. Church by claiming that "no true follower of Christ will hinder us."[47] Whites eliminated Southern Methodism as a true expression of Christianity because of its racial exclusivity, while black church members did the same to African Methodism. Each left the M. E. Church as the only denomination for both black and white Methodists who accepted biblical standards.

Southern Methodists, however, refused to acknowledge the theological charges. As a result, they also denied the important connections between social relations and the practices of religious institutions, connections that were so central to black church members' criticism of racially separate denominations. When challenged on the morality or social implications of segregation, southern churches invoked the doctrine of the spirituality of the churches, claiming to eschew political involvement and thereby refusing to act on social problems. According to ministers in the Louisiana Annual Conference of the Southern Methodist Church, "the civil and religious right of the colored people" was "simply a political question without any moral questions being involved." To advocate such issues from the pulpit was to engage in the supposedly forbidden practice of "preaching politics."[48] Southern Methodists apparently missed the contradiction of calling their own opposition to black interests "spiritual" while characterizing African-American responses as "political." Northern advocates responded that "though our religion is wisely not dogmatic on such subjects, unquestionably it repels at its very heart most of these prejudices." White M. E. church members attacked segregationists' failure to defend separatism from a theological perspective: "We have yet to meet with the first person who advocates separate schools or churches exclusively for colored or white people on Christian principle."[49] Their appeals fell on deaf ears. Over time, increasing numbers of white Christians, including many in the M. E. Church, would similarly refuse to discuss segregation, claiming race relations was a social or political, not a theological, issue. Ironically, theology offered little hope for transforming the church.

Watching the debates among white Methodists, black church members took solace in their denomination's commitment to racial inclusion as central to its identity. Especially reassuring were M. E. pronouncements regarding reunion with Southern Methodists. Given the ongoing tensions, the rival denominations did not yet consider "organic union," which would have reunited them into a single denomination. They did speak of "fraternity" as a first tentative step that would help move them closer to eventual reunion. The role of black Methodists was and would remain the central issue in adjusting relations between northern and southern Methodism. The M. E. Church insisted that neither fraternity nor union with Southern Methodism could come at the cost of abandoning its biracial identity. Hartzell explained that "the Fraternity for which we should work . . . is that brotherly love which regards the colored man, as well as the white." True fraternity remained problematic as long as Southern Methodism maintained its discriminatory attitudes toward black church members. Segregation was a nonnegotiable roadblock. Weighing the demands of fraternity and racial equality, Hartzell concluded that "to let go of the prostrate colored people whom we had taken hold of and are lifting up, so as to have our hands free for embraces with the brethren of the M. E. Church South, is not the best way to do our work." A fellow white laborer in the South insisted that before any negotiations began, Southern Methodists must recognize that "the Methodist Episcopal Church cannot set off her colored members, nor abandon the schools established for them." The Methodist pattern was typical within American Protestantism.

Questions of racial inclusion similarly hindered Presbyterian efforts toward reunion. Within the M. E. Church, black members found comfort in the fact that Hartzell's insistence on racial inclusiveness had episcopal backing. In their 1880 General Conference address, the bishops declared: "We question seriously the propriety of permanent union efforts where the distinctive methods of the Church are yielded to conciliate the prejudices of good men of other denominations. We lose more than the Master gains, while others gain all we lose."[50]

Like that of their black counterparts, the white M. E. rhetoric of inclusion extended beyond ecclesiastical institutions. Radical whites, from Hartzell to Haven to many lesser-known names as well, called for the full inclusion of African Americans in the nation's economic and, especially, political structures. They pointed to the Constitution and its recent amendments guaranteeing the right of citizenship to African Americans and stressed that all people and all regions were charged with "the duty of maintaining it in its fullest integrity." From discrimination in the military to anti-miscegenation laws, white M. E. workers in the South called upon southern states to recognize the full citizenship as well as the full humanity of African Americans. "Color," they charged, "whether white or red, black or yellow, should be incognizable before the laws of the republic." What was true of constitutional and political rights was also true of natural rights, they continued: "The Negro, as a human being, is possessed of all the rights that naturally belong to human beings. . . . No natural right can be named as pertaining to any white man in the South that is not a part of the providential outfit of the black man."[51] That Southerners disagreed with these contentions only signaled the distance between the two sections and the need, in the religious language of the missionaries, for the conversion of the South. As with the competition among black Methodists, the conflict among white Methodists was about more than gaining members. It was about right belief. Like their black colleagues, white members held that right belief was best measured by a church's inclusion of all races. These M. E. calls for inclusion and conversion helped win the confidence of African Americans, even as those calls continued to alienate most southern whites.

Black and white M. E. church members thus shared a confidence in the transformative power of their church in American society. White leaders contended that the church could shape race relations, just as black members had stressed to their African Methodist rivals. On the one hand, racial interaction in religious institutions was relatively innocuous. It lacked the intimacy so threatening to whites in other settings, such as the railroad and streetcars that would become the early targets for legalized segregation. Yet the symbolic importance of religious interracialism could not be overestimated. M. E. advocacy of religious integration placed the conflict within an institution that Southerners put at the center of their society and that they declared to be the primary source of moral authority. Biracial denominations created a counternarrative to the growing emphasis on racial distance emerging in southern society.

The M. E. biracial model, church members argued, would benefit both black and white Southerners. They understood the work of the M. E. Church to extend well beyond spiritual salvation to a radical transformation of southern social and racial order. M. E. church members believed their denomination offered a model of racial equality and inclusion that, if emulated throughout Southern society, would boost the confidence of all African Americans. "The wisdom of our church in establishing mixed churches and conferences in the Southern states," black church members affirmed, is that it made "the colored people to abandon the belief . . . they are so degraded." M. E. missionaries who entered the South on the heels of Union troops were likewise confident that the M. E. Church was the key to reconstructing the South and healing the nation. Over two decades later, despite limited success, white church members argued that the church remained a force for racial transformation among whites. "The work of the Church," wrote one white worker, continues to be important in the South "for its influence upon the white race in securing . . . the recognition of the manhood of the negro."[52]

For this reason, M. E. church members believed their church bore a special burden to advocate racial equality. For southern society to change its view of the emancipated slaves, ministers stressed that churches needed to lead the way. "If we are to have a change of sentiment," blacks and whites in the M. E. Church agreed, "we must begin with the church." And not just any church, they argued. Only the M. E. Church could best lead the nation into a new vision of racial equality. M. E. biracialism could counteract the dangerous example of racially exclusive denominations. They believed the inclusion of both black and white "is a standing proclamation to the world that all distinctions on account of race or color are wrong; and that they are to be warred against until, by Christian unity in the church of God, they are done away with." In New Orleans, pronouncements from the racially mixed New Orleans Preachers' Meeting emboldened African Americans by declaring the M. E. Church sought a "speedy and complete triumph over the prejudices in her own communion and in the nation against Christian brethren, because of their color." Through its calls for racial equality in both church and society, members of the M. E. Church felt confident that "our church has placed herself in the van[guard] in handling and solving these questions, and believes that thus far God has led her."[53]

Despite occasional M. E. claims to monopolize hope, African Americans in the South found multiple avenues for advancing equality and resisting segregation in the 1880s. When the rhetoric was put aside, African Methodist and other black denominations were equally committed to racial equality, and other northern denominations also proceeded in a similar fashion. African Americans also found ways to advance and model their ideal society beyond churches. Cooperation in the Republican Party, and in other political movements such as the Unification movement in Louisiana and the Readjusters in Virginia, took place in the political realm, although politics seemed a rapidly disappearing possibility by the 1880s. Dockworkers along the Mississippi River in New Orleans also occasionally pursued interracial cooperation to advance their labor interests against management. Recreationally, black and white baseball teams played against one another throughout the 1880s, while interracial crowds looked on. On a daily basis, African Americans across the South engaged in small acts of protest to signal their rejection of a white-defined inferiority. From challenging the racial order on streetcars to refusing to utilize segregated facilities, African Americans signaled their hope for an integrated society premised on racial equality.[54] But such resistance was always precarious, and as more and more avenues were closed down, churches increasingly appeared to be the best hope for sustaining racial interaction and a rhetoric of equality. Blacks still had access to the M. E. church in ways they did not in other formerly interracial platforms. As one leading black M. E. church member indicated, "We want to feel, that though the State has not arisen to that state of grace where it can give us equal justice & privileges, that the church of our choice accords freely such privileges."[55]

Together, black and white M. E. church members in the South remained hopeful throughout the 1880s that their church would be the best catalyst to transform the region's race relations. Church members were aware of the increasing oppression limiting black citizens, even within the M. E. Church. They acknowledged that their rhetoric and vision were as much about what might be, as what actually was. They were aware that they faced serious challenges from an increasingly recalcitrant southern white culture. They also overestimated support from white members of their denomination, both north and south. And yet they continued to be optimistic that all was not lost in either church or society, that their vision of a religiously and racially transformed society might yet come into being. To twenty-first-century eyes, the glass appears half empty, at best. But to many M. E. church members, the small victories and resistance were evidence that the glass might be half full. Into the 1890s, the M. E. Church was remarkable for its inclusive racial views and policies, even though much of its rhetoric did not reach fruition. Church members were proud of the accomplishments of their churches in resisting institutional segregation, sustaining their faith in the God who had only recently delivered them from slavery. Already, the M. E. Church was more successful than any other racially mixed denomination in its ability to win converts, form churches, and preserve an interracial denominational identity.[56] Black and white church members were forging a common religious identity that transcended race, evident in their willingness to suffer for their denominational affiliation and in their debates with racially exclusive rivals. In these parallel experiences they moved closer to each other and to the ideal of a unity that valued religious commonalities over racial differences.

Bishop Haven had opened the decade after Reconstruction with his optimism that New Orleans, especially through its M. E. Churches, would lead the racial transformation of church and state alike. Echoes in New Orleans and in the North made clear that Haven was not alone in his optimism. Church members' accomplishments through Reconstruction and into the 1880s signaled a new chapter in race relations rather than continuity with the past. Throughout the 1880s, Crescent City church members pressed ahead with their efforts to construct biracial alliances within and beyond the church in order to bring about the racial transformation they envisioned. From religious governing bodies to educational institutions to moral crusades, they explored the biracialism that formed the basis of their denominational loyalty. So confident was one M. E. minister that he proclaimed the church would be "God's great tidal wave . . . to sweep away caste from the South."[57] But to a city built below sea level, rising water rarely brought good news.

CHAPTER 2

Instituting Interracial Methodism

IN APRIL 1879, the New Orleans police department distributed the following order: "Commanding officers are hereby instructed to notify the preachers of the various colored churches in your precinct that services whenever held must terminate at 10 o'clock, P.M. Under no circumstances must they be allowed to hold services after that hour. Affidavits must be made against preachers violating this order for disturbing the peace." The order affected black churches in all denominations, but it was the city's Methodist Episcopal Preachers' Meeting that successfully challenged the discriminatory ordinance. The interracial association of M. E. clergy argued that the order violated "the sacred right of liberty of worship" guaranteed by the First Amendment. The clergymen reminded city officials that "colored people are American citizens, under the same laws and guaranteed the same protection as are any other class." The city's black and white M. E. preachers presented the mayor with their petitions against the ordinance, complaining "that it pronounces as disturbers of the peace colored persons, for doing that which white persons can do without question or condemnation" and therefore that it also stood in violation of the Civil Rights Act of 1866. The Preachers' Meeting proceeded to issue to the mayor its own warning: "We hereby notify your Honor that the pastors and churches named above will continue their services as their interests or judgment may dictate irrespective of the order named." The mayor revoked the discriminatory policy. In its place, he issued a new mandate that applied to all churches, at least in theory.[1]

The effective protest against the racially restrictive closing ordinance bolstered M. E. church members' contention that the future of race relations remained uncertain in the 1880s. The mayor's quick retreat offered hope that every path did not lead to segregation. Church members joined black political and economic leaders in asserting an ongoing flexibility, in which boundaries of inclusion and exclusion were negotiated situation by situation rather than uniformly predetermined. Studies of the post-Reconstruction South have illuminated the ways in which culture, labor, politics, and even recreation maintained space for flexible black and white relations throughout the 1880s. From interracial labor unions to Republican and third-party political coalitions, African Americans throughout the South found evidence they could turn back the tide of Jim Crow.[2] Viewing the southern experience through the window of biracial denominations further reveals the racial interaction and resistance that contributed to the unsettled character of race relations in the decade after Reconstruction.

The closing ordinance also confirmed M. E. assertions of the close links between racial discrimination in church and society. Concern about this intertwining of sacred and secular segregation stood at the center of members' criticism of their racially exclusive rivals. It was also central to their allegiance to the M. E. Church in New Orleans. Much of the M. E. rhetoric focused on churches influencing society. But the closing-ordinance episode warned church members that the opposite also held true: the political realm could invade the pews. Municipal leaders had limited African-American religious expression by deeming black churches a nuisance and empowering police officers to restrict their activities. Even separate black churches, which were a supposed refuge from racial oppression in the larger social order, were not immune. There would be no boundary between sacred and secular in the effort to restrict black Americans. Yet this very permeability also pointed to the basis of M. E. optimism: the influence could flow in both directions. In the end, church leaders persuaded political leaders to shift from a racially discriminatory to a race-neutral ordinance. The Preachers' Meeting recognized that resisting racial oppression in church and resisting it in society were inextricably intertwined. In moving beyond its original focus on strictly spiritual matters, the M. E. Preachers' Meeting broadened its activities to challenge the right of the secular order to legislate racial inequality. The victory buoyed the church members' confidence that M. E. Church would play an important role in shaping a racial order whose form remained far from fixed.

The biracial character of the New Orleans Preachers' Meeting was the key to overturning the closing order, according to M. E. church members. Neither black Baptists nor rival African Methodists had persuaded the mayor to revoke the closing order, bolstering M. E. claims that their denomination was best poised to lead the fight against discrimination in church and society alike. The Preachers' Meeting's biracial membership distinguished it from any other clerical association in the Crescent City, and supporters argued that this accounted for its success. They lobbied as Methodists and Americans, rather than as black or white, demonstrating their denomination's commitment to a religious and national identity in which race was secondary. Pragmatically, racially mixed organizations combined the concerns of African Americans with the power of white members to create the most effective lobby for racial equality. The biracial cooperation also demonstrated that racial interaction did not undermine a group's effectiveness. Racially exclusive organizations, such as African Methodist denominations, could claim neither the pragmatic nor the ideal advantages of the biracial M. E. Church in the fight for equality.

These often small but symbolically significant gains propelled the ongoing optimism that the M. E. Church would play a crucial role in the creation of a racially inclusive society. Church members were well aware of increasing restrictions against African Americans both within and beyond their church in the decade after Reconstruction. Yet during this same period, M. E. church members were enacting the promise of a biracial denomination. They supported organizations that modeled the racial inclusiveness at the center of their religious identity, moving beyond their denomination's rhetoric of inclusion and its accompanying criticism of racially exclusive rivals. Theirs was a faith not confined by church doors, seeking instead the world beyond the sanctuary. They challenged one offense at a time, and each victory added another brick to a wall that they hoped would turn back the rising tide of Jim Crow. As they pursued interracial endeavors that privileged religious and national identities over racial ones, M. E. church members explored possibilities for biracial interaction that others would find closed in subsequent decades. In the process, black church members experienced the alternation between possibility and disappointment that has always characterized the African-American religious experience.

THE LOUISIANA ANNUAL CONFERENCE was a particularly promising example of racial interaction for M. E. church members in New Orleans. Annual conferences were the regional jurisdiction within the M. E. Church, representing and overseeing the work of local congregations.[3] The annual conferences also elected delegates to the General Conference, which was the denomination-wide gathering that met once every four years and whose responsibilities included electing bishops, establishing annual conference boundaries, and overseeing the denomination's work among African Americans. The Louisiana Annual Conference boundaries, like most M. E. conferences in the South, coincided with those of the state that provided its name. Many of the largest churches in the Louisiana conference were located in and around New Orleans, despite the higher concentration of Protestants in the northern half of the state. During the annual conference meeting each year, Louisiana's M. E. clergy heard reports and developed plans for the upcoming year, worshiped and offered one another spiritual support, and received their ministerial assignments for the next conference year. The white M. E. churches and clergy in New Orleans were a persistent and crucial part of the Louisiana Annual Conference's identity, even though most of the conference membership was black.

Throughout the 1880s, the Louisiana Annual Conference sustained the biracial identity that had been a defining characteristic since its founding. On Christmas Day 1865, meeting in Wesley Chapel in New Orleans, the conference began as the Mississippi Mission Conference of the M. E.

Church. It was the second M. E. annual conference founded in the South since the Civil War. Four men were ordained at that first gathering, three black and one white. Observing the equal treatment and reception of all four candidates, the white secretary of the new conference believed he was witnessing "the commencement of a new era in the South." A year later the conference reported twelve black and five white preachers when it met at the First Street M. E. Church in New Orleans. Two decades later, the conference's biracial character remained central to its mission and identity. Black and white clergy jointly led conference worship services, and conference members insisted the communion rail remain integrated. Segregation was alien to conference proceedings. "There were no distinctions on account of race or color in the annual conference. Men of both races occupied the same pews, were examined and ordained in the same classes," and deliberations occurred "in council with no disadvantage as persons of different color." With districts that included both black and white churches, Louisiana was unique even among integrated annual conferences.[4] Racial interaction characterized the social as well as the administrative aspects of conference life. White ministers stayed with black hosts, and conference members openly walked and dined with one another, to the dismay of many of Louisiana's white citizens. The white Joseph Hartzell recalled occasions when he and his wife lived and worked in New Orleans that "our Negro Pastors spent an evening with us." Hartzell noted that "such a social function in New Orleans in later years would have been severely denounced and might have led to something more serious," contrasting the openness of the 1880s with subsequent decades.[5] Both black and white members were aware of the significance of their accomplishments, noting in their conference minutes that these biracial activities proved "necessarily powerful among the people whom we serve as pastors."[6]

Integrated conference practices occasionally showed signs of trickling down to the congregational level in New Orleans, where most individual M. E. churches were racially separated. At the predominantly white Ames Chapel, for example, black worshipers found comforting the congregation's rejection of a proposal to institute segregated seating. Hartzell considered the efforts at Ames a modest success, though a more objective, but still sympathetic, observer deemed it "a lamentable failure."[7] Some whites also attended black congregations on a regular basis, such as Simpson Chapel, which was the official church of New Orleans University.[8] But even in New Orleans, these were exceptions. Across congregations of every denominational affiliation, black church members rarely received equal treatment in white congregations, even though white visitors to black churches were generally escorted to positions of honor. As a result, M. E. congregations in the Louisiana conference and throughout the South consisted almost exclusively of either white or black members, served by a minister of the same race. Racial affinity had been the M. E. Church's recommended, though not required, strategy. Although invoked more frequently by whites than blacks, church members accepted these patterns of racial affinity as natural and acceptable as long as the racial homogeneity was an expression of choice rather than the product of church legislation. Methodists were no different than any other Protestant congregation, despite some exceptional and usually short-lived experiments.[9] The pattern was also widespread beyond churches. Interracial labor unions, for example, consisted of racially segregated locals. The same was true of the Women's Christian Temperance Union where interracial state WCTU organizations maintained racially distinct local chapters. Deflecting racial mixing from local to regional jurisdictions offered the best strategy for institutionalizing interracial cooperation throughout the South. In the wrong hands, these appeals to racial affinity became tools for white supremacists to justify segregation. Still, M. E. congregations were rarely a focus for integration, as long as they remained open to all, in theory.

Acknowledging congregational demographics should not hide the significance of racially mixed annual conferences. Racial mixing, even at mid-level jurisdictions such as conferences, marked an advance over earlier practices. Neither black clergy nor black churches had been accepted as equal conference members in antebellum Methodism. And after their brief postbellum appearance, biracial conferences would not reemerge in the South until well into the second half of the twentieth century. M. E. biracial annual conferences thus marked a unique and noteworthy moment in the decades after Emancipation. Neither Episcopalians nor Presbyterians accepted black clergy and churches with the same level of equality into their regional jurisdictions, while the more racially progressive Congregationalists lacked a sufficient number of churches to form regional conferences in the South. Opposition from rival denominations indicated the significance of racial integration, even at the conference level. A Southern Methodist minister in New Orleans described as "disgusting" the racial interaction that took place between black and white ministers of the M. E. Church during the 1889 meeting of the Louisiana Annual Conference. The minister reported with horror that white M. E. officials, including a bishop, "slept on Negroes' beds, ate at their tables, walked arm in arm with them along the streets." For many white Southerners, racial interaction at even a formal regional gathering raised the bugaboo of sexual intimacy. In Virginia, the white Dover Baptist Association considered the application for membership of a black congregation. The report rejecting the application warned that "this mingling of the races must lead, more or less rapidly, to amalgamation. . . . Who can contemplate the *mongrelization* of our noble Anglo-Saxon race without emotions of profoundest horror?"[10] While some critics continued to focus on the lack of interracial congregations, M. E.

church members recognized that mixed annual conferences alone were making an impression on southern society.

As a result, advocates of a biracial M. E. Church focused on annual conferences in the late nineteenth century. They would measure their denomination's integration by the inclusiveness of its annual conferences, hoping that its influence would eventually transform individual congregations as well. Annual conferences had long been the bureaucratic level at which American Methodism had debated and resolved questions of inclusion and exclusion. The formation of the A.M.E. and later A.M.E. Zion churches in the early nineteenth century resulted from the decision to deny African-American clergy such as Richard Allen equal standing in the annual conferences. This emphasis on regional jurisdictions contrasted with the congregational focus among both Baptists and Congregationalists and the increasingly national policy-making of Presbyterians. Methodist annual conferences still retained some control in the 1880s, although they too were transitioning toward greater influence of the denomination-wide General Conference in establishing the boundaries of inclusivity. Annual conferences were an important middle and mediating ground between the practices of local congregations and the often idealistic proclamations of the national denomination and its General Conference. Annual conferences were the battleground for Methodist segregation in the late nineteenth century.[11]

By the 1880s, the biracial membership of the Louisiana conference formed an exception, religiously as well as socially. Mixed conferences had once typified M. E. organization in the South. The rash of southern conferences created in the two years following the start of the Louisiana conference also began with biracial memberships. In Georgia, black and white ministers worked together to create an annual conference whose churches boasted 8,000 black members and 2,300 white members at the time of its formal organization in 1867. In Tennessee, an A.M.E. minister described his treatment as an equal at that state's annual conference as justification for switching his affiliation to the M. E. Church. The practice of racially mixed conferences was well-known by 1874, when Southern Methodists listed them as a barrier to reunion with the M. E. Church. But the trend soon shifted. In 1876, the General Conference gave permission to annual conferences to divide along racial lines, provided a majority of black and white members, voting separately, agreed. That few mixed conferences were racially balanced only exacerbated tensions. Along the border states, most were primarily white and favored separation, while those in the Deep South, Louisiana included, were predominantly black and raised greater opposition to separation. By 1884, all but three conferences had voted to segregate, though not without resistance from both black and white anti-caste members. Whites claimed to act in the best interests of advancing

Methodism among white Southerners, while black supporters touted the advantages for leadership and representation. In actuality, white members were often acting out their own racism, and black members were simply making the best of a bad situation. For many years, the divisions undermined rather than facilitated growth. Few white Southerners joined the M. E. Church, while the spreading segregation hindered work among the African-American population that had been the greatest source of M. E. growth in the South. By the early 1880s, only South Carolina and Mississippi joined Louisiana in refusing to divide into racially segregated conferences.[12]

With the trend toward separation, New Orleans Methodists attached even greater significance to the biracial Louisiana Annual Conference. They contended their regional struggle held widespread implications for the church and beyond. Both black and white conference members had led the fight against the 1876 General Conference resolution that permitted conference divisions along racial lines. Louisiana members continued in their conviction that the annual conference was the level at which the fight against segregation in the M. E. Church must continue, despite the decision of many annual conferences to divide. The Louisiana conference refused even to vote on division, considering, in the words of one of its leading clergymen, that "a division on the 'color line' [is] a retrograde movement, a long step backward." The same minister worried that "separation of our annual conferences on the 'color line,' if persisted in, will prove in my opinion the entering wedge to a final separation in the general conference." Black church members acknowledged a growing discrimination. However, they urged annual conferences not to "divide on account of this prejudice. . . . Let us stay together and fight it out." The dangers of segregation far outweighed the increased opportunities for black conference leadership that white members and a few black allies elsewhere had advocated. The Louisiana Annual Conference evidenced the possibility of black and white working together. As a black M. E. leader in neighboring Mississippi argued, similar accomplishments there demonstrated that "our white brethren [sic] who are now laboring in the South, will not be harmed by continuing in the same relation to their colored brethren [sic] that now exists between them."[13] By holding off segregation in Louisiana, church members believed they had demonstrated that racial separation was not inevitable. Nor did the church have to reflect the surrounding society. Louisiana Methodists were aware of discouraging developments in other annual conferences. But they also believed their own accomplishments demonstrated that capitulation was not the only option. The M. E. Church in New Orleans was demonstrating that the rising tide of Jim Crow could be turned back. Against ever-strengthening currents, they would hold fast. The Louisiana conference distinguished itself by never, in its entire history, voting to divide along racial lines.

The segregation debates erupting throughout M. E. annual conferences highlight the complex and highly localized ways that segregation emerged in the South. Whether Methodists or Presbyterians, Episcopalians or Congregationalists, the decision to accept or reject segregation was most often a choice first made by local congregations and regional jurisdictions. Denominational policies came later. So it was with railroads and politics, too, as particular lines and districts chose to separate or exclude black patrons and voters and only later complied with or received the more uniform backing of states and, eventually, the federal government.[14] The different arrangements worked out in various locales demonstrate the discontinuity of racial patterns in the decades after Emancipation with both what went before and what came later. The constantly shifting negotiations and patterns of race relations across churches, annual conferences, and denominational institutions disrupted efforts to establish a simple polarity of integration or segregation. Rather, like other biracial denominations, the M. E. Church developed varying structures that enabled a continuum of racial interaction between the extremes of exclusion and equality. Recognizing this continuum, black and white church members in Louisiana maintained a flexibility that kept race relations far from fixed.

AT THE SAME TIME the M. E. General Conference enabled annual conferences to separate along racial lines, it also provided a strong boost to one of the voices most critical of that very decision. The New Orleans–based *Southwestern Christian Advocate* became the denomination's official newspaper in the South, replacing the *Methodist Advocate* of Atlanta, which had received denominational backing for the previous seven years. The switch to the *Southwestern Christian Advocate* demonstrated that the denomination had not abandoned its commitment to racial equality and inclusion, despite growing concerns to the contrary. The recently displaced *Methodist Advocate* had favored racially separate annual conferences and concessions toward the racial mores of southern whites in its effort to appeal predominantly to white readers. The *Southwestern Christian Advocate*, in contrast, had taken black church members as its primary, but not exclusive, audience and had been a tireless advocate of racial equality and an opponent of racially separate conferences. Joseph Hartzell established the *Southwestern Christian Advocate* in 1873.[15] Although it struggled financially, the newspaper quickly became the most visible and vocal advocate of the denomination's commitment to a biracial identity. The paper defined its mission as a defender of equality and an opponent of caste. Following its elevation to a denominational paper, Hartzell affirmed the paper's unchanging principles: "This paper has from the first waged an unceasing war against the spirit of caste, both in State and Church, and has never once lowered its standard to the demands of the enemies of colored people, or their friends who, from motives of policy, have aided to perpetuate the spirit and fact of caste in Church or State."[16] The *Southwestern Christian Advocate* was a critical voice in the effort to sustain a biracial M. E. identity that would remake southern race relations. No better record exists for understanding the hopes and fears of black M. E. church members as their denomination struggled with questions of racial identity and the limits of inclusion.

The *Southwestern Christian Advocate*'s elevation to denominational status only increased its influence and readership. With the affirmation and financial backing of the M. E. Church's publishing agents, Hartzell expanded the paper in his efforts to bolster biracial support for the greater protection of black rights in church and society alike. Hartzell's success almost ended his role as editor. When the denomination elevated the newspaper to an official publication, it also assumed the right to elect its editor. The 1876 General Conference proceeded to elect a black minister, Hiram Revels, as editor. Hartzell, the white runner-up, received the post only when the editor-elect declined the position. Hartzell continued with his unabashed advocacy on behalf of African Americans, criticizing both his city and his church over their failures to respect racial equality. The *Southwestern Christian Advocate* formed a southern counterpart to the *Zion's Herald* in New England, which had been edited by the radical Gilbert Haven and was the denomination's only other newspaper with an unequivocally anti-caste emphasis. Hartzell urged black and white alike to support the newspaper, pressing white congregations as persistently as black for subscriptions. While the paper claimed to have the largest circulation of any paper in New Orleans, its support poured in from throughout the South. Typical was the Tennessee clergyman who assured potential readers that the newspaper's qualities and commitments "recommends it to the hearty support of every man without regard to color." At the end of 1878, Hartzell proudly reported that of five hundred new subscribers, one hundred came from white congregations. By 1890, a study of the black press reported that the *Southwestern Christian Advocate* "is read by the whites more than is any other Afro-American journal in the Union." Subscription rates fell short of estimating the paper's influence. M. E. workers throughout the South reported that ministers frequently read the *Southwestern Christian Advocate* from the pulpit, ensuring that poor and illiterate black church members were included in its reach.[17] This combination of influence and racial stance had stood at the center of Bishop Gilbert Haven's confidence that the M. E. Church in New Orleans would lead the church and the nation away from the path of segregation.

Hartzell also ensured the *Southwestern Christian Advocate* staff modeled the interracial cooperation he advocated on its pages. In 1881, as soon as he procured the necessary funds, Hartzell hired an African-American assistant editor, A.E.P. Albert. Hartzell's successor, also white, retained Albert. Observers described the relationship between Albert and the successive white editors as one of equal partners rather than a hierarchy of a senior and junior authority: "These two conduct the paper, being jointly editors." Albert frequently wrote editorials, remaining in charge of the day-to-day management of the paper during the frequent absences of both Hartzell and his successor. From 1884 forward, the General Conference elected African Americans as editors, one of whom was Albert. These editors became colleagues, and sometimes rivals, of other black religious editors such as those at the *Georgia Baptist*, the A.M.E. Zion *Star of Zion*, and the A.M.E. *Christian Recorder*, who also spoke passionately on matters of racial equality and inclusion from their respective denominational contexts. At the *Southwestern Christian Advocate*, the tradition of biracial cooperation persisted as white church members continued to assist black editors in managing the paper. The newspaper's racial advocacy and the model of its editors proved an important example to black and white church members, not just in New Orleans but throughout the nation. Many of the *Southwestern Christian Advocate*'s editors went on to other positions of prominence in the denomination, including the episcopacy, testifying to the influence and visibility of the paper's editorship. Even the election of the paper's editors was a biracial affair, standing among the many ballots considered by each quadrennial General Conference of the M. E. Church. Yet this may have also had a conservative influence, as candidates with an accommodationist stance were more attractive to the increasingly conservative white majority by the turn of the century. Nonetheless, a recent historian of Methodism has suggested that, save pulpits and college classrooms, "no institution in the denomination has had more impact upon black education, opinion, and public issues than the *Southwestern Christian Advocate*."[18]

EDUCATIONAL INSTITUTIONS WERE another crucial part of the M. E. work in the South, and New Orleans was no exception. Schools were second only to churches in the effort to construct a new M. E. identity. In the Crescent City, Joseph Hartzell worked with local black M. E. leaders to establish New Orleans University, which opened in 1872 under the auspices of the denomination's Freedmen's Aid Society. Like all M. E. institutions, New Orleans University welcomed students "without regard to race or religion," though it was opened with a particular eye toward serving African Americans. Church-related institutions became the only hope for racially mixed schools, following the end of New Orleans's experiment with integrated public education during Reconstruction. Visitors in 1888 confirmed that the university was "open to both sexes and all races and religions."[19] By 1888, the university had moved to a new building on St. Charles Avenue, where it assumed a visible presence on the most fashionable street in the city's uptown section. Despite calling itself a university, the school began with more of a remedial and high school curriculum than a collegiate one, as was typical for institutions serving freed people. New Orleans University also offered degrees in medicine and theology before these departments were transferred to Meharry Medical College in Nashville and Gammon School of Theology in Atlanta as part of a denominational effort to consolidate resources. The nursing school and associated hospital remained in New Orleans, continuing to offer important medical services to the city's underserved black population. Teacher training quickly became the university's other successful professional program. New Orleans University, along with the Congregational-sponsored Straight University across town, trained most black teachers in the region, thereby exerting considerable influence over the shape and character of public education in New Orleans and throughout Louisiana and the Gulf Coast.[20]

Establishing New Orleans University linked Crescent City Methodism to cities and similar religious institutions throughout the South. Planting schools and colleges stands as the most enduring legacy of northern Protestant missionary efforts in the postbellum South. The unwillingness and inability of southern state governments to establish schools for black citizens left the field of education wide open to churches. Nearly every northern-based denomination sent people and funds south to begin institutions for freed people, whose enthusiasm and attendance testified to the need for and priority of education among the recently emancipated. The schools ranged from rudimentary grade schools to professional training schools and, as with New Orleans University, often tried to meet the whole range of needs within a single institution. By 1878, the M. E. Church had educational institutions in every southern state save Virginia, while Baptists, Presbyterians, and Congregationalists made similar efforts. These schools became the lasting contribution of most biracial denominations, since none matched the success of the M. E. Church in organizing new churches.[21] Located primarily in cities, the schools attracted a wide range of students from surrounding areas and from a variety of religious backgrounds. Few institutions pressed for conversions, though most considered their educational work a form of mission that could result in new members. In New Orleans, for example, the Congregationalist Straight University claimed as many as three-quarters of its students were Roman Catholic. Church-sponsored schools remained the primary source of education for southern blacks well into the twentieth century, and churches continued as the main source of funding for black colleges and universities in the South as late as the 1930s. Most contemporary private black colleges in the South have their roots in these church-sponsored institutions.[22]

But a black college was not the intent of the founders of New Orleans University. M. E. schools such as New Orleans University hoped to fuse the two appeals at the heart of the denomination's success among black Southerners: racial inclusion and education. Meaningful integration proved much more formidable than educational achievement. Church leaders had the most success modeling racial integration in the faculty and governance of the institution. Five years after the university's founding, the Louisiana Annual Conference passed a unanimous resolution urging that "as soon as practicable one or more colored professors should be employed in the School." The rhetoric of such a resolution came more easily than the reality. Especially in its early years, university leaders found it difficult to recruit and retain qualified black professors, given the university's limited financial resources. The desire for black faculty and the lack of candidates meant that faculties across the South had to be integrated, at least until enough black teachers could be trained. The commitment to integration also extended to the university's board of trustees. By the end of Reconstruction, three of the city's black M. E. clerics joined several of the city's prominent white lay and clerical members on the university board. By 1887, the board elected a local black M. E. clergyman as its first black president, and the pattern of biracial leadership continued throughout the school's history.[23] But such accomplishments rarely exerted the desired influence.

The ideal of a racially diverse student body remained elusive. Few white students attended the university. White M. E. leaders in New Orleans occasionally sent their children to the university for a semester or two as evidence of their commitment to interracialism. More often, however, their children attended well-established Methodist universities in the North, such as Wesleyan or Boston University. Native white Southerners avoided the northern church-sponsored schools altogether. The quest for black faculty members only further alienated white Southerners. White no less than black parents recognized the importance of schools in shaping both intellectual and social behavior, and they did not want their children "brainwashed" by northern views on race or politics. Nor did southern whites believe black citizens should receive any more than a rudimentary education, a contention that directly conflicted with the mission of the schools. The founders of New Orleans University encountered opposition in securing a charter from the state legislature, confronted by white claims that such an institution was not necessary. Southern churches eventually constructed their own network of schools and colleges for white students, where children could be socialized into white ways of thinking about race and religion. After considerable debate, the M. E. Church too began erecting white schools in the South in the late 1880s, claiming the new efforts were necessary in order to serve the widest possible population. In a decision echoing its earlier stance on separating annual conferences, the 1884 General Conference decided that "the question of separate or mixed schools . . . is to be left to the choice and administration of those on the ground and more immediately concerned." Despite such setbacks, black Louisianians insisted that education was paramount; its context was secondary. The lack of integrated education was regrettable, one resident conceded, but "what we want is an education, whether it be acquired in a mixed or a colored school it must be had."[24] Like its denominational counterparts, the legacy of its educational institutions would outlast the M. E. Church's commitment to integration.

In New Orleans, the Congregationalist-sponsored Straight University may have most closely approached the M. E. ideal to fuse a biracial identity with an educational mission. Congregationalist schools throughout the South, which were built and sponsored by the American Missionary Association, often had the greatest success in maintaining the semblance of a racially mixed student body.[25] Like New Orleans University, the Congregationalist school maintained open admission policies despite a lack of white interest. Professional departments offered the greatest promise for biracial cooperation. Fifteen of the first twenty graduates from Straight's law school were white.[26] Likewise, the first graduating medical class at New Orleans University included both black and white students. The professional programs had started in reaction to the exclusion of black students from the law and medical schools of Tulane and other leading southern universities. The departments at both universities readily appointed black graduates to their faculties, ensuring their interracial character. Yet neither professional school would survive. Straight's law department closed in 1886, and in 1911 New Orleans University consolidated its medical department with the denomination's medical school in Nashville. Both Straight and New Orleans Universities struggled financially. In 1935, the two schools merged to form Dillard University. Dillard remains a testament both to religious education in the South and to the racially separate basis upon which that legacy had to be built, despite early celebratory efforts to the contrary.

M. E. WOMEN IN NEW ORLEANS also played an active and important role in fostering the denomination's biracial ideal, even as most of the church's celebrated interracial activities centered on the more visible male-dominated institutions. Leading the effort in New Orleans was Jennie Hartzell, whose husband Joseph had begun the *Southwestern Christian Advocate* and played an important role in advancing the denomination's biracial character in the Crescent City. Beginning with four missionaries in 1879, Jennie Hartzell established a biracial mission project that continued to grow for the next decade, becoming the catalyst and model for the formation of the denomination-wide Woman's Home Missionary Society. The woman's home-missionary movement created intimate interracial experiences unlike any other in the church. No less than male ministers and teachers, female missionaries suffered ostracism and sometimes physical threats for the interracial character of their work. Hartzell and her missionaries used a column in the *Southwestern Christian Advocate* to report the previous week's accomplishments. Visiting the city's impoverished black residents in their homes constituted the first duty of the white female missionaries. Once inside the homes, the missionaries provided religious and moral instruction, offered advice on personal habits and home life, taught lessons in sewing and domestic work, and encouraged attendance at M. E. churches and schools. Leaving the comfort of their own churches and homes, these mostly northern women crossed the thresholds of black homes to carry out their work. Each week throughout the 1880s in New Orleans, the missionaries reported between a hundred and a hundred fifty home visits apiece. The missionaries lived in the districts they served, reciprocating the hospitality they received on their visits. In their own homes, the missionaries hosted "mothers' meetings" and gatherings of young women to instruct them in matters both practical and spiritual.[27] Training in the domestic arts was institutionalized at the Peck School in 1888, which, from 1912 onward, was located next to New Orleans University. Regardless of their locale, these female missionaries interacted with black residents far more intimately and regularly than did most M. E. church members who touted their denomination's commitment to biracialism and black missions.

The M. E. missionary women in New Orleans were neither the first nor the largest group of white women to minister to the city's black residents. The success of northern Baptist women had been an important impetus to the M. E. work. Like the Methodists, some of the earliest Baptist work among women had taken place in New Orleans, and its success led to the formation of the Women's Baptist Home Mission Society in 1877. Both the concentration on New Orleans, where Baptists had five missionary women by 1878, and the relation of the women's society to the denomination's other missionary societies became models for the M. E. Woman's Home Missionary Society that was organized in 1880. Baptists in particular focused on missions, along with education, as prime areas of biracial cooperation, especially in the absence of biracial denominational structures. The interracial cooperation within the women's missionary organizations also encouraged an ecumenical spirit. M. E. women considered the Baptists co-laborers rather than rivals in a vast field of work that far exceeded either denomination's ability to meet the need. By the 1880s, these female missionaries came to represent the new class of northern white missionaries to black Southerners. A generation earlier, men had led the charge, often with wives and families in tow, to establish churches and schools. By 1880 a new wave of single women came south to carry out work in black homes and on the fringes of the established church and school institutions. Every large southern city reported the presence of several such missionary women. As in New Orleans, most were Baptist or Methodist, but Congregationalists, Presbyterians, Episcopalians, and nearly every northern-based Protestant denomination with a missionary organization sponsored at least one home missionary in the South.[28] This missionary movement was often rooted in a blatant paternalism that assumed the inferiority of black women. Moreover, the movement's emphasis on the program of racial self-improvement known as uplift often taught skills that were as much about training black women to work as domestics as they were beneficial to the "moral elevation" of the black home. Still, women in home missions would continue as one of the last and often unremarked-upon examples of racial interaction, laying the groundwork for the interracial women's organizations that preceded the Civil Rights movement.

The biracial character of the woman's home-missionary movement in New Orleans stemmed from its concern for both races and not merely from the interaction of white missionaries with black residents. Although Jennie Hartzell began the work with a focus on the needs of the city's black women, concern soon came to include impoverished white residents. By 1884, Josephine Cowgill, one of the original missionaries to New Orleans and superintendent of the work after Hartzell's departure, reported that during the previous seven months "2,726 religious visits among the poor" included "both white and colored." Cowgill's religious and domestic classes in local churches included responsibilities at the white Ames Chapel as well as several of the city's black congregations. The Louisiana home-mission society proclaimed a constancy of its mission without regard to race, promising to "carry its work into destitute localities among the white people just as among the colored people. In all cases aiming at the ultimate salvation of souls and the elevation of the home." Nor was the work limited to white missionaries. Auxiliary societies sprang up in nearly every M. E. congregation in Louisiana, with black women carrying out much of the work themselves and filling the leadership ranks of the state organization. By 1886, Louisiana boasted sixty-seven auxiliary societies and nearly 2,600 members of the Woman's Home Missionary Society.[29] Yet certain lines still could not be crossed. While white women ministered to both black and white, black women were limited to working among their own race.

Black church members celebrated their inclusion in the denomination's Woman's Home Missionary Society as a model for race relations. Throughout Louisiana, black women assumed leadership of the state districts, working alongside the white missionaries who served the region. Society members were especially encouraged by their reception at national conventions where, in inverse proportion to state gatherings, the majority of members were white. In 1884, for example, Louisiana's sole delegate to the National Woman's Home Missionary Conference in Cleveland was

Mrs. M. L. Dale, whose husband was pastor of Wesley Chapel, one of New Orleans's largest M. E. congregations. Dale addressed the conference, ate in common with the other delegates, received warm accommodations in a white home, and upon her return was "happy to say there was no color line visible in that convention." Her reception at the convention contrasted sharply with her experience traveling, when she was forced to ride in a different car once the train crossed into Alabama. A correspondent from the 1889 national convention offered similar assurances that the M. E. Church's Woman's Home Missionary Society still modeled racial inclusion. Suggesting the exceptional nature of such acceptance, the reporter suggested "the Louisiana conference will be pleased to know that their delegates were not snubbed up here but were fraternally granted seats in the delegation and entertained alike. The Methodists (white) up here are Christians and not Negro killers."[30]

FROM THE LOUISIANA ANNUAL CONFERENCE to wider denominational organizations such as the Woman's Home Missionary Society, M. E. church members in the 1880s gained confidence in the transformative power of their church. For church organizations, these accomplishments represented institutional expressions of a biblically and theologically rooted inclusiveness. At the same time, black church members built upon this tentative M. E. interracialism to advance other concerns that they believed transcended racial differences. The budding promise that a religious identity could create a common ground that transcended, or at least made room for, racial differences provided the courage and confidence to advance interracial cooperation in other areas as well. The primary goal was to emulate the model of a common religious identity to create a unified national identity that likewise subordinated racial differences. The progress of the M. E. Church in New Orleans suggested that one day, American citizens might be recognized first and foremost for their citizenship rather than the color of their skin. Yet church members did not simply rush from their local to their national ideals, which perhaps accounts for charges of racial conservatism that have plagued African Americans who remained in the M. E. Church. Nonetheless, throughout the 1880s church members pointed to possibilities for transcending race that echoed accomplishments within the M. E. Church. Such examples built upon M. E. connections, even as they extended beyond them.

Especially in the context of New Orleans, black M. E. church members considered a unified anti-Catholicism as evidence that not only Methodists, but black and white Protestants as a whole, held much in common that overshadowed racial differences. Throughout the 1880s, Methodists in New Orleans shared the national tendency toward anti-Catholicism, publishing warnings in the *Southwestern Christian Advocate* about Roman Cath-

olic efforts to lure Protestants into "the ruinous meshes of a false and se-
ductive system." In many ways, this anti-Catholicism was simply part of
being an American Protestant and a response to the emergence of Catholicism as the single largest Christian denomination in the United States by
the latter half of the nineteenth century. In its basic contours, the rhetoric
of anti-Catholicism among New Orleans black Methodists did not differ
from anti-Catholic sentiment nationwide. They joined criticism prevalent
throughout the nation in expressing fear about unchristian practices, political and religious intolerance, and anti-democratic tendencies among Catholics.[31] Yet it was also a product of the particularity of New Orleans. Black
and white Methodists in New Orleans shared a common struggle to preserve their Protestant identity in a place that stood, more than the rest of
the nation, "under the influence of Romanism." Protestants in New Orleans equated the end of Reconstruction and the return of native Louisianians to office as a Catholic coup that constituted, according to one Congregationalist, "the greatest triumph for the Roman Catholic church ever
achieved in this country."[32]

African Americans used the broader anti-Catholic rhetoric to emphasize
their own particular concerns, even as they repeated many of the arguments
of white anti-Catholicism. In their efforts to preserve and regain their
rights as American citizens, black Protestants demonstrated their own
commitment to the Protestant and democratic principles assumed to stand
at the center of the nation's identity. Black church members charged that
the Catholic Church "has not a single teaching that is not directly opposed
to the cherished political ideas of the American Republic." By pointing to
the ways that Catholicism hindered American ideals, black Methodists felt
they were demonstrating to whites their own understanding of and commitment to American ideals and thus their worthiness for full inclusion in
the American nation. Anti-Catholicism suggested that African Americans
better appreciated American liberty than many white Catholics, who neither valued nor properly utilized the constitutional freedoms to which their
skin color alone seemed to entitle them in the post-Reconstruction South.
African Americans were committed to the American nation and its form
of government. They sustained no loyalty to any foreign power, unlike
Catholics, who supposedly offered their blind obedience to the pope. Patri-
otic denunciations of Catholic intolerance cast African Americans as insiders and Catholics as outsiders to American political ideals. African Americans hoped to demonstrate to skeptical whites their worthiness to remain
participants in a political system that increasingly excluded them. As one
minister explained, "We are as genuine Americans as the white man."[33]

This criticism of Catholic religious practices highlighted African-American claims to stand firmly within the center of the American Protestant
mainstream. By pointing to the errors of Catholicism, African Americans

proved they were as capable as any white person of recognizing what Protestants considered false religion. As one editor argued, "the colored people, no less than the white people of this country, are believers in the Christian religion." Criticizing Catholic rituals also countered the prevalent stereotype that African Americans were more prone to superstition than whites. Especially in New Orleans, black church members wanted to assure their denomination that they were orthodox, despite living in a city that teemed with Catholics and practitioners of voodoo and suffered from a reputation for moral laxity. As the nation debated the place of African Americans in the national polity, black anti-Catholicism joined together religious and racial concerns to demonstrate that "the colored man is a fellow not only in the bonds of Christian brotherhood, but also in the bonds of patriotism and citizenship, and sooner or later it must be recognized."[34]

Anti-Catholic rhetoric also functioned as instruction to fellow black Methodists in New Orleans. The city's pervasive Catholic ethos infiltrated Methodist churches even as Methodist congregations criticized Catholic rituals. That many M. E. church members and even ministers had converted from Catholicism only compounded the difficulties. The New Orleans Preachers' Meeting struggled against the "disposition on the part of some of the pastors and churches to conform in some respects to the ritualistic services of Romanism." The city's M. E. leaders complained of ceremonies for "baptizing banners [and] domestic animals," the use of Roman Catholic objects including the sepulcher and weeping Mary, and the corruption of sacraments, such as the presence of godparents at baptisms. Ministers reported widespread Catholic behavior on the part of their congregants, ranging from excessive celebrations at Christmas and the gathering of Holy Water before Easter, to an elaborate emphasis on All Saints' Day. The repeated criticisms of Catholic practices warned Methodists living in a community with "a strong Roman Catholic sentiment" to keep within the bounds of Methodist orthodoxy.[35]

The warnings extended to whites as well. As an impetus to greater denominational efforts on their behalf, black church members repeated rumors of Catholic designs on the nation's black population. One New Orleans clergyman cautioned that "Rome has her eyes and institutions riveted on the Negroes of this country" and thus the "Protestant world" must "take due notice." The rise in anti-Catholic rhetoric in New Orleans coincided with calls by the American Catholic hierarchy to pay greater attention to the nation's black population and especially with the arrival of a new archbishop in New Orleans who named building up black Catholicism as one of his highest priorities. Other times it was not criticism but backhanded compliments of Catholicism that black Methodists used to encourage greater efforts on their behalf. They skillfully played racial issues against white Protestant fears of Catholic domination, warning that "the Protestants of this land, in their blind adhesion to caste and race prejudices," must not ignore Catholic missionary efforts which were proceeding on claims of being the only religion "offering the Negro communion on terms of equality."[36] Other Protestants also invoked similar missionary concerns. Baptists in New Orleans and Virginia, and Presbyterians as well, used the specter of Catholic conversions to plead for greater attention to black Southerners.[37]

Black Protestants in New Orleans had to maintain a careful balancing act in articulating their anti-Catholicism. Catholics still controlled most of the city's corridors of power, black as well as white. As a result, most criticisms of Catholicism were distant and diffuse, referring to foreign lands or generalized complaints rather than pointed concerns about Catholic behavior in and around New Orleans. Occasionally, however, black Methodists could not resist local illustrations of their wider concerns. Protestant evangelists often encountered, and likely provoked, Catholic intolerance in southern Louisiana, leading many to the conclusion that "Romanism in Louisiana, as elsewhere, is the determined enemy of religious freedom." Black Methodists were especially critical of the Catholic Church's support of the Democratic Party, which was also the party of white supremacy. Also troubling were local white Catholic defenses of lynching in "certain cases" and a call in the archdiocesan newspaper to ensure "that the State shall not again fall under Negro rule." Of greatest concern to local residents were the city's schools. Black Methodists blamed the constriction in local schools, especially at the expense of black residents, on Catholic domination of the school board. Catholics, they reasoned, preferred parochial schools and thus had little concern for the condition of public education. M. E. leaders spoke of a "Romish-Bourbon conspiracy to destroy" the schools in New Orleans and Louisiana.[38]

Anti-Catholicism thus furthered the ongoing effort to create a common bond between black and white members of the M. E. Church, who were equally concerned about Catholic incursions into the American religious landscape. Several nineteenth-century white Methodist writers and clergy had written on the dangers of Catholicism and its threat to religious and civil liberties and the American way of life.[39] The religious rhetoric formed yet another means of constructing a shared identity in which religious continuities transcended racial differences. Both black and white Methodists made vigorous denunciations of Catholicism while asserting the M. E. Church as the embodiment of American Protestant ideals. Noting that most Americans adhering to the errors of Catholicism were white, African Americans argued that racial homogeneity guaranteed neither religious nor national purity. A shared religious identity rooted in Methodism, they suggested, offered a much better basis for constructing community than did racial similarities.

As African Americans struggled with their place as citizens in the years after Reconstruction, anti-Catholicism emerged as one manifestation of the effort to declare a black identity that stood firmly within the American Protestant and democratic mainstream. African Americans hoped to demonstrate their worthiness as citizens and political participants by affirming their religious and political orthodoxy. In depicting the political and religious failures of Catholics, African Americans portrayed Catholics as outsiders while affirming themselves as insiders. Most blacks were American-born, while in New Orleans no less than in the rest of the nation, increasing numbers of Catholics were immigrants and hence political and religious outsiders. National and religious identities offered an alternative to the primacy of racial categorization. But in the end, the situation reversed. Catholic immigrants, from Irish to Italian to Eastern European, successfully cast themselves as white and American, enabling them to emphasize race over religion and thereby portray African Americans as outsiders.[40] In an ironic twist, the outsider became insider, forcing African Americans into the very role they had sought to avoid. Compounding the irony was the white supremacist appropriation of anti-Catholicism in the Ku Klux Klan and the racial rants of politicians such as Tom Watson. Even in the face of a religious rival, a common Protestant and Methodist identity proved unable to transcend differences in race.

THE EFFORTS OF M. E. CHURCH MEMBERS were not the only opportunities for racial interaction in New Orleans, despite a growing trend in the city toward racial separation. Throughout the 1880s there remained many informal opportunities for racial mixing, including baseball contests between black and white teams and interracial facilities on Lake Ponchartrain's beaches.[41] But more formal institutions also facilitated racial cooperation. Interracial labor unions along the city's riverfront provided one of the most promising examples during the 1880s and into the early 1890s. Black and white workers belonged to different locals, but their locals belonged to the same unions and coordinating agencies, which advanced the interests of workers of all races, black and white, native and immigrant. The Cotton Men's Executive Council was an alliance of black and white unions that coordinated efforts across unions to gain wage and work improvements, while the Knights of Labor were also an important force in unifying black and white labor in New Orleans, as it had in much of the South. The interracial labor structure resembled integration in the M. E. Church: local units based on racial affinity, which belonged to larger, coordinating agencies or conferences that accepted both black and white members.

Recognition of black workers and their interests, even in separate unions, was an important challenge to widespread racist assumptions about African Americans in general and black laborers in particular. The interracial labor unions challenged the belief that whites did not always benefit from the exclusion of black laborers, paralleling a central argument that black church members used to explain their denominational loyalty. M. E. church members viewed these encouraging labor developments as part of their larger efforts to resist segregation. The *Southwestern Christian Advocate* took notice of the hope of interracial labor, celebrating a parade of black and white laborers "with positions according to official rank, without discrimination on account of race or previous condition." The biracial labor cooperation provided yet another reason for black citizens to "take courage," for it was evidence that "they are not to be, and will not be forever ignored, despised and abused on account of their color or previous condition." The *Southwestern Christian Advocate*'s editors were so overwhelmed by the interracial labor parade that they suggested it offered greater hope "than any political or ecclesiastical circumstance which has transpired for years." Biracial labor cooperation would ebb and flow with changing political and racial circumstances but continued to impress M. E. leaders well into the twentieth century as a promising model that often exceeded the church in subordinating racial differences.[42]

Politics constituted another area of widespread hope for biracial cooperation that might transform the social order. African Americans throughout the South had tasted the promise and possibility of political participation during Reconstruction. They remained hopeful in subsequent decades, even as opportunities for political involvement rapidly decreased. Methodists in New Orleans were no different. Church members celebrated any mechanism that brought black and white together, whether within or beyond church doors. Nor did they consider political action distinct from religious commitment. In fact, a shared belief in the close relationship of religion and politics formed further common ground for black and white M. E. church members. Joseph Hartzell, for example, seconded the assertion of a fellow Methodist editor who insisted that "every political question today has a religious bearing and must be solved, if solved at all, by the application of Biblical truth." Black church members agreed. The 1880 Louisiana Annual Conference passed a resolution that "whenever any political measure in the State or nation involved moral questions, the pulpit should lead public sentiment in denouncing wrong and defending the right."[43] Both white and subsequent black editors of the *Southwestern Christian Advocate* stressed the intersection of religion and politics on the paper's pages, insisting upon their duty to provide "political information" and not to shy away from "our imperative duty to preach righteousness," even when others perceived such pronouncements as meddling in politics.[44] Ongoing commitment to political involvement demonstrated that M. E. church members considered their church as a way to engage and transform the world and not a place to retreat from it. Theirs was a Methodist view of church that continued the social-reform movements, especially abolitionism, emerging out of the revivals of the Second Great Awakening in the early nineteenth century.

The political involvement of both black and white M. E. clergy demonstrated their shared commitment to the connection between Methodist faith and political action. During Reconstruction, both black and white M. E. clerics sought elective office as an expression of their commitment to bring Christian ethics to bear on the political life of the postwar South. Hartzell, for example, served on the New Orleans school board during the 1875–1876 school year, participating in its experiment with integrated schools. Pierre Landry, a black M. E. cleric who was a minister in New Orleans in the 1880s, first served a term as mayor of Donaldsonville, was a delegate to the 1879 state constitutional convention, and was elected to a term in the Louisiana legislature as late as 1882. Nor were Louisiana Methodists unique. In Mississippi, M. E. clergyman Hiram Revels was elected to local and state positions before filling the seat of former Confederate President Jefferson Davis in the United States Senate.[45] Meanwhile, politics remained a primary concern of the editors of the *Southwestern Christian Advocate*. They used its pages not only to encourage their readers to vote but to vote in specific ways, especially against candidates who threatened black rights, supported the state's lottery, or encouraged electoral corruption and relied upon machine politics.[46]

Churches also became centers of political activity. Ministers emerged as the most effective means for disseminating political messages throughout the community, while church buildings became a primary gathering place for political meetings. These gatherings addressed a broad range of issues affecting the black community. In January 1882, for example, First Street M. E. Church hosted a meeting to petition Congress for a mail ship between the United States and Africa. In August 1888, black M. E. clergy coordinated a meeting to protest violence against the state's black citizens and to establish an emigration bureau and a committee to lobby the state and federal governments for greater protection. Neither black nor white church members lost sight of their commitment to infuse politics with religious concerns in the years after Reconstruction. Black Methodists called upon church members to hold the government responsible for its treatment of black citizens, while white members of the M. E. Church criticized government persecution of black laborers who went on strike in 1880 in Louisiana.[47] These efforts represent an important strain of the often overlooked tradition of political protest among black M. E. church members.

Party affiliation proved one of the clearest shared political commitments that joined black and white M. E. church members and offered hope for a transformed racial order. White M. E. church members in the South, such as those at Ames Chapel in New Orleans, supported the Republican Party. They had been some of its leading figures during Reconstruction, earning them the scorn of most white Southerners but reinforcing their connections to African Americans who likewise supported the Republican Party for its role in freeing the slaves. Black Republican support was widespread throughout the South. Typical was Margery Laporte, a black M. E. church member, who considered the Republican victory in the 1880 national elections a cause for rejoicing and a reason to "look and wait for the change to come" that would benefit black Southerners. The model of interracial cooperation was a primary reason for ongoing black loyalty to the Republican Party. In March 1888, Henry Clay Warmoth began his gubernatorial campaign in New Orleans, where he "was listened to and applauded heartily by a very large and mixed audience of whites and blacks." Later that year, the black editor of the *Southwestern Christian Advocate* declared that the Republican presidential victory, replacing the Democratic incumbent, left his people "buoyant with hope for a brighter future."[48] African Americans across a wide range of religious denominations, including rival African Methodists, were equally supportive of Republicans. Joining ranks with both fellow African Americans and white Republicans revealed the potential for political affiliation to encourage racial interaction and advance interests that transcended racial boundaries, even as political rivals used their party to constrict the electorate along racial lines.

Beyond Louisiana, the political possibilities appeared even more promising. Republicans achieved some post-Reconstruction success in Tennessee, North Carolina, and Virginia. Third-party alternatives were also encouraging, as black Southerners moved beyond the increasingly conservative Republican Party. The most successful interracial political alliance was the Readjusters, a black majority party that governed Virginia from 1879 to 1883. Third parties like the Readjusters were not free from the racism prevalent among white Southerners. Nor did they advocate breaching the social separation of the races upon which white Southerners were so insistent. They did, however, recognize the importance of black voters in challenging Democratic rule and thus supported the black franchise. Black supporters were rewarded with the spoils of political victories and participation in party organization. The Readjuster coalition was always fragile, consisting of black and white Republican and white Democratic voters. As a result, the party was never unified on racial policies, only on the necessity of maintaining a biracial coalition to defeat Democrats. Nonetheless, black Virginians found a new sense of possibility in the political sphere, even as they recognized the limits and challenges they faced. Biracial political alliances, whether Republican or third party, offered alternatives to the prevailing racial order, and the occasional victories by such coalitions, like those of biracial churches, sustained a hope that the alternative might someday prevail. The Readjusters and other independent movements exposed the pliability of southern racism in the 1880s, even though they could not ultimately transcend it. Any presumption of white supremacy as static and hegemonic masks the ways, ranging from the Readjusters to the M. E. Church, in which it was constantly challenged and occasionally undermined. Nor did the legacy of interracial politics end in the 1880s. New interracial movements, mostly notably Populism, would emerge during the next decade to challenge once again the Democratic Party's white-supremacist dominance of the South.[49] These alternatives, more notable for their existence than their failure, inspired black Southerners continually to explore possibilities for interracial cooperation.

METHODISTS IN NEW ORLEANS WELCOMED any opportunity to forge interracial alliances. As their political involvements made clear, they willingly reached beyond specifically religious concerns to identify causes that would protect African-American interests and advance the effort to construct a biracial identity. Church members found common ground on issues beyond black-white tensions, although the concern for African-American citizenship undergirded interest in these other areas. Protests against the anti-Chinese legislation were one such example. In 1879, and again in 1882, the United States Congress passed legislation seeking to bar Chinese immigration to the United States. Whites feared that unchecked immigration would overrun the West and thereby displace white laborers in the emerging labor market along the nation's West Coast. The federal legislation sanctioned discrimination already occurring against the Chinese in California and the West. Black and white church members opposed both the particular restrictions against the Chinese and the more generalized acceptance of discrimination. Whites in the M. E. Church shared African-American concerns about any efforts to curtail the freedoms of a particular race or group who lived or sought to live in the United States. Church members therefore praised President Rutherford B. Hayes's veto of the 1879 anti-Chinese legislation, claiming that the president "by his veto, has saved the national honor, and checked a dangerous precedent in the way of class, or race legislation." Although halfway through his term, Hartzell considered Hayes's veto to be "the very brightest act of his administration." When Congress passed similar anti-Chinese legislation three years later, Methodists and African Americans in general once again heaped praise upon then-President Chester A. Arthur for vetoing the legislation.[50]

Black opposition to the Chinese Bill stemmed most directly from the concern for the rights of African Americans. If governments could legislate discrimination toward the Chinese, it would prove difficult to prevent legal restrictions against African Americans, recent constitutional amendments notwithstanding. It was a prediction most lived to see come true. In a widely published speech given at the Congregationalist-sponsored Straight University in New Orleans, black M. E. minister A.E.P. Albert warned against "this assault upon human rights directed, in this instance, against the Chinese, and over their shoulders, unwarrantedly and uncharitably, against the Negro." Albert warned that the proposed legislation undermined basic constitutional rights guaranteed to all people and the very principles by which God intended all of humanity to live. Whites such as Hartzell shared African-American concerns about legislation to curtail the freedoms of any race or group who sought to live in the United States. They too recognized that bill to be "inspired by race prejudices." Whites pointed to the Constitution as preventing such discrimination against any race. Even more fundamental was the opposition rooted in religious justification: "We insist upon the Christian treatment of every human being."[51] The vocal opposition of white M. E. church members contributed to the sense of common identity with their black Methodist counterparts and reaffirmed their commitment to a racially inclusive church and society.

Yet all was not so idealistic. Even when black and white Methodists agreed on issues, their motivations could, and often did, differ. Whites were worried about restrictions on mission work in China if the Chinese responded with similar exclusionary measures. They also feared the financial ramifications of Chinese retaliation, which would affect trade. The impact would reach the Crescent City, for "the Chinese bill, if it became a law, would lead to a cessation of much of our commerce with China, which is now relied upon as a great feeder of the Southern Pacific Railroad and the shipping in the port of New Orleans."[52] These white arguments illuminated the uncertain place of race relations, even within the M. E. Church. While shared political goals might broaden a sense of biracial identity, the differing motives of black and white belied a genuine unity transcending racial differences. Different motives might unite to advance specific political issues, but for meaningful advances in race relations, all would have to be committed to the righteousness of the cause, regardless of any additional benefits that might result. The inability to engage many whites on the moral and religious dimensions of the discriminatory legislation foreshadowed a growing unwillingness for whites to consider segregation as a religious problem. Also troubling was the widespread Republican support for the anti-Chinese legislation. The same party that had previously protected African Americans was retreating from that role. Political affiliation appeared an increasingly unlikely possibility for expanding the biracial identity that black M. E. church members hoped to extend beyond their churches. In an ominous sign, President Arthur signed the Chinese Bill in 1882.

At one point in the Chinese Bill debate, Hartzell charged that Americans hoped to rid the nation of Chinese "to make room for the friends of beer and whiskey."[53] Like the debate over the rights of Chinese immigrants, the struggle over temperance revealed both the possibilities and the limitations facing M. E. efforts to extend biracialism beyond its own denominational structures. Temperance enjoyed nearly unanimous support within Methodism. From its earliest days under Wesley, temperance formed an important part of Methodist movement. Until the late nineteenth century, Methodists characterized intemperance as a personal sin from which individuals needed to repent. Their reform efforts focused on church discipline and moral persuasion directed at individuals. By the 1880s, however, a growing national sentiment against drinking transformed temperance from a personal to a social and political issue. M. E. church members supported the emphasis on prohibition as a political tool to end the social problems of intemperance. Methodists did not stand alone in the fight against alcohol. They did, however, play a central role in it.[54] Black and white members of the M. E. Church hoped that the biracial support of the temperance movement might expand the acceptance of interracialism in southern society.

Temperance looked especially promising for moving southern society toward a greater degree of racial interaction and cooperation. White and black clergy each established temperance movements within their congregations. At Ames Chapel, the pastor organized a weekly temperance society in 1878 and regularly invited temperance societies to his church for sermons and rallies. At the same time, black pastors pressed the cause among their congregations. A.E.P. Albert, who would rise to prominence as a black M. E. leader, established his reputation in Louisiana by his temperance work, winning the praise of his first congregation for his extensive work against the dangers of alcohol consumption.[55] Temperance work extended beyond simply parallel efforts by each race. In organizations such as the New Orleans Preachers' Meeting, black and white clergy worked together to promote temperance among both races through efforts ranging from petitions and promises for abstinence to interracial meetings. Black and white temperance advocates blamed much of the South's racial antagonism on alcohol. While black and white advocates often disagreed on whose drinking lay at the root of the problem, both concurred that "half of the race troubles in the South begin and end while the contestants are in liquor; and would not occur at all but for the liquor."[56] Biracial temperance work therefore seemed to hold the solution to both the immediate problem of liquor and the larger issue of race relations.

M. E. church members in New Orleans hoped temperance would extend biracial unity outside their denomination and even beyond the church. In 1881, for example, members of the M. E. Church in New Orleans rejoiced that both they and the state's Southern Methodists sent nearly identical resolutions to the state legislature calling for prohibition. Reports from Mississippi strengthened biracial aspirations. In Dekalb, Mississippi, white

Southern Methodists supported a black M. E. temperance advocate, with the result that black and white ministers were "working shoulder to shoulder in this great fight against the demon 'alcohol.' "[57] The following year brought news that a white Southern Methodist minister and a black M. E. presiding elder edited a monthly temperance newspaper together. In North Carolina as well, black and white women created a biracial organization for that state's chapters of the Women's Christian Temperance Union (WCTU).[58] Across the South, church members believed temperance could forge biracial alliances across political as well as religious divisions. The first black editor of the *Southwestern Christian Advocate* assured his readers that "God is not a Democrat, and He is not a Republican as Republican politicians in the United States are now. God is a prohibitionist."[59] African Americans reminded white temperance advocates of the necessity of black votes to winning temperance elections. They hoped the caution would discourage violence against black voters at the polls. The resulting "united voice of the good people of both races" could reverse the nation's moral slide and transform models of race relations along the way. Shared commitments to temperance, church members in New Orleans concluded, might be the best road to racial equality.

But biracial cooperation proved the exception more than rule. White stubbornness was too strong to transcend racial differences, and Jim Crow took a seat in the temperance movement before interracial efforts could solidify. Black advocates received little support and no acknowledgment for their efforts. White leaders blamed black voters and politicians for failures to pass temperance legislation, ensuring they would not have to unite with African Americans and providing additional justification for disfranchisement. National organizations followed suit. Ostracism by the WCTU was especially troubling to black temperance supporters in the M. E. Church in New Orleans. They decried the action of the WCTU convention in Atlanta in 1883 when it voted that "it was best to keep the colored work separate from ours." Appeals to WCTU president Frances Willard failed as she explained her support for a policy of states' rights in which each union could decide for itself on the question of racial inclusion. Willard, like so many white church leaders, bracketed questions of race as political rather than moral and therefore outside her realm of influence or concern. The divisions took their toll on black M. E. church members in Louisiana. Two black M. E. ministers wishing to hear Willard speak at a meeting at a Southern Methodist Church in New Orleans in 1889 were forced to choose between sitting in the colored gallery or leaving the church altogether. The men chose to leave. Willard did address black Methodists in the Crescent City—at a later time and in a separate meeting. At the Louisiana State Convention of the WCTU a week later, delegates

passed resolutions that "the colored people cannot and must not be ignored," even going as far as to called them "our brothers and sisters." The
convention then promptly set apart a time and place "for the colored
women of the town" to hear lectures, call speakers, and conduct their own
business.[60] By 1890, Albert concluded that "the more righteous the white
people of this State grow against . . . the liquor traffic, the more they hate
the Negro. A regular ratio of increase exists between the two facts."[61]

THE CRUMBLING OPTIONS for building an interracial identity did not signal
defeat for African Americans in the M. E. Church in New Orleans. While
disappointing and discouraging, such setbacks did not mark the end of
black church members' hope in an interracial church that might yet transform the nation's race relations. Such optimism undoubtedly failed to acknowledge the frailty of white M. E. support. In New Orleans, white advocates such as Hartzell were rare, and their northern, Republican roots
effectively stymied any influence among native whites. Moreover, Hartzell
and his white colleagues compelled very little following amongst their
northern white brethren, who could appreciate their work without having
to actively promote racial equality. After Reconstruction, black church
members hoped that northern churches would replace northern troops in
enforcing a Christian and constitutional inclusion of African Americans.
Northern churches were unwilling to assume that role. Nonetheless, in a
context of uncertainty where some interracial examples persisted, black
church members refused to give up. Churches were their best hope, not
for retreat but as the means to transform society. In the end, their hope
was premised more on what might be than on what actually was.

A decade after the end of Reconstruction, black M. E. church members
in New Orleans found themselves in a precarious position. The rising tide
of Jim Crow was beating harder and harder against an increasingly fragile
wall of resistance. Methodists in New Orleans and the Louisiana Annual
Conference had sustained impressive interracial accomplishments
throughout the 1880s, demonstrating the as yet unsettled future of race
relations and thereby keeping hope. Nor had the M. E. Church abandoned
its official language of inclusion and its affirmations of equality. But persistent black membership, rather than active inclusion by whites, was keeping
the M. E. Church biracial. At the same time, the potential for wider influence appeared to be shrinking. Although church organizations had preserved the semblance of an interracial character, this biracial model generally failed to extend its reach and transform the larger religious, social, or
political realms. Neither commitment to temperance nor opposition to
Catholicism, despite their popularity among southern whites, had managed
to ease racial tensions between black and white southerners. Black church

members did not lose hope, but at the dawn of the nineteenth century's final decade, they were less confident that the divisions of race would first melt away in New Orleans. Even within the M. E. Church, African Americans would have to depend solely on leaders of their own race in advocating for the racial advances that had once been the concern of black and white Methodists alike.

CHAPTER 3

The Decline of Interracial Methodism

No INDIVIDUAL WAS MORE IMPORTANT than A.E.P. Albert in guiding New Orleans's black Methodists through the turbulent final decade of the nineteenth century. He faced head-on the full fury of the rising tide of Jim Crow in his city, his church, and his country. Albert's uncompromising agitation was rooted in two life-changing transformations. The first was the transition from slavery to freedom. Aristides Elphonso Peter Albert was born a slave on December 10, 1853, on a sugar plantation in St. Charles Parish, Louisiana, thirty-five miles from New Orleans. His father, a white man originally from Bordeaux, France, was the overseer on the plantation where Albert's mother was a slave. Even as a child, Albert thirsted for freedom. Early in the Civil War he tried to escape to Union lines but was caught and returned to his owner. Once freed by Emancipation, Albert never forgot the humiliation of the slavery into which he had been born. He spent the rest of his life advocating on behalf of his race for the fruits of freedom to which their newfound citizenship entitled them.

A religious conversion that followed quickly on the heels of Emancipation was the second transformation that propelled Albert's racial advocacy. Albert was reared a Catholic, which was the faith of his parents and was the predominant faith throughout southern Louisiana. He and his mother maintained their Catholic identity when they moved to New Orleans after Emancipation. They changed course dramatically in 1866, after a falling-out with their parish priest. The priest refused Albert's mother absolution when she denied that Emancipation constituted a mortal sin against the South. Mother and son soon joined the Methodist Episcopal Church, which had recently arrived to preach a gospel of racial equality among freed slaves. Albert's conversion marked the intertwining of religious and racial identities that would inspire his life's work. Soon after, he began a lifetime of service in the M. E. Church, empowered by a denomination that promised to privilege religious over racial identities. Within two years of his conversion, the M. E. Church licensed Albert to preach. He began a classical and theological education in Georgia, attending Atlanta and Clark Universities. In 1878, he received his first ministerial appointment in Houma, Louisiana, where he earned a reputation as an effective temperance worker. Albert returned to New Orleans in 1880, where he continued to work as a minister. In 1881, he became the first graduate of the theological depart-

Figure 3.1. A.E.P. Albert (1853–1910). Courtesy General Commission on Archives and History of the United Methodist Church.

ment at the Congregationalist-sponsored Straight University. From 1881 to 1884, he held an appointment as a presiding elder in the Louisiana Annual Conference, while also serving as assistant editor of the *Southwestern Christian Advocate*. In 1884, he returned to full-time parish ministry for three years in Shreveport, Louisiana.[1] Albert's successful transition from slave to educated freedman, and his movement from Catholicism to Methodism, prepared him for leadership among the racially and religiously diverse communities in New Orleans and beyond.

Albert's untiring defense of the M. E. Church, which he based on its biracial commitment, earned him widespread denominational recognition. In September 1887, a national committee selected Albert to complete an unexpired term as editor of the *Southwestern Christian Advocate*, following the death of the previous occupant. Albert's appointment invigorated the hopes of black Methodists in New Orleans and throughout the South. Albert was not the first African American to serve as editor—his predecessor held that distinction. He was, however, the first native of Louisiana to do so. Louisiana conference members celebrated that the entire denomination would now come to know their conference's rising star, since the newspaper editorship represented the most vocal and visible position available to black church members. Throughout the 1880s, Albert had been a leader in advancing a biracial M. E. identity. Working alongside white leaders such as Joseph Hartzell, Albert had led the charge against the dangers of racially exclusive denominations in the quest for equal rights. Less than a year after his initial appointment, the 1888 General Conference overwhelmingly elected Albert to remain the *Southwestern Christian Advocate*'s editor for a full four-year term. Albert's support extended beyond New Orleans to include the entire denomination. He received the nearly unanimous support of white as well as black General Conference delegates.[2] Frequent mention of Albert as a candidate for bishop led many to hope that he might be the first African American elected to that position. Church members throughout the South understood Albert's rise to leadership as ongoing evidence of their denomination's commitment to a racially inclusive identity.

Following the trajectory of Albert's career broadens our understanding of the ways black Christians responded to racial segregation in the final decade of the nineteenth century. Yet Albert's story is little known, despite his prominence as both a religious and a racial leader. His elusiveness stems from a lack of extant personal sources, despite his being an articulate and assertive leader in both religious and civic spheres. Albert's story emerges almost exclusively on the pages of the *Southwestern Christian Advocate*, and in occasional references in church records. His editorial writings reveal him to have been a man passionately committed to fighting segregation on all fronts, religious and secular. With widespread backing, Albert brought a new level of agitation and radicalism to the black membership of the M. E. Church in the final two decades of the nineteenth century. He thus challenges the accommodationist stereotype associated with New Orleans's black Protestant community and with black M. E. church members as a whole. Albert signaled a new level of agitation as he worked to hold both his church and his nation accountable to their founding principles. Frustrated with a growing racial conservatism within the M. E. Church, he directed at his own denomination many of the criticisms previously reserved for African Methodist rivals. Albert's critiques were not an abandonment of his hope for an interracial M. E. Church but rather a push for a restoration of that ideal. Black church members still believed their church could play a crucial role in transforming the nation's racial order. But they would not wait for denominational changes that would only subsequently influence the secular sphere. Albert pushed for changes in church and society simultaneously, continuing his predecessors' focus on the intimate intertwining of segregation in religious and secular realms. He subordinated all other concerns to the quest for racial equality, including his earlier attention to temperance and denominational rivalries. This new phase of agitation reflected Albert's belief that the racial order remained contested, even as segregation made substantial gains.

ALBERT DIRECTED MUCH OF HIS agitation at the M. E. retreat from racial equality and inclusion during the final decade of the nineteenth century. In the 1880s, M. E. church members had built on the gains of Reconstruction to advance an interracial Methodism they believed would bring about racial equality in church and state alike. By the 1890s, black church members found themselves alone in their calls for equality. White church members softened their racial advocacy as the M. E. Church expanded its efforts to recruit white Southerners. The change was pragmatic rather than theological. M. E. workers recognized they would have little success among white Southerners if they insisted on the primacy of racial inclusion. Mollifying rather than challenging southern white racial mores became the norm. By the turn of the century, northern church members increasingly advanced racial views that conformed to those prevailing among southern whites. Black church members complained that their denomination no longer "maintained the spirit and principles with which our Church entered the southern States."[3] No official pronouncement or policy explicitly dictated a shift of the M. E. commitment to racial equality and inclusion. In fact, much of the rhetoric at the denominational level persisted. But actions spoke louder than words. Albert and his colleagues pointed to abundant evidence in New Orleans and throughout the South of changing M. E. views on race. Surveying the religious and social landscape, Albert acknowledged the tempered hopes and precarious position of African Americans on the eve of the twentieth century: "We praise God that we have escaped out of Egypt and spread the passage of the Red Sea." But nearly thirty years after Emancipation, the journey was incomplete. "We are not yet out of the wilderness. The promised land is yet to be possessed."[4]

Black M. E. church members were not alone in feeling abandoned. Most organizations had made the same compromise. Temperance work, for example, had a promising interracial start. Many black Methodists had supported the Women's Christian Temperance Movement, only to discover that southern racial mores would permeate its organization and reform efforts. Albert had been involved in another temperance organization, the International Order of Good Templars, which suffered a similar fate. British in origin, the Templars asserted the humanity of all people and insisted on integrated lodges and biracial organizations. Southern white Templars revolted, refusing integration and precipitating a division of the international organization. The Templars eventually reunited when they agreed to accept segregated lodges. Labor, which was another promising possibility, fared little better. Common economic interests had enabled dockwork-

ers in New Orleans, and Savannah and Galveston as well, to break the color
line in the 1880s. During that same time, the Knights of Labor succeeded
in attracting white as well as black recruits. But interracial labor cooperation, like temperance work, fell apart in the face of a growing resistance to
integration in the 1890s. Many would go the way of the railway unions,
which strictly excluded black members, although a few organizations continued to accept separate black locals.[5] From labor to social reform, and
from religion to politics, while Southerners' concerns for respectability reconfigured nearly every biracial institution along segregated lines.

Among Methodists, changes in the Freedmen's Aid Society marked the
shift in denominational priorities from black to white Southerners. The
Freedmen's Aid Society had coordinated the M. E. Church's work among
African Americans, especially its educational component. In 1888, the
General Conference voted to expand the name of the Freedmen's Aid
Society to include "and Southern Education Society." The change reflected the growing M. E. emphasis on "white work" in the South. Black
church members reminded the denomination that existing M. E. schools,
such as New Orleans University, remained committed to their founding
principle of admitting students regardless of race. Albert and his colleagues warned that building additional M. E. schools to cater specifically
to whites would undermine the denomination's biracial identity and commitment, as well as draining resources away from financially strapped institutions. Their protests were to little avail. By 1891, twenty-one of the
forty-three schools operated by the renamed Freedmen's Aid and Southern Education Society were for whites. In the previous two years, the number of white schools had nearly doubled, from twelve to twenty-one, while
the reconstituted Freedmen's Aid and Southern Education Society added
only one school for African Americans. In 1908, southern white schools
were transferred to a different denominational society, segregating M. E.
education all the way from the local classroom to national oversight and
funding. Exacerbating racial separation was a shift from classical to industrial education in many of the denomination's black schools.[6] Like most
northern organizations working among black Southerners, the M. E.
Church emphasized the strategy of Christian uplift, which focused on
practical training and personal morality. Rather than educating for equality and inclusion, the schools prepared black students for second-class status. The denomination rationalized the revised educational philosophy,
arguing that it reduced white opposition in the South and increased financial support from the North.

The shifting focus of white M. E. workers in New Orleans reinforced
the denomination's changing racial priorities in the 1890s. The first generation of postbellum missionaries to New Orleans advocated for the rights
of African Americans in both the political and the religious realms. Typical

was Joseph Hartzell, who, even when he served as minister of a primarily white congregation, spent much time, energy, and even large sums of his own money defending African-American interests. When Hartzell left his pastorate, he retained his membership and celebrated important life events, including his son's baptism, in the city's black congregations rather than the predominantly white Ames Chapel where he had served as minister.[7] The new generation of workers had different concerns. From the 1890s forward, white clergy turned their attention toward other white communities in New Orleans, forming missions among French, German, Italian, and Scandinavian peoples. With the exception of a few whites working at New Orleans University, the M. E. Church had left its work among African Americans in New Orleans almost entirely in the hands of its blacks members. White claims of deferring to a new qualified generation of black leaders did not accurately describe the new race relationships. A wall emerged separating the city's black and white work in a way Hartzell and his colleagues would have neither understood nor tolerated. By 1893, a black minister in New Orleans lamented that "times have changed somewhat, and many of those who prate loudest and boast of being the friends of the Negro are found to be very sadly wanting."[8]

Not just in New Orleans but also throughout the denomination advocates for racial equality were neither as prominent nor as vocal as they had been in the first decades after the Civil War. Those who spoke most forcefully on behalf of African Americans, whether black or white, generally failed to gain positions of widespread denominational influence. Hartzell, for example, was promoted through the ranks of the Freedmen's Aid Society, where his advocacy would be expected but not disruptive. When Hartzell was elected to the episcopacy in 1896, it was as a missionary bishop to Africa, confining his authority, and often his physical presence, to the far side of the Atlantic. Other sympathetic whites, such as Bishops Willard Mallalieu and Wilbur Thirkield, rarely used their positions to advocate actively and publicly on behalf of black church members. Unlike the fiery Gilbert Haven in the Reconstruction era, or even Hartzell, they seldom utilized the press or pulpit to call for racial inclusion, preferring more private but less effective methods of persuasion.

By the end of the nineteenth century, most northern whites had become distracted from racial concerns in the South. The declining number of missionaries working among southern blacks and an increasing fraternal dialogue with Southern Methodists only furthered the distance between black church members in the South and whites in the North. Related developments encouraged racialist thinking. The budding alliance between science and religious progressives, especially in defending evolution against fundamentalism, made space for accepting the notion that different races reflected different stages of evolution, with Anglo-Saxons representing the highest possible development. The rise of the Social Gospel also shifted the attention of progressive northern Protestants away from the previous generation's concern with race. The primarily northern challenges of urbanization, industrialization, and immigration replaced the needs of freed people as the focus of social-reform efforts. For many Northerners, the nation's problems were no longer concentrated in the South. Rather, the most pressing concerns were in the North itself. Social Gospel advocates had very little to say on the question of race. At the same time, the Social Gospel looked toward a variety of institutions for the salvation of humans and society, rather than privileging the church as unique in that role. Churches lost their special calling as the means to transform society, especially in the realm of race. Although the Social Gospel was never a formal institutional organization, it represented a decidedly conservative approach to the nation's racial dilemma, just like the churches with which it was connected.[9]

The changing climate left black M. E. church members with little voice in their denomination. Beyond the leadership of black congregations and districts, they were limited to a few administrative positions and the editorship of the *Southwestern Christian Advocate*, whose readership had become almost exclusively African American by the 1890s. The inability to elect a black bishop most clearly demonstrated the limits of black church members' ability to shape denominational discourse and decision making. Black church members knew that by the final decade of the nineteenth century they had numerous qualified candidates, even as whites affirmed their intent to elect a bishop of African descent upon the nomination of a capable candidate. Each General Conference passed resolutions affirming that "color is no bar to the election of any man to the episcopal office." When the time came to elect bishops, however, white delegates failed to cast their votes for African Americans. A black nominee might receive a few token votes early in the balloting, only to have them trickle off as voting proceeded and candidates were eliminated. Even in their best showing, African-American candidates, Albert among them, failed to receive even half the votes necessary for election to the episcopacy.[10] White Methodists, north as well as south, were simply unwilling to elevate a black man to an office where he would have authority over whites. Racial equality was, in most contexts, unacceptable; black authority over white was inconceivable. The same anxiety that kept black voters away from the ballot box and black passengers out of first-class railroad cars kept black Methodists from the episcopacy.

Methodism showed little immunity to the segregationist tendencies making inroads throughout Southern society. Racial separation at youth gatherings was particularly disconcerting, since it provided a moral imprimatur for socializing children into racial separation. Organizers at the 1895

International Epworth League Conference, a gathering of Methodist youth in Chattanooga, attempted to relegate black delegates to a separate section at the rear of the tent. When the delegates sat instead in a middle section, even though they were "away from any immediate contact with any white persons," they were nonetheless "twice ordered away by the ushers in the most offensive manner, even threatened with arrest by the police." At first, African Americans in the M. E. Church blamed the troubles on the other Methodist bodies involved, especially Southern Methodists. However, further investigation revealed not only that the offending usher belonged to the M. E. Church but that the denomination's Epworth secretaries had given approval to the seating arrangements "for the sake of peace" with the southern hosts. Even the revival, a hallmark of American evangelical Christianity once distinguished by its interracial character, bore witness to the rising tide of segregation in New Orleans. Congregationalists in New Orleans reported an integrated revival led by Dwight L. Moody and Ira Sankey, but Methodists were not so successful. Sam Jones, a famous Methodist revivalist from Georgia, spared no one in explicating the sins of his audiences. Jones chastised the wealthy, supported temperance, took a liberal stance on the public role of women, and even preached that religion could, by itself, solve the race problem. Yet Albert complained of Jones's insistence on segregated seating during a series of revival meetings in New Orleans in 1890. By insisting on segregated seating at his revivals, Sam Jones could turn his attention directly to blacks, address them with derogatory names, and blame their troubles on a unique propensity for drink and a desire for material things without the drive to earn the money to pay for them. Jones then preached a message of uplift, stressing accountability and praising the rise of industrial education, which would reinforce the subservient place of black citizens.[11] Like increasing numbers of white Methodists, evangelists appeared less willing to point out the peculiar sins of caste and racism among their white audiences.

This desire to conciliate white Southerners was the most common explanation for the growing M. E. acceptance of racial separation. As a result, northern whites insisted the changing racial practices were merely social and pragmatic, not religious. They rejected black members' efforts to discuss segregation in theological terms, insisting instead on the language of expedience rather than the language of the Bible. Several concerns prompted the new wave of efforts to appease white Southerners. The denomination needed greater growth among southern whites to justify its increased expenditures in building churches and schools for them. Only by proceeding according to the dominant racial mores could it realize the necessary gains. At the same time, interest in reuniting northern and southern Methodism was growing. To facilitate both fraternity and eventual reunion, few white members were willing to press the issue of racial inclusion, which both sides readily acknowledged was the greatest source of tension between the two denominations. In a pragmatic calculus, white members were willing to sacrifice growth and loyalty among black members in order to gain the much larger membership of the Southern Methodist Church. The institutional, financial, and numerical strength of the Southern Methodist Church, which had recovered from the devastation of the Civil War, enabled it to dictate the terms on which reunion might take place. While white Northerners were compromising on racial inclusion, Southern Methodists only hardened their resistance to change. Albert frequently highlighted Southern Methodist intransigence, including nostalgia for the antebellum racial order and ongoing support for the Democratic Party, which had denied black citizenship rights in Louisiana and throughout the South. The M. E. Church, which had entered the South on the premise of racial equality, was courting the ecclesiastical manifestation of white supremacy.

By the 1890s, Albert and his black M. E. colleagues were experiencing a marginalization within their denomination that mirrored their alienation from American society, both north and south. The ways in which white M. E. church members abandoned their southern black counterparts both echoed and reinforced the broader neglect of the nation's black citizens. Northerners who had once claimed the inclusion of black citizens as a central concern had abandoned their rhetoric, often adopting the language and imagery of white supremacy in its place.[12] As old soldiers and new politicians worked to heal sectional tensions, white supremacy became the basis for reunion. The combination of racial prejudice and a desire for national unity silenced the few remaining voices defending African-American interests. At the same time, a decade of white Democratic rule in southern states had marginalized black voices from the South. Few Northerners could speak to the plight of either black citizens or black church members, even if they wanted to.

In the South, the northern silence created wider spaces for the abuses that fueled Albert's racial agitation. White tyranny was increasing with frightening frequency, ranging from lynching and rape to economic marginalization, segregation, and disfranchisement. New Orleans was no longer an exception. In 1889, Albert lamented that "even in this city, every week we hear of colored men being set upon, beaten or cut half to death and taken to the hospital where they have died." Rare was the white resident who defended the rights of black citizens. Even "the better class of white people," who had advocated on behalf of freed persons as recently as the decade after Reconstruction, kept quiet in face of this increased oppression. Black and white residents alike conceded the "growing hatred and hostility" that characterized the "attitude of a large number of the whites in the South toward the Negro," as many church members abandoned the interracial optimism that had inspired them during the previous decade. This worsening climate in the 1890s signaled a new era of race relations that differed markedly from previous decades. African Americans complained that three decades after Emancipation their constitutional rights appeared no greater than they had been before the Civil War. Conditions led some black residents to suggest in 1892 that "the slavery existing in Louisiana today is more galling than the system which existed before the war."[13]

As a civic and religious leader, Albert played a central role in confronting the worsening racial climate in his church and in his city. His widely celebrated leadership among black church members challenges the image of M. E. loyalists as more accommodationist than their African Methodist counterparts. For Albert, white efforts to restrict black citizens necessitated opposition on a variety of fronts. Most pressing, he would not stand by while white vigilantes threatened black lives. Immediate resistance, not patient retreat, formed the appropriate response to physical aggression. He encouraged those threatened with violence to respond in kind. In the litany of equal rights, the right to bear arms was no less important than any other. When confronted by mobs, Albert urged his readers not to turn over their weapons "until you have discharged its contents among your invaders." Albert hinted that violence might be the language white mobs best understood. He preceded his invocations with exhortations to be "peaceable, law-abiding citizens." But when the worst arrived, as it increasingly did in Louisiana and throughout the South, he urged readers to remember his often repeated refrain that "if you must die, see that some one dies with you."[14] Albert conceded violence was not a particularly Christian response. But he also noted that whites who carried out violence, or permitted it to occur, claimed a Christian identity themselves. Black victims who responded in kind should be judged no worse.

The core of Albert's activism, however, focused on his hope for constructive change. Ironically, the declining racial climate engendered optimism that a rigidly segregated society might yet be avoided. While increased violence and efforts to legislate segregation suggested the solidification of a racially stratified society, a countervailing interpretation could also explain those developments. Whites were turning to violence and segregation because they were uncertain and worried about the racial order, not because they were confident of their position in it. By the 1890s, whites directed much of their animosity not at the lower class but rather at middle class blacks who confounded white understandings of racial distinctiveness. Black success, not black failures, propelled white calls for greater separation. Albert and his generation of clerical colleagues represented an important component of that emerging black middle class. Black accomplishments suggested an ability to integrate with middle-class American culture that denied the racial inferiority upon which white supremacy was built. Whites turned to disfranchisement and segregation to prevent such assimilation, revealing their own anxiety that it was already occurring. Laws, no less than violence, became tools to impose a hierarchy that was not always clear. Legislating Jim Crow therefore constituted far more than merely codifying existing practices. Black advances demonstrated that the place of African Americans was neither static nor self-evident, necessitating efforts to legally inscribe black inferiority. The white need to impose a rigid color line was as telling as the forcefulness with which they instituted it. Black citizens recognized in this insecurity the possibility they might yet force the alternative whites so clearly feared.[15]

Politics remained a venue through which many African Americans hoped to achieve the changes they still believed possible. Albert exemplified those black citizens who continued to advocate political participation as not only a right but also a means by which black citizens might exert an influence. Albert's political advocacy aggressively challenged white efforts to suppress the black vote, rejecting any calls for a retreat into racially separate churches or communities to wait for a better day. He used the pages of the *Southwestern Christian Advocate* to emphasize the importance of casting ballots, even if whites resorted to violence and intimidation to discourage African-American voters. Voting was a concrete step toward improving the declining race situation. The mere act of casting a ballot was a significant assertion of one's freedom and citizenship, even in the face of violence and with the knowledge the votes would not be counted fairly. Prior to each election, Albert printed reminders for readers to ensure their voting papers were in order so they could register for the upcoming election. He insisted that black citizens assert their right to vote "at whatever cost" rather than "patiently submit to . . . their political degradation." Albert prodded his readers even when they faced danger at the polling places, invoking the right to vote as the most important of rights and the fulfilling of this duty as the highest expression of patriotism. As each election marked another effort to repress further the rights of African Americans, Albert claimed that the only excuse for not voting was "imminent danger to life in doing so."[16] The 1890s witnessed an increasing need to invoke that very excuse.

Albert's political agitation even led him to question the longstanding black loyalty to the Republican Party. African Americans' membership in the Republican Party had been a nearly universal assumption since the emergence of the black franchise. It had also been an important link joining black and white M. E. church members in South, exemplifying how common identities beyond Methodism could transcend racial differences. But Republicans had retreated from their commitment to black rights. Like the M. E. Church, the Republican Party cast away its interracial commitments to become more attractive to southern whites. In response, Albert called for an end to the fawning "political subserviency" of black Republicans. Albert's cynicism grew when Republican victories in 1888 failed to improve the plight of black Southerners.[17] Under Republican president Benjamin Harrison, African Americans suffered the repeal of the Federal Elections Law and the defeat of the National Education Bill and found no relief from the violence of white mobs. Albert expressed frustration that there appeared "no difference between a Republican and a Democratic administration."[18] His political criticism was rooted in his Christian faith. As a Christian and a Methodist, Albert argued, he must "know no party." Rather, it was his duty "to be true to God, to the just claims of humanity," and to "righteousness," "regardless of what party it benefits or injures." Albert did not recommend the Democratic Party as an automatic default. Rather, he warned that Democratic animosity no longer provided a sufficient reason for African Americans to support the Republican Party. He cautioned Republicans that "the days of [our] adhesion are numbered" since few would risk harm to vote for a party that did not protect them.[19] Those politicians and political parties who best protected the rights of African Americans would earn the black vote.

Albert's threats were not new. Dissatisfaction in previous decades had likewise pushed black voters to seek interracial political alternatives. Especially in New Orleans, some had aligned with Democrats, though even the most elite Creoles of color ultimately found the party's racism unyielding. In neighboring Mississippi, Hiram Revels, a black M. E. minister who briefly represented that state in the United States Senate, had joined with Democrats to overthrow a Republican regime hostile to free people's interests. In Virginia in the early 1880s, the Readjuster Party had forged an interracial alliance to govern the state, while an interracial party also briefly ruled Tennessee. The final decade of the nineteenth century witnessed a new wave of biracial third-party alternatives. The most successful were the Populists, who created a national movement that included recognition of the political rights of black citizens. Widespread black support for Populists in 1892 and 1896 revealed that Albert's dissatisfaction with the Republican Party was widely shared. Emerging out of the Farmer's Alliance movement, Populists tried to unite numerous interests, including the South and West, agrarian and urban workers, and most importantly, black and white. The interracial cooperation among Populists was based on the common interests of black and white workers. Populists elected black party members to leadership positions and to national conventions as evidence of their interracial commitments. In Louisiana, fusion parties had some success, and only fraud prevented a victory over Democrats in 1896. However, the movement rooted in economic self-interest was always fragile. Few white Populists embraced racial equality. Many blamed the 1896 electoral failures on black voters, whom they considered easily manipulated for purposes of electoral fraud. The party soon collapsed as most white populists came to support disfranchisement as the best solution to their political frustrations. Not unlike the M. E. Church in the South, Populists had briefly carried the hope of a new interracial order only to succumb to white self-interest riding a rising tide of Jim Crow.[20] Politics and class, no less than religion, would remain subservient to race.

By the 1890s, racial segregation was coming to intrude upon every aspect of African-American life. The M. E. alienation that Albert protested against therefore formed an important swell reinforcing the large surge of segregation pounding the daily lives of black Southerners. Whites in New Orleans, as elsewhere in the South, became fixated with racial separation. Justifications for segregation ranged from fear of racial contamination through miscegenation, especially as a result of a supposed black sexual aggressiveness, to white assertions of black physical and intellectual inferiority. Jim Crow reared its head at local fairs, where efforts to bolster white attendance meant setting apart specific days for "the colored folks." When Albert tried to admit a respected black M. E. presiding elder to a mental hospital in New Orleans, the facility refused, explaining that "the whites do not like to have colored people thrown in among them, and we deem it best not to attempt it." African Americans were excluded from juries and most forms of civil service. At the same time, businesses routinely discriminated on the basis of race. Whites in New Orleans forced African Americans to shop in "the merest dens," which nonetheless charged "as though they were palaces," while the city's insurance companies annulled policies covering black churches solely on the basis of the congregation's racial makeup.[21] The Grand Army of the Republic, an organization of Union Soldiers, refused during Decoration Day celebrations in the 1890s to affiliate with the black soldiers who had fought by their side during the Civil War. Even prostitutes, in New Orleans no less than Atlanta and Nashville, were segregated. From separate hospitals to separate schools to separate burial grounds, attempts to separate black and white marked every phase of Southerners' lives. Segregation, Albert complained, was inescapable for the black citizen: "It denies him a meal at the restaurant, a glass of soda at the confectionery, a place for his living body at the hotel, and for his dead body in a white cemetery."[22]

Nothing came to represent the offensiveness and the complexity of Jim Crow more than separate railroad cars. Segregating transportation involved some of the earliest attempts to legislate Jim Crow. Railroad cars were places where black and white might otherwise come together as equals in a proximity uncomfortable for whites. By 1890, Louisiana had joined five other southern states in passing separate car laws. Implicit were class concerns, where the largely middle-class black riders challenged the assumptions of white superiority upon which Southerners were to trying erect their racially separate society. More explicit were fears of sexual intimacy, premised on the myth of the Negro as sexual beast. The supposed need to protect white female sexuality remained a central justification for legislating separation, even though white mobs had already set the punishment at lynching, with or without segregation laws. Women of color, of course, did not receive equal protection. Marking black citizens as inferior was one of the fundamental tasks of segregation. White Southerners also relied upon railroad segregation to clarify ambiguous racial identities that might otherwise unknowingly bring "pure" whites into contact with someone of African descent. As a result, white passengers chose from several classes of service, while African Americans all rode in the same type of car regardless of the tickets they purchased. Black passengers never found their accommodations to be equal, while whites violated the separate part of the law. The "colored car" often doubled as the smoking car, where whites also gathered to drink, curse, and engage in otherwise prohibited behavior that railroad conductors and porters permitted and even encouraged for the discomfort of their black passengers.[23]

Albert experienced firsthand the horrors of railroad segregation. He was returning from Houston to New Orleans in 1891, after promoting the *Southwestern Christian Advocate* at a meeting of the Texas Annual Conference. Albert purchased a ticket for a first-class seat and a berth on a sleeper car, though not without resistance from the ticket agent in Houston. He boarded the train, and the sleeping car conductor assigned him a berth. Another conductor then complained that Albert's presence on the sleeping car violated Texas state law, which prohibited white and black passengers from riding in the same car. Soon, "a mob meeting of the passengers was held to protest against the presence of 'the nigger,' and to decide upon the course to be adopted." They telegraphed the sheriff at Beaumont, Texas, to meet the train and arrest Albert. "In the meantime, a beer-bloated 250-pounder was deputized to inquire whether [Albert] did not know" he was not allowed to ride with whites. Albert answered that "he was not responsible, as he accepted the place assigned him by the sleeping-car conductor." Albert continued that "he was just as much entitled to the comforts of a sleeping car as anybody else." If arrested, Albert realized he would be lucky to reach the jail. Just as likely, he would be intercepted and lynched by the inevitable white mob waiting to greet him. Fortunately, the sleeping-car conductor pleaded on Albert's behalf that "such a dignified and cultured Christian gentleman" be shown mercy, focusing on his religious rather than his racial identity. The train mob eventually relented and allowed Albert to proceed to New Orleans. Given Albert's stature, the episode received notice throughout the African-American community.[24]

The combination of Albert's personal experience and his commitment to fighting segregation led to his involvement in what has become the most well-known, albeit unsuccessful, effort to overturn legalized segregation in the late nineteenth century. The 1896 ruling by the United States Supreme Court in *Plessy v. Ferguson*, validating the principle of "separate but equal" accommodations, became the cornerstone upon which white Southerners constructed their system of legalized segregation. The case originated in New Orleans, when Homer Plessy, a light-skinned Creole of color, was arrested for violating Louisiana's 1890 separate-car statute. The carefully planned test case has long been associated with New Orleans's Catholic Creole community. However, Albert was centrally involved in the Citizens Committee that coordinated the Plessy case.[25] His participation highlights ways that black Protestant activists modified earlier strategies in their continued effort to combat segregation.

Albert's advocacy signaled a new degree of racial cooperation and solidarity that transcended the denominational rivalries of previous decades. Up through the 1880s, black M. E. church members had believed a common identity with white Methodists likewise committed to racial equality would best stem the advancing wave of Jim Crow. But the increasing acceptance of racial separation within the M. E. Church forced black leaders to consider alternative strategies. Albert increasingly turned to fellow African Americans rather than to the national church, often favoring organizations outside the church that emphasized common racial concerns rather than religious differences. In 1889 alone, he joined a meeting in January at St. James' A.M.E. Church to protest a racially antagonistic article by a U.S. senator, in April he participated in a "convention of ministers and laymen" of the city's black churches to deplore the violence in Louisiana's rural parishes and the governor's lack of action in response, in September he helped form the Evangelical Alliance in New Orleans to suppress violence against blacks, and in November he served as a vice president of the newly formed Christian Sabbath Union.[26] Although these alliances and organizations were often short-lived, the city's ministers and prominent laymen once again gathered and created a new association when a new issue arose. Albert remained loyal to his denomination and continued to advocate for racial equality in the M. E. Church. And he did not completely abandon the criticism that African Methodists encouraged segregation by their racial distinctiveness. Yet the issues that worried African Americans in New Orleans, including schools, violence, and separate car laws, transcended denominational boundaries. Albert felt as comfortable presiding over a meeting at St. James' A.M.E. or Central Congregational as at Wesley M. E. Church; the issues he addressed affected members of all these denominations.

Albert's support of the Citizens Committee and its Plessy case reveals how the worsening racial climate resulted in changing alliances and strategies within New Orleans's black community. Albert became willing to build bridges with the city's black Catholic community, even though he had maintained a vocal anti-Catholicism ever since his teenage encounter with a racist priest prompted his conversion to Methodism. Opposition to segregation ran deeper than resentments against Catholicism. The Citizens Committee, which coordinated the Plessy case, was organized by leading Creoles of color in New Orleans. Nearly all these Creoles identified themselves as Catholic, though few remained active parishioners. The primary objective of the Citizens Committee was advancing a case to test the constitutionality of Louisiana's separate-car law. Albert's longstanding opposition to railroad segregation, and his own personal experience of its horrors, made his support a logical fit with the Citizens Committee. He was committed to fighting racial discrimination in all its forms, and using the courts was a complementary rather than competing endeavor to his religiously motivated efforts.

Albert might even be considered a grandfather of the Citizens Committee. The committee was not the first organization in New Orleans to press for a challenge of the separate-car law. That distinction fell to the local chapter of the American Citizens' Equal Rights Association (ACERA). Albert had helped organize the ACERA at a national conference in Washington, D.C., in February 1889. Part reform organization and part assistance league, the ACERA emphasized "dispassionate agitation against every specie of injustice visited upon" black citizens. Declaring itself "the slave of no party," the ACERA embodied Albert's commitment to racial equality over political and denominational loyalty. In March 1890, Albert had helped found and was elected president of the central Louisiana chapter of the ACERA, whose members included both black Protestants and Catholic Creoles of color. In language anticipating the work of the Citizens Committee, the ACERA included among its aims the "testing in the courts of the country the cruel and inhuman discriminations visited upon" the region's black residents. The ACERA chapter in Louisiana organized protests and a petition against the state's proposed separate-railroad-car bill, coordinating its strategy with black legislators.[27] When the bill became law, the ACERA chapter began collecting funds to test the law's constitutionality. As Albert continued his appeals on behalf of the ACERA in the winter of 1891, he ominously predicted that "one decision by the Supreme Court of the United States will decide the matter for every state in the Union. Let everybody join in testing the outrageous measure." That spring, the record went silent. There was no mention of the ACERA until October 1891, when Albert began praising the Citizens Committee, which had been founded the previous month to test the separate-car law. Thereafter, Albert printed numerous references to cooperation between the ACERA and the recently formed Citizens Committee.[28]

In New Orleans, Creoles of color had organized the Citizens Committee in September 1891, largely at the urging of Aristide Mary, one of the city's wealthiest Creoles. Mary likely provided the financing that the ACERA was unable to secure. Apparently concerned about the effectiveness of the ACERA, several of the city's leading Creoles decided to reorganize with a more tightly structured and better-funded effort. Albert had nonetheless made a crucial contribution as the president of the ACERA: he built a network of ministers and churches committed to agitating for civil rights that could be marshaled on behalf of the Citizens Committee. Accordingly, the committee, and its organ, the *Crusader*, welcomed Albert and his connections into its fold. Albert's importance was recognized when he was offered the presidency of the *Crusader*, which was edited by his good friend Louis A. Martinet. Albert declined. He did, however, accept the vice presidency. Albert continued as a member of the Citizens Committee until its dissolution in 1897.[29]

Albert served as a conduit between the city's predominantly Catholic and Creole Citizens Committee and the African-American Protestant community in New Orleans, bridging one of the city's longstanding historical divides. His Catholic background, racially mixed parentage, and fluency in French enable him to work with both communities, bringing the radicalism associated with the predominantly Catholic Creoles to the city's Protestant African-American population. A close personal relationship with Louis A. Martinet facilitated Albert's mediating role. Of similar age and background, including white fathers and slave mothers, the two men had much in common. Martinet carried out much of the administrative work of the Citizens Committee and, as editor of the committee's newspaper, the *Crusader*, shared Albert's profession. Both editors directed their efforts toward the same fundamental goals of equal rights and equal protection for black citizens. The two men also shared an educational background: both belonged to the first medical class to graduate from New Orleans University. Albert praised both the interracial and the ecumenical character of that first graduating class, which included black and white, Protestant and Catholic. After graduating, the two men served as colleagues on the medical school faculty. Reciprocal comments of praise for each other's newspapers and work, especially on behalf of equal rights, testified to the warmth of their friendship.[30] The two men forged a friendship that transcended many of the city's boundaries. Like them, more and more people of color in turn-of-the-century New Orleans moved fluidly between uptown and downtown, between French and English, and between Catholic and Protestant institutions. Such alliances increasingly replaced denominational loyalties, playing a central role in the struggle to overthrow Jim Crow.

Nor was Albert the only Methodist involved in the Citizens Committee and the Plessy case. The lead attorney and best-known figure associated with the case, the white Northerner Albion Tourgée, also belonged to the Methodist Episcopal Church. While he is perhaps best known as a novelist who depicted the horrors of southern society for African Americans, Tourgée's brief on behalf of Plessy introduced the notion of color-blindness before the law that provided the framework for the lone dissent in the Supreme Court's 1896 decision. The argument reappeared in the 1954 *Brown v. Board of Education* ruling that overturned the Plessy ruling. Methodism had shaped Tourgée in ways he could not escape. Tourgée grew up in Ohio's Western Reserve with a religiously strict father. He also attended college in western New York where the embers of revivalism occasionally flared up. That same revivalism gave rise to the abolitionist movement, which subsequently motivated many northern white missionaries to aid the freed slaves.[31] Tourgée was one of them. Following service in the Civil War, during which he was twice injured, Tourgée became an attorney and carpetbagger in North Carolina, where he served as a judge. His Methodist faith was an important motivation for his sojourn in the Reconstruction South and his abiding commitment to equal rights. Even so, like Albert, Tourgée coordinated across denominational boundaries, preparing petitions for a range of religious groups, from the Presbyterian General Assembly to Quakers to black Catholics. He also ventured beyond the church in his civil-rights advocacy, working with labor unions, the Republican Party, and the Citizens Committee in New Orleans.

Albert and Tourgée's work on behalf of the Citizens Committee reflected a spark of hope that M. E. church members might yet advance the biracialism so celebrated in previous decades. For the Citizens Committee, as Albert and Tourgée make clear, connections with Methodists proved crucial to their ability to sustain the struggle against segregation. Like Albert, Tourgée had stridently opposed discrimination within the M. E. Church. He had also been a leading voice behind the 1892 General Conference resolution denouncing prejudice and segregation and calling for greater religious and governmental action on behalf of black Americans. While white M. E. supporters were increasingly rare in the M. E. Church, the occasional cry from the likes of Tourgée kept alive the earlier hope that black and white cooperation could transform race relations not only in the church but in society as well. But theirs was a tempered hope by the 1890s. They could no longer wait for a backsliding M. E. Church to transform itself and then transform society in turn. They would have to challenge segregation simultaneously in church and society. Tourgée shared Albert's emphasis on assertive protest and similarly criticized their denomination's accommodationist spirit. The church's lethargy contributed to a cynical turn in Tourgée's religious faith; Albert stayed the course.[32]

Churches were always crucial to Albert's racial advocacy, as his work with the Citizens Committee made clear. He stressed the harmony between the ideals of the M. E. Church and the Citizens Committee, and between the *Southwestern Christian Advocate* and the *Crusader*, which was the Citizens Committee's official paper. During his editorship, Albert used the pages of his Methodist weekly to advocate on behalf of the committee's work, soliciting support and keeping readers informed of developments in the Plessy case. Churches, he insisted, would play a central role in raising funds to resist the separate-car law. Typical was his suggestion that, on Thanksgiving, "a good way to observe it is to conclude the services of the day with a liberal collection from every church to assist in testing the constitutionality of the 'jim crow car law.' " As encouragement, Albert publicized contributions from prominent Methodists, such as the twenty-five-dollar donation from Willard Mallalieu, one of the denomination's sympathetic white bishops. At the same time, Albert continually pressed his denomination to fight segregation, serving on the Louisiana Annual Conference's Committee on the Separate Car Law and supporting resolutions against segregation and discrimination at the denomination-wide General Conference.[33]

Ministers and churches maintained their importance in fighting segregation at the same time the ACERA, the Citizens Committee, and other organizations challenged Jim Crow through legal channels. They were complementary rather than competing efforts. When the Louisiana legislature debated the separate-car bill in 1890, Albert called upon congregations to "flood that body with loud and emphatic protestations." After the legislation passed, Albert stressed the necessity for ministers to generate support to test its constitutionality. Albert printed in the *Southwestern Christian Advocate* sermons for clergy to read from their pulpits, urging them to make opposition to caste legislation "a text for their sermons." Albert's efforts were ecumenical. He coordinated efforts with a cross section of the city's black religious leadership, noting the contributions of Baptist as well as Congregational and A.M.E. churches and clergy. He also urged concrete steps. Recognizing that preachers organized railroad excursions as a way to compete with a popular secular pastime, Albert entreated fellow ministers to cancel all railroad excursions, believing the loss of income would be enough to get the railroads to "cooperate with us in seeking their repeal." Many ministers withdrew their patronage from railroads that required separate cars for black passengers, while church meetings were strategically located so that attendees could avoid using lines that practiced segregation. The Louisiana Annual Conference supported Albert's agitation, passing resolutions to protest the separate-car laws, discouraging any use of the railroads until the law was repealed, and endorsing efforts to raise funds to test the law's constitutionality.[34]

Black religious leaders played an ongoing role in resisting Jim Crow, as Albert's involvement makes clear. But he was far from alone. Even after the devastating Plessy ruling, African Americans refused to be silenced. Black plaintiffs continued to seek redress from abuses that segregation engendered. The suits against railroads, some of them successful, sought damages for a range of abuses including assault, inferior accommodations, and, in a commentary on the ironic inconsistency of segregation, the failure to keep whites out of spaces set aside for black passengers. Clergymen across the spectrum of black Protestantism coordinated and filed lawsuits throughout the Jim Crow era. In 1908, five A.M.E. bishops filed suit on behalf of African Americans for abuses suffered on a railroad excursion. While the episcopal backing offered a higher profile than most cases, ministers throughout the South ensured that the voices of black Southerners be heard within the nation's legal system. Boycotts, like those Albert and his Crescent City colleagues urged, were another weapon African Americans continued to use. The boycotts were widespread and sometimes effective, despite coinciding with the height of abuse against black citizens. Ministers joined other black professionals in leading boycotts, not just in New Orleans but in over twenty-five cities throughout the South. In at least three cities, streetcar companies bowed to the economic pressure and briefly abandoned Jim Crow policies. In Nashville, ministers played a central role in creating an alternative bus line in 1905 to circumvent segregated trolley cars. The entrepreneurial endeavor, which suffered financial collapse after a few months, nonetheless demonstrated the range of efforts black citizens would explore to resist Jim Crow, as well as the central role churches would play in those struggles.[35] The lessons would not be lost when, four decades later, a bus boycott in Montgomery, Alabama, would give rise to the modern Civil Rights movement and would raise to prominence a new ministerial advocate for racial equality: the black Baptist preacher, Martin Luther King, Jr.

Albert's agitation for African-American equality reveals an important strain of black M. E. leadership that was anything but accommodationist or otherworldly. While historians and African Methodist rivals alike have characterized the decision to join the M. E. Church as conservative, Albert's actions suggest just the opposite. There were few within or beyond the church whom Albert did not challenge. He remained as vocal as, and often more vocal than, his critics in rival African Methodist denominations or even among New Orleans's Catholic Creole community. Clearly separating Albert from the accommodationist camp, a white Louisianian once complained to Booker T. Washington of "the fiery opposition of men such as Albert, of the [Southwestern Christian Advocate], etc."[36] Nor was that agitation disconnected from Albert's M. E. identity. While many charged that Albert's racial advocacy moved beyond religious concerns, Albert could not have disagreed more. Albert had converted to the M. E. Church because of its racial inclusion. He believed that working on behalf of the Citizens Committee, working against the Republican Party, and protecting the lives of black citizens were all a part of his responsibility as a Methodist leader. He was bringing the voice of the church to bear on what he considered fundamentally moral and religious questions. The church was failing if it was concerned only about what occurred within its doors, although its record there was increasingly problematic as well. Albert believed the church had to speak out against injustice wherever it occurred, or else it had failed to be the church. Albert's efforts marked an ongoing hope, however diminished, that the church might yet turn back segregation. Ironically, Albert had greater success engaging whites outside the church than within his own denomination. Race relations remained a social rather than a spiritual concern to most white church members. Black Methodists would continue to fight a losing battle until white Christians shared the conviction that segregation was a religious issue.

Advocating for black equality brought Albert increasing recognition, not all of it favorable. Especially outside Louisiana, he came under fire from white church leaders. Critics characterized his support of the Citizens Committee and similar organizations as unnecessary and even traitorous. Bishop John Newman, who was among the first M. E. missionaries in New Orleans and had overseen Albert's conversion to Methodism, argued that "the Negroes have blundered in forming leagues to gain their rights." Newman claimed that setting a group apart because of racial or ethnic similarities was "wrong," especially in light of M. E. Church's claim to respect the universal brotherhood of all peoples. The inconsistency of M. E. support for separate churches and annual conferences apparently escaped Newman. Albert responded that organizations such as the ACERA and the Citizens Committee made no special claims for African Americans, they only sought the same rights to which every other American citizen was entitled. While these race organizations hoped to "arouse the Negroes of this country to utilize every means in their power . . . to see that their rights are accorded them," Albert argued they were not, strictly speaking, race leagues. He likened them to the anti-slavery societies of earlier generations, which were open to all people who supported freedom, regardless of race. The leaders of the ACERA and Citizens Committee had deliberately chosen organizational names that did not exclude any race from membership. Albert affirmed that he, too, was "opposed to race segregations and clannishness." That groups advocating racial equality and justice resulted primarily in "the association of one particular race" was not the fault of Albert or his black colleagues.[37]

Albert's defense failed to move the denomination's white majority. Albert had not given up on the church, but the church gave up on him. The 1892 General Conference refused to reelect Albert to another term as editor of the *Southwestern Christian Advocate*. Four years earlier, Albert had been elected by an overwhelming majority. At that time his racial advocacy appeared to carry not only the support of the black Methodist community in New Orleans but also of the entire denomination. But the nation's racial climate continued to deteriorate. During the next four years the white majority became uncomfortable with Albert's constant agitation for equal rights, even though he had nearly tripled the number of newspaper subscriptions. His willingness to transcend denominational rivalries to form racial alliances made white church members nervous. Albert's involvement with the ACERA and Citizens Committee drew attention to his activities just as the M. E. Church prepared for the 1892 General Conference that voted him out of office. The editorship of the *Southwestern Christian Advocate* was the most prominent M. E. position held by an African American, and the denomination proved unwilling to continue providing Albert with a platform from which he could agitate both politically and religiously against segregation. In a General Conference in which less than 10 percent of the delegates were black, the voting was extremely close. Albert lost 244 to 227. Only three votes went to candidates other than Albert and the victor.[38]

Among the many late-nineteenth-century black editors who lost their positions, Albert was relatively fortunate. Many who spoke forcefully on racial issues were physically threatened and driven away rather than merely voted out of office. Ida B. Wells had to flee Memphis after her press was destroyed following her editorials against lynching. Black editors in Alabama, Mississippi, and cities throughout the South who protested racial oppression were similarly driven out of town and lost all their possessions.[39] The church that could no longer tolerate Albert nonetheless provided a context for protecting his life, given its ability to control editorial content through the regular election of newspaper editors.

Supporters joined Albert in blaming his loss on the influence of conservative white votes. In his farewell editorial, Albert noted the unanimous support given him by the delegates from the conferences the *Southwestern Christian Advocate* served: "There was not a single defection." In the one office to which an African American would be elected at the 1892 General Conference, the denomination refused to honor the will of its members who were most affected by the decision. Four months earlier, the Louisiana Annual Conference had passed resolutions in favor of Albert's reelection. In order that white General Conference delegates might unmistakably know the will of the black conferences who patronized the paper, all the black conferences, except one, seconded Albert's nomination. The one black conference that did not rise to second Albert's nomination was his opponent's home conference and one that had never adopted the paper as its official organ. Support for Albert stood so strong among the denomination's black members that they had hoped to nominate him for bishop, an honor Albert declined out his desire to continue as editor. When white delegates rejected the nearly unanimous wishes of the black delegates, it bore a striking resemblance to the ability of southern whites to elect Democratic candidates, even in the face of a black Republican majority. Still, Albert encouraged black church members to support the victor and the *Southwestern Christian Advocate*. His frustration was with white manipulation, not with his opponent.[40]

Albert did not appear surprised at his removal, only disappointed. Just three months earlier, Albert had completed his medical degree at New Orleans University. Albert claimed his pursuit of a medical education held no significance beyond fulfilling a curiosity. Yet he also admitted that the practice of medicine might provide a means to serve his race "should the occasion require." A mere three months after completing his M.D., the occasion arose. He began practicing medicine immediately upon his return from the 1892 General Conference, advertising his services in both the *Southwestern Christian Advocate* and the *Crusader*. He continued to alternate between medicine and service to the church for the remainder of his life. Albert had been a rising star in the M. E. Church, but his assertive stance on behalf of equal rights was too much for the predominantly white denomination. The man who held the highest-profile position of his race, and was even talked about as a candidate for bishop, never again held a denominational post. Albert remained an elder statesman in New Orleans but no longer spoke to or for the denomination. He served as a presiding elder from 1893 to 1896, as vice president and then president of an M. E. academy outside of New Orleans until 1901, and as pastor of Wesley M. E. Church in New Orleans for the next two years. From 1903 to 1905, he practiced medicine full-time, before returning to the pastorate for another two years. In 1908, Albert returned to his alma mater, the Flint Medical School of New Orleans University, where he continued as a professor until his death in 1910.[41]

In the meantime, African Americans in New Orleans and throughout the M. E. Church heard a new voice and a new strategy. Edward W. S. Hammond replaced Albert as editor of the *Southwestern Christian Advocate* in June 1892. Hammond was born free in Baltimore in 1842, although both of his parents had been slaves. He attended schools for free people of color and then earned his collegiate and theological degrees at Lincoln University near Oxford, Pennsylvania. Hammond belonged to the Lexington Annual Conference, where he ministered to congregations in Ohio and Kentucky. In 1888 he received an honorary Doctor of Divinity degree from

New Orleans University. In the years immediately preceding his election as editor, Hammond served as a presiding elder in Ohio.[42]

Hammond represented a shift from Albert's agitation toward a more accommodationist approach that better suited most whites. Louis Martinet, Albert's close friend and fellow editor in New Orleans, complained that the M. E. Church had "discharged Dr. Albert as editor of the *Southwestern Christian Advocate* for a man *less* aggressive, *more* conservative." Howard Henderson, a white Methodist editor from St. Louis, offered an extended commentary on the dynamics surrounding Hammond's victory over Albert. Henderson conceded that Hammond's election "was accomplished by the white vote—the colored members supporting mostly Dr. Albert." Hammond's conservatism appealed to the white majority who favored him over Albert. Henderson expressed relief in the change, for it "is indicative of a more conservative spirit, as Dr. H. is a cautious, courteous, educated man, who will provoke no strife." Henderson and the denomination's white majority felt confident that Hammond's "unobtrusive" character, in contrast with Albert's, would bring about an improvement in the relations between the races. Never having lived in Louisiana, Hammond lacked Albert's connections to New Orleans's racial activists who had so threatened the denomination's white members. Physical appearance may have played a role in Hammond's election. Henderson celebrated Hammond's appearance as "a pure Negro, while Albert is a mulatto." In an age obsessed with the shade of one's skin, the ambiguous appearance of many mixed-race persons threatened to undermine white efforts to maintain racial separation. Places set apart only for whites might become unknowingly contaminated. Whites also feared that those with light skin, such as Albert, were more likely to challenge the color line than those like Hammond, who stood no chance of crossing it. Reassured by Hammond's triumph, Henderson encouraged other African Americans to imitate Hammond's conservatism as the key to resolving racial tension. Henderson claimed that "as colored men approach his type, they draw the white men nearer to them," apparently unaware of the irony of such commentary coming from one with obvious sympathies for maintaining racial separation.[43]

True to white expectations, Hammond advocated a gradualist philosophy of racial uplift, in contrast to Albert's agitation for immediate recognition of political and legal rights. Hammond shared the same ultimate goal as Albert, an acceptance of the equality of African Americans in both church and state, but he envisioned a different timeline and process than Albert. African Americans needed to earn rather than demand the respect and recognition of whites. They must not confront whites with a sense of entitlement, even if the constitution required the recognition of black civil rights. Hammond's uplift perspective blamed "the present strained relations between the races" more on the failure of African Americans to develop their own moral and intellectual character than on the moral and legal shortcomings of their white oppressors.[44] He advocated a patient program of moral uplift and education, in which the church would play a central role. Absent were Albert's earlier calls for political participation or legal challenges to the prevailing racial order. Whether addressing lynching or a desire to remain in the M. E. Church, Hammond advocated reflection on "our personal sins" and the development of "civilization and moral culture" as the best response. Over time, the moral and intellectual development of the race would persuade whites that "there is nothing in race or blood, in color or hair," that justified any sort of domination of "one race of people over another."[45]

Hammond's commitment to uplift linked him to a growing cadre of uplift advocates in the African-American community. Booker T. Washington stood foremost among them. In Washington, Hammond believed the black community had found "a safe leader." Attention to uplift was neither new nor unique, even within M. E. work in the South, but its emergence as an alternative rather than complement to agitation made significant gains near the turn of the century. Much of the shift resulted from growing white insistence on personal uplift over public advocacy and the flow of assistance to those, such as Washington, who advocated such views. Many black leaders accepted the changing emphasis and the role of white patronage as necessary to survival in the worsening racial climate.[46] Their strategy focused on survival over integration and was more about preventing losses than making gains in the interracial arena. Along with this emphasis on deference, the shift toward industrial education, famously endorsed by Washington at the 1895 Cotton States and International Exhibition in Atlanta, was a leading measure of the predominance of the accommodationism so often associated with uplift. When Washington made his famous speech, Hammond was confident that "untold good will result therefrom."[47] Though Washington was often critical of black ministers as uneducated and otherworldly, clergy like Hammond, across a wide range of denominations, were crucial in advancing Washington's model of industrial education. Whereas Albert advocated the value of a classical education, Hammond stressed that "the education of the hand for our people is quite as important as that of the head and the heart." Along with Booker T. Washington's Tuskegee Institute, similar schools such as Hampton Institute and the M. E. schools offering industrial rather than classical education made the greatest gains in this era. Hammond argued that industrial education would also encourage "home building and character building," as well as enabling black workers to compete in the marketplace. The educational leg of racial uplift would continually reinforce the leg of moral uplift. Nor was the M. E. Church the only denomination to favor this shift. Baptists in Louisiana similarly emphasized uplift, stressing that the "church and the school room" must represent what the African American "is doing for himself and for his own elevation."[48] The southern black turn to pragmatic over idealistic needs formed a necessary response to the northern white preference for pragmatic reunion with the South rather than the idealistic push for racial equality.

Albert's and Hammond's different approaches reveal the complexity of race leadership in the late nineteenth century, for religious no less than secular black leaders. African Americans were far from united on the best approach for advancing racial interests, not only across different denominations but even within the same traditions. A constantly shifting racial climate only complicated their efforts against an increasingly unified white supremacy. Privileging the Washington–Du Bois polarities, which is a caricature in itself, obscures the frequency with which African Americans moved along a continuum of strategies to counter racial discrimination. Black leaders were not inflexible. In advancing similar goals, leaders like Albert and Hammond had much in common. Both men envisioned an end to violence and dreamed of racial equality, and both insisted upon the central role of the M. E. Church in achieving that vision. Yet both also advocated transdenominational racial alliances in response to the growing complicity of the M. E. Church in the spread of segregation. Nor did they advocate passivity or resignation. African-American agency remained crucial to both men. Whether emphasizing agitation or uplift, Albert and Hammond each asserted the ability of African Americans to bring about an improvement in their condition and a change in society's treatment of them. They even borrowed from each other. Education was a central tenet of Hammond's uplift ideology. Yet Albert, like all African Americans, also privileged the importance of education for African Americans. Albert's commitment to education was evident in his tenures as vice president and later president of Gilbert Academy in nearby Baldwin, Louisiana, from 1896 to 1901. Occasionally, Albert even sounded like Hammond, urging his readers to "let politics take of itself, and build up the race educationally, morally, and materially." Likewise, Hammond recognized that some degree of legal and political agitation was necessary for African Americans to achieve true equality. He conceded that in order to turn the tide of racial oppression, at times it became necessary that the "tremendous energies of the pulpit be brought into the political arena."[49] As a result, Albert gave his unequivocal support to Hammond, and Hammond supported Albert's ongoing work in New Orleans and in the Louisiana Annual Conference.

In the end, Hammond found no more job security than had Albert. At the 1896 General Conference, Hammond lost a close election for the editorship to Isaiah B. Scott. The first ballot produced no victor. In an apparent protest, forty-five presumably black delegates voted for A.E.P. Albert. Albert was clearly not in a position to win, but the votes cast for him prevented any candidate from winning a majority. On the second ballot, Scott secured his election with 265 votes to Hammond's 152. Scott was a native of Kentucky, where he was born free in 1854. He attended the M. E. Central Tennessee College and then worked in the Texas Annual Conference. At the time of his election as editor of the *Southwestern Christian Advocate*, Scott was the president of Wiley University, an M. E. school in Marshall, Texas. White Methodists described Scott as being "identified with all intelligent movements for the improvement of his race" and claimed he was "highly respected by both races."[50] The reasons for Scott's election remain unclear, as he appeared similar in temperament to Hammond and remained more closely identified with Hammond's uplift strategy than Albert's philosophy of racial agitation.

ALBERT AND HAMMOND, AND SCOTT AS WELL, shared another fateful similarity as race leaders and editors of the *Southwestern Christian Advocate*: none could stem the rising tide of Jim Crow in either church or society. The separate-but-equal ruling in the 1896 *Plessy v. Ferguson* case provided cover for enacting Jim Crow legislation throughout New Orleans and Louisiana. The disfranchisement of black voters in the 1898 Louisiana Constitution was another important development on the road to segregation. Polling booths joined railroad cars as a primary place where blacks might come as equal to whites, so white efforts to exclude black voters matched the vehemence with which they imposed racial separation on railroads. The primary disfranchisement clause was based on an educational qualification. Subsequent clauses, however, offered ways for illiterate whites to qualify based on property requirements if they or their ancestors were entitled to vote on January 1, 1867, or, in the case of foreigners, if they had registered to vote by January 1, 1898.[51] Polling officials used a double standard in administering the literacy tests required by the new constitution. Whites invariably found assistance from sympathetic clerks or party managers who often failed black registrants for "incomplete" answers that nonetheless exceeded the standard for even the most literate white voter. To add insult to injury, Louisiana passed its disfranchising constitution during a Republican administration, and President William McKinley neither protested nor punished Louisiana for its new constitution. While the 1898 constitution did not disfranchise every black voter, its effect was devastating. Even in New Orleans, which had one of the highest concentrations of educated and property-holding black residents in the entire nation, the new constitution effectively curtailed the black vote. In the year before disfranchisement, black voters constituted 22.5 percent of the electorate in New Orleans. In the two elections after disfranchisement, the percentage of black voters dropped to 3.7 and 3.6 respectively.[52]

Despite vocal opposition, neither Albert nor Hammond could prevent similar patterns of exclusion within the Louisiana Annual Conference. The M. E. Church in Louisiana had long resisted racial segregation, but in the 1890s it fell victim to the separation becoming so pervasive in the schools, railroad cars, and political halls of New Orleans. Both Albert and Hammond opposed segregating the Louisiana Annual Conference along racial lines. Albert considered such segregation "a great blunder and an unpardonable sin." Hammond likewise praised the annual conference's long-standing resistance to segregation and the presence of both black and white members, claiming "it would be a sin to even suggest a breaking up of this delightful relationship." Annual conferences that divided racially, both men argued, made the M. E. Church no different than racially exclusive denominations, justifying and reinforcing Jim Crow practices throughout society.[53] Such divisions also encouraged discrimination against African Americans within the M. E. Church, most noticeably the failure to elect a bishop of African descent. The Louisiana Annual Conference's biracial membership set it apart from most M. E. annual conferences and from other Protestant denominations that had segregated their regional jurisdictions.[54] For more than a decade after Reconstruction, the Louisiana Annual Conference remained unified in its opposition to segregation, not once entertaining a motion to divide the conference along racial lines.

During the 1890s, however, the Louisiana Annual Conference began its long crawl toward racial segregation. Annual conferences in the M. E. Church were subdivided into geographically organized districts. The white work in New Orleans had always been part of one of the two New Orleans districts and thereby in the same district with several black congregations. In 1887, a shift began taking place. The Louisiana conference created a new district, the Mission District, for its white work. That first year, the Mission District consisted only of the old Ames Church, by then renamed St. Charles Avenue M. E. Church, and a mission for Swedish immigrants living in the Crescent City. Altogether, the Mission District claimed barely a hundred members. The membership of the other five districts in the Louisiana conference ranged from 1,569 to 3,343.[55] Over the next four years, white congregations outside New Orleans united with the Mission District, reinforcing its identity as a district defined by racial rather than geographical boundaries. French and Italian missions in New Orleans later joined with the Swedish missions as members of the Mission District. In 1896, all the white congregations and missions in Louisiana withdrew, except those in New Orleans, to join with white congregations in Texas. Together, they created the all-white Gulf Mission Conference, which was the beginning of a new and racially separate annual conference. The General Conference defined the boundaries of the Gulf Mission in first racial, and only secondarily, geographic terms. Outside of New Orleans, the Louisiana conference had become completely segregated, and even within New Orleans, whites and blacks continued to work in different districts. In 1901, the remaining white churches in New Orleans left the Louisiana conference and joined the Gulf Mission Conference, which now included all of the white M. E. congregations from Texas to the Florida panhandle. In 1904, the Gulf Mission Conference dropped its designation as a "mission" conference, becoming a regular annual conference in the M. E. Church.[56]

The Louisiana conference in general, and New Orleans in particular, had been the loudest opponent of annual conference segregation and had resisted its imposition the longest. But New Orleans and Louisiana, by institutional reorganization rather than a vote of members, had capitulated, thirty-five years after the conference's interracial founding and a quarter century after annual conferences first received permission to divide. Whites had left rather than forcing black members out, but the outcome was the same. In allowing white churches to withdraw, rather than requiring a vote by the majority of the annual conference, the denomination denied the Louisiana Annual Conference the right to determine its own fate. Denominational rather than local decision-making determined the racial character of the M. E. Church. The Louisiana conference was left as a segregated conference whose boundaries were defined as simply "the colored work in the State of Louisiana." Not until 1971 would black and white churches again belong to the same district in the Louisiana Annual Conference.[57]

New Orleans's racial climate deteriorated significantly between the time A.E.P. Albert became editor of the *Southwestern Christian Advocate* in 1887 and the turn of the century. The city that a decade earlier had been known for its liberal racial policies deserted that promise by the end of the 1890s. The exclusion of blacks from city politics, combined with increasing violent outbreaks on the levees and across the city, led African Americans to conclude that "it will be difficult to find a city on the American continent where the life of a Negro is held in [more] contempt than in New Orleans." New Orleans's black residents were left "talking of the great times they *used to have*," as the city's Jim Crow laws and practices became among the most oppressive of any city in the South. Reflecting on the particularities of New Orleans at the beginning of the next century, *Southwestern Christian Advocate* editor I. B. Scott acknowledged that "it would seem that our city should be extremely liberal on the color question, but to the contrary we dare say there is no city in the South more sensitive in this particular."[58]

By the turn of the century, the racial practices of the M. E. Church in New Orleans reflected those of society at large. Albert lamented that "no one who has put himself to any trouble to know, will deny that American prejudice, in church and state, in pulpit and pew, in the halls of legislation and in the courts of justice, asserts itself incessantly and everywhere, against this people." These parallel impulses of segregation in church and society enabled segregation's hegemony in the South. Both followed a similar pattern, moving from local option to statewide conformity. State laws had replaced local ordinance and transportation-company preferences regarding railroad and streetcar segregation, and constitutional amendments dictated voting patterns that local politicians had previously controlled. Likewise, the M. E. denomination created explicit racial boundaries for its conferences, eliminating the flexibility that had once been a hallmark of annual conferences. Yet leaders like Albert and Hammond reveal that Jim Crow came to pervade both religious and secular institutions only by a long, complicated, and tortuous road. Race relations, especially in the M. E. Church, operated along a continuum rather than at the polar opposites of exclusion or inclusion. Segregation looked different in different places, as the strong protest tradition in New Orleans revealed. Into the 1890s, much depended on the circumstances of place, time, and people involved. This suggested a still-unsettled character that sustained black church members, even as their denomination increasingly reinforced patterns of segregation. They pointed out that as a denomination, the M. E. Church still included both black and white members, which was more than could be said of other Methodist denominations. This fact alone led Hammond to affirm that "the colored man will stay in the Methodist Episcopal Church."[59] But on the brink of a new century, black church members would have to reconsider and renegotiate their place in their church and its role in their pursuit of racial equality.

CHAPTER 4

Renegotiating Black Methodist Episcopal Identity

On July 27, 1900, a black man named Robert Charles shot twenty-four white people, including four policemen, while hiding in a house in New Orleans. Four days earlier, Charles had shot three police officers: the first when confronted as he and a friend waited for their dates, and two others when the police arrived at Charles's room to arrest him for the earlier scuffle. Charles evaded the arresting officers that first night and remained in hiding a few blocks away. The confrontation ended four days later when a white mob set the house where he was hiding on fire. The angry crowd shot Charles and finally stomped him to death when he tried to escape the flames. In the four days between the initial skirmish and Charles's death, New Orleans erupted in waves of violence that included "fully armed" mobs that "roamed the streets hunting Negroes." When rioters encountered African Americans, "they were fired upon at sight; some were shot, others were beaten with clubs or cut with knives." Even after his death, mobs continued exacting retribution on the city's black residents, whom they held responsible for Charles's behavior. In the end, over a dozen black citizens died, and many more suffered serious injury.[1]

The Charles riot epitomized rather than deviated from the racial trends gripping New Orleans at the turn of the century. In the weeks prior to the riot, Isaiah B. Scott, editor of the Methodist Episcopal Church's *Southwestern Christian Advocate*, had ruminated on the decade-long deterioration of race relations in New Orleans. He lamented disfranchisement and legalized segregation of public facilities, from railroads to restrooms. Only a month before the riot came another troubling development: the New Orleans school board prohibited education past the fifth grade for black students.[2] The capitulation to segregation appeared complete in the city that had experimented with interracial schools a quarter century earlier. In an eerie premonition the week before the riot, editor Scott mourned that "it would seem that our city should be extremely liberal on the color question; but to the contrary we dare say there is no city in the South more sensitive." With the Charles riot came confirmation. Once considered unique for its racial liberalism by both residents and visitors, New Orleans's racial order had become more typical than distinctive in the American South. The Crescent City matched the racial oppressiveness of other urban centers such as Wilmington, North Carolina, and Atlanta, Georgia, which suffered outbreaks of racial violence in 1898 and 1906 respectively. For some of New Orleans's "best colored citizens," the riots destroyed any hope for racial reconciliation. Many sold their homes and property, often at great loss, to move elsewhere and begin again their quest for equal rights and equal protection.[3]

Even so, events surrounding the Charles riot provided a basis for hope amid a sea of despair. No single event could destroy the hopes of African-American Southerners, and this outbreak of urban violence would be no different. White residents had offered black citizens more protection than during the city's previous violent outbreaks, such as the 1866 attacks on the constitutional convention at the Mechanics Institute and the 1874 Battle of Liberty Place. During the 1900 Charles riots, many of New Orleans's white residents, especially its "best citizens," condemned the mob violence and helped end the brutality and looting. White businessmen cautioned rioters that racial discord "paralyzes business" and that racial harmony benefited the interests of capital and labor alike. Also notable were many individual acts on behalf of black citizens. When a mob boarded a streetcar to assail an elderly black man, an equally old white woman "threw her dress skirt over him and defied them to touch him, and they didn't." She refused to move until the rioters left. *Southwestern Christian Advocate* editor Scott likewise benefited from white concern. Upon learning he was out of town during the outbreak, two white neighbors reassured his wife they would defend her, even offering special police protection for his house. As a result, Scott offered a paradoxical interpretation of the recent racial upheaval. The better class of black citizen, he asserted, "feels better toward his white neighbors than he has at any time since the war."[4]

The contradictory messages emerging from the Charles riots exemplified the complexity of race relations at the turn of the century. African Americans belonging to the M. E. Church faced equally complicated developments within their own denomination during the first two decades of the twentieth century. The struggles in church and society reinforced one another, strengthening the connections between racial developments in each. Black M. E. church members spent much of the early twentieth century seeking their voice in American society and renegotiating their place in their church. In the midst of these reconfigurations, black church members interpreted developments in their denomination as simultaneously hopeful and discouraging—the same way they had interpreted events surrounding the Charles riot. These M. E. developments transposed into new keys the chords marking the alternation between optimism and despair that had long characterized the African-American religious experience. Black church members remained faithful to the M. E. Church, even as those chords increasingly sounded in minor keys.

DISCOURAGED BY THE DECLINING racial climate, African Americans searched for ways to displace race as the primary category of identification.

Appeals for interracial class solidarity became the new hope to improve the nation's racial order. The idea of class-based alliances was not new, as interracial possibilities ranging from labor unions, to temperance, to the Populist Party, were all built upon a presumed class solidarity. With renewed vigor at the turn of the century, African Americans argued that the interests of the growing black middle class coincided with those of whites and that cooperation would be advantageous to both. Middle-class blacks were also trying to dissociate themselves from the lower and criminal classes, whose behavior whites universalized to undermine the status of all black citizens. Privileging commonalities along class lines would humanize race relations and disrupt the construction of black citizens as "other," which was a necessary component of white supremacy. Black leaders conceived of class in broad terms, since few African Americans could match the salaries and economic status of their white counterparts. References to class therefore invoked a range meanings, including education, social refinement, economic and vocational aspirations, political concerns, respectability within one's community and in the eyes of the law, and, frequently, religious affiliation.

The shift toward class alliances to ease racial discrimination signaled the growing competition churches faced in the black community. By the turn of the century, many African Americans were discouraged by the inability of churches and religious leaders to enact substantive and lasting improvements for black citizens. Many looked outside the church for solutions, while some left the church altogether. Where clergymen had once been the undisputed leaders in the African-American community, a new group of educators, scholars, and artists emerged to challenge ministerial authority. From Booker T. Washington and W.E.B. Du Bois, to poets such as Paul Dunbar and writers and teachers like Julia Cooper, African Americans heard a cacophony of voices and strategies for responding to segregation. Some praised the accomplishments of the church and maintained hope for its future role. Others encouraged black Americans to look beyond religious institutions as the key to survival. Even among black M. E. leaders, few maintained that their church alone could resolve racial conflicts. Across the spectrum of differing ideological positions, fostering class interests was a nearly universal strategy. Race leaders stressed the cultural, educational, and economic accomplishments of African Americans since Emancipation. This progress foreshadowed even greater gains, which would provide the foundation for lasting alliances with similarly educated and concerned white citizens that would result in the betterment of each race and of American society as a whole.[5]

Religious leaders were quick to endorse interracial class alliances. As churches less frequently claimed a leading role in the nation's racial struggles, M. E. clergy embraced the strategies of the new generation of black leaders. In the 1880s, black M. E. church members had offered their de-nomination as the foremost opportunity to create common identities that transcended racial differences. A decade later, A.E.P. Albert and E.W.S. Hammond emphasized racial solidarity as the best response to spreading segregation. After the turn of the century, black M. E. leaders looked be-yond both religious identity and racial solidarity. In New Orleans, the Charles riot formed the impetus for Isaiah B. Scott, an M. E. clergyman and editor of the *Southwestern Christian Advocate*, to advocate class as a basis for improving race relations. The individual acts of compassion Scott observed had fostered his hope in biracial alliances that were rooted in common economic and civil interests. The Charles riot taught the city's black residents an important lesson: The African American's "only hope is to keep close to the best white citizens of our city . . . [who] will stand by him in the time of need." This class solidarity would replace the emphasis on racial solidarity, which whites had used to judge all black citizens by the actions of the race's worst members. Whites might yet learn that race, for black no less than white, could not predict characteristics such as education, refinement, or intelligence. As a start, Scott urged blacks to dissociate themselves from the "bad element" of the race. The fate of those who had harbored Charles proved the folly of mixing with such bad elements: the mob murdered one accomplice while the police arrested the others for aiding and harboring a criminal. Other denominations reached the same conclusions. Black Baptists, whose state convention was meeting in New Orleans at the time of the riot, likewise condemned Charles. A month later, the National Baptist Convention met in New Orleans and urged its members to create a class distinctiveness by keeping away from "the shift-less, idle, ignorant, no 'count negroes."[6] Throughout the first two decades of the twentieth century, black M. E. leaders stood among those who joined with black cultural and educational leaders to promote class solidarity as the best hope for racial reconciliation.

Competing forms of racial interaction in New Orleans undoubtedly fos-tered religious leaders' interest in class alliances. Perceptions of lower-class immorality threatened both the reputation and the uplift efforts of the city's black middle class. Three traditions for which New Orleans was fa-mous, or infamous, stood at the heart of religious leaders' concerns. The first was Mardi Gras, whose masks and costumes fostered interracial con-tact and the inversion of racial hierarchies. But Mardi Gras, according to Methodist leaders, was low culture, and Catholic to boot. Even as it under-mined racial separation, Mardi Gras offered little hope for racial advance-ment, given its limited duration and the public preoccupation with "the license and shameless conduct of loose characters in certain parts of the city." Jazz, the Crescent City's most famous creation, was little better. While racially mixed crowds from different classes gathered to hear the new music, religious leaders once again saw little hope for its redeeming value. Especially troubling was a "music that appeals to the bodily senses" but was "not conducive to heart culture or the development of the Christian graces." Such music was also found in the brothels that were at the center of the city's third vice: prostitution. Between 1897 and 1917, prostitution was legal in the Storyville section of New Orleans. Much of the appeal of Storyville was the lure of crossing the color line, which, in 1897, was merely socially taboo. A decade later it became illegal. Beyond the morally problematic practice of prostitution, the large number of women of color working in Storyville's brothels reinforced and preyed upon white stereotypes of lurid black sexuality. The M. E. Church in particular had struggled with prostitution in New Orleans, as the municipally established boundaries for Storyville included Union Chapel, one of the city's largest black M. E. churches. Despite filing a lawsuit, the church was unable to convince the city to change the boundaries. Church leaders lamented the power of the interracial sex trade over the moral protection of its parishioners. They hoped that interracial alliances among the higher classes might restore morality to the city.[7]

At the *Southwestern Christian Advocate*, the class-based rhetoric against segregation continued with Scott's editorial replacement. Robert E. Jones was elected the paper's editor in 1904 and quickly became one of New Orleans's preeminent civil and religious leaders. Born in Greensboro, North Carolina, in 1872, Robert Elijah Jones was licensed to preach by the North Carolina Annual Conference in 1891. A graduate of Bennett College in North Carolina and Gammon Theological Seminary in Atlanta, Jones served in M. E. schools and churches in North Carolina before moving to New Orleans in 1897 as assistant manager of the *Southwestern Christian Advocate*. In 1901 he became an M. E. Sunday school agent, working with congregations throughout the Gulf States. Jones edited the *Southwestern Christian Advocate* from 1904 until 1920, making him the longest serving editor in the history of the paper. During his tenure in New Orleans, Jones participated in a variety of civic activities, including organizing the local Negro Business League, serving as the first president of the colored YMCA, and becoming a founding trustee of Dillard University. After retiring in 1944, Jones returned to the Gulf States as superintendent of Gulfside, a seaside camp and conference grounds in Waveland, Mississippi, which he had founded in the 1920s for black M. E. church members.[8] Throughout his career, Jones was a tireless advocate not only within the M. E. Church but also for fellow African Americans in New Orleans and throughout the South.

Jones used his editorship to amplify and justify calls for class-based alliances. Like other leaders of his era, he highlighted the accomplishments of African Americans only two generations removed from slavery, pointing

Figure 4.1. Robert Elijah Jones (1872–1960).
Courtesy General Commission on Archives and
History of the United Methodist Church.

to statistics on literacy, education, and personal-property ownership. He
offered this as evidence to whites of a growing black middle class whose
interests coincided with similarly educated and professional whites. Testimonies of black accomplishments, printed in religious and secular black
papers alike, proved the distance of the black middle class from the criminal
and lower classes. Jones hoped that as whites learned of class differences
within the African-American community that mirrored those among
whites, they would be willing to associate across racial lines. As a result,
black citizens would no longer be subject to the "unwarranted, illegitimate
judging, for the most part, by the American people, of ALL Negroes by
the acts of the lowest and vilest of the race." Class interests would prove
to be stronger and more rewarding bonds of association than racial affinity.
In appealing for class sympathy across racial lines, Jones insisted that "it is
to our interest to clearly demonstrate to the country and to the world our

aloofness from the worthless Negro." Just as his predecessor had denounced those who harbored Charles in the 1900 riots in New Orleans, Jones announced his relief that during and after the 1906 Atlanta riots, M. E. clergy were "on the alert in denouncing and holding up this criminal element" among the black race.[9]

But whites considered a rising black middle class a source of anxiety, not reassurance. Impoverished or criminal blacks were not those who most worried white Southerners. Rather, the rising middle class posed the greatest threat. Educated, economically self-sufficient African Americans who conformed to white middle-class values threatened the belief in black inferiority that formed the foundation of white supremacy. The resulting confusion necessitated segregation as a tool to enforce the racial hierarchy that was not always self-evident. The racial interaction that whites found so threatening—in shopping districts, on trains, and in polling booths—generally involved the black middle class rather than the lower classes of whom black leaders were so critical. As a result, segregation was aimed more directly at the literate, educated, politically savvy voter and the well-dressed first-class train passenger than at the unemployed or impoverished laborer, whose presence was less threatening to whites' sense of racial superiority.[10] Ongoing white interactions with black laborers and domestics were not threatening because they enacted rather than disrupted the racial hierarchies whites hoped to codify. From the white perspective, the middle, not the lower, class had stepped out of place. And it was the black middle class they sought to return to its rightful location, which was away from whites. Or so they claimed.

In practice, segregation was inconsistent, both in its enforcement and in its effects. Jones was fond of highlighting the failure of segregation to protect whites from most of the nation's crimes, which were committed by whites rather than the anomalous black criminal such as Robert Charles. Attacking a favorite southern white bogeyman, Jones paraded statistics showing more white men in Chicago committed rape than did black men throughout the entire nation.[11] Nor had the *Plessy v. Ferguson* decision ensured the separation white Southerners professed to desire. Interracial liaisons, evidenced in the appeal of Storyville, and the proliferation of people of obviously racially mixed ancestry testified to ongoing sexual fascination with African Americans, white rhetoric of contamination and sexual purity notwithstanding.[12] The resulting complexity of skin color made segregation based on appearances difficult to enforce, as Jones was well aware. A streetcar conductor once asked Jones, who appeared very light-skinned, to move out of the colored section into the white seats.[13]

The failures of streetcar segregation were especially galling, as New Orleans's system made clear. When the Crescent City mandated separate streetcars in 1902, transportation companies instituted what many African

Americans considered the most offensive method of separation. Rather than providing separate trolleys, each streetcar had movable screens to separate black and white riders. Jones characterized the screens as "an utter failure." Whites frequently "packed into the Negro compartment," even when there was standing room in the white section in front of the screen.[14] At the same time, black riders sat in the white section when they accompanied whites, generally as nannies. This practice encouraged the very interaction Jim Crow advocates claimed to abhor: the proximity of black and white that might result in physical contact. Jones complained that black servants who sat with white passengers often embodied the shortcomings of the race, while the best representatives of the race had to sit or stand in cramped quarters behind the screens. The Reverend Dr. M.C.B. Mason, a national leader in the M. E. Church, had to ride behind the screen on a New Orleans street car, while "directly in front of him on the next seat, but on the other side of the screen in the apartment allotted to white people sat a Negro girl with her clothes carelessly and loosely pinned on, her clothes soiled and her hair unkempt. She was undoubtedly of low intellectual calibre, and certainly not tidy in appearance." The girl sat in front of the screen because she had in her arms a white child for whom she cared. An equally ill-clad man could sit next to white women without commotion, simply because he carried a white child. "A well-behaved, well-clad, self-respecting Negro" who did the same "would have been bruised, driven from the car and given a heavy fine"—or worse.[15] Streetcar encounters revealed that segregation was more about enacting hierarchy than ensuring separation. Given the failure of segregation to separate, Jones pressed for identities reorganized on the basis of class rather than race.

Black Methodist considerations tapped into a broader conversation about race and class within the African-American community in the early twentieth century. W.E.B. Du Bois, especially since the 1903 publication of his *The Souls of Black Folk*, was challenging Booker T. Washington as spokesman for the race. Du Bois rejected Washington's emphasis on industrial education and his relegation of civil rights and integration as secondary to self-sufficiency. M. E. leaders such as Isaiah Scott and Robert Jones echoed Du Bois, who stressed the importance of classical liberal arts and university education for training black leaders who could then advance the interests of the entire race. These leaders, whom Du Bois called "the talented tenth," would earn the respect of the equivalent class of whites with whom they would work to improve the nation's race relations. At the same time, these race leaders would elevate the mass of black citizens away from the worst vices, facilitating their uplift and integration into American society. Such advocacy hearkened back to the agitation of earlier M. E. leaders such as A.E.P. Albert, who, like Du Bois, asserted the equality of black and white citizens and insisted upon the immediate recognition of such equality. Gradualism troubled Jones as well. An obituary remembered Jones as one who "maintained an uncompromising position in his written and verbal pronouncements against such fiendish practices as segregation, economic oppression, disfranchisement, and lynching even in such danger zones as the states of Mississippi and Louisiana."[16] Like A.E.P. Albert before him, Jones's actions challenged the claim that those who remained in the M. E. Church were fundamentally accommodationist in their approach to race relations.

Yet black church leaders' emphasis on class also drew upon more conservative racial strategies. Booker T. Washington stood as the best-known but far from the only advocate of a more accommodationist approach. Many black church members, from the M. E. Church to the women's convention of the National Baptist convention, embraced the industrial training at the heart of Washington's program. They too emphasized improving the behavior of the race and maintaining distance from the worst element, but without the corresponding agitation of white citizens for civil rights. This pragmatic gradualism fell short of the immediacy Du Bois urged. These accommodationist class advocates believed that a change in black behavior would eventually win white support. It was the same argument that E.W.S. Hammond, who had replaced Albert at the *Southwestern Christian Advocate*, had made. The resulting class alliances would then open further doors to both interracial cooperation and racial uplift. Jones could articulate this uplift component as well, stressing the role of preachers and church-school teachers to educate black citizens for moral and civic responsibility. Most black religious leaders, including Jones, have been identified with this Washingtonian perspective. However, his actions, and those of most religious leaders, made clear that most black citizens did not draw an either/or distinction between strategies of racial advancement. Jones, like so many others, could draw from both Washington and Du Bois to construct a strategy that would best advance the interests of black M. E. church members as both Methodists and African Americans.

Within the M. E. Church, Jones's advocacy of class translated into calls for a new understanding of the denomination's black members. When the denomination first came south to help the freedmen, it worked with and among them as an expression of charity. Fifty years later, black church members complained the M. E. Church still regarded its work among African Americans as philanthropy. Black church members wanted recognition as equal members of the denomination, not wards of charity. Jones acknowledged that "the Church has been concerned as to what help it may offer the Negro, and as to how it may better his condition. But the great question of justice, of equality, and of human brotherhood is seldom if ever squarely faced in the councils of the Christian Church." Philanthropy functioned as a way to sustain black church members' inferiority. Charity,

Jones complained, "is a species of bribery or slavery that develops weaklings and often reminds the beneficiary that 'you wear our collar and, therefore, you must do as we suggest.' " African Americans called for a change in perception, hoping to replace paternalism with brotherly love. "If we will keep in mind," Jones urged, "that the Negro does not want philanthropy but justice, that the Negro wants a chance and not charity," the church will make great headway in its struggle over race relations.[17]

Many similarly called for the end of the term "freedmen" in the church's work among African Americans, most notably in regard to the Freedmen's Aid Society. By World War I, few black church members had been alive during slavery, and they had different needs than those who had been emancipated, as well as a different relationship to the M. E. Church. The continued use of "freedmen" to describe the church's work among its black members enabled it to persist in depicting them as "being clothed in filthy rags of slavery and smacking of the unwashed reproach of Egypt" and suffering from "a malignant and offensive ignorance."[18] In 1920, the denomination changed the agency's name from the Freedmen's Aid Society to the Board of Education for Negroes. The change eliminated the offending slave reference but highlighted the ongoing separateness of black M. E. church members and their educational institutions.

RENAMING THE FREEDMEN'S AID SOCIETY was just one of many ways African Americans struggled both for and against reconsiderations of their place in the M. E. Church in the early twentieth century. In previous decades, these questions of inclusion and exclusion were resolved primarily at the local and regional levels. By the turn of the century, however, the battle to retain integrated annual conferences had been lost, and debates about the role of black church members shifted to denomination-wide considerations.[19] The General Conference had become the last bastion of interracial contact in the M. E. Church, and black church members were determined to maintain this bulwark to preserve and expand their role in the denomination. Two issues dominated that struggle, each highlighting the increasingly complicated and deteriorating relationship between the denomination and its black members. Neither problem was new, but both changed course between 1900 and 1920. One, the quest for an African-American bishop, primarily concerned the denomination's black members. The other, unification between the M. E. and Southern Methodist churches, concerned black and white Methodists throughout the nation. Both typified the simultaneous experiences of hope and alienation so familiar to black Americans. And church leaders from New Orleans figured prominently in each development.

The uncertain place of black M. E. church members stood at the center of renewed debates over unification with Southern Methodism. The two denominations had divided in 1844 over the issue of slavery. Following the Civil War, both churches, but especially the M. E. Church, encroached upon each other's territory. Sectional tensions persisted into the late nineteenth century, and discussions between the two churches focused on the notion of fraternity, which was an agreement to get along as separate members of the larger Methodist tradition. As conditions in both church and society shifted in the early years of the twentieth century, the focus of conversation shifted from fraternity to organic union, which would be the restoration of a unified Methodist Church that would permanently heal the schism of 1844. Even as the character of negotiations changed, the central point of contention remained the same: the role of black church members in a unified denomination.[20]

Renewed interest in Methodist unification echoed the reunion sentiment sweeping the nation as a whole. From his perspective as both a religious and racial leader, Jones was certain that within the M. E. Church "the cause for letting the Negro alone is due in no little measure to the propaganda of reconciliation between the North and the South." Time was mending the divisions that once divided North and South. Even Civil War commemorations were taking on a national rather than sectional tenor. New military conflicts hastened the healing and asserted a united American identity to the world. The Spanish-American War began the process at the turn of the century. On the heels of that victory, President William McKinley affirmed the sentiments of many Americans, north and south: "We are reunited. Sectionalism has disappeared." Two decades later, World War I nearly completed the creation of unified national identity—with one exception: the new national vision was one of whiteness only. Northerners had increasingly accepted, and even adopted, southern whites' racial views. Few were willing to agitate for a racial equality that would jeopardize the growing harmony with the South. Nor did white patriots recognize the glaring inconsistency of a nation fighting for democracy abroad while denying those same rights to its own citizens. Even President Woodrow Wilson saw no incongruity in segregating the civil service and then urging American participation in World War I with the insistence that "the world must be made safe for democracy." The protests of black soldiers who fought for that democracy only to face worsening discrimination at home went unacknowledged. In all aspects—politically, economically, and geographically—the rhetoric of reunion excluded the nation's black citizens. The drive for a unified Methodism was no different.[21]

The M. E. Church's changing attitude toward its black members was evident in the unification negotiations. In the late nineteenth century, M. E. leaders refused to discuss reunion with Southern Methodists because of the southern church's rampant racial prejudice. Southern attitudes had not changed in the twentieth century. Leaders in the southern church continued to argue racial divisions were "heaven-born," and they invested "race antipathy with divine authority." Nor did Southerners repudiate their decision to set apart black members into the racially segregated Colored Methodist Episcopal Church. But such segregationist and racist ideology was no longer a stumbling block to cooperation. M. E. leaders did not reject Southern Methodist demands that any unified organization marginalize, if not exclude, African Americans. Absent were voices of active white leaders like Joseph Hartzell, who had earlier insisted on reconciliation "with our colored brother counted in." Gone as well were episcopal declarations like the Bishops' Address of 1880, which rejected any talk of union "where the distinctive methods of the Church are yielded to conciliate the prejudices" of southern whites. A common identity among black and white church members, based upon opposition to racially exclusive rivals, had once been a hallmark of M. E. identity. But the M. E. Church had exchanged its loyalties. Union with Southern Methodists took precedence over the equality, and possibly the inclusion, of its own black members. Even the New England–based *Zion's Herald*, once edited by radical Gilbert Haven and long a defender of racial inclusivity, favored a unification proposal that placed black church members in an inferior position. Black church members lamented that "we have now reached a period in the Church's history when the anxiety for Organic Union is so great [that] a large number of people would have it at the expense of the sacrifice of the principle for which the Church has so long stood."[22]

Black church members feared Methodist unification would end the denomination's biracial identity, which had been central to their decision to join and remain loyal to the M. E. Church. As negotiations moved from the language of fraternity to that of union, the search for harmony led M. E. leaders to consider setting apart their black members into a separate jurisdiction and possibly a separate denomination. Unlike African Methodists, who chose separation as a means of empowerment, M. E. separation would constitute forced segregation that ignored the wishes of those affected. It would be no different than the separate and unequal segregation found on railroad cars and in classrooms. The people who had been invited in on the principle of equality would be ushered out on the basis of inequality. W.E.B. Du Bois charged that the once-promising M. E. Church seemed "determined to consummate one of the greatest crimes against the Negro race since slavery" to clear the way for union with Southern Methodists. Other biracial denominations offered little hope. Northern Presbyterians had created separate black presbyteries by 1906 as a part of their own reunion efforts. Despite that concession, a Presbyterian leader acknowledged that "the real obstacle in the way of Presbyterian union as also in the way of Methodist union is the color line."[23] Any hope that a common religious identity might transcend race, and thereby transform society, evaporated as whites courted union with their southern counterparts.

Even the unification negotiations modeled the exclusionary practices that would characterize a reunited denomination. For many years, consultations on union were all-white affairs, even though the fate of African Americans constituted the "paramount question" of the negotiations. These discussions explored setting aside the black members of the M. E. Church into a separate denomination, either on their own or in conjunction with the African Methodist churches. Other plans considered a separate colored jurisdiction within the new denomination, which would be a part of the denomination in name only. Black members decried their exclusion from decisions that would permanently alter their relationship with the M. E. Church. They argued it violated both the laws and the traditions of Methodism to segregate or limit the role of any conference "without the consent of these conferences." The discussions were akin to all-white southern legislatures passing Jim Crow ordinances. Especially troubling were efforts to create a single black Methodist denomination, a plan formulated in the absence of the black members of the M. E. Church and without the participation of the African Methodist denominations.[24] Jones and other denominational leaders warned that not only did African Americans feel competent to negotiate their own alliances, but "self-respect would compel us to repudiate, disregard, and refuse any sort of an alliance which we did not make absolutely of our initiative and liking." Finally, in response to widespread complaints, the 1916 General Conference appointed Jones and a black layman, I. Garland Penn, to represent the church's black membership on the denomination's unification-negotiating committee. Between 1916 and 1920, the Committee on Unification negotiated a plan that created a unified denomination with an additional conference level, called a jurisdiction, which would be inserted between annual conferences and the General Conference. All white members would be placed into regional jurisdictions, with black members funneled into a single separate jurisdiction that was racially, not regionally, defined. The jurisdictional system guaranteed black representation in the General Conference and on national boards, although such representation was apportioned differently from the white regional jurisdictions.[25]

The resulting plan for unification revealed the importance of the North in the spread of segregation in the United States. In its willingness to marginalize black members to achieve unification, the M. E. delegation had compromised more than had those from the southern church. What was true among Methodists was true for Northerners more broadly. By the early decades of the twentieth century, it was changes in northern white attitudes, not southern white attitudes, than enabled the widespread implementation of Jim Crow. Although segregation began primarily in local and particular instances in the South, it was only with northern acquiescence and institutionalization, as in the M. E. Church, that segregation emerged as a uniform and national system. M. E. capitulation was far from distinctive, taking place in the context of widespread northern acceptance of segregation that ranged from railroads to the federal bureaucracy. Northerners, no less than Southerners, bore the burden for the creation of a universally segregated society. It was neither a problem nor a practice confined to the South.

Meanwhile, white Methodists in New Orleans acted as though unification had already taken place. In June 1916, the city's white M. E. and Southern Methodist congregations held a series of meetings, exclusive of the city's black congregations, to celebrate the move toward organic union. White clergy, both M. E. and Southern Methodist, also organized the Methodist Preachers' Union of New Orleans.[26] Such exclusion stood in stark contrast to the interracial achievements of earlier generations. In the decade after Reconstruction, black and white M. E. clergyman had formed the New Orleans Preachers' Meeting. The integrated organization challenged racial discrimination both in New Orleans and in the M. E. denomination. It protested municipal efforts to restrict the hours of worship in black churches, advocated for a black bishop, and rejected segregating the Louisiana Annual Conference. In the twentieth century, the interest in Methodist union pushed aside the ideals of the Preachers' Meeting in favor of segregated gatherings. The interracial Methodist tradition in New Orleans give way to organizations that valued racial similarities over a common religious affiliation.

Still, black church members did not oppose unification in theory. They believed a unified American Methodism could move a step closer to the universal inclusiveness that had initially attracted them to the M. E. Church. Robert Jones stood among unification's most vocal proponents, black or white, no doubt contributing to his appointment on the denomination's Commission on Unification in 1916. Jones considered unification a way to ease the sectional tensions that plagued both church and nation, as well as a means to move the church toward the ideal of being "as universal as Christ."[27] Jones combined his interest in unification with the issue to which he was most committed: racial equality. He thus emphasized that any form of union must not compromise the standing and rights of the denomination's black members. As long as a unified church did not ask African Americans to assume an inferior place in church and society, the denomination's black members were as supportive of union as any other group within the M. E. Church.[28] Black supporters who argued for the potential benefits of unification echoed the faith of earlier generations that a biracial church might yet be the means to transform society.

In 1920, African Americans achieved a partial victory in the unification debates. Once again, a refreshing moment of hope intruded into the long draught of despair. Despite an apparent determination to consummate union, both sides pulled back in 1920 because of sizable pockets of objection within each denomination. Race remained the source of contention. Conservative Southern Methodists held that even a separate racial jurisdiction did not create sufficient separation. According to the *New Orleans Christian Advocate*, "setting the Negro apart in a separate Church . . . is the only completely satisfactory solution of this problem." At the same time, Jones's participation in the negotiations had enabled the black church members to voice their concerns directly. As a result, African Americans were neither asked to leave nor placed in a distinctly racial jurisdiction. Black church members retained their General Conference standing. In the midst of a deeply segregated nation, theirs would remain, at least officially, a biracial organization. But the reprieve was only temporary. Both denominations were committed to moving forward to create a workable plan of unification. It remained clear that any plan would, in some form, compromise the standing of the church's black members. When the two denominations finally joined together in 1939, along with the Methodist Protestant church, they used virtually the same plan as proposed in 1918. The new unified denomination siphoned all its black members into the separate Central Jurisdiction, where they remained until 1968.[29]

THE STRUGGLE FOR A BLACK bishop formed the other major issue surrounding reconsiderations of the role of black church members. Calls for a bishop of African descent had been one of the most persistent pleas of African-American members. At nearly every quadrennial General Conference since 1872, the predominantly white delegates to the national convention affirmed that color posed no bar to elected office in the M. E. Church and recommended the election of a black bishop. But these same delegates consistently gave only white candidates the two-thirds majority necessary for election to the denomination's highest office. *Southwestern Christian Advocate* editor Isaiah B. Scott recognized that whites voted for resolutions supporting a colored episcopacy because they knew they could "let it go— it doesn't amount to anything anyway."[30] The early-twentieth-century agitation for a black bishop provided one of the clearest continuities with previous generations. Yet the new century also witnessed the first progress. Two significant episcopal elections framed the first two decades of the twentieth century—elections that both advanced and revealed the limitations of African-American struggles for equality in the M. E. Church.

The first turning point in the quest for a black bishop came at the 1904 General Conference. New Orleans resident and *Southwestern Christian Advocate* editor Isaiah B. Scott played the starring role. At first, the 1904

General Conference appeared headed down the well-worn path of electing only white bishops. African-American delegates had once again presented resolutions requesting the election of a bishop of African descent. Before the Committee on Episcopacy could consider the resolutions and make recommendations, the General Conference proceeded to elect eight new bishops. To no one's surprise, all of the new bishops were white. The next order of business was the election of a missionary bishop to Africa. Scott, who had already edited the *Southwestern Christian Advocate* longer than any of his predecessors, appeared headed for yet another term as editor until his supporters among the colored annual conferences presented him as a candidate for the missionary episcopacy. General Conference delegates decisively elected Scott on the first ballot, where he garnered nearly 85 percent of the votes. Only two other candidates, one of whom was white, received more than ten votes.[31] After more than thirty years of resolutions and pleadings, the M. E. Church had elected an African American to the episcopacy.

Black church members rejoiced in Scott's election as a missionary bishop. Never before had the entire General Conference, a predominantly white body, elected a man of African descent to the denomination's highest office. Nor did Scott's election constitute a "special" election. The General Conference elected Scott in the same manner it elected its other missionary bishops, who served overseas from China to Africa. Neither special legislation nor resolutions required that the missionary bishop to Africa be of African descent. Joseph Hartzell, the other missionary bishop to Africa, was white, as were several of Scott's challengers. Also noteworthy was Scott's status as coordinate bishop to Africa, marking his equality with Hartzell with whom he would serve. Scott's service alongside Hartzell was especially fitting, since Hartzell had founded the *Southwestern Christian Advocate* and had been a leading white voice for racial equality in New Orleans and throughout the denomination. It was an especially proud moment for the M. E. Church in New Orleans. The two men, black and white, working side by side as equals created a "sign of hope" that "the Methodist Episcopal Church was willing to trust large responsibilities in the hands of the colored man." As a coordinate bishop, Scott would make the M. E. Church the only denomination in which black and white bishops worked side by side without restriction.[32]

Still, Scott's election was only a modest gain. Even Robert E. Jones, Scott's successor at the *Southwestern Christian Advocate* and among those most optimistic about the significance of Scott's elevation to the episcopacy, conceded that "this election will not wholly satisfy the demands of our colored membership." Scott's election failed to provide a sufficient response to the long-standing call for a bishop of African descent. As a missionary bishop, his episcopal authority was restricted to his assigned territory across the Atlantic. In contrast, bishops who were general superintendents could preside over any conference, including those served by missionary bishops. Such limitations confined Scott to Africa and prevented him from ministering to African Americans in the South who had been calling for the election of a black bishop. Whites had finally acceded to the election of an African American, but only to a bishopric that limited his contact with whites by sending him to a distant continent to serve those assumed to be "his" people. So obvious was the affront that an A.M.E. publication charged the M. E. Church with creating a "Jim Crow Episcopacy."[33] The door to equality had, perhaps, opened a bit more, but the threshold had not been crossed.

The limitations of Scott's episcopacy focused renewed attention on the failure to elect a black man to the general superintendency. As church members continued their calls for a black bishop, they stressed different arguments than previous generations had. Earlier appeals had emphasized the need to silence African Methodist rivals, who highlighted the lack of black M. E. bishops to win converts. The rivalry with African Methodist denominations had waned under M. E. church leaders such as A.E.P. Albert and E.W.S. Hammond, who expanded interdenominational cooperation in their efforts to resist Jim Crow. By 1915, denominational animosity had subsided so much that Jones claimed "we all rejoice in the good work that the African Methodist Episcopal Church has done."[34] Black M. E. church leaders realized that neglect by their own denomination, rather than the criticism of rivals, posed the greatest threat to black church members' loyalty in the early twentieth century. Those leaving the M. E. Church felt pushed out by their own denomination as much as wooed by their rivals. Accordingly, arguments for black bishops shifted to emphasize the nurture of the M. E. Church's own members more than responding to charges from rival denominations. Echoing the broader class concerns of the era, black church members argued that race leaders would advance the programs of moral, spiritual, and educational uplift that would lead "the masses of their own people" toward recognition as equal citizens in both the church and the nation. Methodists pointed with particular optimism to New Orleans, where "the marvelous achievements of the Negro Methodists of the New Orleans Area under their own leaders, are an unanswerable argument for indigenous leadership from bottom to top."[35]

Arguments for a bishop of African descent focused especially on the declining effectiveness of the white bishops who presided over the denomination's black church members. In the decades after Emancipation, bishops had stood among the strongest supporters of African Americans who affiliated with the M. E. Church. After the turn of the century, however, the episcopal consensus supporting African Americans broke down. Bishops generally neglected the colored conferences under their supervision, and a few were downright hostile in their administration of annual conference meetings. Some even favored excluding black members altogether. Bishop Earl Cranston, for example, became obsessed with improving relations with Southern Methodists. Although Cranston would never ask black members to leave, a more sympathetic bishop conceded to Jones that "I think he might go into his closet, shut the door, and thank the Lord if you volunteered to go out."[36] Even those who were supportive found their effectiveness severely limited, foremost among them Wilbur Thirkield, who was the son-in-law of the leading nineteenth-century white M. E. advocate for racial equality, Gilbert Haven. Southern white hostility to racial interaction had restricted the ability of white leaders to communicate directly with black followers. White congregations in the South therefore received preferential treatment, although in many places, as in New Orleans, they claimed only a small percentage of the city's M. E. church members. Unlike black bishops, who would be free to travel with black members and minister in their homes and gathering places, even the most sympathetic whites found that their "supervision has been confined chiefly to the presiding at annual conferences." Black bishops, on the other hand, would know and could respond to the particular challenges and struggles that black members faced in ways white bishops never could. A plea for compassion, rather a fight against external competition, now motivated the call for bishops of African descent: "We do not base our appeal for a colored bishop . . . on the fact that the election of one would quiet the agitation . . . nor upon the fact that our people are taunted by other churches with being under white bosses . . . but upon the crying need of the work itself for adequate episcopal supervision for this the most needy part of the church."[37]

Early twentieth-century debates about electing a black bishop centered around the proposed Bishops for Races and Languages amendment. At the same 1904 General Conference that elected Scott to the missionary episcopacy, proposals began circulating to create a similarly limited episcopacy for African Americans in the United States. Calls for a black episcopacy had always rested upon a tacit understanding that bishops of color would preside only over colored annual conferences—mostly because that was where black church members wanted them and would benefit from their presence, but also to reassure white members they would not be subject to black supervision. Actual legislative limits on a black episcopacy would not be necessary, since black M. E. leaders, from clergy to presiding elders, had always been selected with the understanding they would serve only black church members.[38] The Races and Languages amendment signaled the white desire to make explicit and binding what had long been an implicit part of the cry for a bishop of color. Not surprisingly, the proposed amendment came from a white annual conference. Only with the proposed amendment could they ensure a black bishop would have not authority to preside over whites, since the denomination's constitution prohibited any restrictions on the authority of bishops elected as general superintendents. The amendment would create a new category of bishop who would be assigned "for work among particular races or languages" while also "limiting their episcopal jurisdiction to the same respectively." A bishop for races and languages would have the authority of a general superintendent, but only within his assigned jurisdiction; he would be a missionary bishop to African Americans. The push for the amendment revealed the conflicting meanings of segregation. On the one hand, it marked a growing acceptance of segregation within the M. E. Church that matched its acceptability throughout the nation. On the other hand, codifying what had always been assumed revealed an underlying fragility that betrayed the supposed fixed limits of racial interaction. The need to ensure that African Americans not rise to positions of authority over whites suggested it was not the impossibility that many whites wished it were.[39]

Black church members' willingness to consider the Races and Languages amendment signaled significant concessions on their part. Previous generations had rejected any episcopacy that would differentiate between black and white bishops, from the mechanics of their election to the exercise of their duty. Tacit understandings that a black bishop would minister to his own people were acceptable, and even assumed, but constitutional restrictions were not. Nonetheless, the M. E. retreat from its earlier commitment to racial equality led many African Americans to reconsider the best strategy of electing a black bishop for service in the United States. The amendment appeared to offer a workable solution for both races. African Americans would receive the episcopal supervision they desired, while whites found reassurance they would not be subject to African-American authority. In a speech supporting the proposal, one black clergyman acknowledged that it was time to be practical, considering the failed results of thirty years of recommendations that the church elect a black bishop on the basis of equality. The Races and Languages amendment offered the best, and probably the only, way that African Americans could obtain any form of black episcopal supervision. The election of Isaiah Scott as missionary bishop a few days earlier made clear that African Americans stood a greater likelihood of election if they accepted restrictions rather than holding out for total equality. Most saw little option but to accept the compromise. The 1904 General Conference passed the Races and Languages amendment by an overwhelming vote of 517 to 27, endorsing Jim Crow within a denomination that had long trumpeted its commitment to racial equality.[40] The M. E. Church was not alone. That same year, black Episcopalians proposed their national convention consider the establishment of "special Missionary Districts for races and languages" in order to facilitate the election of that denomination's first black bishop.[41] Neither church's proposal succeeded.

Following the 1904 General Conference both black and white M. E. church members lost their enthusiasm for the Races and Languages amendment. The second step for approving a constitutional change required each annual conference to vote on the amendment prior to the subsequent General Conference, four years later. By the time annual conferences began their voting in late 1907 and early 1908, the momentum had shifted from support to opposition. Opponents blamed the initial enthusiasm on the fact that it was pushed through in the closing hours of the nearly month-long 1904 General Conference. They suggested white delegates offered it as compensation for the failure to elect a bishop of African descent and to inspire loyalty among the church's black members during the four years between General Conferences. After the 1904 conference ended, black Methodists in Louisiana and throughout the South reasserted their long-standing contention that a bishop elected under special provisions failed to fulfill the call for a bishop of African descent. Ernest Lyon, a clergyman with deep roots in New Orleans, declared that "as members of the Methodist Episcopal Church we have a right to expect that they be elected under the same general rule which applies to the election of white Bishops." The proposed amendment signaled a step backward in the struggle against segregation, further institutionalizing racial distinctions within the M. E. Church. Compounding the opposition was a rumor, fueled by liberal white Northerners, that the 1908 General Conference would be willing and able to elect a black bishop to the general superintendency without restrictions. The members of the Louisiana Annual Conference unanimously opposed the amendment.[42] Meanwhile, white apprehensions about even a limited black episcopacy assured the amendment's demise. Similar concerns within the Episcopal Church ensured its proposal for special missionary districts and bishops was likewise tabled.[43]

The promise of a black bishop in 1908 failed to materialize. The General Conference elected eight whites to the office of bishop, just as they had at the previous denominational gathering, and as they would continue to do at subsequent meetings. At the same 1908 General Conference, the denomination's Committee on Episcopacy ceased its dual traditions of affirming that color was no bar to elected office and recommending that the conference elect a bishop of African descent.[44] Perhaps the growing field of qualified candidates led the committee to fear that its resolutions, long merely rhetorical, might become reality. More than ever, black church members recognized the need to reconsider their strategy for electing a bishop of their own race.

African Americans responded very differently when the 1912 General Conference revived the Bishops for Races and Languages amendment. A people once welcomed with the promise of equality accepted marginalization as their best means of survival. As in 1904, the proposed amendment passed the 1912 General Conference by a large margin, 520 to 45. African-American delegates strongly supported the amendment and, unlike in the past, continued to support the proposal when voted upon in annual conferences in late 1915 and early 1916. Over forty years of frustration led African Americans to conclude that the only chance for electing a black bishop for service within the United States resided in a limited episcopacy. The Races and Languages amendment would enable African Americans to achieve their goal of black episcopal supervision, despite the limitations it imposed. Jones urged black church members to face "squarely and sensibly" the reality that electing a black general superintendent in the near future was "not at all probable, if not impossible."[45] In a complete inversion of their vote on the same amendment eight years earlier, clergy in the Louisiana Annual Conference approved the amendment 151 to 1, while the laity approved it by a 96-to-1 margin. A prominent laymen explained that each colored conference "changed from the position they took in 1908 to advocacy of the amendment purely because they believed as most of our people are believing, that a Bishop under this amendment is all that the Church will give them."[46] Church members who, after Emancipation, had believed that equality was within reach in the M. E. Church, agreed a half century later to codify their inferiority in the church. Nonetheless, the Races and Languages amendment once again failed, despite widespread support among the black church members it would affect. A majority of annual conferences approved the proposal, but not the two-thirds necessary to enact a constitutional change. White opposition ranged from prejudice, to a few lingering supporters of racial equality, to immigrant constituencies who feared the amendment would hinder their own integration into the episcopacy. Assessing the most recent developments, Jones observed that "there was a time when it was claimed by not a few that when a Negro was qualified for the Episcopacy he would be elevated. Now you would have to fine-tooth comb the entire Church to get a man who actually believes that that is at all possible. To state the proposition plainly," Jones continued, "to qualify for the general superintendency in the Methodist Episcopal Church, one must be white."[47]

Just when the debate seemed deadlocked, the bishop struggle dramatically changed course in 1920. The General Conference voted to add a special ballot for the election of two black bishops to serve as general superintendents. Robert E. Jones was the first to rise victoriously to the bishops' bench. In the midst of despair came a moment of hope. The century had opened with the election of one New Orleans resident and *Southwestern*

Figure 4.2. Louisiana Annual Conference, Bishop Robert E. Jones, presiding (seated, front right). Courtesy Arthur P. Bedou Photographs, Xavier University Archives and Special Collections, New Orleans.

Christian Advocate editor, Isaiah B. Scott, to a limited episcopacy in faraway Africa. The second decade ended with the rise of another New Orleans leader and *Southwestern Christian Advocate* editor, Robert E. Jones, to the episcopacy as a general superintendent. Black Methodists in New Orleans were especially proud that Jones had been the first of the two black bishops elected in 1920, and by an overwhelming margin. Following Jones's victory on the first ballot, Matthew W. Clair was elected on the third ballot. The new black bishops faced fewer explicit restrictions than African Americans had been willing to accept during the previous decade. Jones and Clair were elected without any of the formal restrictions proposed in the Races and Languages amendment. They were general superintendents. Episcopalians, in contrast, succeeded in electing only suffragan bishops, whose work was constitutionally limited to African Americans within their own dioceses. M. E. General Conference members acknowledged the significance of the moment and spontaneously broke into song, singing "Mine Eyes Have Seen the Glory of the Coming of the Lord." The General Conference assigned Jones to New Orleans, in recognition of its importance among black Methodists and of Jones's stature in the Crescent City. Upon his return home, Jones received a hero's welcome. Further celebrations ensued in November 1920 when Jones first presided over the Central Alabama (colored) Annual Conference, the first time an African American had presided with "complete episcopal prerogative" in the M. E. Church.[48]

Convenience, as much as compassion, enabled the election of black bishops in 1920. Changes in the M. E. Church as a whole rather than a newfound concern for the denomination's black members made possible the long-awaited victory. By 1920, the M. E. Church approved a plan of "districting" all of its bishops so that each was assigned a specific territory and group of annual conferences to supervise between General Conferences. The denomination had previously rejected districting because it ran counter to the Methodist ideal of itinerant bishops. However, the growth of the denomination and the nation had made itinerancy impractical. By the time the General Conference assigned its black bishops to specific conferences in 1920, it was an accepted practice for all bishops, rather than an exception as would have previously been the case under the Races and Languages amendment.[49] The white majority granted African Americans their own bishop only when the restrictions implicitly placed upon him mirrored rather than challenged practices accepted within the rest of the church.

As was so often the case for black church members, a moment of great hope was once again tempered by disappointment. The election of Jones and Clair as bishops still fell short of the more than half-century quest for equality within the M. E. Church. The General Conference elected the black bishops on a separate ballot on which only black candidates could be nominated. In separating the episcopal elections by race, the denomination conceded that African Americans remained unequal and inferior. Ironically, the denomination used calls for racial equality in that year's Episcopal Address to justify using a separate ballot to elect bishops of color. Separate balloting also ensured that the remaining twelve bishops elected to the general superintendency in 1920 would be white. Furthermore, the election took place with the understanding that the black bishops would preside exclusively over black annual conferences. White conferences would not have to be subject to black bishops, despite the election of Jones and Clair as general superintendents. Without actually creating a special episcopacy, black and white alike recognized that black bishops would function as if elected to the restricted episcopacy proposed under the Races and Languages amendment. No such assumptions existed for white general superintendents who could, and did, continue to preside at colored conferences. With separate districts and special episcopal elections, the M. E. Church took yet another large step in institutionalizing within its own walls the racial segregation it had once so strongly opposed.[50]

A FUTURE FULL OF OPTIMISM in 1880 had collapsed by 1920. Gone was the hope for a biracial M. E. identity that could transcend racial differences, even with recent advances on the bishop question and the retreat from unification negotiations. The M. E. Church was understood to have undergone a shift of wills: whereas black members once believed that "the M. E. Church *will* act" on their behalf, they now asked "what *will* the M. E. Church do" with its African-American members? The parallels to the slavery debate a century earlier were striking. The General Conference had spoken forcefully against slavery in the 1780s, then tempered its opposition until it was silent in 1820. A century later it followed the same path on equality of black members, from optimistic statements in the 1880s to racial retreat by 1920. Once again, black church members lamented that their denomination had moved from leader to follower in race relations by the early twentieth century. If the church did not take further steps to resist segregation within its own walls, "it must lose its leadership in the spiritual and social life of America." The M. E. Church remained the largest Protestant denomination that included both black and white members, and its backtracking on racial equality would have a devastating influence on its own members and among African Americans in general.[51] Among biracial Protestant denominations, the M. E. Church had already gone the furthest in separating its black members. Presbyterians, Episcopalians, and Lutherans all had separate regional bodies for black members, but none had proposed or created the equivalent of the M. E. Central Jurisdiction to isolate black members so completely. The M. E. Church had become a segregated denomination in practice, if not in law. The racial division ranged from separate education societies and school facilities to separate accommodations and entertainment at national board meetings, not to mention separate churches, conferences, and soon jurisdictions. M. E. segregation began in fits and starts, much like segregation on railroad cars and in other public spaces, spreading unevenly until it had become pervasive and uniform across both the denomination and the nation. The church hoping to overturn the southern racial order found itself transformed instead.

Jones even suggested race relations in M. E. Church ran "counter to the spirit of the times in which we live." Church leaders found increasing examples of secular interaction that contrasted with the declining possibilities in their own denomination. The white business leaders who had provided protection during the Charles riot were just one example. Labor unions represented another hopeful model. After witnessing the 1904 Labor Day parade, where black and white union laborers marched side by side, Jones suggested it might be labor, rather than religion, that would "conquer the race antipathies." Nor were the patterns limited to the laboring classes. Jones noted that "white physicians and colored physicians confer quite frequently and with a good deal more satisfaction to each other than white preachers and colored preachers." The M. E. Church seemed to recede even in comparison with the government in protecting and advancing the rights of African Americans. Among the examples black church members cited was the 1917 Supreme Court decision that declared residential-segregation ordinances unconstitutional.[52] This came at the very time the M. E. Church considered isolating its black members in a separate jurisdiction, or even a separate denomination. How ironic, Jones pointed out, that the church had fallen so far behind social trends that it advanced a principle "tabooed by the highest tribunal in the land." Employment opportunities presented a similar contrast. While the United States government sent African Americans overseas to teach from Brazil to the Philippines, the M. E. Church refused to send African-American missionaries anywhere besides Africa, where work would be restricted to "no race save his own."[53] The rhetoric clearly overestimated federal advocacy, as the United States government had just gone to great lengths to segregate its bureaucracy. M. E. frustration came more from their denomination's conformity than its deviation from wider racial practices. The exceptions to racial segregation that had once largely occurred within the M. E. Church now happened almost entirely outside of it.

Despite Methodist complaints, the racial transformations did not distinguish the M. E. Church from other denominations. Nearly every American denomination had instituted some form of racial separation, whether through formally divided jurisdictions or informal parting. Even recent interracial upstarts found the surge of Jim Crow too overwhelming. Among the most striking examples is Pentecostalism. In 1906, the Pentecostal movement emerged from the revivals on Azusa Street in Los Angeles. Though its origins were complex, William Seymour, an African American leading the Azusa Street revivals, played a central role. Emphasizing the baptism of the spirit, and most noted for its participants speaking in tongues as a sign of that baptism, the Pentecostal revivals at Azusa Street attracted an interracial and international congregation that cast aside worldly markers such as race, class, and gender, at least in worship. The interracial worship continued to characterize Pentecostalism as it spread across the United States and into the South. The interracial and egalitarian possibilities must have seemed intoxicating at first. Several early organizations appointed black and white leaders, and predominantly white audiences frequently invited African-American preachers to speak. Black preachers often baptized whites converts, and C. H. Mason's Church of God in Christ baptized many of the white clergy that would go on to form the largest Pentecostal denomination, the Assemblies of God. The black Mason led revivals specifically for whites that attracted thousands in Arkansas and Tennessee. But entrenched racial patterns quickly proved too much for these new, liberated, and spirit-filled religious expressions. By 1924, and earlier in most cases, Pentecostal organizations had divided into racially separate denominations that had very little contact with one another. In the few cases where black and white remained, they nonetheless formed separate jurisdictions. The Pentecostal shift from integration to segregation was more typical than extraordinary, except perhaps in its rapidity. In one notable contrast to the prevailing pattern, however, most Pentecostal separations resulted from white withdrawal rather than by excluding black members or by black self-separation.[54]

SURVEYING THE DEMISE of their denomination's commitment to racial inclusion, black M. E. church members wondered how Methodists could justify segregation from a theological perspective. White church leaders denied the relevance of the criticism. They argued racial separation was a question of institutional expediency and social conformity rather than one with theological or moral implications. As a social and political practice, segregation was an issue about which the church neither could nor should take a position. Denying a religious framework also enabled white church leaders to dismiss critical black voices as irrelevant. At the same time, bracketing theological discussions created space for the M. E. Church to adopt racial separation as a pragmatic necessity. White church leaders had long invoked the social custom of racial affinity as the most beneficial means to advance Methodism, especially in the South. Adapting to social custom contributed to the denomination's quest for respectability and its ability to compete in the American religious marketplace. Institutional growth, not theology or ethics, was the framework for evaluating the question of racial segregation. Methodists had made the same decision regarding slavery one hundred years earlier, retreating from their opposition in order to advance Methodist growth in the South. The pragmatic sentiment was widespread among northern Protestants who organized religious institutions in the postbellum South. A Congregationalist in Atlanta, arguing for separate churches to facilitate the widest possible work, ridiculed the contention that "we turn aside from nearly all the white population of the South simply because they are not willing to join themselves to a church composed wholly, or almost wholly, of colored people."[55]

White church leaders simply ignored black criticisms that segregation constituted a theological and moral failing for which the church would be judged. To white leaders, it was a social convention, not an injustice, and early-twentieth-century whites would not bring religious language to discussions of segregation. The silence recalled earlier commentaries on slavery, which southern churches characterized as a "civil and domestic institution" whose regulation was limited to the state and was therefore not a proper arena of action for churches, which were to focus on spiritual matters alone. Having gained legal validation in courts, segregation was a legal and political issue to be debated and resolved in those arenas. The role of churches was to ensure that, both within their own institutions and without, African Americans did not suffer abuse within the context of their socially and legally prescribed separate spheres. The morality of segregation was not measured by its presence but only in how it was administered. Methodists, or most other American Christians for that matter, would not associate segregation with the problem of equal rights until the 1940s. Only then did white Americans reevaluate segregation in theological categories that highlighted its inconsistency with Christian claims of equality. Only with that reconsideration would black members develop sufficient momentum to overturn the church's segregated institutions.[56] The intervening silence was telling. Widespread and sophisticated biblical defenses of slavery had emerged only when religious language began attacking slavery. The lack of theologically grounded pro-segregation defenses suggests the corresponding absence of any substantial or sustained religious critique of segregation.

As white church leaders turned to the social and political arena that they invested with authority to shape race relations, they encountered a worldview that embraced black inferiority and the resulting corollary of racial separation. The 1898 Spanish-American War, in which the United States took possession of Cuba, Puerto Rico, and the Philippines, signaled the emergence of a new wave of American imperialism. Assumptions of racial and religious superiority undergirded the conquests, reinforcing a long tradition that presumed the inferiority of non-Christian peoples. The same assumptions of racial hierarchy and the need for a civilizing white Christian presence had inspired both overseas M. E. missions and the denomination's work among black Southerners. By the early twentieth century, a growing science and anthropology of race, including social Darwinism, reinforced ideas of innate racial differences. Many of these cultural observations found expression in M. E. publications and sermons, which used the language of "dominant races" and invoked common assumptions of an "essential race superiority." Typical was the Boston Memorial Day sermon that argued "the Anglo-Saxon is the dominant race of the world."[57] Few could miss the domestic as well as international implications of such assertions.

Northern discussions of segregation therefore lacked the more the explicit religious reasoning promulgated in southern Protestantism. Yet even in the South, religious defenses of segregation tended to be vague, lacking the close biblical readings and theological analysis that had characterized the antebellum pro-slavery defense. Most southern evangelicals shared a conviction that God had created inherent differences in the black and white races, which justified a perpetually inferior position for African Americans. This reasoning proceeded largely from observations of the existing social order rather than specific biblical references, although the curse of Ham (Gen. 9:20–27) was occasionally invoked to justify black subjugation. This southern Protestant racial ideology, which conflated God and nature, was consistent across regions and denominations. Southern Methodists in New Orleans praised "that social distinction between the white and black races which Nature, God and the best instincts of mankind have so far preserved." Searching the Scriptures for any command to racial integration, the Virginia Baptist Convention concluded it "did not think we are required by the law of God to carry out this policy." Southerners argued that patterns of racial affinity represented a divinely implanted will that would be sinful to overturn. In this logic, segregation became a measure of faithfulness. "The color line is distinctly drawn by Jehovah Himself," a southern Presbyterian warned, and it would be "a sin and a crime to obliterate it." Like most Southerners, church leaders argued that segregation was necessary to prevent miscegenation, which they assumed was the most egregious violation of the divine command of racial separation. Virginia Baptists asserted that "God has made the two races widely different. . . . [W]e take it for granted it was not the purpose of the Creator that they should be blended." Churches did not shirk from their regulatory responsibilities. The Virginia Baptist General Convention took three years to consider and ultimately reject a proposal to exchange delegates with a black Baptist association, warning that "religious and social intercourse are closely, if not inseparably connected." They feared religious fraternity would put black Baptist delegates "in juxtaposition with our wives and our daughters," facilitating a social interaction that would, according to the logic of southern sexual anxieties, lead to miscegenation and intermarriage.[58] The link between segregation and divine law was so rooted in the southern white psyche that it did not require explicit articulation. As Lillian Smith, the incisive white commentator on southern racial mores, remembered from her own southern upbringing,

> I do not remember how or when, but by the time I had learned God is love . . .
> I had learned that God so loved the world that He gave his only begotten Son
> that we might have segregated churches. . . . I learned it is possible to be a Christian and a white southerner simultaneously . . . to pray at night and ride a Jim
> Crow car the next morning and to feel comfortable in doing both.[59]

The same fear of racial mixing motivated many white Northerners who dominated the M. E. Church, even if they did not articulate them in the same religious language as their southern counterparts. Repeated assurances by black M. E. church members that their assertions of religious equality were not demands for unwanted social interaction testified to ongoing white anxiety about maintaining limits on racial interaction. Black church members found themselves coddling white egos and calming white racial fears. They prefaced appeals to interracial contact with paeans to the benefits of contact with white leaders, celebrating "your ideas, your ideals, ambitions and purpose." On the other hand, they reassured white church members of the limits of their demands. In calls for a black bishop, for example, they promised that "there is no contention for a Negro to preside over white conferences" nor any desire to assign black ministers to white congregations. Equality of opportunity, they claimed, did not require the social mixing that whites claimed to abhor. "It is not a question of the drawing room or parlor," explained one minister. "It is not even a question of eating and drinking, as some vainly think and dread." The link between religious fraternity and social fraternization was not as direct as whites charged. Jones reminded anxious whites that neither intermarriage nor rape resulted from the work of the earliest generation of white laborers in New Orleans, whose interactions with black members exceeded any taking place in 1920.[60] In a jab African Americans enjoyed taking, Jones assured nervous whites that "the percentage of Negroes who desire to marry and associate with white people is so insignificant as to be imperceptible." Most episodes of sexual aggression involved white men attacking black women. Nonetheless, renewed white anxieties about miscegenation, exemplified in the popularity of the film *Birth of a Nation* and the subsequent rebirth of the Ku Klux Klan, which blamed the nation's troubles on African Americans and racial mixing, complicated black leaders' efforts. Race relations in the early twentieth century were so fragile that even black church leaders found themselves on the defensive against charges of ulterior social and, by implication, sexual motives.[61]

At the same time, Methodist understandings of the church eased the seeming incongruity between Christianity and segregated religious institutions, even without reference to the broader social or political context. Long before the unification negotiations, the denomination had accepted separate churches and annual conferences, as Southern Methodists were fond of reminding their northern counterparts. Adding racially defined jurisdictions to enable reunion simply expanded the existing conference system in a manner consistent with several generations of Methodist practice. White Methodists also maintained distinctions between ecclesiastical organization and religious fellowship. Unlike black church members, white M. E. leaders did not consider religious institutions a manifestation of religious belief. Unification advocate Bishop Earl Cranston argued that a system of racially separate conferences and jurisdictions "is not a segregated relation. It is an ecclesiastical fellowship representing but one spiritual communion." In addition to its twenty black annual conferences in 1920, the M. E. Church also had a Japanese, a Chinese, two Norwegian-Danish, two Hispanic, six Swedish, and ten German annual conferences. To white leaders, the sum of the whole, rather than the character of any of its individual parts, was the only way to judge the M. E. Church. Moreover, the primary mission of the M. E. Church, with its evangelical, revival roots, was the salvation of souls. White leaders believed receiving God's grace and accepting salvation was not contingent on a biracial congregation, conference, or even denomination. Theirs was a human-centered understanding of church, created by and reflecting the human-made social order. Only in subsequent generations would Methodists, like Catholics, reconceptualize the church as the body of Christ and therefore a community that transcended rather than recreated human boundaries.[62]

Why did African Americans remain in the M. E. Church in the face of such persistent marginalization? They stayed because they believed. Unlike their white counterparts, they believed that the racial organization of churches was fundamentally a religious issue. They believed the Christian faith and the Methodist Church offered the path to both spiritual and racial salvation. They kept their faith because of a confidence in the transformative power of Christianity, rightly preached and rightly practiced. Reading the New Testament for themselves, black church members learned to "make a firsthand interpretation of the fundamentals enunciated by our common Lord." They concluded that true Christianity demanded an end to racial divisions. According to Jones, African Americans remained Christians because in the midst of seeming despair, the biblical message of God's redemption offered hope that "the Gospel is to bring peace between the two races."[63] Jones argued that the Christian Scriptures recorded the unfolding of an increasingly universalistic church, whose mission was to include all the peoples of the earth. African Americans thus sustained a confidence in the truth and righteousness of Christianity, even as the institutional expression of that faith fell short of the biblical ideal. African Americans were confident that they stood at the center of God's promise of salvation. Only three generations earlier, God had fulfilled the promise to deliver the slaves from bondage. The God of their ancestors would not abandon them, and so they remained faithful to their church.

African Americans also found in Christianity an assertion of a divinely ordained equality that countered white invocations of natural hierarchies. Black church members formed an equal part of God's creation, no less than any other race or people. If anyone objected to African Americans or any other nonwhite race belonging to the Christian Church, Jones suggested it was neither the problem nor the fault of the darker races. "The Negro," Jones reminded white Christians, "is not of his own making. God made him and made him a part of a common humanity." If whites were dissatisfied with the presence of black church members and anticipated the extinction of the race, as some argued in this period, whites should go to the source of the so-called problem: "Blame the Creator. He made them."[64]

Moreover, as a people who were "God-made," African Americans reminded white antagonists of their shared belief in God's goodness: "God never made a mistake." Invoking widely shared doctrines, ranging from creation to the sovereignty of God, black Christians pointed out that they were placed "in this world by the same loving, wise, far-seeing Divine Providence as the most favored peoples of the earth." Christianity became a means to demonstrate to whites, in the context of their own belief systems, that "the Negro has a divine right in the brotherhood of Christian believers" and in the world.[65]

Ongoing loyalty to the M. E. Church in particular stemmed from an insistence that it most closely expressed the faith at the root of African-American adherence to Christianity. Black Methodists pointed to John Wesley's racial inclusiveness and the early Methodist opposition to slavery and racial exclusion. African Americans had been part of the American Methodist mission from the very beginning. Among their heroes was Harry Hoosier, known as "Black Harry," who was an early Methodist preacher who traveled with Francis Asbury, sometimes attracting larger crowds than Asbury himself. While not denying that other churches, especially African Methodists, had done much to help the race, African Americans in the M. E. Church asserted that "we have stayed with the Church because of the principles for which she stood." Jones warned white church members that "the Methodist Episcopal Church cannot turn out its Negro members without doing violence to its best traditions."[66] By remaining in the church and pushing it to be more Methodist and more Christian, African Americans also hoped to vindicate their decision to affiliate with the M. E. Church rather than any other Methodist or Christian denominations.

But membership was not merely racial self-interest. Black church members argued that their ongoing presence would save the denomination. They insisted on the crucial nexus between belief and institutions, in contrast to white apologists who denied any link between spiritual and institutional communion. Black church members would play a prophetic role by holding the denomination accountable to the faith it proclaimed. They would remain for the integrity of Methodism and not only for their own benefit. The greatest test of American Methodism, Jones argued, was what "we are doing for ten million Negroes in America. It is not whether we can preach brotherhood to all the world, but whether we can practice brotherhood in our neighborhood." The presence of African Americans would help the M. E. pass that test, moving all peoples closer to salvation. The M. E. Church's integrity rested on its treatment of its black members, since a church that failed to follow the inclusiveness demanded by Christianity could no longer be called a Christian church. As Jones explained, "Any church that is worth the name must be as universal as Christ and as comprehensive as his invitation to salvation." Black church members were also concerned about the integrity of their church worldwide. Their ongoing membership would be crucial to M. E. success in the mission field, where three-fourths of the people were nonwhite: "Nothing so discredits the Christian religion as the inability of the American Church to accept in its fellowship its converts among the Negroes," Jones warned. An all-white denomination would make the M. E. Church "a laughingstock for enlightenment" rather a force for evangelization. The stature of white Methodists would increase only as they treated black church members with integrity.[67] The fates of black and white Methodists were inextricably bound together, in spite of Jim Crow.

African-American church members were unwilling to abandon all influence in the denomination they loved. They had not conceded the interpretation of faith to whites who had tried to shape it for their own self-interests, despite their unequal status. Institutional power did not control faith itself. Many black M. E. church members had helped build their church, both locally and denominationally, and they would not relinquish its identity and faith to white supremacists. As a leading black Methodist and future bishop explained, "We helped to make her great, and we have a right and title to her glory and power, and we do not intend to surrender that right." In the face of white racism, only ongoing black membership maintained any semblance of theological integrity in the M. E. Church.[68] As a result, only African Americans' presence could preserve the character and future of the denomination. Their love for their church and its ideal, even if not yet realized, meant they would not destroy the very institution that had saved their souls and might yet save society as well. Black M. E. loyalty did not rest on a desire for material gain, as critics sometimes charged. Nor did members understand themselves as accommodationist. Just the opposite. M. E. loyalists charged that to run away would be to give in. Remaining and fighting for right was more courageous than cowardly. If black leaders simply wanted a black episcopacy, they could have left for African Methodism and had it immediately. Instead, they chose to remain, enduring assaults from black and white alike, to fight for righteousness within the denomination they loved. By their faithfulness, they ensured that they, and not whites alone, would speak for Methodist Episcopal identity in the twentieth century. By necessity, they had to remain as an antidote to apostasy until the entire denomination was healed of racial antipathy.

This African-American loyalty to a denomination trying to exclude them paralleled patriotism in a country that had similarly marginalized them. Blacks' commitment to the M. E. Church equaled their determination to remain in the United States, even as the nation legalized segregation, practiced disfranchisement, and tolerated lynchings. Most black Americans were no more willing to leave for Africa than M. E. church members were interested in joining African Methodism. They firmly rejected African emigration and colonization schemes, preferring instead to cast their lot with the American nation. Even Isaiah Scott, who later went to Africa as a missionary bishop, shared Jones's sentiment that "the Negro is in this country to stay."[69] African Americans had helped build the nation, forming the backbone of much of its economic system, especially in the South, and had most recently demonstrated their patriotism and loyalty as troops in World War I, even as the nation failed to grant them the very freedoms for which it was fighting in Europe.[70] African Americans argued that commitment to democracy necessitated their remaining a part of the United States. The American nation could only prove a successful experiment in democracy if it accepted and included its black residents with the equality of citizenship that the Constitution guaranteed them, just as the M. E. Church would be a true Christian church only as it accepted its black members as true brothers. While much of the nation was focused on the challenges of massive immigration in the early twentieth century, this anxiety missed the real danger. "In the last analysis," a Methodist leader warned, "American democracy is to be tested and judged by its solution of the problem of the Negro."[71] A mass exodus or exclusion of African Americans would only prove the nation a failure—a failure that could only worsen the quest for democracy by oppressed peoples around the world.

M. E. church members insisted African-American loyalty to the church and to the nation were not merely parallel but intimately intertwined. In a sermon entitled "The Democracy of Love," Jones outlined the connections between Christianity and democracy. "Democracy is the twin sister of Christianity," he claimed. Christianity formed a necessary foundation for a democratic society, for "Christianity, the essence of Christ's teachings, is the basis of all democracy." As a result, "Christianity and democracy are inseparable," and thus "they rise or fall together." The presence of African Americans was crucial to the success of both, and the failure in one would inevitability prove the collapse of the other. Loyalty to Christianity and the M. E. Church therefore articulated a commitment to democracy and the American nation, and vice versa. In the midst of the unification debate, Jones claimed that for the church to divide along the color line would be an act which was "as undemocratic, as un-American, as it is unchristian."[72] The intersection of American and Methodist loyalty had been a persistent part of M. E. identity. Nearly forty years before Jones's sermon weaving together Christianity and democracy, a layman in Louisiana, born into slavery and later a Union soldier, reflected on both the idealism and pragmatism undergirding his own decision to remain in both the M. E. Church and in Louisiana:

> My plan is for us to stay right in this country with the white people, and to be so scattered in and among them that they can't hurt one of us without hurting some of their own number. That's my plan, and that is one of my reasons why I

am in the Methodist Episcopal Church. God's plan seems to be to pattern this country after heaven. He is bringing here all nations, kindreds, and tongues of people and mixing them into one homogeneous whole; and I do not believe we should seek to frustrate his plan by any vain attempts to colonize ourselves into any corner to ourselves.[73]

As the soldier's vision revealed, Christianity offered the promise of the eventual triumph of God's justice in social as well as salvific realms. Confidence in God's justice enabled African Americans to remain faithful to Christianity even as many churches practiced the racial discrimination that contradicted African-American understandings of the true Christian church. Black Christians affirmed that God would reward their faithfulness. Anticipating Martin Luther King Jr.'s understanding of redemptive suffering, they believed they would be rewarded and the world transformed because of the oppression they endured. Reflecting on the sacrifices of black soldiers in World War I, Jones suggested that "if this war vouchsafes to the Negro his full American citizenship, so that he shall face nowhere in America unjust, unfair, un-American discrimination, it will have been worth all the precious blood which the Negro has shed, even though that blood be much and costly."[74] The inverse was true as well. Those who caused the suffering would be held accountable for their actions. As a black Baptist minister reminded his Methodist brethren: "Vengeance is mine, and I will repay, saith the Lord!"[75]

Confidence in God's sovereignty did not constitute mere escapism nor limit God's actions to the afterlife. African Americans remained faithful Christians because they believed that God ultimately controlled earthly events as well. "God is a direct and potential force in human affairs," Jones encouraged; therefore, African Americans had reason to hope that through the power of God, a solution to the race problem would come. With God, they maintained, right always triumphed.[76] Far more than downplaying the current suffering, pointing to future hope and judgment functioned as a prophetic call for white Christians to be true to their faith in the present. In the midst of debates on union, Jones reminded his white colleagues that "it is only a short time before all of us must work this program [of racial cooperation] in heaven." Jones went on to offer, "I am willing to begin here so as to get accustomed to it."[77] Visions of heaven were not excuses to suffer but rather calls to transform the world to more closely approximate that which God intended. The threat of God's future judgment would stand as incentive for whites to change their behavior before it was too late.

Black M. E. church members did not lose faith *in* their church, just as they had not lost the faith *of* their church. Against the swell of segregation, black M. E. church members sustained a hope that their denomination retained the potential to improve race relations in both church and society. Forty years earlier, black and white church members in New Orleans had advanced an interracialism that positioned their denomination at the forefront of the challenges of race relations. Keeping alive the memory of past possibilities sustained a hope of what they might yet accomplish. Despite its backsliding on segregation, no other Protestant denomination could claim to include both black and white to the extent of the M. E. Church. The denomination's General Conference, one church member argued, probably constituted not only the largest but also one of the few bodies in which both African Americans and whites had representation and where whites could interact with African Americans who were not servants.

And there were hopeful signs on the horizon. The 1920 Bishops' Address reasserted the need for the church to be at the forefront of healing the nation's racial divisions, which had recently flared in a new round of urban rioting in northern as well as southern cities. During the 1920s, church publications increased their protests against racial injustice, though it would be another generation before segregation was widely accepted as an injustice. A few solitary white voices, reviving the calls of Hartzell and his colleagues decades earlier, once again began to question racial separation and called upon the church to fight segregation within its own ranks and in society at large. By the end of the decade, church members could point to concrete signs their denomination was making progress. In the 1928 General Conference, Jones became the first bishop of color to preside over a session of the General Conference. The next General Conference committed to meeting only in cities that would guarantee equal treatment of black and white members, a policy that both the board of bishops and the women's auxiliaries had already adopted.[78] With these promising, but admittedly small, advances, Jones argued that the M. E. Church might yet recover its commitment to racial inclusion and achieve the role its loyal black church members had long envisioned: "The schoolmaster of the world in race relationships."[79]

CHAPTER 5

Interracial Catholicism in New Orleans

IN 1874, THE RECENTLY ARRIVED Joseph Hartzell observed religious interactions in New Orleans that would have shocked the sensibilities of most Americans, northern as well as southern. During visits to the city's leading Catholic churches, the Methodist Episcopal clergyman observed that "lips of every shade, by hundreds press with devout kisses the same crucifixes, and fingers of as great variety in color, are dipped in the 'holy water,' . . . in the renting of pews colored families have a chance, and we have seen them sitting as others in every part of the house."[1] Hartzell, who figured so prominently in the struggle for a biracial Methodist Episcopal Church, had discovered examples of integration that exceeded even his own goals. Catholic integration in New Orleans presented a striking contrast to the predominant pattern of racial homogeneity in the city's Protestant congregations. During the next four decades, the possibilities and limitations of mixed parishes would remain at the center of Catholic debates over religious and racial identity in New Orleans.

The distinctive Crescent City Catholicism that had so impressed Hartzell underwent dramatic changes in the decades surrounding the turn of the twentieth century. Nowhere were those transformations more evident than in the changing place of Catholics of color. Although Hartzell's observations testified to a promising past, they occurred on the cusp of a downward spiral away from racially mixed Catholic congregations. But the shift to segregated Catholic parishes was neither immediate nor certain in the decades after Reconstruction. Black and white Catholics trod a protracted and halting path towards racially separate churches, constantly renegotiating their relationship with each other and with their church. Throughout the era, black Catholics raised powerful critiques of racial divisions within and beyond the church, paralleling M. E. criticisms of racially separate denominations. This resistance delayed the emergence of black parishes in New Orleans until the second decade of the twentieth century. At the same time, white Catholic leaders spoke and acted in contradictory ways. Those who claimed to act in the best interests of the city's Catholics of color often undermined the struggle against segregation, while those who had little concern for racial equality inadvertently delayed the swelling tide of Jim Crow.

NEW ORLEANS REMAINED a distinctly Catholic city at the end of Reconstruction, distinct from the predominantly Protestant South and from Catholicism in the rest of the United States. American Catholicism outside Louisiana was English in origin and traced its institutional roots to colonial Maryland, even though French and Spanish missionaries had been the first to reach territories that would eventually become the United States. Despite its Catholic roots and governor, Maryland's early laws required toleration, and the colony never established Catholicism as an official or state-sponsored religion. Protestants soon outnumbered Catholics in Maryland, as they did throughout the American colonies, leaving Catholicism a minority tradition in a religiously competitive and Protestant-dominated culture. Catholics had become the largest Christian denomination in the United States by 1850, though they were still substantially outnumbered by Protestants as a whole. Achieving a plurality did little to stem the marginal place of most nineteenth-century American Catholics. Protestant critiques of Catholic dogma conflated with political accusations linking "popery" to antidemocratic tyranny ensured varying degrees of anti-Catholicism in most places where Protestants outnumbered Catholics. At the same time, Catholicism continued to be concentrated in the urban North, meaning very few African Americans outside of Maryland and Louisiana had come under its influence. The overall demographic character of American Catholicism in the late nineteenth century remained northern, urban, and white, even after a century of rapid growth.[2]

Immigration was the defining characteristic of the Catholic Church in nineteenth-century America. Most of the church's growth was fueled by immigration, first from Ireland and Germany, and later from southern and eastern Europe. Concentrated first in Baltimore, New York, and Boston, these Catholic immigrants spread along the eastern seaboard and into the urban centers of the Midwest, especially Chicago, St. Louis, and Milwaukee. The massive foreign influx fueled a nativist movement that compounded and was often conflated with anti-Catholicism. At the same time, tensions between immigrant groups fostered major disagreements among American Catholics, especially Irish and German. National-language parishes emerged as a strategy to dissipate tensions and retain the swelling ranks of immigrants with close linguistic and cultural ties to their European homelands. These parishes functioned as a way station on the road to a new American identity, albeit a Catholic one. As a sign of their "Americanness," these northern white Catholics readily accepted the racial separation so prevalent throughout the nation and so central to the United States' bipartite racial order.[3]

The Catholic Church in New Orleans followed a distinct trajectory, accounting for its different character and racial patterns that so amazed nineteenth-century visitors. Catholicism came to southern Louisiana under the auspices of French colonialism. Catholic missionaries were official members of imperially sponsored settlements whose mandate from the king, no less than the church, was to ensure the Catholic identity of all who inhabited the colony, whether colonist, native, or slave. Until it became its own diocese in 1793, Louisiana Catholicism was subject first to Quebec, and later to Santiago, Cuba, but never to any Anglo-Catholic province.[4] Little changed when Spain acquired Louisiana in 1763. Even after the Louisiana Purchase in 1803, the ongoing mission status of the Catholic Church in the United States kept the Archdiocese of Louisiana an outpost of the Society for the Propagation of the Faith in Lyon, France. Nor did Catholics in southern Louisiana face the anti-Catholicism their counterparts to the North endured, since Louisianians first belonged to a state-sponsored religion that excluded all others and later, under policies of tolerance, maintained their numerical superiority. Unlike Catholicism in the North, Catholic dominance in New Orleans derived as much from natural increase as from European immigration. Even its immigration patterns were different. While receiving its share of German, Irish, and Italian Catholic immigrants, early-nineteenth-century immigration also came from or through Caribbean colonies, bolstering rather than diluting the distinctive French and Spanish identity of Crescent City Catholicism. Louisiana also lagged in the development of a native clergy and continued to receive the vast majority of its priests, nuns, and episcopal leaders from Europe and, particularly, France.

Crescent City Catholicism's distinctive background fostered the interracial practices that differentiated New Orleans from both American Catholic and southern Protestant racial patterns. Catholic interracialism, as Hartzell observed as late as 1874, played an important role in upholding the city's reputation for racial tolerance.[5] From the first stages of settlement and conquest, the Latin Catholicism of the French and then Spanish colonists in Louisiana differed from the racial rigidity of the Anglo-Saxon Protestants and English Catholics who colonized North America's eastern seaboard. French colonial slave laws, known as the *Code Noir*, required the conversion of slaves to Catholicism and hence their inclusion in the colonial church. This requirement, in conjunction with the Catholic system of parish organization in which all the residents of a particular area made up the parish, resulted in the emergence of interracial churches that ministered to every shade in colonial Louisiana. Racially inclusive worship and rituals in the colonial era contrasted with the predominantly Protestant English colonies to the North, where British colonists and clergy were uncertain whether churches and slave owners held any religious obligations to their slaves. The church remained a locus of racial interaction, evidenced in the frequency with which whites stood as sponsors at black baptisms. French and, especially, Spanish clergy extended the sacraments to Catholics of color as relative equals and even recognized and encouraged slave marriages. Catholic inclusion nurtured a loyalty among the city's black residents that outlived both French colonialism and African slavery.[6]

The racial liberalism so evident in New Orleans's Catholic churches also resulted from the city's unique three-caste racial structure. Between the typically American categories of black and white emerged a middle caste of free people of color in Louisiana, later known as Creoles of color. The largest and most influential Creole community was in New Orleans, although other communities emerged in southern Louisiana and throughout the Gulf Coast region. This third racial category, often of mixed ancestry, complicated race relations by confusing the supposedly clear and absolute racial distinctions upon which divisions elsewhere in America were premised. By the antebellum era, free people of color occupied a distinct legal and social position that provided privileges unknown to persons of African descent living elsewhere in the United States. Nowhere was this distinctiveness more apparent than in the city's Catholic churches, which were among the central institutions that originally fostered a unique Creole identity. This middle racial caste would later stall the rise of segregation because the imposition of strict separation in the United States depended, almost by definition, on the existence of only two categories. When segregation reconfigured the racial order in New Orleans, it affected Catholic Creoles of color more than any other group. The changing place of Creoles of color reveals the constantly shifting racial practices and meanings in New Orleans, as well as highlighting strategies used to implement Jim Crow throughout the American South.

Postbellum Creoles who endured the shifting racial categories traced their identity to the free people of color, or *gens de colour libre*, who were their ancestors in colonial and antebellum Louisiana. From the first colonial settlement, gender ratios favored the interracial liaisons that gave rise to the city's free population. Within New Orleans's white population, men outnumbered women well into the nineteenth century. At the same time, women of African descent outnumbered men, especially among free people of color. The large community of freed slaves arose from the tendency of French and later Spanish colonists, unlike their Anglo-American neighbors to the north, to free the offspring of their interracial liaisons. Especially under Spanish rule (1763–1803), slave codes further encouraged the manumission of large numbers of slaves. Louisiana colonists treated the growing class of free people of color as socially and racially distinct from the enslaved, often providing them with education, property, and income. The gap between free and slave widened as freed people gained socioeconomic status by learning skilled trades that made them vital to New Orleans's growing economy. Militia service was another way that free African Americans earned special recognition and set themselves apart from slaves and free people elsewhere in North America. Between 1791 and 1809, an influx of refugees from the Haitian revolution bolstered the size, skill, and standing of the city's free population. Only a few years after the American takeover in 1803, free people of color were a quarter of New Orleans's population and had secured a distinct place in the city's emerging three-caste order.[7]

Legal codes also played an important role in constructing New Orleans's tripartite racial organization. The French colonial *Code Noir* outlined a wide range of rights that distinguished freed persons from the enslaved. Free people of color could inherit and own property, invoke the protection of the laws of the colony, sue in court, and even testify against whites. Under American rule, the Louisiana legislature placed greater restrictions on slaves. Such legislation only strengthened the free people's unique status because it did not place comparable constraints upon them. Instead, the protections the French and Spanish colonial governments had granted free people of color continued in force throughout most of the antebellum era. Louisiana state laws further institutionalized New Orleans's triracial order by isolating free people of color as equally separate from both slaves and whites. Nineteenth-century marriage statutes, for example, placed as strong a prohibition on marriage between free persons and slaves as they did between free people of color and whites. The city even provided three separate cemeteries, one each for slaves, free people of color, and whites. The state's judicial branch likewise upheld the city's tripartite structure. In an 1860 opinion concerning the African Methodist Episcopal congregation in New Orleans, the Louisiana Supreme Court outlined the unique legal status of free people of color. While the court ruled that slaves "are strangers to our Constitutions," it also recognized free people of color as a distinct class: "As far as it concerns everything, except political rights, free people of color appear to possess all other rights of persons, whether absolute or relative."[8]

Still, the emergence of free people of color as a distinct caste would not have occurred without the approbation of the Catholic Church. The church welcomed children of interracial liaisons into its midst, partly in response to French colonial policy that dictated that all inhabitants must be Catholic. Priests baptized, confirmed, married, and buried persons of mixed parentage, reflecting the more racially liberal Latin Catholicism of New Orleans's colonists and clergy. Catholic leaders also encouraged white fathers to acknowledge and support their mixed-race children. On rare occasions the church even blessed unions across racial lines.[9] The acquiescence of the Catholic Church suggested a moral and religious assent to the interracial liaisons that resulted in New Orleans's growing free population. The church's acceptance also cultivated the centrality of a Catholic religious affiliation with a mixed-race, that is, Creole, identity.[10] Creoles of color thereby became crucial to the strength of New Orleans Catholicism, forming the majority of attendees and financial supporters in several of the city's parishes. As late as 1875, a priest conceded that he did not want to offend Creoles in his congregation "because they are the chief support."[11]

As the Catholic Church welcomed free people of color, it also affirmed their distinctiveness from slaves, further institutionalizing the city's triracial order. Priests acknowledged Creoles' middle status as they refused to perform marriages between free and slave as steadfastly as they resisted marriage between free and white. Likewise, Catholic officials utilized a tripartite classification in sacramental registers, categorizing people as either slave, free, or white.[12] The Archdiocese of New Orleans allowed free people of color to create their own separate societies, denying slaves the same freedom. Catechetical schools, the Christian Doctrine Society at St. Louis Cathedral, and a separate women's religious order, the Sisters of the Holy Family, exemplified the range of Catholic organizations serving the city's free population. Church seating also reflected the city's unique racial order. When congregations instituted separate seating, the most important distinction remained between free people of color and slaves, not between black and white. At St. Augustine Church, for example, Creoles rented nearly half the pews in the center of the sanctuary, while slaves sat on benches along the sides. So pervasive was the tripartite order that it sometimes found recognition in antebellum Protestant churches. At St. Paul's Methodist Church, white members and free persons of color worshiped on the ground floor, while slaves sat in the balcony.[13]

The accomplishments of free people of color were crucial in preserving the relative racial liberalism in New Orleans. Taking advantage of educational, economic, and social freedoms unavailable to people of color elsewhere in the United States, they achieved a cultural standing, economic status, and educational sophistication that challenged the stereotypes of black inferiority with which whites justified racial separation. Some free people of color founded schools in New Orleans, while others sent their children to France to advance educational opportunities. Among the free population were doctors, publishers, military leaders, and artists. New Orleans's free community formed literary journals, including the first published poetry by people of color in the United States.[14] These cultural and social accomplishments enabled free people to assert their place in New Orleans society in ways that kept racial possibilities open, even as the same people faced concrete limits. The distinct recognition accorded Creoles, both socially and legally, was of the accomplishments of their class even as it was also an effort to restrict the benefits that recognition accorded. White New Orleanians would continue to insist on the inferiority of any people of African descent and therefore prevent any social conflation of whites and Creoles of color. Nonetheless, the liberal treatment of freed slaves and children of mixed liaisons, as well as the acknowledgment of the accomplishments of free people, testified to at least a grudging recognition that racial identities were not nearly as fixed and caste-bound as the nation's predominant biracial system suggested. One consequence was ongoing and regular racial interaction in New Orleans, especially in the city's Catholic churches. Religious institutions, and especially Catholic sanctuaries, would remain an important locus that challenged the supposed pervasiveness of racial separation in the American South.

The triracial order that New Orleans Catholicism fostered was far from unique, even as it formed another measure of the city's distance from the rest of the United States. Multi-tiered racial orders were common in many predominantly Catholic societies in the Caribbean and South America. In this wider context of the Western Hemisphere, New Orleans emerges as a fault line between the binary and fixed racial order of British North America and the more complex and fluid racial orders of nations to the South. The Crescent City's shifting positions between these options illuminate the complex and varied constructions of race and racial systems available to societies emerging from African slavery. Among North Americans, Creoles of color may have shared the closest links to and awareness of these alternate systems, given their common heritage and even familial ties to residents of Caribbean and South American societies. During the Civil War, Creoles urged the Union government to follow the example of French colonies, which granted immediate legal equality upon emancipation, rather than the English model of emancipation without citizenship or equality.[15] But they were not the only ones to highlight the implications of alternatives to the American racial binary. The bishop of Erie, for example, extolled as a model for the United States the more equitable treatment of racial differences "in the central and southern republics of the continent." Even a white Methodist noted that "throughout Central and Southern America . . . our prejudices against amalgamation . . . are comparatively unknown," challenging the common assertion that opposition to racial mixing was universal, "invincible," and perhaps even divinely ordained. These multilayered racial systems that fostered greater freedom for former slaves, most notably in Brazil, challenged the claims of white residents that the emergence of segregation marked a necessary evolution from a slaveholding past and the inevitable structure of free societies where black and white lived together. New Orleans's racial order thereby emerged within a spectrum of racial possibilities.[16] With these alternate guideposts, the shifting recognition of Creole distinctiveness reveals the changing meanings of race in New Orleans. Most notably, the place of Creoles measured the movement of the city and church toward a typically American biracial structure of mandated segregation.

THE RACIAL CLIMATE THAT EMERGED out of New Orleans's tripartite structure opened a window to interracial worship that was not easily closed when the winds of Jim Crow began to blow. Black and white worshiped together during the antebellum era, illustrating Catholicism's role in fostering the city's relatively liberal racial climate. Catholics of color were an important constituency in most parishes, given the equal proportion between black and white among the New Orleans Catholic population at the turn of the nineteenth century. By 1810, Catholics of color constituted nearly two-thirds of the membership of St. Louis Cathedral, their numbers bolstered by waves of immigrants fleeing political upheaval and violence in Haiti and Cuba at the end of the eighteenth and beginning of the nineteenth centuries. Antebellum visitors to the cathedral frequently commented on its integrated membership. A popular stop for visitors, St. Louis Cathedral overlooked the city's square and was the dominant structure visible to travelers who arrived by ship on the Mississippi River. In 1845, one traveler reported his surprise at what he witnessed within the cathedral: "Never had I seen such a mixture of conditions and colors . . . white children and black, with every shade between, knelt side by side. In the house of prayer they made no distinction of rank or colour. The most ardent abolitionist could not have desired more perfect equality." Others expressed their similar astonishment that "within the edifice there is no separation" according to race. In other parishes as well, sacramental reports and parish registers testified to the interracial character of New Orleans Catholicism in the antebellum era.[17]

Integrated seating distinguished Catholic worshipers from their Protestant counterparts but not from examples of racial interaction throughout antebellum New Orleans society. The accomplishments of free people often facilitated racial interaction, so that, one black observer of New Orleans explained, "there is a great deal of sociability between the free colored and the rich whites." Elsewhere, notably Washington, D.C., large antebellum free populations likewise achieved integrated seating in Catholic churches. But mixing in New Orleans, in social life as well as in Catholic churches, extended beyond free people of color to include slaves. In a pattern that would persist into the twentieth century, neighborhoods in New Orleans lacked the racial boundaries typical of many urban areas. Black and white homes were interspersed throughout the city and sometimes within buildings. Slaves often lived in quarters behind their master's home rather than in separate slave compounds or districts. This proximity resulted in black and white socializing together in local bars and restaurants, even after the city passed regulations prohibiting such interactions. According to a Creole nun reflecting on antebellum race relations, "we have always been like one and the same family, going to the same church, sitting in the same pews, and many of them sleeping in the same bed." Although whites always maintained their superior position, the extent of racial mingling was nonetheless remarkable.[18]

Catholic inclusivity fostered the loyalty of a black population accustomed the city's relatively liberal racial climate. Given the "temporary oblivion of all worldly distinctions" during Catholic worship, one British visitor observed, "Can it be wondered, therefore, that the slaves in Louisiana are all Catholics?" Free people, as well, remained an important part of the antebellum Catholic landscape. The large free black population contributed to the financial stability of the city's Catholic churches. Creoles of color supplied much of the funding to build the new St. Augustine Church, which opened in 1841. Free blacks rented half of the new church's pews, with many of the aisle seats were reserved for slaves. Together, slave and free blacks totaled nearly half of the congregation's membership, with free people of color playing an important role by their ongoing support of the church's budget. St. Augustine was the first of many parishes to become closely linked with Creole identity and continued to be an important place of worship for the city's black Catholics into the twentieth century.[19]

Catholic women of color contributed to New Orleans's interracial character, living a theology that privileged a common religious identity over racial differences. The Sisters of the Holy Family, a religious order founded by free women of color, included white children among those they instructed, as did a smaller short-lived order in the postbellum era, the Sisters of Our Lady of Lourdes. Though often rebuffed, both orders reached across racial lines to express the universal ideal of Catholicism, asserting that all people were equal before God and thus equal in the Catholic Church. The Holy Family Sisters were the nation's second order of black women religious, following the Oblate Sisters of Providence, which had been founded in 1828 by free women of color in Baltimore who were part of that city's Haitian refugee community. Black laywomen in New Orleans also formed a vital part of the city's Catholic congregations, giving "generously" of "their domestic services to the Church." Other black laywomen of means gave property to the church or used their wealth to aid the poor of the community.[20] Whether religious or lay, black Catholic women in the antebellum era worked to preserve Catholicism's interracial character in New Orleans, helping the church to prosper as a result.

Crescent City Catholicism retained an interracial character even after the turmoil of the Civil War and Reconstruction, as Joseph Hartzell's observations of St. Louis Cathedral made clear. Priests continued to minister to black as well as white parishioners, forming the basis of Catholic historian Roger Baudier's claim that after the "War Between the States," "in most churches, the Negro was permitted and there was very generally no interference with his practice of his religion."[21] Many parishes with only small black Catholic populations opened schools for black Catholics and established lay devotional and social societies for black members. Catholic sisters testified to the inclusion of all people by ministering to both black and white residents. The Sisters of Mercy visited prisoners, providing instruction without regard to color. Well into the 1890s, such interracial service persisted. The Sisters of the Good Shepherd opened an asylum to serve, at the donor's insistence, both black and white orphans. Even religious institutions built along segregated lines attracted biracial interest. When the Sisters of the Holy Family laid a cornerstone for a new orphanage for children of color in downtown New Orleans in 1891, the event attracted not only black Catholics but also "many whites."[22]

Catholic parishes in New Orleans remained mixed because the city's Catholics of color were loyal to the church and continued to attend Catholic services, sometimes with greater regularity than white parishioners. Occasional Catholic proclamations of the universality of the church and common humanity of all races reinforced the historic loyalty of black Catholics in Louisiana. They continued to seek the sacraments, religious instruction, and, where available, parochial education. Nor was participation limited to Creoles. Former slaves raised in Catholic households were an important part of the city's Catholic landscape. A Catholic reporter in New Orleans noted in 1892 that "the freed slaves here of Catholic owners cling to the faith in which they were raised with a tenacity that is wonderful." The rapid increase in parishes had not isolated black Catholics into particular churches. The same reporter noted that "during the ceremonies of Holy Week not one church did I visit without seeing therein a goodly number of them."[23] Even as Catholics of color were pushed into separate galleries or benches in the back, their simultaneous presence with white Catholics provided an encouraging contrast to the racially separate congregations among the city's Protestants.

The persistence of mixed parishes in postbellum New Orleans was striking, though not entirely unique in southern Catholicism. Black and white Catholics worshiped in the same sanctuary in many Catholic churches in the South. An 1883 article on Catholics of color noted that "you will find some of them in every Catholic congregation in the Southern cities."[24] The small Catholic populations in most southern communities, white as well as black, made the erection of separate parishes impractical. Unlike in New Orleans, most of these churches followed the more traditionally American patterns of separate seating and the separate administration of the sacraments. In addition, dioceses both north and south established separate black churches as soon as they had a critical mass of black parishioners, and sometimes before. Not so in New Orleans. A confluence of multiple and sometimes conflicting racial, religious, and social interests combined to delay the emergence of separate parishes in New Orleans.

WHILE BLACK CATHOLICS UNAMBIGUOUSLY opposed segregation, the motives of church officials were less idealistic. Their contribution to ongoing racially mixed worship was neglect rather than active support of equality. Priests and bishops in New Orleans offered pragmatic rather than ideological resistance when Roman and American officials pressed for additional work among black Catholics. Crescent City prelates justified their failure to address the needs of black Catholics with the claim that "everything that could be done up to now was being done for the Negroes." Catholic leaders in New Orleans, supported by fellow southern bishops, insisted that any decisions regarding black Catholics be left to local diocesan control rather than be mandated by Roman, or even American, councils. Bishop Martin of nearby Natchitoches believed that the treatment of black Catholics was simply a local concern and was "no business of the bishops and theologians who know nothing about the negro race."[25] These arguments, echoed by other southern bishops, bore a striking resemblance to the Confederate rhetoric of states' rights and subsequent protests against Reconstruction, which claimed southern politicians best knew how to deal with the "race problem."

New Orleans clerics succeeded in making their approach official church policy in the United States. American Catholic leaders gathered at the Second Plenary Council in Baltimore in 1866 to consider a number of questions raised by Roman officials, among them care for the recently emancipated slaves. In a sign of New Orleans's growing influence, Archbishop Spalding of Baltimore, who led the conference, requested that Archbishop Jean Marie Odin of New Orleans prepare materials for and lead the discussion on black Catholics. In a personal note, Spalding informed Odin that "we shall especially want the benefit of your experience in devising the most effectual means for saving the poor emancipated slaves." Although some prelates favored forming separate churches, Odin and his assistant Napoleon Perche, who would succeed him as archbishop, proved the crucial voices in persuading the council to postpone any specific requirements to create separate missions or churches.[26] Invoking expediency and an emphasis on local control, neither Odin nor the council based their objections to separate black work upon doctrines of universality or concern for the equal rights of black church members. This inability to discuss ministry to African Americans in explicitly theological language or in reference to biblical mandates would remain characteristic of the American Catholic hierarchy's approach to racial concerns well into the twentieth century. Crescent City prelates considered black Catholics a practical or social issue best understood and resolved within the predominant southern political and racial idioms, which provided more widely accepted implications than did theological doctrines such as creation, atonement, or the universal church.

As a result of New Orleans's influence, the Catholic Church in the United States lacked a national policy or program for the care of African Americans. The 1866 Second Plenary Council left decisions regarding black Catholics entirely in the hands of local prelates, urging but not requiring that each diocese containing black Catholics hold a council to discuss the matter. The plenary meeting offered neither a policy for work among African Americans nor a means for funding such missions, though several bishops favored creating separate churches. American bishops also rejected Vatican interest in a special delegate or prefect to oversee work among black Catholics in the United States. At the same time, northern bishops were reluctant to expend energy or resources on what many considered a local problem, especially as they faced their own financial difficulties and an influx of Catholic immigrants. As James McCloskey of New York explained, "In no way was the conscience of the bishops of New York burdened in regard to the black."[27] Nor did Archbishop Odin of New Orleans push for financial backing from the North, apparently glad to forgo aid for autonomy.

The Catholic approach stood in stark contrast to Protestants, who had formed national agencies, such as the Methodist Episcopal Freedmen's Aid Society and Congregationalist American Missionary Association, to coordinate work among African Americans. These denominational agencies raised funds, sent personnel, and coordinated the organization of churches and schools throughout the South. For at least two decades after Emancipation, Protestant denominations considered the conversion and care of African Americans a national and denomination-wide priority. In contrast, a white Catholic sympathizer complained that among Catholics, parochial schools, divorce, and religiously mixed marriages are "in every way . . . propounded, sifted, discussed." But, he continued, "It is rarely . . . that from Catholic sources we hear a word on the 'negro problem.' " Not until 1884, at the Third Plenary Council, did Catholics begin a national effort directed at black Americans. Even then, it was merely a collection made once a year to be distributed by the newly created Commission for Catholic Missions Among the Colored People and the Indians. After an initial collection in 1887, donations declined. Even so, as late as 1904, the funds went largely untapped as many prelates made little effort to access them.[28] The future of black Catholics was in the hands of local bishops reluctant to make much effort.

In New Orleans, this pattern of neglect persisted throughout the 1870s and 1880s, forestalling the segregated parishes that might emerge from new efforts directed toward black Catholics. Odin never held a council to discuss the care of black Catholics, despite the central role he had played in the Second Plenary Council's decision to leave racial concern to local bishops. Napoleon Perche, archbishop from 1870 to 1883, followed the example set by his predecessors. Although he did convene a local council, he did not include black work on the agenda. Other provinces, such as Cincinnati, followed New Orleans's example of excluding blacks as a topic of discussion in their councils. Perche claimed black Catholics in New Orleans received sufficient attention from the current diocesan clergy and institutions, even though they experienced increasing ostracism within their parish churches and could not enroll in parochial schools attended by whites. Perche acknowledged black opposition to separate parishes, but like so many whites who failed to listen to black voices, mistakenly interpreted the opposition as an acceptance of an inferior place rather than as resistance to racial segregation. When pressed, Perche finally conceded that black Catholics in the city's non-French districts might benefit from greater attention. Still, he made no further efforts to address their needs. Perche's successor, Archbishop Leray, continued the laissez-faire approach. Leray opposed opening a school for black children in an area teeming with potential students, despite the desire of the Sisters of Mercy to staff it, and even though Catholic children were attending a nearby Protestant school. From Mobile to St. Louis, many bishops across the South remained indifferent to the Catholics of color under their care. For the Third Plenary Council in Baltimore in 1884, the New Orleans archdiocese was once again asked to guide the consideration of black Catholics. Leray simply ignored requests for information and failed to submit any reports or recommendations. He then disregarded the plenary council's injunction to initiate the formation of separate parishes for black Catholics. Inaction pervaded the entirety of Leray's administration. When Francis Janssens replaced Leray in 1888, he repeatedly encountered evidence of the previous lack of concern for black Catholics, including his 1893 discovery that "we have nothing in our archives relating to the colored people."[29] Nonetheless, long-standing dedication to the status quo enabled black Catholics in New Orleans to continue worshiping in the same churches as whites, rather than being set apart into special parishes or missions as was occurring in much of the nation.

Inaction on questions of racial justice, though troubling to some, stood well within the American Catholic tradition. The prevailing understanding of the church as an institution, combined with the actual place of Roman Catholicism in the South, kept Catholic leaders relatively silent on racial issues, from slavery in the nineteenth through segregation in the early twentieth century. Catholic understandings of the church stressed the alignment of church and state. Foreign-born prelates, such as those in New Orleans, advocated a European-style Catholicism. They rejected the American model of church-state separation that gave religious institutions the freedom to criticize political and social policies. First slavery and, later, segregation fell under the responsibility of the state rather than the church, and therefore Catholics rarely engaged such questions, which they considered beyond religious responsibility. The "perfect society" model of the church under which these prelates labored fostered a disconnection between faith and social action. American and sometimes Vatican officials repeatedly instructed postbellum Catholic leaders to refrain from political questions in public and in the pulpit, continuing the practice from the slavery era. In addition, the marginal and persecuted place of Catholicism, especially in the South, meant Catholic leaders were reluctant to take action or make statements that would create controversy and jeopardize the precarious reputation and standing of the church in the United States. Close ties between Catholics and the Democratic Party, which in the South was the party of white supremacy, further stifled church efforts on behalf of black Catholics.

Still, for all the talk of a hierarchical church and the authority of Rome, local concerns determined the character of much of Catholicism outside strict doctrinal issues. The American laity was shaping the church even more than they recognized. For Catholic leaders, winning souls was the highest priority, and accommodation on social and political issues—slavery and segregation among them—remained an important part of their strategy. Social concerns focused on caring for individuals rather than changing the broader socio-economic context in which people lived. Orphanages and schools constituted the appropriate spheres of action, although prelates sometimes neglected even these. Calls to moral responsibility focused on acts of personal charity, not on social justice, to bring people to the church; the soul's status in heaven was privileged over the person's place in society. Church leaders therefore criticized as immoral individual acts of brutality against black citizens but not the larger socio-political context that fostered the violence. Even the growing Vatican concern for black Catholics focused on including African Americans within the church rather than addressing broader concerns about American race prejudice.[30]

American Catholic leaders also disagreed on the religious character of African Americans, further undermining any coordinated efforts on behalf of black Catholics. As Catholic leaders debated their views on black personhood, they mirrored discussions that kept the place of African Americans in the sociopolitical order equally uncertain in the decades after Emancipation. Catholic teaching never denied black humanity, nor the presence of souls that needed saving; but neither did it insist on racial equality. Catholicism, no less than other Christian traditions, had long articulated an understanding of human differences that need not be transcended in this world. The prevailing "perfect society" model of the church, a medieval construction that dominated into the twentieth century, conceptualized humanity in a hierarchical series of categories, each with reciprocal duties. Fulfilling one's place in the hierarchy, rather than improving it, marked human faithfulness to the church and to God. Racial differences were easily grafted onto this model so that separation by race, no less than any other category, was neither problematic nor inconsistent with other church doctrines. An 1883 Catholic editorial against race prejudice invoked a divinely ordered hierarchy to assure its readers that "the Christian doctrine that all men are brethren . . . does not, indeed, level men in the human sense . . . does not break down those barriers that are the metes and bound of the gifts of Providence in the natural and civil order."

American Catholics, like most white Americans, differed only on the degree of inherent separation between the races, not whether such separation existed. Some, such as Bishop Verot of Savannah and Florida, and Bishop Gross, who succeeded Verot in Savannah, emphasized the humanity and promise of African Americans as both Catholics and American citizens. Yet their affirmations also contained the paternalism and assumptions of white superiority prevalent in most liberal racial rhetoric in the late nineteenth century. In a sermon at the Third Plenary Council in Baltimore in 1884, Gross asserted the common humanity of people, who "were created by the same God, are children of the same common father and mother," yet also repeatedly invoked the moral inferiority of African Americans who, in the words of a Mississippi bishop, needed to "acquire more of the manner & thoughts of the white people." Those seeing black potential favored efforts to convert and minister to African Americans, including bishops in Savannah, Florida, and Charleston. But others, among them archbishops in St. Louis and Baltimore, saw an unbreachable distance between black and white, arguing that nothing could be done for African Americans and therefore any effort on their behalf squandered scarce resources.[31]

Both clergy and lay responses reinforced the archbishops' philosophy of neglect in New Orleans. Like the episcopacy, most clerical concerns about separate churches were pragmatic rather than theological. Parish priests did not want to alienate powerful whites in their congregations who objected to separate black work. Ironically, some white members suggested that separate facilities alongside white churches might convey equality rather than inferiority. Whites would invert their reasoning in subsequent decades, building alternate facilities to institutionalize inequality. In the meantime, whites rejected any effort toward black members that implied equality. White parishioners opposed sharing their clergy with black Catholics. At the Sacred Heart of Jesus parish in New Orleans, white members went so far as to petition the superior of their priest's order for a replacement. Their complaint reflected jealousy and echoed underlying Catholic conceptions of the relation of religion and race: "He takes more interest in the negroes than is due to them, and further, from the altar, he has spoken of the negro, with such favor, and to such an extent that we are becoming greatly dissatisfied; we do not think that questions of race should be discussed by the reverend pastor at the altar." From Washington and Savannah in the east, and even in northern communities such as Philadelphia, through Arkansas and into the Deep South, white Catholics were nearly unanimous in their complaints against any priest who wanted to devote more time to African-American parishioners. A priest in neighboring Mississippi warned of the consequences facing a cleric who directed any of his ministrations toward black parishioners: "The white man associating with Negroes, let it for ever so holy a purpose, loses caste and is ostracized." Others expressed more immediate fears, echoing those of the white Methodist Protestants who labored in the South. Few were willing to risk the destruction of their property, remembering that outraged whites in New Orleans had torched the school for black children in one of the city's Redemptorist parishes.[32]

Others invoked economic concerns in their opposition to separate black churches. Bishops and priests refused to use diocesan or parish funds to create separate black institutions. Most clergy were unwilling to risk scarce resources on black facilities unlikely to become self-supporting. Like many southern dioceses, New Orleans was plagued by debt, which had reached $600,000 by 1879. The white laity, impoverished by the Civil War and opposed to promoting racial equality, refused to support such endeavors. Efforts to have the Oblate Sisters of Providence, a black order from Baltimore, open an asylum and school for black children during Reconstruction failed owing to a lack of funds to support them. What few facilities already existed for Catholics of color fell into a state of disrepair that far exceeded that of white institutions in even the poorest parishes. Priests complained on the one hand that black parishioners were unable and unwilling to provide funds for separate institutions. The bishop in neighboring Natchez, Mississippi, voiced what many whites expressed subtly: "Since the Catholic colored people . . . do not try to support a priest, they don't deserve any & I cannot afford to give them one."[33] On the other hand, many clergy in New Orleans opposed separate parishes because they wanted to retain access to black Catholic contributions, especially among the relatively well-off Creoles of color. One priest in a French parish confided that he did not want his black members to withdraw "because they are the chief support."[34]

The lack of priests became another widespread obstacle to the formation of separate black churches. Crescent City archbishops and their colleagues throughout the South faced a clerical shortage in the late nineteenth century. Many southern priests already received insufficient financial support. As a result, a New Orleans archbishop pointed out, "It is very difficult to obtain priests." On the further challenge of recruiting priests to work among black Catholics, the same prelate warned, "how much more difficult to secure missionaries to open a field, new and uncompromising, which will present a life of hardship, of disappointment, and of continual self-sacrifice!" Despite the difficulty of recruiting additional workers, the New Orleans hierarchy was unwilling to utilize existing priests for separate work among African Americans. Clerics already taxed by existing parish responsibilities would be unable to look after additional separate congregations of black Catholics. When two priests desiring to undertake work among black Catholics presented themselves to Archbishop Janssens in 1889, even he, an untiring advocate of separate parishes, lamented, "I cannot spare them for this special work."[35] Instead, Janssens would pursue separate churches only if he could secure an outside religious order to undertake the work. He could then avoid losing his own parish priests, while also passing along to the religious order the financial responsibility for the segregated work. Economics more than theology drove the delayed emergence of segregated parishes in New Orleans. A ministry dedicated to black Catholics in New Orleans would have to wait for external funding and outside religious orders. In the meantime, the city's Catholic churches remained open to Catholics of all races.

THE PERSISTENCE OF MIXED PARISHES could not overcome equally longstanding traditions of racial antagonism and segregation in New Orleans's Catholic institutions. Inclusion did not extend to equality. After Louisiana became part of the United States in 1803, the influx of English-speaking American settlers and growing interaction with the rest of the American South began to stem the tide of racial liberalism in New Orleans. At mid-century, Catholic leaders in New Orleans, as throughout the South, supported the Confederacy and the racial order it advocated. Several Louisiana priests worked as Confederate chaplains, including Francis Xavier Leray, who, with little change in his racial views, served as archbishop of New Orleans from 1883 to 1887. Women religious also supported the Confederate effort, ministering to troops on battlefields and in hospitals. The few clergy who dissented, supporting the Union and abolition during the war and advocating racial equality afterward, found themselves ostracized by archdiocesan leaders.[36]

   Catholic officials endorsed views signaling their hostility to racial equality in the aftermath of the Civil War. The experiences of Reconstruction nurtured racial antagonism, even among the supposedly liberal French clergy and parishioners. White Southerners found especially bothersome the rash of black candidates elected to office. The French-born Napoleon Perche, who served as archbishop of New Orleans from 1870 to 1883, stood among the most vigorous supporters of the Confederacy and all things southern, including the white Redeemer government that marked the end of Reconstruction and thus what was widely called "Negro domination" in Louisiana politics. Despite official dictums discouraging political pronouncements, Catholic leaders felt no danger in doing so when their views harmonized with the white majority. Perche was so grateful for the end of Reconstruction in 1877 that he issued a pastoral letter calling for a day of prayer and thanksgiving celebrating the removal of the "political strifes under which we were groaning" and hence "an end to the broils which afflicted and desolated our State and which, had they been protracted any longer, would have brought upon all of us a complete ruin."[37] Catholic leaders in Louisiana thus made no secret of their political leanings and support for the Democratic Party. In New Orleans and throughout the South, Democrats were first and foremost the party of white supremacy. A priest visiting New Orleans near the end of Reconstruction observed that the "Archbishop & Priests side more or less openly against Republicans & hence against the Negroes." The same visitor noted that one New Orleans priest had to leave the city because he supported the Republican Party during Reconstruction.[38]

Black Catholics encountered growing resistance to their presence in Crescent City churches in the final decades of the nineteenth century. As one of the city's black nuns observed, the discrimination marked a significant change from the antebellum era: "It is only since the Civil War that this state has become so very prejudiced and the people of this city have so many hard feelings against the colored class." By 1875, Peter Benoit, an English priest surveying the possibilities for work among black Catholics in New Orleans, concluded that "the impassable barrier between White & Black exists here as everywhere else." Benoit cited, among his examples, the Little Sisters of the Poor. The sisters had recently obtained permission to admit black residents to their home for the elderly. "They must however go about it prudently," a sister confided to Benoit, for the whites in and around the home "[would] not like to be put in intercourse with negroes according to the general strong feelings I find here." Sympathetic clergymen fared no better. Benoit noted that priests who attempted to work among African Americans likewise "required exceptional courage and had to face bitter opposition" from their congregations and a lack of support from their superiors.[39]

White Catholics at all levels organized their religious environment on a segregated basis. The passive neglect of preceding generations veered to active exclusion, even without erecting separate black parishes. Priests proved unwilling to dedicate their time and effort to serving African Americans, sharing their superiors' aversion to work among black Catholics. Instead, Crescent City clergy ministered in ways that encouraged the involvement of white Catholics and discouraged black participation. As early as 1875, visitors to New Orleans remarked that priests required the children of different races to make their first communion on different days. The same visitor observed a priest in St. Louis Cathedral refuse communion to a black soldier. Reports from Mater Dolorosa in the uptown section, as well as from St. Rose of Lima downtown, confirmed that clergymen separated children by race for catechetical instruction, first communion, and confirmation, as well as in parish celebrations and processions. At Mater Dolorosa, priests permitted the parish's black school children to attend mass in the church only once a year, Easter Sunday, and even then only at the six o'clock mass. Priests had also long structured parish societies, organizations, and confraternities along segregated lines. The separate

Colored Christian Doctrine Society at St. Louis Cathedral dated from 1823. At the uptown St. Mary's and downtown St. Rose of Lima, priests organized both children's and adults' societies according to race.[40]

Segregation extended well into the ranks and orders of Catholic leaders. Unlike Crescent City Methodists, the Archdiocese of New Orleans had no black clergymen to serve its black membership. Nationwide, only five African Americans were ordained to the priesthood in the nineteenth century, and none engaged in any sustained ministry in the South. Presuming to speak for black church members, whites rejected the idea of black priests in the Reconstruction era with the unsubstantiated claim "that a Negro-Priest [would] find no favor with his race." The struggle for black priests resembled the quest of black M. E. church members for a black bishop. White Catholics feared that black priests would preside over white Catholics, just as white M. E. church members feared a black bishop would preside over white conferences. Black Catholics endured taunts for belonging to a tradition lacking black leaders, just as black M. E. church members suffered at African Methodist hands for a lack of black bishops. Especially in Louisiana, a Catholic worker complained, "the non-Catholic colored people constantly remark that the Catholics have white priests whilst they have ministers of their own color."[41] American bishops, like the M. E. General Conference delegates, ignored church leaders' calls for black clerical vocations. The Vatican had a policy of seeking native clergy in its mission areas since the seventeenth century, and ordinations in Africa began in the eighteenth century. Yet American bishops refused to nurture black vocations, with only a handful of exceptions. At first they simply ignored the subject, but by the end of the nineteenth century many expressed open hostility toward the possibility. Not even a segregated priesthood proved acceptable, even though black priests would fill the growing need for clergy to serve black Catholics as well as quiet critiques from both Rome and rival Protestant traditions. As with southern Episcopalians, the combination of prejudice and paternalism created a desire to keep black Catholics under white leadership. Jean Laval, vicar general of the archdiocese at the turn of the century and later pastor of St. Louis Cathedral, believed that "in America no Negro should be ordained. Just as illegitimate sons are declared irregular by Canon Law, so, to settle the whole question, the Negroes could be declared irregular because they are held in contempt by white people." Most priests and bishops in New Orleans agreed with Laval. Into the twentieth century, New Orleans and the Gulf Coast area would continue to play a central role in the debate over black priests in the United States.[42]

Women's opportunities presented a striking contrast to those available to men. Religious vocations were open to women of color, although segregation too limited their choices. The Sisters of the Holy Family, an order founded in New Orleans by Creoles of color nearly two decades before the outbreak of the Civil War, arose because its founding members could neither join nor found a congregation of mixed women. The bishop then prevented Marie-Jeanne Aliquot, who had worked with Henriette Delisle and Juliette Gaudin to begin the Sisters of the Holy Family, from joining the order because she was white. Another short-lived women's order in New Orleans, the Sisters of Our Lady of Lourdes, arose because the members had been ejected from a convent during their postulancy in 1882 upon the discovery that they had traces of African blood. Racial proscriptions restricted both the membership and the work of these women's orders. The Holy Family Sisters received ongoing diocesan support only because they labored among the city's black residents. For a brief period of time the Holy Family Sisters taught catechism to white students, but covertly. Likewise, the short-lived Sisters of Our Lady of Lourdes attempted to cross the color line and teach white students at their school in the French Quarter. The sisters were unable to retain a sufficient number of students to support the order, leading to its demise. The survival of the Holy Family Sisters was crucial to black Catholicism in New Orleans and the communities throughout the South in which they worked. In the face of the widespread white neglect, the sisters were often the only ones who regularly tended to the needs of Catholics of color. "It was the Sisters of the Holy Family unquestionably who were mainly responsible for the maintenance of the Faith among members of their race," conceded a leading historian of Louisiana Catholicism. Their expanding religious roles, especially as the opportunities for black men decreased, paralleled the ways that black women throughout the South took on "political" responsibilities as disfranchisement excluded black men from the electorate. In religion, as in politics, their gendered roles made their work less threatening to many whites, even as they addressed the very issues over which whites hoped to retain control.[43]

As women of color, however, the Holy Family Sisters endured the humiliations of racial prejudice and segregation on an almost daily basis. Their religious identity did not prevent the discrimination associated with their racial identity. Even permission to wear the habit that would mark their religious identity was delayed for over thirty years after their founding. The white Sisters of St. Joseph then led an effort to have the Holy Family Sisters remove the habit they waited so long to wear, clearly threatened by the equality their dress implied. By the late 1880s, the Holy Family Sisters had lost their place in St. Louis Cathedral. They were pushed to the rear by white orders who, though founded after the Holy Family Sisters, insisted on sitting in front of them. Even a gate on Holy Family Sisters' assigned pew failed to keep out the trespassers who refused to accept any suggestion of equality, let alone subordination, to their sisters of color. Priests who helped the sisters "received a great many insults," not unlike priests who worked with the black laity. The sisters also endured discrimination when they ventured onto the streets, despite the predominance of Catholicism in New Orleans. In a representative incident in 1893, a streetcar conductor forced three Holy Family Sisters to pay full fare although the line regularly allowed white nuns to travel free of charge.[44]

White orders also experienced the constraints of segregation. Legal scholars have noted how segregation restricted white as well as black space, albeit in different ways and without the demeaning and damaging consequences. Corollary limits operated in the religious realm. Catholic leaders believed any order working with black Catholics needed to be devoted to that mission alone. Those who worked in black sacred space should not cross into white, and vice versa. When Archbishop Janssens began considering black churches in New Orleans, he insisted that religious congregations seeking to minister to the diocese's black Catholics not work among whites. He contended that only when they directed their attention exclusively to black Catholics would priests be able to "reclaim the poor dark negroes & lead them back to the church."[45] Janssens found confirmation in his position from John Slattery, head of the Josephite order headquartered in Baltimore that was dedicated to exclusive work among African Americans. Slattery claimed that in order to preserve the order's mission, a Josephite priest had to work exclusively with African Americans, "because from the moment he begins to visit the Whites, his love for his Blacks is on the wane." Another Josephite priest admitted that white parishioners forced orders ministering to African Americans to make their work racially exclusive. White church members frequently threatened to leave parishes where the priest would "humiliate himself with Negroes," or abused priests who tried to minister to both races. The prejudice fell upon white women religious as well. Janssens reported that "the prejudice of white Catholics against the colored Catholics was so great that they did not want to have their children taught by the same Sisters."[46] This insistence on distinct orders with exclusive service to black Catholics would become the standard for racially segregated parishes throughout the nation.

Separate schools formed the longest standing example of segregation within New Orleans Catholicism. Catholics in New Orleans had educated black residents as early as the colonial period but did so in an unbroken chain of segregated classrooms. Schools for white children had never welcomed students of color. The Ursulines first established classes for the religious instruction of slave girls and women in New Orleans in the early eighteenth century. In the nineteenth century, the Sisters of the Holy Family took over the Ursulines' schools for black children, while several city parishes began instructing the children of black parishioners. By this time education was restricted to free blacks only. Elsewhere in the city, women opened private schools, often in their homes, to educate free people of color. Whether operated by parishes or private individuals, these schools struggled financially in often dilapidated buildings and frequently offered little more than catechetical teaching. When possible, the city's black elite sent their children to Paris for their education.[47]

Pervasive neglect and prejudice, combined with a lack of money and teachers, hindered the Catholic response to black educational needs in the postbellum era. Protestant denominations, such as the M. E. Church, emphasized educational institutions as a key to their "colored work" from the moment they arrived on the heels of Union troops. Serious efforts to develop schools for black Catholic children did not get under way until almost 1890. During Reconstruction, Catholic leaders used the city's integrated public schools as an excuse to avoid erecting parochial schools for black children.[48] At the end of Reconstruction, however, one of the white Redeemer government's first actions was to segregate the public schools, leaving the Catholic Church behind in the competition with Protestants to provide education for black children. When Catholics did begin schools for black children, they emphasized the lowest grades, in contrast to Protestant schools such as New Orleans (Methodist Episcopal) and Straight (Congregational) universities, which offered a comprehensive education from preparatory work through collegiate and professional training. White Catholics also erected schools on a strictly segregated basis, unlike Protestant schools, which theoretically remained open to all races.

Segregated Catholic schools expanded in the post-Reconstruction era. The Third Plenary Council of Baltimore in 1884 provided new impetus as it stressed the importance of Catholic education to retain children in the faith and to counter the growing systematization and strengthening of public schools. The council committed the church to a comprehensive system of parochial education, leading to a renewed vigor in creating parish schools. When Archbishop Janssens arrived in New Orleans shortly after the council, he sought to bring his diocese into conformity with the wishes of the American hierarchy and pushed for the foundation of regular parochial schools in each parish. As Catholics, African Americans were not to be excluded from the overall project. But the pressures on race dictated that education for black Catholics be carried out on a separate basis. If teachers or priests admitted black children to white educational facilities, they soon learned that "the school may be deserted by whites." Direct contact was not necessary. In one parish, a nun reported that simply "the proximity of the Negro school has proved fatal to the white department."[49]

The number of black children in Catholic schools in New Orleans nearly doubled between 1888 and 1893.[50] This expansion resulted partly from the new impetus to provide parochial education for all Catholic children. Archbishop Janssens, who oversaw this first expansion of parochial education in New Orleans, also recognized the benefits of schools for keeping

Figure 5.1. St. Louis School. Previously known as the Widow Couvent School or Catholic Indigent Orphan School. Originally opened in 1841, the school served not only orphans but also children of the city's Creoles of color. The Creole community administered and staffed the school until it was destroyed by a hurricane in 1915. Katharine Drexel then donated funds to rebuild the facilities, renamed it the St. Louis School, and staffed it with her order, the Sisters of the Blessed Sacrament. Shortly thereafter, the school became associated with the recently created Holy Redeemer parish. Courtesy Archives of the Archdiocese of New Orleans.

black members in the church. Janssens feared that Catholics who attended Protestant schools often left Catholicism to join Methodist or Baptist churches. Janssens admitted, "There is nothing in my administration of the Diocese that worries me more than our colored people; to see what is done by the Protestants to capture them, & how often they succeed." He considered black Catholic schools "the means to counteract the evil" and fulfill his sense of calling to keep black Catholics from leaving the church.[51] Yet in creating a separate school system for African Americans, Janssens instituted structures that reinforced the segregationist practices occurring in the secular realm, from railroads to public schools, rather than offering a viable alternative to the racism he claimed to oppose.

The Catholic Indigent Orphan Institute constituted the one viable option for a quality education for New Orleans's black residents. Sometimes called the Couvent School, the institute was the gift of Marie Couvent, a wealthy black woman who died in 1837 and left money and property to found a school for the city's indigent black orphans. The school began in 1841 with ties to the Catholic Church but also free from the control of any parish or episcopal authorities. Black Catholics championed the Indigent Orphan School as a response to their children's exclusion from both public and parochial schools and not as an attempt to perpetuate segregation. The school represented a choice of self-separation and self-determination because of the lack of viable educational alternatives. It was not a statement in favor of racial separation. For this reason, the school sustained the support of the city's black community and its few black philanthropists in a way that the archdiocese's segregated institutions could not. Operated by an independent board that, along with its faculty and staff, was all black, the Indigent Orphan School accepted paying students in addition to sustaining its mission of providing education for orphans. The school soon became the central focus of educational efforts among the city's Creole elite, remaining so into the twentieth century. Most of the city's black authors and poets, and many who led protests against both religious and secular segregation, were students, teachers, or board members of the Couvent school.[52] The changing degree of control Catholics of color maintained over the Couvent school would serve as an important measure of their place in the landscape of New Orleans Catholicism.

The growth of separate Catholic schools illuminates the complexity of religious and racial relations in late-nineteenth-century New Orleans. The schools, just like the separate orders for black women, provided opportunities otherwise unavailable to African Americans. Black Catholics had not been left out of the national expansion of parochial education, unlike their growing exclusion from many other aspects of parish life. Education represented the largest effort on behalf of black Catholics, in New Orleans as in dioceses across the South. At the very moment that the New Orleans public school system restricted the opportunities and resources for black children, Catholic schools expanded black educational options. Yet like the public schools, black Catholic schools were vastly inferior to their white counterparts. Janssens conceded that the schools were "in miserable buildings with more miserable furniture."[53] A shortage of teachers further hampered the quality of education and the number of grades that the schools could offer. The increasing number of explicitly black schools helped institutionalize the ideal of segregation in New Orleans Catholicism.

BY 1890, BLACK CATHOLICS IN NEW ORLEANS, like their M. E. colleagues, found themselves in a declining but still undetermined position. Catholics of color recognized that neglect in some cases, and outright hostility in others, signaled their growing marginalization from the city's white Catholics. Yet the recent expansion of educational opportunities made clear that the church had not abandoned its black members and could respond to their needs when it chose to. Although the 1884 Third Plenary Council of Baltimore adopted a policy of separate parishes, New Orleans still lacked even one in 1890. There were also occasional countervailing voices to those becoming bolder in their declarations of black inferiority and their opposition to nurturing black leaders for the church. In the early 1890s, the possibility of a black priesthood seemed stronger than ever. In 1887, white seminarians in Maryland voted to welcome a black student, and in 1892, Archbishop Janssens sent two more black students to study for the priesthood. The rhetoric was not all negative. White assertions of the common humanity of all people were sometimes expanded to claim a future spiritual brotherhood with African Americans and the imperative to "be alive to their earthly needs." In the North, Archbishop John Ireland of St. Paul repeatedly opposed separate schools and asserted his belief in racial equality and the need for racial integration in all Catholic institutions, and throughout American society as well. The voices were admittedly lonely, but they had not been silenced altogether. Catholic hopes echoed those of black M. E. church members who advanced an ideal of a religious identity transcending racial differences. As late as 1892, the president of a national gathering of black Catholics believed that his Church could best lead the world to "realize the fact that the bond of grace and face are much stronger than flesh and blood."[54]

Catholics in New Orleans responded in opposite ways to the despair of uncertainty tinged with moments of hope. On one side, numerous black Catholics left the church because of the clerical and episcopal reluctance to dedicate men and money for their salvation. They found the hierarchy's resistance to special work for black Catholics degrading because it represented the pragmatic and economic concern to preserve limited resources rather than any ideological opposition to racial separation. Subsequent moves toward segregation drove still others away, their exit accelerated by the interpretation some prelates gave to their opposition to separate churches. Archbishop Perche, for example, interpreted black calls for integration to mean "the Negroes themselves preferred to keep their inferior condition among the Whites rather than to be an exclusively black congregation."[55] The prelate appeared unable or unwilling to conceive of alternate interpretations of black Catholic resistance to segregation.

Yet the hierarchy's failure to erect separate black institutions also had a paradoxical side. In a society increasingly hostile to anyone of African descent, some black Catholics found affirmation in the midst of neglect. Many remained in the church because its disregard delayed segregation and thereby enabled black Catholics to continue worshiping in mixed parishes—an unusual occurrence among both Catholics and Protestants by the 1890s. Even the M. E. Church never claimed a significant number of interracial congregations. Well into the 1890s, the pervasive inaction of Crescent City bishops preserved a religious space where black Catholics could uphold their belief and hope in a Catholic Church that welcomed all regardless of race. Black Catholics declared their equality by attending the same church and partaking of the same Mass as white parishioners who claimed a racial superiority over them in nearly every other aspect of New Orleans life. Soon, white Catholics would challenge even this small assertion of Christian equality.

CHAPTER 6

The Decline of Interracial Catholicism

THE 1890S WAS A TURBULENT DECADE for black Catholics in New Orleans. The rising tide of Jim Crow was pushing them out of railroad cars and classrooms alike. Church sanctuaries stood among the institutions black Catholics hoped they might yet preserve from total separation, since they remained one of the few places where black and white still gathered in the same space. But the battle against segregation was not easy. Like those who tried to contain the Mississippi River that periodically flooded the Crescent City, Catholics of color braced themselves against forces beyond their control. The waves that carried the threat of segregation could come from many directions, both secular and religious. In 1895, the current that so concerned the city's Catholics of color came from an unexpected source. Francis Janssens was not an obvious culprit for provoking black anxieties. As archbishop of New Orleans, Janssens had shown more concern than any of his predecessors about the condition of black Catholics. At the eye of the brewing storm between Janssens and black Catholics was St. Katherine's, the first parish erected exclusively for black Catholics in New Orleans.

St. Katherine's began with great fanfare on May 19, 1895. The opening of the first racially segregated Catholic church was a newsworthy event, even in the predominantly Catholic City. St. Katherine's stood a few blocks upriver from Canal Street, which marked the informal boundary between New Orleans's primarily French and Creole downtown population and the upriver American and African-American neighborhoods. The church occupied the former sanctuary of the St. Joseph parish, which had built a new building a few blocks away. Janssens celebrated the new church as an unparalleled gain for the city's black Catholics, contrasting his accomplishments with his predecessors' inaction. The archbishop had overcome numerous obstacles to open St. Katherine's, which he considered evidence of his long-standing concern for Catholics of color. But the significance of St. Katherine's was far more complex than Janssens's appraisal suggested. Most black Catholics avoided the new parish, considering it a regression for their church and their city. These conflicting interpretations ensured the legacy of St. Katherine's remained highly contested. The various responses to the new separate church affected the pattern of segregated parishes in New Orleans for a generation. The many strains of religion and race in New Orleans in the 1890s, especially as they coalesced around the issue of segregation, came together in the events surrounding the erection of St. Katherine's.[1]

The contested opening of St. Katherine's also illuminates the importance of individual parishes in the emergence of segregated Catholicism. The contrast with Methodists is striking. Black M. E. congregations were never integrated, and thus segregation struggles occurred at the regional and national levels. Catholics, by contrast, were never racially mixed beyond the parish level. As a result, only with an eye to the local do the experiences of most Catholics come into focus, despite the supposed universal and institutional character of Catholicism. The controversy surrounding St. Katherine's exemplifies the local, uneven, and highly contested emergence of racial segregation in American Catholicism. Diverse pressures from below, more than uniform implementation from above, led to separate churches. With origins in discrete episodes spread over several decades, churches, no less than separate railroad cars or restricted ballot boxes, demonstrate the regionally specific and varied origins of racial segregation. Only later did segregation spread uniformly across institutions that linked southern communities to become a consistent system of racial ordering.

THE ABSENCE OF SEPARATE BLACK PARISHES distinguished New Orleans from other centers of black Catholicism in the United States in the 1890s. The nation's first separate black parish began in Baltimore in 1863. Within three years, others opened in Washington, D.C., and Cincinnati. At the Second Plenary Council in 1866, the nation's bishops failed to reach an agreement on separate churches, largely because of the laissez-faire approach advocated by the New Orleans delegation. With this policy of local discretion, many bishops proceeded to erect separate churches in communities with concentrations of black Catholics, including Charleston, Savannah, Louisville, and St. Louis. American Catholic leaders officially called for the creation of separate churches and schools at the Third Plenary Council in 1884. Making separation an official strategy answered Vatican calls for a consistent approach, since Rome was displeased with the bishops' 1866 decision to defer to local discretion. A new wave of black parishes soon opened, not only in the South, but also in northern cities such as Pittsburgh, New York, and St. Paul. With twenty separate black Catholic parishes by 1890, American Catholic leaders had complied with the 1884 decree to establish segregated churches—except in New Orleans.[2] Crescent City archbishops refused to erect separate parishes despite the nation's largest concentration of black Catholics and despite an increasingly hostile racial environment in church and state alike. Although mixed parishes continued to distinguish New Orleans from Catholic practices in the rest of the nation, the long-standing patterns of neglect betrayed any suggestion that racial liberalism was the cause.

Black Catholics were surprised to discover that Francis Janssens would be the prelate who changed course and introduced segregated parishes into New Orleans. Born in Tilburg, Holland, in 1843, Janssens was the first non-French archbishop of New Orleans. Janssens attended seminary in Holland and finished his education at the American College in Louvain, Belgium, following his decision to become a missionary in the United States. After his ordination in Ghent, Janssens left Europe in 1868 for St. Peter's Cathedral in Richmond, Virginia. Working in the immediate aftermath of the Civil War in Richmond, Janssens first became acquainted with the plight of the nation's African-American population and the particular struggles of those claiming the Catholic faith. Janssens quickly rose to prominence in the diocese, filling administrative posts for the three bishops under whom he labored. Among the bishops was James Gibbons, later archbishop of Baltimore and Cardinal, with whom Janssens developed a life-long friendship and a shared interest in the welfare of black Catholics. In 1881 Janssens rose to the episcopacy of Natchez, Mississippi, where he expressed frustration at his inability to provide clerical or financial support to the diocese's black Catholics. In 1888, he received the papal bull elevating him to the see of New Orleans, where he remained as archbishop until his death in 1897. Janssens kept a diary during his tenure as archbishop, although it was mostly a ledger of his visitations and meetings rather than a means for reflecting on his struggles to better the lives of black Catholics.[3] The turmoil that accompanied Janssens's efforts on behalf of Louisiana's black Catholics emerges instead through his correspondence, the press, and his interactions with the city's black Catholic population.

Janssens arrived just as white New Orleanians dismantled the optimism of the 1880s and instituted new levels of racial discrimination. The resulting racism differed from other southern communities not in its substance but in its distance from the freedoms black New Orleanians had achieved in the two decades after Emancipation. The state had been under Democratic rule for a decade when Janssens was appointed to New Orleans, and shortly thereafter city and state leaders worked to ensure racial separation became part of Louisiana's legal code. Black residents were no longer permitted to ride in first-class railroad cars and were forced into separate waiting rooms as they awaited their inferior coaches. Interracial labor cooperation along the city's waterfront evaporated. Personal relations were restricted as well, as the state legislature prohibited interracial marriages. From baseball to bicycling to boxing, sporting events were segregated, as white fans ostracized white teams who dared compete against black athletes. Whites argued formal segregation was necessary to order southern society. Politics was no different. Whites were firmly in control

Figure 6.1. Archbishop Francis Janssens (1843–1897). Courtesy Archives of the Archdiocese of New Orleans.

of the Republican Party by the middle of the decade, and a few years later a new constitution deprived most black residents of the right to vote. Rising violence against black residents manifested a growing spirit of vigilantism, including lynchings, in which whites felt free to punish, without fear of retribution, even the perception of black disrespect.

The city's black Catholics found Janssens's responses to the declining racial climate encouraging, especially compared with his predecessors' silence. His concern ranged well beyond the treatment of black Catholics to include the abuses people of color endured in every aspect of their lives. Janssens frequently defended African Americans and criticized those seeking to oppress the black Catholics under his care. In his official capacity as archbishop, Janssens "protested sharply" the growing episodes of violence and lynching against black residents in both New Orleans and the rural parishes in the late 1880s and early 1890s. Janssens also criticized the Louisiana state legislature's attempt to pass anti-miscegenation legislation in

1892, characterizing the bill as "unjust and uncalled for" and an infringe-ment upon human and religious liberty as well as the laws of the Catholic Church. Even the city's black Methodists praised the archbishop's defense of civil rights. As late as 1896, Janssens questioned the authority of the "Regulators" who roamed the countryside terrorizing and brutalizing in-nocent black citizens, calling upon the state to "disband and punish them." Janssens served in the South at a time when federal efforts on behalf of freed slaves had long since ended, and even many Protestant organizations had softened their rhetoric of racial equality. Few whites had either the desire or the courage to match Janssens's challenges to the growing asser-tions of white supremacy. Even some of the most critical Creoles of color were filled with "admiration and gratitude" toward the archbishop for his work on behalf of Louisiana's black citizens. Louis Martinet, who would become a major opponent over St. Katherine's, acknowledged that under Janssens's tenure, "the Catholic Church is more of a safeguard to us in matters affecting the equality of men than any other church."[4]

Catholics of color also found reassuring Janssens's insistence that racial oppression and exclusion were religious issues at their root. His was an unusual assertion among American Catholic leaders. Black Catholics cele-brated Janssens as a leader who articulated the basis of their own loyalty to the church. He believed Catholicism, as a universal church, was rooted in a gospel that advocated equality over inequity, inclusion over exclusion, and a call to minister to the impoverished and marginalized. Janssens's hope for Catholicism mirrored the basis of interracial efforts among black and white members of the M. E. Church in New Orleans. Each believed a shared religious identity could eventually transcend and heal the region's racial animosities. Janssens thus emphasized the equality of African Ameri-cans within the Catholic Church. He believed that the races "now meet on common ground in the Church" and hoped that Catholicism would foster a common identity for black and white in New Orleans. In a sermon to a predominantly black congregation, Janssens assured the parishioners that they "belong to God, because he created you and his breath has given life to your souls." Janssens continued, asserting the equality of all Catholics: "The church is one general, immense brotherhood, and should not know any distinction between its members." The archbishop wanted the black members of his flock to understand that the Catholic "church accepts them all as her common children," despite developments that might suggest oth-erwise. Janssens felt a "great responsibility to preserve the faith among our Catholic negroes." His actions were "actuated solely by a desire for their religious betterment and advancement," resulting from his belief that he would have "to give account to the Lord" for the spiritual welfare of the black Catholics under his care. Accordingly, he defended the religiosity of black Catholics against charges of inferiority, claiming that "when the negro has been brought up in the knowledge and practice of religion, he is as constant as any white Catholic under the circumstances."[5] In theory, Janssens found no basis for separating Catholics on the basis of color.

Janssens made work on behalf of African-American Catholics in New Orleans a priority, dedicating himself to ending the Catholic Church's neglect of its black members. His activities as well as his rhetoric reflected this concern and distinguished him from his predecessors, who had either remained silent or denied the needs of the city's black Catholics. The archbishop repeatedly spoke of his concern for the religious welfare of black Catholics in Louisiana, not only in public sermons and published writings but in his private correspondence as well. Janssens made certain to interact with all races during his episcopal tours, visiting black schools as well as white schools, and keeping specific notes in his diary to ensure he neglected no one under his care. He also publicized the poor condition of existing Catholic schools and asylums for African Americans in an effort to increase donations to them. To repair the neglect of his predecessors, he helped raise funds among both black and white donors to renovate facilities for the Holy Family Sisters, their girls' orphanage and old-folks' home, as well as for the Indigent Orphan School. He also facilitated the construction of an asylum for orphan boys and old men, as well as several new schools for African-American children. Janssens's efforts were the first systematic and visible efforts of the diocese on behalf of African Americans since the Civil War.[6]

Janssens also worked to end racial injustice in the church. He publicly defended priests who ministered to black church members against the wishes of their predominantly white congregations. Janssens restored the black women's order, the Sisters of the Holy Family, to its rightful place in the city's cathedral after several orders of white nuns had refused to sit behind their sisters of color. When the white orders protested his re-arrangement, Janssens revealed his ability to be firm yet compassionate in dealing with racial difficulties. According to a Holy Family sister, those who complained about the black sisters' presence would "soon get the worst of it" from the archbishop. Yet in the next sentence, the same witness recorded that "he very soon calmed them all down and made them respect him and attend to their warm fires." Janssens also earned high marks in the black community for his efforts to foster clerical vocations among Catholics of color. Janssens's advocacy extended to national Catholic journals. He reminded his readers of a long Catholic tradition of promoting native clergy throughout the world and, in a paternalism characteristic of even the most liberal racial advocates, argued that African Americans could overcome their faults to make highly effective priests for work among their own people. Janssens sent two candidates north to study for the priesthood in 1892. Although neither made it to ordination, Janssens remained a strong advocate for black priests. He believed that as the church demonstrated its support for black members, the masses who had left "will return when they see greater interest is taken in them."[7]

Unlike his predecessors, Janssens both noticed and was concerned about the seeming exodus of black Catholics. The declines weighed heavily on the archbishop, who believed the inclusion of black Catholics formed an important component of his calling to the see of New Orleans. Stemming the losses continued as a priority throughout Janssens's tenure. Janssens never missed an opportunity to remind an audience or correspondent that his diocese contained a larger number of black Catholics than any other diocese in the country. His estimates ranged from 75,000 to 100,000, from which he deduced that approximately two-thirds of the nation's black Catholics lived within the boundaries of his episcopal jurisdiction. Janssens figured that in New Orleans alone, the church had lost nearly 20,000 African-American members in the two decades since the Civil War. He lamented that his diocese's losses alone probably equaled half the number of black Catholics living in the United States outside of Louisiana. During his episcopacy, Janssens watched the number of black baptisms remain stable, despite significant growth in the overall population of African Americans in New Orleans. These losses distinguished New Orleans from other cities. The small number of black Catholics elsewhere meant that most dioceses merely sought to win African Americans, whereas Janssens was working to prevent their defection. "In other Dioceses," Janssens pointed out, "they look out for conversions of the colored people, and I have to look out against perversions." Janssens feared Baptist and Methodist gains in Louisiana came largely at the expense of the Catholic Church. Among those who remained Catholic, Janssens felt "many were Catholics merely by name," since by 1890 few adults actually attended church or fulfilled their Easter Duty of receiving communion once a year.[8]

Black Catholics took solace in Janssens's recognition that their declining participation resulted from widespread discrimination in the city's Catholic churches. Janssens was the first prelate to acknowledge their "frequent grievances and complaints of discrimination against them." Separate seating was the most common and fastest-growing form of religious segregation in the city's Catholic churches. Already, separate seating on railroads and streetcars stood among the most widespread manifestations of race prejudice in New Orleans and throughout the South. Similar practices behind religious doors were equally offensive. The seeds of separate seating had been sown well before the final decades of the nineteenth century, despite instances of interracial worship that attracted the attention of visitors. At St. Augustine Church, for example, slaves had to sit on smaller pews along the side aisles even though free people of color rented a large number of pews and made contributions towards construction costs. The primarily Irish uptown parishes were more deliberate in their antebellum discrimination, and the separation only strengthened after the Civil War. By the time Janssens arrived, segregated seating had also made inroads in the traditionally French downtown parishes where most Creoles of color lived. Segregation cycled in an out of the cathedral throughout the postbellum era. Shortly after the Civil War, black worshipers were forced to sit on a long board installed along the back and side walls even in St. Louis Cathedral, the landmark travelers had praised for its mix of races sitting and kneeling side by side in the antebellum era. The English Catholic leader Herbert Vaughan reported on his visit to New Orleans in 1872 the case of Mr. Delaraze, a black Catholic who rented a pew at St. Louis Cathedral but was still forced to sit in a segregated section behind the altar. Vaughan also reported instances where black Catholics had donated large sums for the erection of a new church, yet were "refused places except at the end of the church." Three years later, on his 1875 visit to New Orleans, Canon Peter Benoit observed segregated seating throughout the French section of the city, where black Catholics had to "occupy pews on one of the aisles & the poorer ones kneel on the altar steps."[9]

By the 1890s, black and white no longer mixed freely in New Orleans's Catholic churches. The Catholic ideal, Janssens claimed, was "that any one might occupy any pew or any seat anywhere in the church." But the archbishop conceded that "the feeling between the two races make[s] such an intermixture impossible." Contrary to Janssens's assertion, the feeling was not between the two races but rather of white toward black. Black parishioners welcomed mixed seating and parishes, but such practices "would drive the whites away." Worship no longer constituted an integrated experience even if black and white continued to worship in the same building. Racial proscriptions tightened so much that black Catholics had virtually no choice as to which pews they would occupy. Whites chose the best seats, and black worshipers had "a special place assigned to them" in order to preserve a separation between the races.[10] Sometimes the segregation completely excluded seats. At Mater Dolorosa, the Holy Family Sisters reported that when their school children received first communion, only a few family members could attend and with the provision that they "stand in the back of the church, as it was supposed to be too small" to allow them to sit and thereby mix with white parishioners.[11]

Elsewhere, white priests and parishioners discouraged black attendance altogether. When African Americans attended Mass, whites subjected them to "petty persecutions" to discourage future attendance. Other times whites protested suggestions of equality by threatening to leave their parish and thereby undermine its financial viability. City residents did not resort to the violence and threats of white "Regulators" in the countryside, who expanded their efforts "to prevent the [colored] Cath. to come to church."

Nonetheless, where visitors had once reported surprise at racial mixing in the city's Catholic churches, by the late nineteenth century they most often quoted whites who made clear that "we do not wish them to be mixed with us." As an early missionary to black Catholics in Louisiana bemoaned, "the whites who call themselves Catholics do not want the colored in church and resort to every sort of meanness to keep them out."[12] Priests did their part as well. Janssens lamented the widespread exclusion of black Catholics from worship in the 1890s. Priests prevented black Catholics from participating as lay assistants in worship services and ensured both the altar and choir loft were off limits. Black children could not serve as altar boys or acolytes, nor could their parents sing in the church choir or serve as ushers. At Our Lady of Sacred Heart, the first pastor ministered primarily to black parishioners. His successor, however, disbanded the parish's societies for black members, with the result that his congregation became almost entirely white. The parish alternated back and forth in its inclusiveness, based on the whims of its priests, until the 1915 hurricane destroyed the building, and several area parishes were reconfigured along racially exclusive lines. Meanwhile, an unnamed priest in New Orleans bragged that, despite four thousand African Americans living within his parish boundaries, he had intimidated them sufficiently so that "the Negroes no longer ruled his church."[13] By 1890, the once-promising New Orleans offered little hope that racially mixed parishes could survive.

Janssens's solution to the widespread discrimination came as a great disappointment to black Catholics in New Orleans. The first prelate to acknowledge the need for increased attention to Catholics of color nonetheless pursued solutions that further marginalized the identity of those he hoped to return to the church. His strategy relied on a highly racialized approach that emphasized division over integration. To care for his long-neglected black flock, Janssens would erect separate schools, societies, and most notably, separate parishes, all served by separate religious orders and funded by separate donations. Janssens never wavered from his concern for Catholics of color, nor from his commitment to ensure their presence and participation in the Catholic Church. But he never considered integration as a solution to the problem that so troubled him. Even before his arrival in New Orleans, Janssens reached the conclusion he would stubbornly retain the rest of his life: only with separate churches would African Americans either return or convert to Catholicism.

The call for separate churches stemmed from Janssens's firsthand observations of the suffering and blatant inequality within mixed parishes. The neglect that had preserved interracial parishes had not prevented a rising discrimination that turned many away. In separate churches, Janssens concluded, black members would find the equality denied them elsewhere. He believed providing resources and facilities that did not have to be shared with whites would best benefit disadvantaged and abused black Catholics. In an imperfect world, the best solution was the protection that racial separation could provide. Not once did Janssens couch his advocacy of racially separate churches in the language of divine ordinance or suggest they modeled ideal social relations. Rather, his was a pragmatic concession. Prejudice among white Catholics had grown so strong, he warned, that "we cannot prudently extend the same privileges of indiscriminate pews, or rank in possessions, etc." to black parishioners. The wider social context of an increasingly segregated order had infected the sentiment in the pews to the point that it made "intermixture impossible." While he did not feel capable of changing the white sentiment that created the larger social and political context in which he ministered, Janssens was confident that having the freedom to sit anywhere, and having their own altar boys, ushers, and choirs, would eliminate the sense of inferiority that had driven many black Catholics away. He argued that a church just for the city's black Catholics would "give them a stimulus to come to their churches & to practice their religion."[14] Janssens continued to articulate his plan within the framework of its benefits to black Catholics, although the advantages to whites were equally at work.

Janssens recognized that the city's black Catholics were being pulled as well as pushed out their churches. The swelling ranks of the city's Protestant churches bore testimony to the losses. Though not unfounded, the conversions are difficult to quantify. Protestants did report Catholic desertions in New Orleans, especially under Janssens's predecessors. But the movement flowed both ways, as Protestants also occasionally lost members to Catholic churches. Both Protestants and Catholics frequently overestimated each other's gains in order to spur their own denominations to action. Like many whites, Janssens invoked racial affinity, believing those who joined Baptist and Methodist churches were most attracted to the racially homogenous membership of those congregations. By emulating the Protestant model, he believed he could compete on an equal basis with Protestant denominations.[15] Janssens failed to recognize that many of these black Protestants, especially those in the M. E. Church in New Orleans, were themselves protesting the segregated character of their religious institutions.

Concerns about Protestant competition were evident in Janssens's promotion of parochial schools for black Catholics. He stressed the role of schools in every request for funds he made. Separate schools, where black children would not have to compete with or suffer abuse from white students, were a cornerstone of Janssens's efforts to win back those who had left because of a lack of sufficient educational opportunities. "The school is our special hope & reliance for the future," Janssens asserted, "especially in the City, where our colored Catholics have such a great opportunity to frequent Protestant high schools & Universities and in consequence many become very careless and a few are lost to the faith." Enrollment reports confirmed his fears. At the Congregationalist Straight University, as many as three-quarters of its students came from Roman Catholic homes. Janssens spent considerable effort soliciting funds to expand schools for black Catholics. Typical was Janssens's plea for a small donation for the school in the Carrollton neighborhood, which would enable him to improve the school facility, eliminate tuition, and thereby "get back the colored Catholic children, which are enticed by this free Swedenborgian school." Other times he urged his clergy to make greater efforts. At St. Rose of Lima parish, for instance, Janssens's prodding led the priest to begin a school in the back of the church for the parish's black families. Still, the school, like all founded for black children, was relegated to an inferior space, suffered from a lack of funds and a limited enrollment, and emphasized catechetical instruction over a full grade-school curriculum.[16]

But separate schools were only a stepping-stone to Janssens's goal of a separate church for black Catholics in New Orleans. The new parish would build on the gains begun by parochial schools. Successful schools would convince black Catholics and reluctant clergymen that separate churches would prove equally beneficial. When Janssens sent out an appeal for sisters to teach in black schools, he based his argument on the belief that a successful separate school would "convince our people & clergy that separated churches are as necessary as separate schools." Janssens's strategy was not unique. Prelates throughout the nation had used black schools as the nucleus for organizing separate black parishes. In accordance with Janssens's strategy, the first pastor of St. Katherine's reported that renovations for the new sanctuary did not begin "until the school's life was assured."[17]

In his advocacy of racially separate parishes, Janssens advanced the prevailing approach for working among black Catholics in the United States. The consensus in favor of separate churches had emerged at the 1884 Plenary Council, in contrast to the divisions at the 1866 council. Nearly all who advocated for and worked with black Catholics had coalesced around an agreement that white prejudice, even in religious contexts, necessitated separating black Catholics from their oppressors. In Savannah, Georgia, for example, the bishop argued in 1886 that the coordinated efforts by native whites and immigrants to exclude black parishioners necessitated the formation of a separate church. In St. Paul, Minnesota, as well, John Ireland, one of the nation's preeminent archbishops and most forceful opponents of "color line," nonetheless admitted that "for the time being in view of conditions which we do not accept, but which we must consider, separate churches are more pleasant and more profitable for the colored people." Ireland's concession came at the dedication of a separate black church in St. Paul. Religious orders working among black Catholics were similarly inclined. The Josephite Fathers, who would eventually lead most of New Orleans's separate black parishes, committed themselves exclusively to black parishes after difficulties trying to sustain a mixed parish in Prince Georges County, Maryland, in the 1870s. As the Josephites moved south, persistent racism against black Catholics reaffirmed their decision to focus on separate churches. The Holy Ghost Fathers, a missionary order from Germany known as the Spiritans, also dedicated themselves to working solely with black Catholics after observing the hostility of white Catholics toward black parishioners in the upper South. In a tradition consistent with their approach to slavery, Catholics understood their calling to ameliorate the effects of the existing social and political order, not to overturn it.[18] Throughout the United States, Catholic leaders justified segregated parishes by the need to protect black Catholics. Despite this explanation, white parishioners understood the separation in reverse: it protected them from the supposed dangers of contact with blacks.

Janssens remained so convinced that a separate parish would benefit the city's black Catholics that he proceeded with his plans for St. Katherine's with little concern for opposing viewpoints. He acknowledged opposition from both clergy and the city's black residents but gave it little regard as he pushed ahead with his search for funding and priests to open a separate parish in New Orleans. The archbishop denied that a separate church would further the divisions between the races, given the prejudice already existing among most of the city's white Catholics. He brushed aside complaints from prominent black Catholics, claiming those who complained the loudest "never set foot in the church." In his defense, Janssens also emphasized that black Catholics would not be compelled to attend a segregated church. He simply offered it as an alternative to those who felt uncomfortable elsewhere.[19] Even among his own clergy, Janssens conceded that "very few favor the experiment of separate churches," although more for practical concerns about funding and losing members than an ideological commitment to integration. Usually one to listen to the opinions of his consultors and flock, Janssens pushed ahead with the full authority and prerogatives of his episcopal position on the issue of separate parishes. Janssens's determination contrasted with that of other prelates, such as Bishop Heslin in Mississippi, who promised to abandon plans for a separate church in Natchez if he did not have the support of the majority of the area's black Catholics. In New Orleans, Janssens was unwavering in his confidence that he would be proven correct and that all, black and white, clergy and lay, would come to appreciate the benefits of a separate parish.[20] While acknowledging St. Katherine's might alienate some, Janssens believed most "will fall in line as soon as they shall see that the Church is intended for their good & results in no harm to them." The success of the first parish would turn opponents into supporters of additional black parishes throughout the city and countryside.[21] In the meantime, Janssens sustained an extensive and very public defense of his efforts to open a separate parish for the benefit of the city's black Catholics.

Janssens's determination complicated the world of black Catholics, who thought they finally had an ally in the episcopacy. But in erecting space to include more black Catholics, the archbishop also ensured a religious separateness that paralleled their exclusion in nearly every other aspect of their lives. For Catholics of color, the supposed step forward was several steps backward. Janssens never considered integration as a solution to the problem, even as his correspondence reveals he was deeply troubled by the neglect of black Catholics. The archbishop's commitment to the dignity of African Americans had led him to make bold proposals, such as a black priesthood and a school to nurture religious vocations among African Americans. He had also spoken bravely against the violent racism of white supremacists in Louisiana. Yet this commitment to separate institutions advocated the same response as the white supremacists he deplored, despite their very different aims. Janssens believed separate churches, schools, and even religious orders would improve the self-respect and spiritual well-being of Louisiana's black Catholics. White supremacists invoked segregation to accomplish the exact opposite goals of subordination and degradation. They also used separate churches as evidence that both black and white preferred a segregated society. The crucial difference was that for Janssens, separation was a temporary means to a very different end; for white supremacists, segregation was the end itself. As Janssens's tenure reveals, the relationship between racism and segregation was a complicated one in the American South. The same prelate who rejected many of the South's assumptions of black inferiority and believed he was acting against the pervasive grip of racism nonetheless played a crucial role in moving Catholic churches in New Orleans toward total racial segregation. Others who uncritically demeaned and neglected black Catholics were slower to institute segregation, including the archbishops who both preceded and followed Janssens. In Janssens, black Catholics in New Orleans had the most dangerous of potential allies: one who in the name of good could inflict much harm.

Janssens's persistence paid off. In 1893 he secured assurances from Katharine Drexel that she would contribute funds to renovate the old St. Joseph Church, which stood empty after the congregation built a new sanctuary nearby. Drexel was one of three daughters of Francis Drexel, a Philadelphia banker who became a multimillionaire during the California gold rush. Upon his death in 1885, the elder Drexel left his three daughters a fourteen-million-dollar trust, with the income to be divided among them. Each of the daughters continued the family's tradition of charity, especially toward African Americans and Indians. Katharine became a nun in 1887 and used her inheritance to found the Sisters of the Blessed Sacrament for work among Indians and Negroes, of which she remained superior general until 1937. After her two sisters died childless, the entire Drexel estate reverted to Katharine and her order. Drexel developed a close relationship with Janssens, sharing a concern for African Americans, including the need for separate parishes for black Catholics and for separate orders to minister to them. In honor of Drexel's charity, Janssens named the new church after her patron saint, St. Katharine of Sienna. Thereafter, Drexel and the Sisters of the Blessed Sacrament continued as the primary source of support for separate black churches and schools in New Orleans.[22]

When he also found an order of priests to staff the new church, Janssens had cleared the other major obstacle to opening a separate parish. After being turned down by several orders, Janssens prevailed upon the Vincentians to minister to the new congregation of African Americans. The Vincentians, founded by St. Vincent de Paul and formally known as the Congregation of the Mission, already served the nearby St. Joseph Church. The Vincentians fell short of Janssens's desire for an order that labored solely among the city's black Catholics. Nonetheless their proximity, and the fact that their congregation at St. Joseph Church had formerly occupied the building that would become St. Katherine's, made them an acceptable choice. The order would assume financial responsibility for the parish, relieving Janssens of having to support it. In his insistence that the separate parish be erected without the use of diocesan funds or clergy, Janssens's conditions harmonized with those of his predecessors and with prelates throughout the nation.[23] What distinguished Janssens was the zeal with which he pursued both financing and priests

On May 19, 1895, St. Katherine's opened, representing the culmination of Janssen's commitment to separate institutions for black Catholics. Janssens held a grand opening Mass in which he affirmed his love for African Americans and their equality before God. Janssens also stressed that black Catholics were only invited, not forced, to attend St. Katherine's. They could continue in their local parishes if they preferred. This voluntary caveat distinguished his vision of racial separation from the involuntary character of other forms of segregation in southern society. The dedication featured many firsts for black Catholics, including black choirs, altar boys, and ushers. Janssens had originally claimed that St. Katherine's and his program of separate churches "is merely experimental, and if it does not prove successful it will of course be abandoned." In the planning stages he also confessed his own uncertainty about the project, recognizing that "the special church for the colored people may prove a failure."[24] Even before it opened, however, Janssens reneged on his promises to wait. He predicted unqualified success and commenced planning for churches in the French-speaking section of the city, as well as in the countryside.

A confluence of events had enabled Janssens to open St. Katherine's in May 1895. Funding from Drexel and staffing by the Vincentians allowed Janssens to overcome the most pressing obstacles. But St. Katherine's was also the product of winds blowing beyond Crescent City Catholicism. While Janssens actively pressed for a separate parish in a way his predecessors had not, he also did so in a context that more actively encouraged segregation than in previous decades, especially in New Orleans. The city itself had become increasingly Americanized as English speakers and American-born and educated businessmen and politicians dominated city affairs.[25] With that shift came biracial perspectives that emphasized segregation as a solution to the "race problem." At the same time Janssens pushed the development of St. Katherine's, city and state officials were legislating segregation into most public spaces, and many private ones as well. The national capitulation to segregation also took its toll. St. Katherine's opened only one year before the Supreme Court ruled in favor of separate-but-equal in the *Plessy v. Ferguson* case that emerged from New Orleans. The North was acceding to segregation in the interest of political and social reunion with the South. The same year that St. Katherine's opened, Booker T. Washington gave his famous Atlanta Compromise speech, wherein he urged gradualism and racial separation as the most expedient way to order the post-Emancipation South.

Catholic liberalism formed another important backdrop to the emergence of separate parishes. During the late 1880s and through the 1890s, American Catholic leaders debated the nature of the Catholic Church and its relationship to the United States, in a conflict known as the Americanist controversy. Liberals pushed for Catholic immigrants and the Catholic Church to adapt to the American context. They also hoped to overcome the distance between Catholic faith and social action, which derived from the "perfect society" model of the church that emphasized Catholicism's unchanging character and kept the church apart from the political and social questions confronting individual nations. Conservatives upheld this long-standing conception of the church, resisting change and preserving ethnic Catholic identities and the national parishes that nurtured them. Neither Janssens nor the challenges of black Catholics figured prominently in the Americanist controversy, whose specific conflicts revolved around parochial schools, secret societies, labor unions, and religious freedom. Nonetheless, Janssens's tenure in New Orleans coincided with the ascendancy of the Americanist wing, and his advocacy of separate parishes, his writing for *The Catholic World*, published by the Americanist-leaning Paulist order, his criticism of racism, advocacy for black priests, and connections to Archbishop James Gibbons in Baltimore, all suggested Janssens's sympathies with the liberal faction. His belief the Catholic Church could help solve the American racial dilemma and his willingness to adopt the

Figure 6.2. St. Katherine's Church. Photograph taken July 4, 1939. Copyright ©
The Historic New Orleans Collection. Photographer: Clarence John Laughlin,
accession no. 1983.47.4.542.

prevailing social custom of segregation also reflected the liberal emphasis on adapting Catholicism to the American context. Leading liberal bishops, including Janssens's mentor, James Gibbons in Baltimore, and John Ireland in St. Paul, were among the few to speak to issues of race and had also advocated separate parishes for black Catholics. Janssens's turn to separate parishes also reflected his quest for the respectability of the Catholic church in New Orleans, both among the American hierarchy, then dominated by liberals, and in American society more broadly. This desire for acceptance by the American mainstream, which was defined as white in racial terms, also placed Janssens well within the Americanist wing. Janssens's approach contrasted with that of his French-born predecessors, whose inaction on behalf of black Catholics was just one measure of their sympathies with the conservative wing of the American church.

Yet the question of separate black parishes also cut across the liberal/conservative divide. Justification for black parishes often derived from the pervasive presence of national-language parishes, around which conservative support coalesced. Most conservatives did not denounce racially segregated parishes, though few considered them a priority within their understanding of the church and its role in American society. Black parishes, therefore, did not end with the papal denunciation of the Americanist agenda in 1899, even though it dampened enthusiasm for racial reform. Before long, separate parishes would become one principle upon which both liberal and conservative leaders could agree. Janssens's efforts, though aggravating to the black Catholics under his care, were entirely consistent with the larger Catholic ethos within which he labored.[26]

Janssens considered the erection of St. Katherine's the capstone of his career. With its opening, he believed he had succeeded in his mission and persuaded the members of his diocese, black and white, of the benefits of separate parishes. The archbishop boasted of the full congregation at the dedication, which included many whites. But he spoke particularly of the black members of the congregation "who seemed delighted" in one report and "overdelighted" in another. The opening mass was an auspicious occasion, Janssens wrote to Drexel, "and it fills me with great hopes for the future." Only a few months after its opening, he pronounced St. Katherine's an unqualified success. Janssens had invested too much time, energy, and money in the face of significant opposition to admit anything but triumph. In the months before its opening, Janssens proclaimed his confidence that St. Katherine's would be an unmitigated victory and stopped calling it an experiment he would terminate if it failed. In the remaining two years before his death, the archbishop expounded the success of St. Katherine's and the benefits of separate parishes to potential benefactors, hoping to raise financial support for additional separate parishes in New Orleans's French-speaking neighborhoods.[27]

BUT THE OPENING OF ST. KATHERINE's marked an episode of resistance even more than it signaled the ability of the Catholic hierarchy to impose its will upon black Catholics in New Orleans. Historians have traditionally emphasized Janssens's maneuvering in recounting the story of St. Katherine's, crediting him with implementing segregated parishes in New Orleans. In these narratives, the black community's resistance remains subordinated to Janssens's accomplishments.[28] But St. Katherine's did not achieve the stature that either Janssens or subsequent historians accorded it. Protests before, during, and after the dedication of St. Katherine's delayed the further spread of segregation within the Crescent City's Catholic parishes. This substantial and largely successful opposition forms the real significance of St. Katherine's, especially when measured against Janssens's original hopes for the new church.

Opponents to St. Katherine's drew upon a long tradition of Afro-Creole protest in New Orleans. Much of this protest was rooted in the ideals of the French Revolution, which refugees fleeing the revolution in St. Domingue transmitted to New Orleans at the turn of the nineteenth century. Alliances with white French radicals in New Orleans provided free people of color with a modicum of protection from the wave of racial oppression that accompanied Louisiana's Americanization during the nineteenth century. During Reconstruction, Afro-Creoles played a central role in constructing the most radical and racially inclusive of all southern state constitutions. In the final decades of the nineteenth century, Afro-Creoles had resisted the segregation of New Orleans streetcars in the 1870s and had successfully challenged railroad segregation on interstate travel in the 1892 State Supreme Court case, *Abbot v. Hicks*.[29]

Within the Catholic Church as well, Afro-Creoles resisted efforts of church officials to suppress their independence. At midcentury, they successfully confronted Catholic authorities in disputes over control of the Indigent Orphan School. The school had been a gift of a wealthy Creole woman of color, Marie Couvent, and was intended for the education of orphans in the city. Creole leaders forced the archdiocese to release funds to open the school in 1847, when, ten years after Couvent's death, the church had failed to establish the school according to her wishes.[30] Archdiocesan officials were reluctant to release the funds designated for the school because Couvent's will stipulated that the institution remain free from clerical supervision. Once opened, the school, which was administered and staffed by black residents, quickly extended its reach beyond orphans to become the preeminent educational institution for people of color in New Orleans. School-board members continued their association with racial advocacy through their financial contributions, writing, and organizational work against the rash of segregation in the final decade of the nineteenth century.

During the 1890s, the ongoing Creole protest tradition was most evident in the work of the Citizens Committee. Formally named the Citizens Committee to Test the Constitutionality of the Separate Car Law, the Citizen's Committee was formed in September 1891, largely through the generosity of Aristide Mary, a wealthy Creole and benefactor to both Catholic and black interests throughout New Orleans. The Citizens Committee also adopted as its official newspaper the *Crusader*, which was edited by Louis Martinet, a lawyer, physician, and good friend of A.E.P. Albert, the M. E. minister and editor of the *Southwestern Christian Advocate*. The committee is most famous for advancing the case of Homer Plessy, a light-skinned Creole, who deliberately violated Louisiana's 1890 law requiring black and white passengers to ride in separate railroad cars. The Citizens Committee carefully staged Plessy's 1892 arrest to ensure a conviction could be appealed on constitutional grounds. The Louisiana Supreme Court upheld the conviction, as did a 7 to 1 majority in the United States Supreme Court in 1896. The U.S. Supreme Court denied any constitutional violation, based on the presumption that separate accommodations were legal if they were required to be equal. The Court appeared untroubled by failure to uphold the "equal" part of segregation statutes. From that 1896 ruling in *Plessy v. Ferguson* came the language of "separate but equal" with which whites legitimated segregation for the next sixty years.[31]

The Citizens Committee's Plessy case was only one in a broad array of late-nineteenth-century lawsuits against railroad segregation. The resources at the Citizens Committee's disposal, rather than court challenges to separate-car laws, are what distinguished the Creole-dominated effort in New Orleans from other lawsuits by black Southerners. Throughout the 1880s, African Americans filed legal suits against railroads for failing to honor first-class tickets and demanding damages for the suffering that often ensued. Women filed many of these suits; some of them were victorious. Black women were especially vulnerable when forced to ride in the smoking car, where white men not suited to ride with white "ladies" were also relegated. By the early 1890s, African Americans began filing a new wave of cases. Like the effort that would result in the Plessy case, these suits were filed by men, belonging to committees organized for the specific purpose of challenging Jim Crow. These men, like the Creoles in New Orleans, came from the South's black middle class. Unlike the earlier wave of cases, these latter cases challenged the legality of segregation rather than seeking damages for its consequences. African Americans in five other states were advancing constitutional cases at the time the Supreme Court issued its Plessy decision in 1896. The Court's overwhelming verdict against Plessy reveals that a different place of origin would not have impacted the outcome.[32]

Railroad segregation and legal strategy were not the only issues that attracted the attention of the Citizens Committee. Most of the preparation for the Plessy case had been completed by early 1893, so the committee focused its attention beyond transportation in New Orleans, including rumors of a separate Catholic parish. Most of the committee's Creole members were Catholic by birth, if no longer in practice. Their protests demonstrated an ongoing concern about the significance of Catholic inclusivity and a conviction that church practices would shape race relations in the larger social and political order. They made their concerns known to Janssens. Creoles had earlier praised the archbishop's defenses of black rights. The relationship turned acrimonious, especially with those involved in the Citizens Committee and the *Crusader*, when Janssens tried to enlist their help "to create public sentiment in favor of erecting a Colored Catholic asylum for girls." Creoles withheld support, "objecting to making it a race affair." Thereafter, the archbishop complained of a politically influential mulatto elite, by which he meant the French-speaking Creoles of color. A year before opening St. Katherine's, Janssens deplored the "light mulattoes & politicians, who abuse me in public print for attempting to begin a new church for the colored people." The archbishop termed their tendency to "look with disfavor upon separate churches" the most troubling Creole characteristic.[33] The New Orleans prelate was not alone in associating Creoles with opposition to separate churches. A priest trying to establish a black congregation in Natchez, Mississippi, complained that "the yellow ones here are so stuck up and so imbued with the equality idea that they spurn having a church of their own and won't quit going to the white people's church."[34] Those sharing similar views were apparently unaware that often darker-skinned African Americans, Methodist Episcopalian as well as Catholic, also opposed segregated churches.

Nor were Afro-Creoles in New Orleans the only Catholics of color to protest the rising tide of segregation in church and society. The early 1890s witnessed a nationwide upsurge in black Catholic protest. Between 1889 and 1894, African-American Catholics held five annual congresses to address concerns of black Catholics and black Americans. The Colored Catholic Congresses were the first national gathering of black Catholics, who, unlike other communities of American Catholics, lacked a priesthood to organize and advocate on their behalf. The congresses were the idea of Daniel Rudd, the owner and editor of the only explicitly black Catholic newspaper in America, the *American Catholic Tribune*. The congresses heard speeches and passed resolutions on a variety of topics, from pragmatic concerns for more schools and religious institutions, to increasingly activist protests against discrimination and segregation within American Catholic churches and beyond. Delegates professed their ongoing loyalty to Catholicism and their confidence that only this universally inclusive church could advance the interests of black Americans. Their careful combination of affirmation and criticism mirrored the language of black M. E. church members, who likewise insisted on their denomination's promise while lamenting its discriminatory tendencies. No less than A.E.P. Albert and his colleagues in the M. E. Church, these black Catholics recognized the link between segregation in church and society. As a delegate to the 1890 Congress reminded his audience, "the struggle of the Church is like unto the struggle of the Colored man in this country."[35] The congresses remained under the auspices of the church, meeting only with the permission the bishop in whose province they gathered. The hierarchy's watchful eye may have limited the assertiveness and effectiveness of the congresses, whose attendance dwindled from a hundred in 1889 to thirty-eight by 1894. The movement also struggled to maintain a national character, attracting most of its delegates from the northern and border states and lamenting the near absence of delegates from New Orleans and the Deep South. The end of the Congresses and Rudd's *American Catholic Tribune* bore a striking similarity to Albert's ouster from the M. E. *Southwestern Christian Advocate* only a few years earlier. Both resulted from the discomfort black radicalism created within a predominantly white denomination. Combined with the Plessy loss and corresponding end of the *Crusader*, events in the 1890s revealed the difficulty facing any organized protest against racial discrimination. Still, the African-American congresses outlasted the larger Catholic congress movement by white laity, which managed to meet only two times in the same period. It had also laid the foundation for the emergence of the Federated Colored Catholics in 1920s.[36]

In New Orleans, the protests against St. Katherine's, and against segregation more generally, reflected the complex position of Creoles in a city undergoing a racial transformation. During the late nineteenth century, Crescent City whites were instituting the typically American binary form of segregation, which distinguished only between black and white. Gone was room for any middle caste. White Creoles played a crucial role in this transformation. The term "Creole" had long lacked a specific racial designation, referring to all people born in Louisiana who had French or Spanish ancestry, as distinguished from those whose roots included British or northern European ancestry. This French-American divide, which included people of African descent on both sides, had long been the crucial division in New Orleans, evident in everything from language and religion to place of residence and architecture. By the late nineteenth century, New Orleans had undergone a reorientation. Basic divisions shifted from a cultural to a racial axis, divided between black and white. The long-standing links between Creoles, both black and white, combined with the sometimes ambiguous appearances in which one's race was not visibly clear, threatened to confuse the emerging color line and undermine the separation it was premised upon. White Creoles started insisting that whiteness was intrinsic to Creole identity, as part of their effort to ensure they ended up on the white side of the color line. Stirring up the waters was George Washington Cable, the white New Orleans native and writer, whose representation of Creole culture insisted on the centrality of interracial liaisons and the inclusion of people of color as "Creoles." Leading nineteenth-century Louisiana historian Charles Gayarré led a tireless campaign in opposition, insisting on the white racial purity of Creole identity, which he then fused with the pervasive white supremacy. Even the Catholic Church joined the effort to redefine "Creole" in racial rather than ethnic terms. In 1894, the archdiocesan newspaper printed reassurances that, although "in the North the idea is prevalent that a Creole has negro blood ... it is entirely wrong."[37]

These attempts to reconfigure New Orleans's racial order provoked Creole protests against segregation. On the one hand, a strain of self-preservation to remain apart from African Americans motivated the Creole opposition. Protesting against segregation was consistent with efforts to preserve a distinct Creole identity. Crescent City whites were instituting the typically American binary form of segregation, which distinguished only between black and white. Absent was a distinct place for Creoles of color, whom whites hoped to reclassify as black. The biracial segregation characteristic of separate parishes would deny such differences in organizing Catholics solely by a perceived presence or absence of African blood, rather than alternative categories such as culture, language, education, or even place of residence. Retaining any claim to a unique social status or cultural identity would become difficult if forced into the same parishes as everyone else the church deemed "black." Creoles invoked the long tradition of their acceptance into mixed congregations, which was also an acknowledgment of the difference between their ancestors and those of African Americans. Their protests also highlighted a cultural distinctiveness as they called upon the French ideals of *liberté*, *égalité*, and *fraternité* in addition to the African-American emphasis on the Declaration of Independence. For Creole leaders such as Rodolphe Desdunes, the cultural, linguistic, and residential differences between the Creole or "Latin Negro," and the "Anglo-Saxon or American Negro" continued their significance at the turn of the twentieth century.[38] Creoles would find it difficult to convince both whites and other blacks that they retained any claim to a distinct social position if forced into the same churches as African Americans. Protesting separate parishes remained in the interest of those seeking to preserve distinctions within the black community.

On the other hand, Creole protests against St. Katherine's revealed a self-conscious diminishing of differences with African Americans. As it softened the distinctions between the Creole and African-American communities, the rhetoric and the support for the Citizens Committee marked a crucial shift among the city's black population. The interests of these once-distinct castes increasingly coincided as both suffered under the weight of a racial oppression that denied any differences among people of African descent. Whether seeking to preserve their own distinct identity and position, or simply resisting the broader tendency to homogenize and discriminate broadly on the basis of an "impurity" of blood, Creoles found increasing reason to make common cause with their African-American neighbors. Most Creoles underscored St. Katherine's offensiveness to all black citizens and Catholics, rather than invoking the more elitist and self-interested arguments sometimes associated with earlier Creole strategies. Even Rodolphe Desdunes, one of the most ardent defenders of Creole distinctiveness, nonetheless assured the Citizens Committee's supporters that its opposition to segregation, in churches as well as on railroad cars, sought to protect and defend "the plain and common people" who were "the poor, the defenseless, the toiler, whether in the field, on the levee, in the shop or factory," and thereby "the plain and common people."[39] The changes among black no less than white residents signaled the shifting meanings of race in New Orleans and formed an important measure of the city's ongoing Americanization. Ironically, this movement toward common cause was itself a tacit recognition of the very biracialism Creoles were protesting.

As a result, the Citizens Committee protesting both religious and railroad segregation drew upon a wider membership than the Creole elite with which it is most often associated. By the 1890s, black Catholics no less than Protestants reached beyond their denominational boundaries to coordinate resistance to the rising tide of Jim Crow. In a city once noted for its preeminent Catholic-Protestant divide, black Protestants supported both the committee's legal challenges and its opposition to St. Katherine's. E.W.S. Hammond, a black Methodist and editor of the *Southwestern Christian Advocate*, suggested that Janssens's pursuit of St. Katherine's "is, in our judgment, a surrender to a most cruel prejudice, and mars an otherwise honorable record." The trend was not unique to New Orleans. Ministers from a variety of Protestant denominations, for example, attended the first African-American Catholic Congress in 1889. The Citizens Committee in New Orleans built upon the work of M. E. minister A.E.P. Albert and continued to rely upon him as a board member and conduit to the city's Protestant community. Rodolphe Desdunes, a leading organizer of the Citizens Committee, solicited a broad base of support, including many of the city's Protestant congregations.[40] Besides the M. E. Church, leaders of the city's Congregationalist and African Methodist congregations also supported the Citizens Committee. Many of the ecumenical relationships had been nurtured in Protestant schools such as Straight and New Orleans

Universities, which the city's black Catholics relied upon because of a lack of similar Catholic institutions. Opposition to St. Katherine's extended beyond class as well as religious differences. In January 1894, a group of 150 black Catholics signed a letter of protest addressed to Archbishop Janssens to call his "attention to the injustice designed against us, in the endeavor to establish a church, exclusively for colored people in the Parish of St. Joseph, against our wishes or consent." The names on the list represented a cross section of the city's African-American population in age, profession, education, and places of residence. Opposition to the parish was widespread, not just among the educated elite with French roots, but also among the poor, the English speaking, and those who lived uptown in predominantly American neighborhoods.[41]

Women too played an important role in protesting the erection of St. Katherine's. A young woman, sixteen years of age, first made the Citizens Committee aware of Janssens's plan to create a separate parish in the old St. Joseph Church when she wrote "a vigorous letter against a movement to make a separate Catholic church edifice, exclusively for the colored Catholics of this city." An elderly woman who belonged to St. Joseph Church made headlines with her refusal to sign a petition in support of creating a separate church in her parish. She invoked the many "plain thinking people" who had been raised in St. Joseph parish and had no interest in leaving for a church consisting only of African Americans. Women also ensured the solvency of the Citizens Committee. Women's organizations in New Orleans accounted for nearly a quarter of the groups that made donations.[42] The women that Janssens hoped would be the foundation of the new parish failed to provide the support he envisioned.

These diverse and sometimes divided communities of black Catholics in New Orleans united with near unanimous opposition to Janssens's hope to introduce segregated parishes. The protesters mounted an "organized and bitter opposition" in which they promised to "put forth every possible effort to counteract such ungodly attempts" to open a separate parish for black Catholics.[43] The effort was a public one, including an almost nonstop flood of newspaper articles emphasizing the injustice of separate churches for the city's black residents. The arguments against St. Katherine's recalled those made by the city's black Methodists against the racially divisive character of African Methodism in the 1880s and against segregation within their denominational structures in subsequent decades. Unlike Methodists, however, Catholics focused on the local congregation rather than access to the hierarchy or larger denominational structures.

Black Catholics feared a separate parish would accentuate racial differences and unnecessarily draw the "color line." Black M. E. church members had likewise invoked appeals to the color line to prevent segregating their Louisiana Annual Conference. In a city that claimed a long tradition of

minimizing rather than emphasizing racial differences, a church that would
further the growing sense of racial distinction remained unwelcome. "Such
distinctions are unnecessary and even harmful, and we must deplore and
discourage them," explained Rodolphe Desdunes in protesting St. Katherine's. Black Catholics not only blamed Janssens but also directed their ire
at Katharine Drexel for providing the funds. They feared that, with the aid
of Drexel's nearly unlimited resources, the archbishop would "finally push
the color line to the point of exclusion." Black Catholics believed Janssens
wished "to separate the races & to widen the gap which exists between the
white and [colored] population." Specifically, they feared they would be
denied entrance to the churches in which they currently worshiped, despite
Janssens's reassurances that no one would be compelled to attend a separate
parish against his or her will. Even as Janssens emphasized the voluntary
nature of St. Katherine's at its opening, most remained skeptical, sensing
as did the black writer and New Orleans native Alice Ruth Moore (later
Dunbar-Nelson), that "it won't be long before such gentle means as a quiet
discrimination all along the parishes will force the colored worshippers
into the 'Jim Crow' church."[44]

Those opposing separate parishes also warned that church segregation
affected the political and civil rights of African Americans, just as their
Methodist counterparts had. The Citizens Committee that developed cases
testing the constitutionality of railroad segregation also filed cases against
a variety of forms of segregation, including schools, juries, and suffrage.
Segregation in the Catholic Church was equally dangerous. Janssens complained that those who protested against his experiment with a separate
church were the same persons who "aim at a greater equality with the
whites, politically & socially." Indeed, Rodolphe Desdunes argued that
New Orleans Catholics should reject Drexel's gift of a separate church
because "separation in one form may bring separation in another." Desdunes believed the Catholic Church carried significant influence in Louisiana, citing Janssens's opposition as a crucial factor in the failure of anti-
miscegenation legislation in 1892. They feared Janssens's support of separate parishes would be equally influential, but with the opposite result of
condoning Jim Crow. The last thing black Catholics needed was for their
church to endorse, through its own actions, the explosion of segregation
legislation in Louisiana in the 1890s. The church increasingly appeared as
the last hope against the rising tide of Jim Crow. "If men are divided by,
or in, the Church," Desdunes wondered, "where can they be united in the
bonds of faith and love of truth and justice?"[45]

Most pointedly, protesters charged that separate parishes violated the
very essence of Catholicism. In rhetoric unique among white Christians,
Janssens had long characterized the need to include African Americans in
the church as a religious and not merely a social issue. Creoles took him

at his word, highlighting the inconsistency between his rhetoric and the reality he was constructing. Alice Moore complained that by separating the races and preventing all people from receiving the communion bread together as equals, the Catholic Church undermined its claims to universality and destroyed "the most beautiful portion of the Catholic creed." "The strength and glory of the Catholic Church," Desdunes agreed, had always been that it knew "no race, no color, nationality; but brotherhood union and concert of action." Protesters also reminded New Orleans Catholics that separate parishes contradicted papal wishes, even if they were the preference of American Catholic leaders.[46] Elsewhere in the United States, black Catholics made good on such warnings, presenting their grievances to the Vatican in a largely unsuccessful quest for redress. Like Methodists, black Catholics argued that establishing separate churches and separate schools ignored the fundamental Christian doctrine of "the Fatherhood of God and the brotherhood of man." Whereas Christ ministered among the most lowly and made no distinction among the people he served, Janssens and Drexel made unnecessary distinctions among God's creatures and thus practiced "the very reverse of what the gospel teaches." Catholic doctrine taught, and Janssens had clearly affirmed, that God created humans of all races. Accordingly, the protesters argued, "There can be no such thing as a separate Catholic church" if the Catholic Church was to be true to its origins and to the Christian faith.[47]

The opposition to St. Katherine's was part of a black Catholic debate occurring in cities across the country. Black Catholics in other communities resisted episcopal efforts to place them in separate parishes, including Natchez, Charleston, and Savannah. Like their Crescent City counterparts, opponents in these cities continued to worship in their local parishes or stopped attending church altogether. Elsewhere, however, Catholics of color were more welcoming of separate facilities. In some cases they, rather than white bishops, initiated requests for a separate parish. African Americans in Cincinnati, Baltimore, and Washington, D.C., all advocated on behalf of a separate parish in their community. Proximity to black neighborhoods and freedom from racial discrimination were the leading reasons black Catholics requested their own churches. Other times class interest prevailed, as it increasingly did among black Protestants as well. Black Catholics at the higher end of the socioeconomic spectrum wanted to avoid the association with lower classes they feared would undermine attempts at assimilation. All denied segregation was the ideal end, but supporters conceded that the immediate future of black Catholics would be better served in a protected environment that would enable the fullest expression of their faith. Supporters pointed to national-language parishes as an appropriate analogy, suggesting both a temporary duration and evidence that separation did not condone inferiority. Speeches at the Colored Catholic

Congresses were similarly divided, with some favoring and others opposing the expansion of racially separate parishes.[48]

No less than their Protestant counterparts, black Catholics in the United States disagreed over what strategies served their best interests. Few communities were unanimous in their support or opposition. A vote in Jackson, Mississippi, recorded eleven in favor and eight against erecting a separate parish. Even in New Orleans, small groups of black Catholics had asked for a separate church on more than one occasion. Janssens clung to a single letter from a trio of non-Creole Catholics supporting his efforts at St. Katherine's.[49] The arguments for and against separate parishes bore a striking resemblance to the debates between M. E. and A.M.E. church members over racially separate denominations, even if Catholic disagreements lacked the ferocity that sometimes characterized Methodist rivalries. From politics to religion, African Americans displayed a healthy disagreement on how to advance the interests of their race. The contributions of Catholics of color in New Orleans reveal the extent to which any monolithic understanding of either a black church or racial identity was more the construction of white opponents than black self-understanding.

The overwhelming opposition in New Orleans resulted in a formidable "storm of opposition" leading up to the opening of St. Katherine's. Protesters kept the archbishop "deluged with petitions, some lengthy, some pithy, some with many signatures, some with a few signatures that meant something." Others formed delegations who repeatedly visited the archbishop to persuade him of the practical and theological dangers of his plan. The determined archbishop complained to his supporters of being "kept busy receiving delegations of objectors who besieged him with reasons why this thing could not be." Janssens and his visitors agreed that the current "prejudices which obtained in the churches" caused many Catholics of color to leave the church. But they could not agree on a solution. The archbishop proposed St. Katherine's because he felt he needed to remove African Americans from the specter of violence in interracial parishes. Challenging the violence itself was not an option he considered. Preserving the stability and support of his white parishioners was an important but largely unacknowledged part of Janssens's calculus. He believed separate churches would be sufficient to stem the seeming exodus. His opponents believed just the opposite: "If the Catholic authorities desire to lose their communicants among the colored population of this city, the surest and most direct way to it is the organization of separate church edifices."[50]

When representatives of the Citizens Committee failed to convince Janssens to abandon the project three months before its opening, the committee called for a full meeting of all its members to consider further action. The committee noted that Janssens continued to press for the separate parish "in total disregard of timely warnings, and proper complaints

on the part of *The Daily Crusader*, an authorized organ of the people."
The committee passed a resolution calling on black Catholics to "show
their disapproval of the same by abstaining from the dedication services
and from any subsequent frequenting of said church." Desdunes also encouraged a public denunciation of Drexel's gift of funds to open St. Katherine's.[51] Previously, prominent Creole philanthropists Thomy Lafon
and Aristide Mary had created their own boycott by refusing to donate
funds for the separate parish, even though both had given generously to
support other Catholic projects such as orphan asylums and the Indigent
Orphan School.

The persistent opposition sowed seeds of doubt that betrayed Janssens's
public expressions of confidence. In private correspondence, Janssens conceded that his plan for a separate church "may prove a failure" because of
the "lack of interest on the part of the colored people." The priest overseeing renovations for St. Katherine's confessed similar doubts in a letter
to Drexel's attorney who coordinated the financial arrangements. "The
formation of 'a congregation or parish for the Colored people of New
Orleans' may be an impossibility," the priest admitted, "owing to the opposition of the Colored people themselves." The same priest nonetheless recommended proceeding with the project, since the influence of the protests
would not be known until the church opened.[52] The protesters' effectiveness remained a point of contention between black Catholics and white
church leaders well after St. Katherine's opened. But the ongoing debates
testified that the protesters made an impact.

Black Catholics matched Janssens's intransigence. Their efforts limited
the success of the new racial parish, Janssens's triumphant claims to the
contrary. Most black Catholics chose not to attend St. Katherine's. While
Janssens boasted of a packed congregation at the opening mass, many
more refused to participate. Women, whose support would be necessary
to Janssens's success, joined the boycott of the opening of St. Katherine's.
One black woman praised "the young ladies who declined to add humiliation and shame to the burden their people already carry in refusing to join
the Jim Crow choir or take part in this masquerade of the Fatherhood of
God and the brotherhood of man." Most black Catholics continued to
avoid St. Katherine's in its first months and years. The separate church
attracted neither existing black Catholics nor new converts. Over its first
five years, only thirteen adults received baptism at St. Katherine's, falling
well short of the rush of conversions Janssens anticipated. Black Catholics
also failed to support the new church financially. Most preferred to remain
in their previous parishes, even at the cost of enduring discrimination.
Even those who lived near St. Katherine's remained a part of St. Joseph
Church, as ongoing pastoral visits to African Americans in the parish visi-
tation register make clear. Not until the end of the first decade of the

twentieth century did St. Katherine's attract enough parishioners to warrant an assistant pastor.[53]

Black Catholic resistance to St. Katherine's dealt a serious blow to the growth of segregated parishes in New Orleans. Early opposition prevented Janssens from obtaining a religious order that would dedicate itself solely to black work. St. Katherine's ongoing struggles stymied efforts to recruit a dedicated order to start another black parish. Potential financial donors were likewise hesitant to contribute to what they considered a questionable undertaking, Janssens's enthusiasm aside. Continuing resistance undermined Janssens's dream of a separate parish for French-speaking black Catholics. It also brought his plan for segregated churches throughout the city to an abrupt halt. No new black parishes opened in New Orleans for fourteen years. A full two decades passed before a separate church opened downtown, where Janssens had hoped to start his second black parish shortly after opening St. Katherine's. Janssens's efforts coincided with the height of black resistance in New Orleans to all forms of segregation. Only a few years later, with the Citizens Committee disbanded and the *Crusader* no longer in circulation after the loss in the Plessy case, the outcome might have been different. But in the early 1890s, the Citizen's Committee and the *Crusader* were at their strongest in the fight against segregation. At the very moment Janssens tried to introduce segregation into the Catholic Church, black Catholics could and did create a successful opposition.

THE LESSONS OF ST. KATHERINE'S were not lost on Janssens's successor, Louis Placide Chapelle. During his episcopal tenure (1898–1905), Chapelle played a crucial role in delaying the further spread of separate parishes in the years following the opening of St. Katherine's. Numerous factors contributed to Chapelle's reversion to the pattern of ignoring the Crescent City's black Catholics. The French-born Chapelle, like the Frenchmen who preceded Janssens, advocated a conservative understanding of the church. Chapelle's appointment to New Orleans came at the height of the Americanist controversy, and he was therefore reluctant to advance any project, including black parishes, that might suggest liberal sympathies. Chapelle's conservative credentials were underscored by his expressions of gratitude for Pope Leo XIII's apostolic letter condemning Americanism and his appointment as apostolic delegate to Cuba and Puerto Rico. This additional responsibility distracted Chapelle from the needs of his archdiocese, white as well as black. Observers in Louisiana also suggested that racial bigotry was at work. In his previous postings, which included parishes in Baltimore and Washington, and as archbishop of Santa Fe, Chapelle failed to nurture compassion for the plight of black Catholics. His disregard for African Americans was apparently well known. A priest working with black Catholics in rural Louisiana conceded that the archbishop's lack of enthusiasm for this work, as well as his opposition to black priests, was hardly surprising, "knowing Chapelle's views on the negro."[54]

Ongoing black resistance to St. Katherine's discouraged Chapelle from pursuing additional segregated work. Although the city's vocal civil-rights paper, the *Crusader*, had ceased publication by the time of Chapelle's arrival, leading black figures such as Louis Martinet and Rodolphe Desdunes had not changed their opinions about the detrimental influence of separate churches upon both race relations and the truth claims of the Catholic Church. Chapelle also recognized that the city's black Catholics failed to support St. Katherine's to the degree Janssens predicted. During Chapelle's tenure, the number of communions served annually at St. Katherine's increased by a mere hundred, while the number of baptisms and school enrollment remained the same. Most of the city's black Catholics continued to attend their neighborhood parishes rather than traveling to the segregated church. Katharine Drexel, the church's benefactor, reported her disappointment during a visit in 1904, when only seventy-five people attended the Sunday morning Mass. "The Colored prefer to go to Church with the Whites," Drexel recorded in her notebook. Uninterested in expending scarce resources in the face of resistance, Chapelle abandoned Janssens's plan to establish a second separate parish in the downtown and largely French-speaking section of the city. Before his death, Janssens had signed a contract with the Assumptionist Order to found the new separate church and had agreed to assist them in purchasing property on Esplanade Avenue. Shortly after arriving in New Orleans, Chapelle tabled the project indefinitely, claiming it needed additional study.[55]

Chapelle neglected every opportunity to minister to black Catholics in the Archdiocese of New Orleans. The prelate refused to open a single school in New Orleans for African Americans, while the few schools already in existence failed to register significant growth. When the Holy Family Sisters sought permission to begin new schools, Chapelle repeatedly ignored their requests. He made no effort to secure the funding necessary to sustain even the existing work among African Americans, let alone begin new work. Chapelle's lack of appeals to Katharine Drexel stood in stark contrast to Janssens's repeated requests for funds and extensive correspondence with the Philadelphia benefactor. Compared to Janssens's vast narratives, Chapelle made only minimal notations in the annual Reports to the Commission for the Catholic Missions Among the Colored People and Indians. Most years Chapelle did not even complete the commission reports, delegating the responsibility to an assistant. More importantly, while Janssens contended that no sum of money would be sufficient to meet the needs of black Catholics in New Orleans, Chapelle or his delegate generally asked for only four or five thousand dollars, with no additional explanation. Some years, Chapelle failed to submit any report or request for funds. As a result, commission allocations to New Orleans decreased.[56] The neglect recreated earlier patterns, wherein some black Catholics took advantage of the space and remained in mixed parishes. Many others resented the lack of attention. The number of black Catholics attending sacraments and schools continued to decline while Chapelle did nothing to stem the losses.

BLACK CATHOLICS IN EARLY-TWENTIETH-CENTURY New Orleans continued to live in the shadow of the racial struggles of the 1890s. In 1897, Archbishop Janssens had died suddenly while on his way to Europe. That same year, the Citizen's Committee disbanded following the U.S. Supreme Court ruling in *Plessy v. Ferguson*. But the efforts of both shaped the outlook of black New Orleanians well into the first decade of the twentieth century. The supporters of the archbishop and of the Citizens Committee could each look with both pride and concern at the developments in New Orleans Catholicism. The contest surrounding St. Katherine's marked a shaky middle ground in the transformation of racial and religious culture in New Orleans. None could be certain of the ultimate fate of racial segregation in the Catholic Church, given the conflicting interpretations of St. Katherine's success. On the one hand, the Catholic hierarchy had succeeded in extending racial segregation into the sanctuary, which had been the last bastion of Catholic interracial activity. On the other hand, black resistance halted the further spread of segregated churches within the city. In the midst of a seemingly worsening racial situation, the future remained uncertain—and that alone was reason to hope.

CHAPTER 7

Renegotiating Black Catholic Identity

THE 1909 OPENING OF ST. DOMINIC CHURCH marked the beginning of a new era of racially separate parishes in New Orleans. In March of that year, Josephite priest Pierre Lebeau arrived in the uptown Carrollton section of New Orleans to open St. Dominic's, the Crescent City's second exclusively black Catholic parish. The new congregation consisted of African Americans who formerly belonged to the Mater Dolorosa Church, which also included white Catholics of French and German ancestry. Mater Dolorosa had just constructed a larger and more conveniently located building. But it was not for everyone. The Sunday before moving to the new facility, the Mater Dolorosa priest informed the church's black members that they would remain in the old building to form a new parish. St. Dominic's church would be staffed by the Josephite Fathers, an order from Baltimore dedicated to working among African Americans. Money to purchase the old church building came from the Philadelphia philanthropist Katharine Drexel, who provided a $5,000 gift for the down payment, just as she had for New Orleans's first separate black parish in 1895. The need for assistance heightened black parishioners' sense of betrayal. They complained to their new pastor that "they contributed for the new church and if they knew of the change they would have kept their money for their church." A few weeks later the already shocked parishioners suffered another setback. Archbishop James Blenk denied permission for Father John Plantevigne, one of the nation's few black Catholic priests and a Louisiana native, to lead the opening mission intended to generate enthusiasm for the new church.[1]

Parish life would never be the same for black Catholics in New Orleans. Despite its troubled opening, St. Dominic's was soon flourishing, evidenced by large attendance at Sunday Mass, a successful parish school, and impressive numbers of annual first communions, confirmations, and conversions.[2] The immediate success of St. Dominic's formed a striking contrast to the ongoing struggles of St. Katherine's, the city's first black parish. The future of church segregation had remained uncertain as St. Katherine's struggled in the years following its opening. Despite the late Archbishop Janssens's plan to rapidly expand the number of separate churches after erecting St. Katherine's in 1895, nearly fifteen years had elapsed before a second finally began. The formation of St. Dominic's, on the other hand, heralded an onslaught of new separate black parishes. Gone was any doubt about the future of segregation, as six additional black parishes began in the decade after St. Dominic's opened. Between 1910 and 1920, white Catholics in New Orleans implemented their conviction that separation would resolve the "Negro problem," both within the church and beyond.

THE LULL BETWEEN ST. KATHERINE'S IN 1895 and St. Dominic's in 1909 affected the city's black Catholics in contradictory ways. On a symbolic level, the plans for a segregated archdiocese came to a halt. On a practical level, however, the context and consequences of the status quo were more problematic. The seeming stasis was a product of widespread neglect of archdiocesan needs, just as it had been under the postbellum French archbishops who preceded Francis Janssens. It was not grounded in any planned or intended opposition to segregation. That same silence enabled increased oppression of the city's black Catholics. Church leaders ignored the discrimination Catholics of color endured in their neighborhood parishes. Schools suffered as well. Under Archbishop Chapelle (1897–1905), the Archdiocese of New Orleans also neglected its relationship with the two major sources of support for black Catholic schools, the Negro and Indian Commission, and Katharine Drexel, a philanthropist and the founder and superior of the Sisters of the Blessed Sacrament. Chapelle's failure to secure funding for schools occurred at the same time the public schools restricted black education past the fifth grade and ignored overcrowding and damaged facilities.[3] White lay leaders also contributed to declining educational opportunities as they decreased funding for black Catholic schools. In some cases, parishes closed their school for black children to preserve resources for the white children's school. Meanwhile, both parochial and public educational opportunities for whites expanded. The Catholic Church in New Orleans contributed to the widening gap between the races, even as church structures appeared unchanged.

White Catholics took advantage of the laissez-faire management to marginalize black church members. Most parishes completed the move to segregated seating by the first decade of the twentieth century. The large numbers of black Catholics in New Orleans meant that many priests originally needed to provide equal numbers of pews for black and white worshipers. Most reduced the number of pews for black Catholics as white animosity increased. While the priest at Mater Dolorosa told Pierre Lebeau he kept twelve pews for black parishioners, Lebeau's investigation produced a different conclusion: "The people say they had only two." Already nearly universal in uptown English-speaking churches, segregated seating also made its way into the more traditionally interracial downtown congregations. Among the most dramatic changes were those at St. Louis Cathedral.

By the turn of the century, the same church that had once amazed visitors with different races kneeling side by side, forced black worshipers to sit on a "long board" installed along the side and rear walls.[4]

Divisions inside the church reinforced hardening racial lines throughout New Orleans and the South. The 1896 *Plessy v. Ferguson* U.S. Supreme Court verdict upholding the doctrine of "separate but equal" unleashed a torrent of segregation statutes that affected every aspect of southern life. Louisiana had proceeded with its implementation of Jim Crow, segregating virtually every public space and form of transportation, including New Orleans streetcars in 1902. The 1898 state constitution disfranchised most of Louisiana's black voters. The Robert Charles race riot in the summer of 1900 further accentuated racial divisions and signaled a new wave of white vigilante justice that accompanied the hardening of Jim Crow practices. At the national level, a new national unity that excluded African Americans replaced lingering Civil War animosities. Military celebrations brought together white veterans from the nation's wars while ignoring the contributions of black troops. The exclusion was particularly offensive to the black community in New Orleans, where black troops had made contributions in the War of 1812 and the Civil War, as well as the more recent Spanish-American conflicts in Cuba and the Philippines.[5]

The rising racial tensions in New Orleans led early-twentieth-century prelates to reconsider the possibility of segregated parishes. They recognized that white Catholics were no more tolerant of racial equality than were whites in any other New Orleans institution. Many black Catholics were leaving the church in response to their marginalization, and dilapidated or nonexistent parish schools for black children made it difficult to keep the rising generation in the church. The proliferation of Protestant schools compounded Catholic educational problems. The three Protestant universities in New Orleans attracted black students because of a lack of Catholic alternatives, sometimes leading to the conversion of entire families. Catholic leaders turned to racially segregated parishes, which became the widely accepted solution for ministering to black Catholics. In the Crescent City, the expansion of separate parishes played a central role in the tenures of both Archbishop James H. Blenk and his successor, John William Shaw.

Archbishops Blenk and Shaw marked the appearance of a new American leadership for the Catholic Church in New Orleans. This native identification ensured that segregation emerged as both men's answer to the growing racial tensions. Blenk's commitment to Catholicism stemmed from his conversion from Protestantism at the age of thirteen, which also fueled his agitation about losing Catholic children to Protestant ranks. A member of the Marist order, Blenk served as a professor and then president of Jefferson College in Louisiana, as a parish priest in the Algiers section of New

Orleans, and as bishop of Puerto Rico, prior to his elevation to the see of New Orleans in 1906. Although born in Bavaria, Blenk moved with his parents to New Orleans as a child. He considered himself, and was looked upon by others, as a native Southerner. His views on race testified to his thorough assimilation of southern ways of thinking, which emphasized appeasing whites concerns regardless of the consequences for black church members. Blenk had long-standing ties to racial separatism. The Marists had taken over Jefferson College, where Blenk taught and was later vice president and president, to prevent its use to educate freed slaves. Blenk had conducted his parish missions on a segregated basis while serving as a priest in New Orleans in the late 1890s.[6] Three years after his episcopal appointment to the Crescent City, Blenk presided over the 1909 opening of the racially separate St. Dominic's. He remained archbishop until his death in 1917.

John William Shaw succeeded Blenk as archbishop of New Orleans in 1918. Shaw was a true southern native, born and reared in Mobile, Alabama, in the aftermath of the Civil War. After education and ordination in Ireland and Rome, Shaw returned to Mobile as a parish priest. He moved quickly through the ranks of the diocese of Mobile prior to his appointment as bishop of San Antonio, Texas, in 1910. Thoroughly imbued with southern racial views, Shaw vigorously continued the program of separate parishes begun under Blenk. Shaw, who served until his death in 1934, also continued Blenk's efforts to consolidate control of the archdiocese's affairs under the authority of the archbishop.[7] Together, the two archbishops signaled a dramatic shift from their predecessors in their treatment of black Catholics. The expansion of separate parishes formed the primary measure of that transformation.

Like their white counterparts within and beyond the church, Blenk and Shaw turned to segregation as the answer to the "Negro problem." That the problem originated with whites rather than blacks seemed not to have occurred to these or any other white leaders. Racial prejudice did not distinguish this new breed of southern archbishop. What differentiated Blenk and Shaw from earlier prelates were their efforts to provide a parish life for black Catholics. Blenk claimed that care for black Catholics was "a burden that was weighing very heavily upon me" and emphasized his hope "in due course of time to make provision for all my people and give them all a chance to save their immortal souls." Blenk began by reestablishing the lines of support his predecessor had severed, especially with Katharine Drexel. He also supported the Holy Family Sisters' efforts to establish additional educational facilities and encouraged financial support for their undertakings. Still, separate churches were the most important part of Blenk's, no less than Shaw's, efforts. Both men insisted their advocacy of separate parishes stemmed from a hope to include, rather than a desire to exclude, Catholics of color. Given the pervasive racial tensions, Blenk confided to Katharine Drexel, "I am convinced that with tact and the necessary caution the racial feelings and natural differences can be best adjusted by having separate churches in the South for white and Colored races." [8]

Blenk's assertion came only days after he opened St. Dominic's, which set in motion a new tide of religious segregation that would reach its peak a decade later. In dedicating the new separate parish, Blenk pointed to St. Katherine's as the model for black churches. Crescent City Catholics have likewise ascribed to St. Katherine's the title of "Mother of the city's black Catholic parishes." Yet New Orleans's second separate parish was not a direct offspring of the first. Although Blenk claimed the success of St. Katherine's motivated him to establish St. Dominic's, its predecessor evidenced little enthusiasm for separate parishes. On the eve of St. Dominic's opening, Josephite priest Pierre Lebeau added his voice to a decade of dismal observations: "St. Katherine's is not so well attended" as its pastor claimed. As a result, St. Dominic's reflected strategic changes for erecting separate parishes. St. Dominic's arose in an altered racial and religious climate from the opening of St. Katherine's nearly fifteen years earlier. The different strategies and context resulted in a parish that flourished almost immediately. It, more than St. Katherine's, became the model upon which the archdiocese erected six additional separate parishes between 1915 and 1920.[9]

St. Dominic's founders did follow the pattern established by St. Katherine's in one important way: using buildings abandoned by white Catholics. Church leaders repeatedly utilized this strategy in opening separate parishes in New Orleans. The decision to begin a church for black Catholics frequently coincided with the decision of a white congregation to build a new church facility. The construction of a new St. Joseph's church building had provided the impetus for Janssens to renovate the old facility to create St. Katherine's. Similarly, the priest at Mater Dolorosa had proposed in 1909 that the Josephites purchase the decaying and poorly located church buildings his congregation planned to abandon for a prime location and new edifice on Carrollton Avenue. In a twist on the same idea, in 1919, Holy Redeemer purchased an old Presbyterian church that had failed in a largely Creole district in downtown New Orleans.[10]

Using abandoned buildings reinforced the inequality that inevitably accompanied segregation. The disparity between black and white Catholic churches betrayed the hierarchy's claims that separate churches preserved the equality of all Catholics, regardless of color. The new white facilities that excluded blacks were imposing edifices built on prominent city thoroughfares. Black parishes remained on side streets in small and often dilapidated facilities. At the same time, black parishes generally had to pay market value for the abandoned buildings, further subsidizing the construction of new white-only sanctuaries. The dazzling new edifices reminded African Americans of the structural inequality infesting Crescent City Catholicism. On the occasions when Blenk had to construct new buildings for black parishes, he insisted they not have prominent or visible locations. In Thibodaux, south of New Orleans, Blenk agreed to establish a separate black parish only on the condition "that the intended church & school should not be placed on the front street." The decaying buildings into which black Catholics were shepherded bore a striking resemblance to the inferior conditions they encountered daily on segregated streetcars and railroads and in segregated schools, restaurants, and theaters. Pierre Lebeau, St. Dominic's priest, acknowledged that "the whites around here don't care much for us," forcing him to appeal to outside agencies to keep his church and school operational. In 1914, Lebeau pleaded for five hundred dollars for modern toilets and sewage when city authorities threatened to cite him for the church's inadequate facilities.[11] The following year a hurricane destroyed St. Dominic's, while a few blocks away the new Mater Dolorosa escaped unscathed.

Segregating black Catholics into deserted facilities was not without its occasional poetic justice. Bigger and newer was not always better. St. Joseph Church, whose old sanctuary had become St. Katherine's, had to dismantle its bell towers because their excessive weight threatened to collapse the ceiling. Other times the ironies took longer to emerge. St. Ann's moved to ensure its survival, abandoning a building in an increasingly black neighborhood for a large new complex on a prominent street centrally located to its white parishioners. By the 1970s, St. Ann's had closed while St. Peter Claver, the black parish that had purchased the old sanctuary, had survived and was also using the facilities at St. Ann's for community work. Elsewhere, using existing buildings undermined the goal of racial separation. Abandoned buildings converted to black parishes were not always located in predominantly black neighborhoods, especially when the desire for bigger facilities or a more prominent location, rather than changing residential demographics, motivated a congregation's move. St. Dominic's, for example, was in a predominantly white neighborhood at some distance from most of its black parishioners. The same was true for the downtown Holy Redeemer congregation, where, its priest lamented, "one of the disadvantages is that the people concerned live mostly in one end of the parish, white people and big business flanking the church." Those attending the separate black parishes ensured that the surrounding white residents would be confronted with a regular influx of Catholics of color into "their" neighborhoods. Many Catholics of color simply continued to attend the more convenient and predominantly white parishes. Either way, the result fell short of the segregationist ideal.[12]

Regardless of location, Josephites staffed nearly all of New Orleans's black parishes. The opening of St. Dominic's began the long relationship between the Josephites and black Catholics in New Orleans. St. Joseph's Society of the Sacred Heart, commonly called the Josephites, ministered exclusively to African Americans, unlike the Vincentian order serving St. Katherine's. Archbishop Janssens had been unable to secure an order that would restrict its work to the city's black Catholics when he opened St. Katherine's in 1895. This difficulty constituted yet another unacknowledged failure accompanying the city's first black parish. In accepting the Vincentian offer, Janssens used an order that also served the nearby white St. Joseph parish from which St. Katherine's emerged, and to whom the priests at St. Katherine's remained subject until 1920. In contrast, each Josephite, regardless of his place or type of ministry, made a vow never to "take up any other work which might cause me to abandon, or in any way neglect the special care of the Negroes." Even before their arrival in New Orleans, the Josephites decided to work exclusively in racially separate institutions as the best means to maintain their vows of service to African Americans. The availability and enthusiasm of the Josephites, who were not yet firmly established when Janssens arrived in New Orleans, provided a crucial element enabling the rapid expansion of separate parishes in the early twentieth century. Largely at the urging of Pierre LeBeau, the Louisiana native who opened St. Dominic's, the Josephites made the preservation of the Catholic faith among black Louisianians a priority. In the Josephites, Blenk and, later, Shaw found the means to implement their vision of a segregated Catholicism. Nor were they alone. Nationwide, the Josephites would serve a majority of the nation's separate black parishes. New Orleans was typical, where Josephites served six of the seven separate churches erected between 1909 and 1920. Holy Ghost parish formed the one exception. Begun in 1915, it was staffed by the Holy Ghost Fathers, a German order also dedicated to service among African Americans. Outside of New Orleans, most non-Josephite black parishes were served by the Holy Ghost Fathers, the Society of the Divine Word, or the Society for African Missions.[13]

Women religious served with the same restrictions. Only orders that worked exclusively among the city's Catholics of color could teach in black Catholic schools. At St. Dominic's, the Sisters of the Holy Family staffed the parish school. As the Josephites founded additional parishes and schools, they relied upon either the Sisters of the Holy Family or the Sisters of the Blessed Sacrament for teachers. New Orleans's social and racial climate limited the Sisters of the Holy Family, who were women of color, to working among members of their own race. Though white, the Sisters of the Blessed Sacrament, which was the order founded by Katharine Drexel, took vows restricting their work to African or Native Americans. Drexel required that the institutions she supported with funds or teachers be exclusively for the communities the Sisters of the Blessed Sacrament were dedicated to serving. She structured her contracts so that failure to adhere to these requirements would result in the forfeiture of funds and the departure of her order.[14]

The Josephites, Sisters of the Blessed Sacrament, and other orders working in separate parishes contributed to the segregated and inferior position of the black church members that were the focus of their ministries. This reliance on outside resources revealed both the separateness and the inequality of black Catholics in New Orleans. Using missionary orders to minister among African Americans implied the inferiority of black Catholics who needed this additional assistance relative to their white counterparts. This differentiation paralleled black M. E. churches and schools, which continued under the supervision of the Freedmen's Aid Society well into the twentieth century. Reliance on separate orders kept not only black and white Catholics separate but also those who ministered to them. The arrival of the Josephites and women's teaching orders signaled to other priests and nuns that they no longer needed to be concerned with black Catholics. The priest at Mater Dolorosa, whose black members had become the new St. Dominic Church, admitted relief at the arrival of the Josephites since he and his fellow priests "never knew how to handle the colored."[15] The individual priests and nuns who came to New Orleans often did so at great personal sacrifice and in a genuine desire to minister to a community they believed the church improperly neglected. However, they carried out their work in a way that strengthened rather than challenged the prevailing racial separation. The new flurry of work that began with St. Dominic's in 1909 brought increased resources and opportunities to many black Catholics in New Orleans, but did so in a manner that only furthered the distance between black and white. Southern racial relations constrained Catholic work among African Americans, even though Catholics belonged to a church whose worldwide reach made it more universal and more diverse than any other Christian tradition.

John Plantevigne's exclusion from the opening mission at St. Dominic's captured the marginalization and racism that undergirded the wave of new black parishes. Even separate churches could not shelter black Catholics from the prevailing prejudice in their church and city. Plantevigne, a Creole of color who grew up in Point Coupee Parish, upriver from New Orleans, became in 1907 the third man of color ordained by the Josephites, and only the eighth African-American priest in the United States. Shortly after his ordination, Plantevigne returned to Louisiana, saying his first Mass at St. Katherine's in New Orleans, then proceeding to say Mass in the church of his childhood in Chenel. After returning to the Josephite house in Baltimore, Plantevigne's superiors assigned him to a mission band that traveled to the South in 1908. The missioners had planned to give a two-week mis-

Figure 7.1. John J. Plantevigne (1871–1913). Courtesy Josephite Archive.

sion as part of the opening festivities at St. Dominic's in March 1909. The mission held great significance since Plantevigne would be engaged in extensive preaching and conversion work and not merely limited to saying Mass as he had during his trip to Louisiana two years earlier.[16]

But Plantevigne's hopes were dashed before they could be realized. Archbishop Blenk denied Plantevigne permission to come to New Orleans and participate in the mission. Plantevigne responded that "death would have been more welcome than such news." Blenk feared that a black priest might upset the city's white residents, hence his request that Plantevigne not come to New Orleans. While claiming to have in mind the best interests of "the dear Colored people of the parish of St. Dominic," the archbishop also informed Plantevigne that black Catholic interests must be advanced only by the "most prudent means." Testifying to the hardening racial climate in New Orleans, Blenk expressed his concern about "overzeal" and "any action that might stir up prejudices and suspicions" and thereby endanger the work among the city's black Catholics.[17] In the archbishop's calculus, white racial anxieties took precedence over the religious benefits that might accrue to black Catholics.

Plantevigne's vigorous defense did little to change Blenk's mind. He tried to reason with Blenk, hoping the prelate's objections were merely a failure to understand Plantevigne's success as a missionary priest elsewhere in the South. From Baltimore to Mobile, Plantevigne argued, he had "met with no objection from neither bishops, priests nor laymen white or colored." "Surely New Orleans," Plantevigne continued, "a city where there are so many Catholics ought not be the exception." He warned that his rejection would do "untold harm to the cause of the Catholic Church among my people." Many black Catholics in Louisiana were already suspicious of the church's attitude toward them and troubled by their treatment in mixed congregations. Preventing a black priest from working among his own people would do little to reassure them. Plantevigne had written proudly to friends and relatives in the Crescent City that he would participate in the mission at St. Dominic's. He recounted to Blenk that prior to his leaving for Baltimore to study for the priesthood, "those who were against the Catholic Church predicted just such obstacles." He warned that Protestants would gain ammunition to win converts as word spread that Blenk practiced the very discriminations they predicted, even against a priest from his own diocese.[18]

White Josephite priests agreed with Plantevigne's assessment. His missionary partner feared "the already large crop of Colored Apostates will be considerably augmented" as word leaked out of Plantevigne's absence. And leak it did. In Scranton, Mississippi, a Josephite priest reported an increasing bitterness on the part of black parishioners against the church and its leaders. He feared it would take two generations before the area's black Catholics would trust the white hierarchy.[19] Nonetheless, Blenk remained unapologetic and unconcerned about alienating those whose interests he claimed to have at heart. Plantevigne stayed behind in Mississippi while his fellow white missioners conducted the two-week mission at St. Dominic's. The hierarchy's desire to appease white Catholic sensibilities continued to define black Catholic experience, even after they had been set apart in separate parishes.

The events surrounding his rejection proved too much for Plantevigne. He warned Blenk that because of his rejection "my life has been most miserable and my course changed altogether by your stand." Indeed it had. Soon afterward, he became disillusioned and left mission work in the South. Within four years, at age forty-two, Plantevigne died of the combined effects of tuberculosis and a nervous breakdown. In a final blow, Archbishop Blenk refused to admit the return of Plantevigne's body to New Orleans for burial, fearing it might provoke racial outbursts. The loss was especially painful in the Plantevigne family. A brother, Albert, who was a graduate of Straight University in New Orleans and a Congregationalist minister, had been murdered in 1903 while attempting to open a school for black children near the brothers' hometown.[20]

Plantevigne's exclusion from the St. Dominic's mission struck a fatal blow to hopes for a black priesthood. Blenk's opposition to a temporary missioner paled in comparison with his hostility against a regular parish appointment for a black priest. Only white priests would serve black churches, even though the city's black Protestant congregations enjoyed the benefit of black ministers. Black Catholics suffered abuse from Protestants who questioned the church's racial commitments, just as African Methodists had criticized the M. E. Church for its lack of black bishops. Blenk reasserted his objection to black priests when he rejected the suggestion of the Josephite superior that Plantevigne be appointed to the church in the all-black community of Palmetto, Louisiana. Blenk did allow another black Josephite, John Dorsey, to conduct missions at St. Dominic's in 1910 and 1914. However, when the congregation petitioned in 1916 to have Dorsey replace their deceased pastor, Blenk refused. Southern prelates universally shared Blenk's aversion to black priests. Northern bishops and congregations were equally unlikely to accept a black priest, whose ministry would inevitably include whites.

The Josephite decision to abandon black priestly vocations was partly a reaction to Blenk's actions at St. Dominic's. Shortly thereafter, the Josephites closed the doors of their college and seminary to African Americans. The Holy Ghost Fathers made a similar decision, conceding widespread racial prejudice. Black congregations already enduring the humiliation of segregation were deprived even of the benefit of a black clergy. Within American Protestantism, separate congregations had created a safe space for black ministers, even in biracial denominations such as the M. E. Church. Not so in American Catholicism. Neither repeated calls from Catholics of color nor a renewed Vatican emphasis on fostering native clergy mattered. Whiteness became a requirement for priestly service, even to Catholics of color. Blenk's successor, Archbishop Shaw, was of the same mind. In 1920 he affirmed that while a "colored priesthood" might eventually prove useful, it was not yet an "opportune" time "to make the experiment." Like the rationale for separate parishes, the exclusion of African Americans from the priesthood was not couched in theological language but rather a pragmatic and social framework. Maintaining social order trumped modeling Christian inclusiveness. Over the next generation, few African Americans anywhere would be accepted to study for the priesthood, none would be Josephites, and none would serve in Louisiana.[21]

OTHER CHARACTERISTICS OF ST. DOMINIC's opening also shaped subsequent black Catholic experience in New Orleans. In a pattern that began with St. Dominic's, Archbishop Blenk invoked the full authority of his episcopal office to avoid any publicity surrounding new black parishes. By hiding their plans, Catholic leaders avoided the prolonged public debate that preceded and accompanied the erection of St. Katherine's in 1895. As a result, the creation of St. Dominic's failed to attract the press attention, black or white, that surrounded St. Katherine's. Nor did Blenk make its opening Mass the grand celebration that Janssens insisted upon for the dedication of St. Katherine's.

The strategy of last-minute announcements became the standard in New Orleans. The opening of St. Peter Claver in 1920 followed a model nearly identical to that used to create St. Dominic's a decade earlier. The new church constituted the eighth separate church to open in New Orleans. St. Peter Claver was erected for the black congregants at St. Ann's, whose white members were moving to a newly constructed facility in a more prominent location and in a neighborhood with a greater concentration of whites. However, the Josephite superior coordinating the opening admitted he was "somewhat uneasy" about black reaction to their removal from St. Ann's. The Superior thus asked that the creation of the new parish not be announced to the members of St. Ann's until the Josephite priest for St. Peter Claver was in place and ready to begin work.[22]

The stealthy openings further marginalized the voices of black Catholics. Janssens had engaged in extended conversation with the city's black residents concerning the merits of separate churches, even as he pushed ahead with his program to establish St. Katherine's. Archbishops Blenk and Shaw, in contrast, made no effort to continue that discussion when they started new black churches. The exclusion of black voices paralleled disfranchisement in the political sphere, where African Americans found themselves silenced even on matters concerning their own governance. Janssens listened to the concerns of black Catholics, responding in the press and receiving and conversing with opponents in his own home. Janssens also searched for supporters of St. Katherine's among the city's black Catholics, invoking any hint of encouragement to defend his project. Blenk and Shaw, on the other hand, never acknowledged the views of the city's black Catholics. Blenk wrote Drexel in search of "any suggestion coming from your devoted and experienced dealings with Colored People," but there is no evidence he ever consulted the city's black Catholics on the same topic. While the twentieth-century archbishops willingly heeded the calls of their own priests for more separate churches, protests within the black community went unnoticed or, more likely, ignored. Archbishop Shaw, the native of Mobile, offered his own southern roots as reason enough to proceed without needing to consult with the city's black Catholic population regarding separate parishes: "Needless to say I a Southerner do not believe that the Good Lord ever intended that the races should fraternize to such an extent."[23]

Catholic understandings of the church enabled, or even fostered, Blenk and Shaw's insistence on a process of episcopal fiat that ignored the voices of black parishioners. The preeminent and long-standing model of the church emphasized its institutional characteristics and vested authority and power solely in the clergy and hierarchy. Like prelates around the world, Archbishops Blenk and Shaw worked comfortably within this model of "the church as institution." Combined with the rejection of black priests, this understanding of the church was particularly devastating to black Catholics. Excluding African Americans from the clergy and episcopacy rendered black voices mute, not just inferior. White leaders proceeded to think and act for black Catholics without any compulsion to listen to those on whose behalf they acted. In the absence of those black voices, separate churches, led by white clergy, seemed the obvious solution to their own perceptions of racial animosities. The lack of black clerics in the ranks of power enabled a nearly unstoppable momentum. Only the combination of black priests and a reconception of the church from being an institution to being the mystical body of Christ would reverse the trend.[24]

Beginning with St. Dominic's, black Catholics were simply pushed out of mixed congregations rather than being invited into separate parishes. In the debate prior to the opening of St. Katherine's in 1895, and again at its dedication, Archbishop Janssens emphasized that the new separate parish existed only for the convenience of black Catholics. They were free to attend their traditional parishes, just as Irish, French, and Germans could choose between national parishes and the church closest to their home. Janssens believed that black Catholics would prefer to worship in a separate congregation, and as word of its success spread, most would freely choose to attend a separate parish rather than a predominantly white or mixed one. His intent for a separate church, Janssens assured his critics, was to increase rather than limit the choices of the city's black Catholics.

No similar claim accompanied the opening of St. Dominic's or any subsequent separate parish in New Orleans. Instead the city's white Catholics, from bishop to layperson, engaged in tactics to ensure that black Catholics attended separate churches as soon as they opened. The new wave of separate parishes decreased rather than increased options. Efforts to force black members out ranged from the last-minute announcements that they would not be joining a congregation's move to a new facility, to episodes where white ushers turned black Catholics away because they now had their own separate church. The priests from the departing white congregations and the new separate black churches worked together to ensure the desired division of the races. The newly appointed pastor of St. Peter Claver admitted that "it will be necessary to wean children from schools they attend, and the parents, from the churches they support" in order to separate them from the departing St. Ann's. The pastor focused especially on the children, forming devotional groups among them "with a view to wean them from other churches." The priest at St. Ann's was all too willing to assist by discouraging black attendance at his congregation. Similarly, the rector of the nearby and previously interracial Annunciation parish "told his colored at Masses Sunday to join the Holy Redeemer Church," a separate parish that opened in downtown New Orleans at the end of 1919.[25]

The Catholic hierarchy was equally deliberate in maneuvering black Catholics toward separate parishes. When Corpus Christi opened in 1916, Blenk required that the sacramental records of black parishioners in surrounding churches be transferred to the new separate parish. Since Catholics were encouraged to receive sacraments in their home parish, the archbishop hoped the transfer of records would convince black Catholics to redefine Corpus Christi as their home parish. Beginning with St. Dominic's, Blenk also created territorial boundaries for separate parishes. Specifying boundaries made explicit his desire to redirect black Catholics into segregated churches and eliminate the emphasis on choice that accompanied Janssens's erection of St. Katherine's. With a comprehensive system of territorial racial parishes, Blenk and, later, Shaw concluded that black Catholics would have little reason to attend to the white territorial parishes.[26] Finally, by closing black schools in all but separate black parishes, the hierarchy provided the final push to move many of the city's black Catholics out of the churches of their birth and into the growing ranks of separate parishes. The mythical model of "separate but equal" arose within the church no less than in the secular world.

Blenk and Shaw proceeded to open a total of six separate parishes for black Catholics in New Orleans between 1915 and 1920. The Church of the Blessed Sacrament, the third separate parish in New Orleans, was erected in 1915 in conjunction with the founding of the city's first black Catholic high school, Xavier. Holy Ghost Parish, staffed by priests belonging to the Holy Ghost Fathers, joined Blessed Sacrament and St. Dominic's in the uptown section of New Orleans in 1916. Except for All Saints, which opened in the Algiers neighborhood in 1919, the remaining parishes were all located in the downtown districts and were all staffed by Josephite fathers. They included Corpus Christi, which began in 1916 and quickly became the nation's largest black Catholic Church; Holy Redeemer, which started in an old Presbyterian church in 1919; and St. Peter Claver, which opened in the former St. Ann's building in 1920.

CATHOLIC CONCEPTIONS OF CHURCH AND SOCIETY facilitated the rapid expansion of separate parishes. Segregation appeared consistent with this larger Catholic worldview, although it was neither a logical nor a necessary outcome of it. At a most basic level, white Catholics did not consider racism in general, and segregation more specifically, a moral, doctrinal, theological, or even Catholic concern. The widespread understanding of the church as a "perfect society," which dated to the Middle Ages, stressed the universal church's distance from particular cultures. This model had long discouraged concern for specific social issues embedded in individual societies, among them slavery and race in the United States. Nineteenth-century American Catholic leaders had declined to condemn slavery or secession, bracketing them as political issues that were inappropriate for church involvement. Catholics differed from most antebellum Protestants in this regard, who engaged in detailed biblical and theological debates defending or opposing slavery. The church also maintained its distance from post-Emancipation debates about race relations, dismissing them as social and political matters rather than the purview of religion. This centuries-long tradition of distancing church and society left most Catholics without a theological toolbox for applying church doctrine to specific social concerns. Nonetheless, the corresponding silence of white Methodists makes clear that even a tradition of biblically critiquing social practices did not ensure its application to the challenges of race in America. For white Catholics and white Methodists alike, compartmentalizing segregation and church enabled religious leaders to accept racial divisions without any sense they compromised the integrity of their faith. It also eliminated the need for theological language to justify the rapid expansion of segregated parishes.[27]

Pragmatic rather than religious concerns dominated the arguments for separate parishes. The Catholic emphasis on expediency over theology paralleled the same insistence within M. E. unification negotiations, which took place during the same years that separate parishes in New Orleans so rapidly expanded. Pointing to the suffering and marginalization black Catholics suffered in mixed churches, Archbishops Blenk and Shaw stressed that racially separate churches would provide the greatest opportunity for black involvement in the social aspects of parish life, including schools, sanctuary seating, assisting in worship, and participation and leadership in parish societies and sodalities. The bishops also acknowledged the comfort segregated churches would provide white Catholics. The social standing of the Catholic Church also figured into the calculus supporting racially separate churches. Catholics argued their powerlessness, not to mention their unwillingness, to challenge racial antipathies. As Blenk explained to Katharine Drexel, "race feelings run high here, and racial differences cannot be obliterated." Catholic leaders were also keenly aware of the inferior status of their denomination compared with Protestantism, especially in the South. They were reluctant to advocate social policies that ran counter to the national consensus. By the early twentieth century, Catholics were gaining acceptance within the larger American political culture and did not want to jeopardize the fruits of that long-awaited recognition. The strong alliance between the Catholic Church and the Democratic Party, which was not only the party of segregation in the South but also the party of the Catholic laboring classes in the North, further dampened Catholic opposition to segregation. A new wave of anti-Catholicism in the decade before World War I only raised Catholic anxieties and encouraged adherence to the dominant white propensity toward segregation. Better to accept and work within prevailing customs than once again raise the specter of anti-Americanism that had plagued many nineteenth-century Catholics.[28]

The lack of religious reasoning suggests how strongly church leaders believed their racial views did not contradict church teachings. Archbishop Shaw captured the reinforcing relationship between religious and social views when he declared that "I a Southerner do not believe that the Good Lord ever intended that the races should fraternize." He assumed his preferred social order maintained the theological validity of divine intent. In the prevailing understanding of the church that lasted into the 1940s, Catholics invoked a long tradition of church teaching that affirmed the divinely appointed hierarchical character of both church and society. In 1870, the First Vatican Council asserted that "the church of Christ is not a community of equals in which all the faithful have the same rights. It is a society of unequals."[29] Also pervasive was the belief that racial affinity, in which like attracts like, was the "expression of an underlying truth" of a divinely ordained order. In a circular argument, the seeming instinctiveness of racial prejudice became evidence of its divine origins. Like Protestants, few white Catholics considered any possibility except their superiority to Africans, and all nonwhites for that matter. Within this context, neither Blenk nor Shaw, nor any other southern bishop, asserted the equality of African Americans. The bishop of Savannah went so far as to criticize President Theodore Roosevelt for dining with Booker T. Washington, lamenting the racial equality and respect that such an invitation implied. By not recognizing as natural rights much of what segregation denied black citizens, including voting, Catholic theology even validated aspects of the broader civic and social segregation. Early-twentieth-century bishops vigorously defended these traditional views. They were emboldened by their success in quashing the recent Americanist controversy, whose leaders had challenged these long-standing models of the church and the theological assumptions that undergirded them. The resulting Catholic retrenchment against modernism stifled theological creativity, nowhere more so than in the American context. Not until Pope Pius XII (1939–1958) pushed the church to consider the widest social implications of its teachings and Catholicism shifted to emphasize its members over its institutions, would a theological movement arise to challenge the racism at the root of segregation. And not until 1958 did either the pope or the bishops of the United States explicitly condemn segregation as sinful.[30]

This is not to suggest earlier Catholic leaders were unconcerned about African Americans. They simply focused on effects rather than causes. As they had with slavery, Catholics remained critical of the abuses inflicted on black Americans, condemning the rioting and lynching that pervaded southern society. Mostly, however, their attention to black Catholics focused on spiritual concerns. White leaders distinguished between the effectiveness of the church's mission and the racial composition of its institutions, paralleling arguments of white M. E. church leaders. The focus of the church was the salvation of individual souls, which required a relationship between God and believer mediated by a priest and the sacraments. The larger context in which that mediation took place did not affect the efficacy of the work. Even leaders concerned about racial issues stressed that the church was not accountable for, nor primarily concerned with, the larger social conditions in which it ministered. To those who were critical of the church's seeming inaction against racism, a Josephite responded: "The Church is not responsible for social conditions which exist in the South." Another Josephite completed the implication of such thinking: "This is the South . . . and you and I can't change it." The transformation the church hoped to affect was in the individual believer, not in the social order. Blenk was quick to insist that "*in religious matters*" separate churches offered "the same rights, privileges and blessings." Separate churches did not undermine the salvific role of the church. The church was called to maximize the number of souls it saved within the constraints of the society in which it labored. Archbishops from Janssens in 1888 to Shaw in 1920 all argued that separate parishes expanded the opportunities to minister to Catholics of color, given the white hostility that inhibited priestly effectiveness in racially mixed churches.[31]

Despite this unreceptive context, black Catholics and a few renegade whites invoked explicitly theological arguments to criticize segregated churches, in particular, and racial discrimination more broadly. John Plantevigne, the black priest whom Blenk prohibited from conducting a mission among black Catholics in New Orleans, asserted the equality of black and white and lambasted the inconsistency of segregation with the universal claims of the Catholic Church. A fellow black Josephite, John Dorsey, likewise charged it was Catholicism's "God-given mission to rid the church of race prejudice." Among the lone white voices was John Slattery, onetime superior of the Josephites whose cynicism eventually led him away from Catholicism and Christianity altogether. Despite a typically American condescension and paternalism, Slattery had long criticized the gap between the church's teachings and its treatment of African Americans as "uncatholic" and "sheer dishonesty."[32] The often overlooked theological doctrines black Catholics invoked, foremost among them the universality of the church and the common humanity of all people created in God's image, offered the basis for creating a church that would open the floodgates to an oppressed people seeking such affirmations. Church leaders claimed the inclusion of these lost souls was a priority. But they also concluded the social risks accompanying a radical racial message outweighed the professed desire to increase black membership.

EVEN AS EARLY-TWENTIETH-CENTURY Catholic leaders relied upon long-standing understandings of the church, recent changes within New Orleans, the archdiocese, and the African-American community also enabled the growth and acceptance of the six new separate churches erected between 1915 and 1920. The Americanization of New Orleans culture proved a crucial factor in the growth of separate churches in New Orleans. In the secular arena, Americanization meant the conformity of New Orleans with the linguistic, cultural, and racial views of the rest of the United States. This perspective on race was steadfastly biracial, emphasizing the difference between black and white, the necessity of keeping the races separate, and the lack of any middle ground between the two. The Americanization of New Orleans Catholicism incorporated these same themes, as Catholic leaders in New Orleans brought their region into harmony with Catholic practices throughout the United States. American Catholics had long considered New Orleans Catholicism different from that practiced in the rest of the nation. Its French and Spanish roots, as well as the considerable black Catholic population, distinguished the archdiocese from most of American Catholicism, which traced its roots to colonial English Catholics in Maryland. Beginning with Janssens, and accelerating under Blenk and Shaw, Crescent City archbishops maneuvered New Orleans toward the mainstream of American Catholicism. Consolidating episcopal authority, establishing parochial schools, and implementing racial segregation were the ways New Orleans's Catholic leadership demonstrated the archdiocese's "Americanness." In church no less than society, white leaders created an American national unity with white racial superiority as its linchpin.

Changes in the archdiocesan clergy and leadership fostered the Americanization of New Orleans Catholicism. The two archbishops who oversaw the rapid expansion of separate parishes, Blenk and Shaw, were themselves

American, both having grown up in the South. These prelates advocated a particularly southern perspective on matters of race, typified in Shaw's denial that "the Good Lord ever intended that the races should fraternize." Parish clergy serving in New Orleans were also increasingly American in birth and outlook, in contrast to the predominantly foreign-born clerics of the nineteenth century. The number of American and even Southern-born priests increased especially after 1915, when World War I restricted the ability of European priests to travel to the United States.[33] Whereas the previous generation of European priests had largely opposed Janssens's effort to establish separate churches, the American priests of the early twentieth century were nearly unanimous in supporting the expansion of segregated parishes. The archdiocese further reduced the likelihood of clerical opposition to religious segregation by turning to the American orders of the Josephite Fathers and the Sisters of the Blessed Sacrament to staff its separate churches and schools.

The language Catholic leaders used to reflect on racial issues also marked the Americanization of the Crescent City and its Catholic churches. The common nomenclature of "the race problem" or "the Negro problem" pervaded Blenk and Shaw's descriptions of the challenges of caring for black Catholics. Previous French prelates denied any such problem existed, even when pressed by American or Vatican officials. The urge to respond to the perceived problem indicated a shift from all but Janssens, their only non-French predecessor. Shaw's challenge to "let America see what the Catholic Church can make out of the colored man" articulated a concern for both America and Catholics of color that would have been inconceivable a generation earlier. The admission of a "problem" signaled the emergence of more American modes of thinking and constrained the new leaders to advancing equally American racial solutions. Their agreed-upon response, asserting the homogeneity and inferiority of all people of color, as well as the need to segregate them, marked the acceptance of American over Gallic or Latin American alternatives. Gone were the complex hierarchies of the tripartite racial order that characterized much of the nineteenth century and persisted in many countries to the South. Instead, Catholic and political leaders alike resorted to a simple binary segregation that divided the world into black and white. The shifting ways that New Orleanians understood race stood at the center of the changes taking place in the Crescent City.

By the turn of the century, these Americanizing patterns had reconfigured the divisions among New Orleans's Catholic population. Through much of the previous century, differences in language and cultural heritage, especially French versus American, and Catholic versus Protestant, had been as formidable a division as race. Since the colonial era, "Creole" functioned as the term to distinguish between the two groups, without regard

to race. By the turn of the century, however, white Creoles paid more attention to race than to language and culture. They adopted the biracial classification characteristic of American racial thought as they moved outside
the downtown districts and increasingly interacted with the city's American
residents. White Creoles argued that purity from African blood was a fundamental characteristic of a Creole, a claim that the Louisiana courts upheld. The church concurred with this changing definition, characterizing
as "entirely wrong" the northern assumption "that a Creole has negro
blood." Creoles of color became, in the language and minds of whites, no
different than the African Americans who were descendants of slaves and
lived in the uptown sections of New Orleans. Likewise, the Louisiana legislature, whose anti-miscegenation legislation previously restricted intermarriage between any of three groups—Negroes, free people of color or
coloreds, and whites—collapsed its classification in 1910 to forbid marriage
or concubinage between the two categories of white and black. From disfranchisement to laws that segregated everything from prostitutes to
neighborhoods, white New Orleanians whitewashed a two-centuries-old
Creole identity to create a strict black-wide divide. White Creoles adopted
the typically American "one-drop rule," which precluded any classification
but "black" for a person even suspected of having a single African ancestor.
Differentiation based on status, culture, language, or previous condition
became secondary, and often insignificant.[34]

As a result, Creoles of color lost their unique status and found themselves
lumped together with those they had long looked down upon. In the 1860s,
the animosity between Creoles of color and African Americans was so great
that both groups refused to march side by side in a procession at the
Church of Notre Dame de Bon Secours. Among the city's most prominent
Creoles of color was Rodolphe Desdunes, who was a writer and leader
in the *Crusader*'s challenge to both railroad segregation and the church
segregation at St. Katherine's. During that struggle, Janssens had identified
Creoles of color as a distinct community. Desdunes lamented by 1907 the
evidence of their declining status: "the treatment we receive in the courts
of justice, at the hands of judges, lawyers and police authorities in the presence of our offenders; the slurs and disrespectful epithets showered upon
the race, without regard for sex, age or cause."[35] Nor did Archbishops Blenk
and Shaw acknowledge differences between the city's Creole-of-color and
African-American communities. Adapting the either/or categories of black
and white blinded the whites to diversity within the black community.
These homogenized stereotypes had troubled M. E. church leaders such
as Robert E. Jones as much as Creole leaders like Desdunes. Even those
who could trace their roots through several generations of free people of
color to French or Spanish colonists were now classified as simply "black"
and subject to the same humiliations of segregation as were other often

darker-skinned, less educated, and poorer African Americans. Although Catholicism had long been an important characteristic of Creole culture, the church's increasing emphasis on race signaled that a shared religious identity was incapable of transcending racial differences. The same Catholic church that had once played an important role in recognizing Creole distinctiveness was dismantling that same identity as it erected separate parishes along a strict black/white binary.

The triumph of English over French facilitated the reconfiguration to the typically American and mutually exclusive categories of black and white. The shift toward English had been taking place for well over a generation. Shortly after the opening of St. Katherine's in 1895, an article in the archdiocesan newspaper noted the growing use of English in Louisiana, which it noted was the nation's language as well as the language of instruction in the city's public schools. Most of New Orleans's Catholic churches included at least one English service by the turn of the century. At St. Rose of Lima, which had been a strictly French-speaking congregation, the pastor began offering an English sermon series in 1911 and, by the end of World War I, marked all parish entries in English. The language shift took place among black as well as white residents. As late as 1909, Archbishop Blenk stressed that French "is very much necessary for work among Louisiana Colored Catholics." Three years later, however, a Josephite investigating mission opportunities in the downtown region warned his superior that "the colored here want good english speaking priests." By 1917, the pastor of Corpus Christi, in what had been the heart of French-speaking New Orleans, reported that "the french is almost obsolete and it is no use trying to revive it."[36]

As the city became more uniform in its language, it put greater emphasis on alternate forms of categorization and separation, and especially on that typically American form of division: race. The widespread use of English contributed to the decline of interracial worship and the marginalization of black Catholics in New Orleans. For the city's white Catholics, especially in the downtown parishes, the absence of the French language in the streets and in churches offered one less reason why black and white Catholics in those districts should worship with each other and away from the city's uptown English-speaking residents. The widespread use of English also indicated that national-language parishes were no longer necessary. German, Italian, and Irish parishes had become more racial than national, functioning as means to preserve all-white congregations, especially when African Americans moved into the surrounding neighborhoods. In non-national parishes as well, white Catholics welcomed European immigrants into their churches to bolster their parish's identity as a white church. In a pattern typical throughout American Catholicism, Italians, Irish, and especially Sicilians, all of whom had once been labeled "nonwhite," became "white" and were welcome to sit and worship where black Catholics could not. From Philadelphia to Savannah, alliances with immigrants became a typically American way to harden the color line.[37] As other ethnic groups' assimilation and adoption of English marked their entry into "regular" Catholic churches, black New Orleanians saw their use of English coinciding with their exclusion from these same "regular" Catholic churches, some of which their families had belonged to for generations.

The Archdiocese of New Orleans advanced the project of Americanization as it simultaneously ended national parishes and erected racially segregated Catholic churches. Separate churches and schools had long been the philosophy of the American hierarchy, dating back to the pronouncements of the Third Plenary Council of Baltimore in 1884. In addition, the American church placed greater emphasis on instituting a system of regular territorial parishes throughout the nation's dioceses. New Orleans parishes had long lacked specific boundaries, a problem compounded by the several national parishes, which by definition lacked territorial boundaries. Yet Blenk recognized that white Catholics in New Orleans would oppose a system of regular territorial parishes unless they knew that black and white would not be forced to attend the same churches. Parishioners at Holy Trinity, a downtown German church, resisted becoming a territorial parish out of an unwillingness to share their church with the population of "mostly negroes" that was moving into the blocks surrounding the church. Blenk resolved the conflict by removing black Catholics from the new system of territorial parishes and placing them in a separate territorial system for Catholics of color. The New Orleans archdiocese thereby contributed to the national Catholic project of stressing a common white American identity over ethnic differences. The church, like the nation, maximized racial differences as it minimized ethnicity, ostracizing native-born black members as "other" even as it embraced ethnic newcomers as both white and American.[38]

National-language parishes were a common but problematic example that white Catholics used to justify racially segregated parishes. They, and sometimes black supporters as well, pointed to the abundance of German, Italian, Polish, and other ethnic parishes in cities throughout the United States to argue that separate black parishes were neither unique nor inferior. But the comparison was not apt. Black parishioners were being pushed out of parishes to which they had belonged for generations, while national parishes were the first stop for immigrants newly arrived in the United States. National parishes helped assimilate immigrants into American churches and society, while separate parishes funneled African Americans out of both. While national parishes also functioned to preserve immigrants' cultures, whites had no similar concern in advocating separate black congregations. Distinctively African-American liturgies would not emerge until after Vatican II in the latter twentieth century.[39] Besides cultural concerns, national parishes were primarily a concession to language differences. But black Catholics had no more trouble understanding their parish priest than did their white counterparts. Whereas national parishes were served by a priest of the same nationality, Archbishop Blenk ensured that black churches would not have the benefit of black clergy. By 1920 the continued appeal to the example of national parishes rang hollow. Bishops' commitment to ethnic churches had waned in favor of assimilation, and the Vatican discouraged them in favor of canonical territorial parishes. Nonetheless, the creation of racially separate parishes continued unabated.

The creation of two territorial parish systems both reflected and reinforced the city's emerging biracial order. Each parish system shared the same geography but claimed entirely different constituents. Suddenly there were two Catholic churches serving each neighborhood, one for white parishioners and the other for black. Church leaders divided the city's once-unified Catholicism, creating a parallel, albeit unequal, Catholic world for all whom the church deemed "black." Creole and white neighbors who once attended the same church now attended different churches based on racial identity, as Creoles and European immigrants alike were reduced to the seemingly simple categories of black and white. Gone from the new system was any recognition of the once-distinct place accorded the city's Creoles of color. The unacknowledged irony was that in the name of creating territorial parishes, place of residence became secondary to race in determining congregational affiliation. Efforts to abandon national and ethnic parishes did not result in a true territorial parish system, as the Vatican had called for, but rather a system of racially organized parishes that were only secondarily ordered along a territorial scheme.[40]

Changes in American Catholicism as a whole also accelerated the expansion of segregated parishes in the 1910s. In 1908 the Vatican had reclassified American Catholicism, eliminating its designation a missionary church. With the change came a shift in Vatican supervision, from the Congregation for the Propagation of the Faith to the Consistorial Congregation. The Consistorial Congregation took a new interest in black Catholics in the United States, especially as reports of their neglect and suffering filtered in. The wave of new black churches and schools in the latter half of the decade was partly an answer to Vatican inquiries about American efforts on behalf of black citizens, even though the Vatican had not advocated segregated parishes as the desired response. At the same time, a new interest in coordinating work among black Catholics lent increased support to separate parishes as a nationally consistent response to Vatican concerns. In 1907, the American hierarchy created the Catholic Board for Mission Work Among the Colored People to dispense funding and encourage the creation of new institutions for black Catholics. In reply to a Vatican inquiry, the board's director concluded that Catholics made the greatest gains where black and white worshiped in separate churches. The increasingly national reach of missionary orders such as the Josephites and the Sisters of the Blessed Sacrament further coordinated a national emphasis on segregated churches and schools. Finally, a new pope (Pius X) in 1903 pushed bishops to assert their authority over both clergy and laity. His agenda, which represented the last gasp of the institutional or "perfect society" model of the church, emboldened Archbishops Blenk and Shaw to institute their vision for segregated churches with little concern for any lay opposition that may have emerged.[41]

By 1920, American Catholicism had developed a coherent, if not carefully organized, strategy of segregating black Catholics into separate parishes. The result was an American Catholicism widely segregated from top to bottom, not unlike the M. E. Church of the mid-twentieth century. Wherever there were sufficient numbers, black Catholics were shepherded into separate parishes served by separate orders, in northern as well as southern dioceses. Catholic institutions closed their doors to African Americans, including the Catholic University of America in 1914. Seminaries likewise rejected the possibility of racially mixed student bodies, claiming bishops would no longer send candidates to institutions that welcomed black students. American Catholic leaders looked to New Orleans as a leader in ministry to black Catholics, and its implementation of separate parishes became a model for dioceses as diverse as Cleveland, St. Louis, and Los Angeles. Once exceptional for its racial fluidity and inclusion, New Orleans had become exemplary in its widespread acceptance and advocacy of Catholic segregation.[42]

The pervasive segregation represented the ultimate index of Americanization for Crescent City Catholicism. The pursuit of national unity at the expense of racial unity echoed similar sacrifices made by Protestants. During this very same period, the M. E. Church quest for union with Southern Methodism led it to consider casting off its black members into a separate denomination. It also mirrored a process taking place in the nation at large, which was healing its Civil War divisions through the recreation of an American identity defined in exclusively white terms. As Catholic leaders in New Orleans turned to the models of both the American church hierarchy and the practices of southern society to soothe white racial anxieties, they refused to look beyond or challenge the available patterns. Unwilling to stake out a prophetic role that challenged established practices, the Catholic Church in New Orleans capitulated to the existing paradigm for race relations. Lay members were no better. Typical was the refusal of white Catholic societies to admit representatives of black societies, forcing them to unite with other black Catholics through the Gulf Coast rather than with white coreligionists in New Orleans. Racial divisions became so universal that the language of "white churches" and "colored churches" pervaded both black and white descriptions of the city's religious landscape.[43] The language testified to a racial marginalization that became the basis of white Catholic unity with the rest of American Catholicism and with southern white society more generally.

Changes within New Orleans's black Catholic communities joined with transformations within the church and in the city's white cultures in facilitating the expansion of separate parishes in New Orleans between 1915 and 1920. The same social and political changes that emboldened white Catholics to impose separate parishes, including the 1896 *Plessy v. Ferguson* ruling, disfranchisement, and the spread of Jim Crow legislation, also affected black residents' responses to the rising tide of segregation. The hardening racial distinctions and discrimination that accompanied segregation created mutually reinforcing patterns that furthered the exclusion of black Catholics from the city's churches. The worsening racial climate limited the ability of black New Orleanians to resist discrimination at the same time it enabled white Catholics to assert more forcefully the prevailing white supremacy.

Black Catholics faced greater constrictions on the times and places they could worship as the archdiocese committed to a system of separate churches. White Catholics interpreted the erection of special black parishes as the church's endorsement of the system of segregation that pervaded nearly every other aspect of Crescent City life. Churches not designated "colored churches" increasingly ostracized and rejected Catholics of color. Separate churches provided white Catholics one more excuse to avoid interaction with black citizens. In the neighborhood around St. Dominic's, parish priest Pierre Lebeau confirmed that "the white people don't know or don't want to know the colored people." Originally, most churches implemented separate seating. Following the opening of St. Katherine's, for example, the nearby St. Joseph Church posted a sign reserving the last two pews "for Colored people only." Likewise, the 1909 opening of St. Dominic's prompted a nearby pastor to force his black parishioners to sit in a few rear pews, apparently in the hope they would choose to attend the separate St. Dominic's instead.[44]

By the second decade of the twentieth century, increasing numbers of churches simply turned Catholics of color away. Black parishioners often faced resistance from white priests or lay leaders, who justified their actions by pointing out that special churches had been set aside for black Catholics. One church member complained to Archbishop Shaw that, despite being a member of a congregation for many years, in 1919 he was suddenly prevented from entering by an usher who claimed that Mass "is strictly for white[s] and negroes are not admitted." Church law forbade discrimination and the withholding of sacraments, but the ethos of segregation and the expansion of separate churches emboldened white Catholics to practice such restrictions anyway. A member of St. Dominic's who frequently passed by the white Mater Dolorosa church remembered that "if you stopped in front of the door on the street and it looked like you thought you were coming in, somebody from Mater Dolorosa would come out there and ask you what you want. They didn't allow blacks to go in there at all." Black Catholics throughout the nation reported similar incidents. Typical was the experience of a black teenager in St. Louis, Missouri, who stopped for confession in a white church. The priest obliged, but afterward told him, "Don't come back here to confession any more. Go to your own church!" Most churches decreased the frequency with which they administered the sacrament of baptism for black parents, while others refused to baptize black children altogether. A Josephite priest reported the impact his order's arrival had on black Catholicism in New Orleans: "The white churches seem to be taking our coming as a good excuse to freeze the Colored out."[45] Catholics who had once merely been pushed toward the back were escorted out the door altogether.

At the same time, Jim Crow's economic consequences stifled black Catholics' ability to engage in effective and vocal protests against their marginalization. As late as the 1890s, prominent Creoles of color such as Thomy Lafon and Aristide Mary had funded organizations such as the Citizens Committee and its newspaper, the *Crusader*. Both men and the institutions they supported had been persistent opponents of the 1895 opening of St. Katherine's, the city's first separate parish. Lafon and Mary died by the turn of the century, and pervasive discrimination prevented others from accumulating resources to fund additional efforts. The pattern was typical of cities across the South, where previously influential light-skinned elites experienced a dramatic decline in status and wealth by the early twentieth century. Rare was the individual, or even community, that could afford the costly litigation necessary to challenge white supremacy or support independent newspapers. Not until the 1920s, with the emergence of a local NAACP chapter, a new generation of race activists such as A. P. Tureaud, and a new voice for the black community, the *Louisiana Weekly*, would the black Catholic population in New Orleans once again engage in broad-based organization to advocate for racial equality.[46] The intervening vacuum facilitated archdiocesan efforts to open segregated churches without sustained publicity or organized opposition from the city's black communities.

Changes at the Indigent Orphan School demonstrated the impact of diminished resources on the black community, in general, and on Creoles of color in particular. In 1847, the city's free people of color had enough influence to compel reluctant church officials to begin the school as specified in the bequest of the school's benefactor, Marie Couvent. Couvent's will placed the school in an unusual relationship to the church. She insisted on its administration by an independent board drawn from the black community, leaving only its spiritual supervision under the authority of the church. This provision enabled the city's black residents to maintain control over the school throughout the nineteenth century. In 1884, Archbishop Leray continued the attempt of his predecessor to take over the school from the board to return it to the jurisdiction of the church as a regular parochial school. Led by Rodolphe Desdunes, the board firmly resisted, reorganizing itself and maintaining the central role of people of color as directors, teachers, and administrators. A decade later, with its facilities near ruin, Creole philanthropists Thomy Lafon and Aristide Mary provided funds to rehabilitate the buildings. The school continued its traditional role of recruiting students and faculty from among the elite members of the city's black community.[47]

In 1915 disaster struck. A hurricane destroyed the school's buildings and supplies. The board, one of the city's few independent black organizations, struggled to raise the necessary funds to rebuild the school. It turned first to the black community within New Orleans and then widened its appeal through advertisements in all of the city's newspapers. The effort fell far short. The pressures of Jim Crow reduced the ability of the black community to raise funds to support its institutions, and the board found it necessary to apply for outside help. The reliance on external support marked the school's conformity with the rest of the city's black Catholic churches and schools. The school's board appealed to Katharine Drexel and her Sisters of the Blessed Sacrament for the funds to rebuild. The board worked through Samuel Kelly, a Josephite priest and pastor of the nearby Corpus Christi Church, to negotiate with Drexel, who agreed to provide the two thousand dollars necessary to reopen the school.[48]

The school's board of directors agreed to a number of concessions that revealed the weakened position of black Catholics in New Orleans. Unable to raise the support themselves, and virtually ignored by the city's white Catholics, the board sacrificed much of the school's distinctiveness to ensure its survival. The school that emerged was not a true continuation of the Indigent Orphan School. To receive Drexel's gift, the school that had been run entirely by black educators since before the Civil War had to turn over its administration to the white Sisters of the Blessed Sacrament, who would also provide the teachers for the school. The new school was placed under the supervision of a priest who was white. If the school ever failed to retain a priest as spiritual advisor, it had to return Drexel's donation. Drexel also insisted on a reduction in scope. She insisted on opening with only two classes, allowing for only two grades, or a maximum of four if each teacher agreed to teach a combination class. Additional grades could be added in subsequent years as salaries and teachers became available. Finally, Drexel insisted that the name be changed to the St. Louis School and that the school be officially associated with Holy Redeemer church when the parish was erected in 1919. The board, whose chair had been the business manager of the *Crusader* that had so eloquently protested Drexel's role in supporting the city's first separate black parish, agreed unanimously to all of Drexel's terms. They further promised to rely upon Drexel or her designated representative in determining the direction of the school and its work. The once-esteemed Indigent Orphan School had become little more than the elementary parochial school of the city's sixth separate black parish.[49]

MANY BLACK CATHOLICS IN NEW ORLEANS came to support the new segregated parishes, despite the troubling logic and methods white leaders used in creating them. As late as 1915, most of the city's black Catholics still attended mixed churches rather than either of the exclusive congregations. By 1920, the inverse was true, when a vast majority of the city's Catholics claimed separate churches as their home parishes. Most of this growth occurred downtown, where three separate parishes opened between 1916 and 1920. These downtown districts had been the center of protest against the city's first separate church and were home to many who traced their ancestry to the city's elite free people of color. Yet these same neighborhoods swelled the rolls of separate parishes by 1920. Corpus Christi, for instance, quickly became the largest black Catholic Church in the nation. Over the next generation, Corpus Christi gave rise to six additional separate congregations within its original boundaries. Even at St. Katherine's, the pastor reported that by 1919, "pews that once went empty are now filled: people that never came here are coming now."[50]

Catholics of color who sought any semblance of spiritual life had little choice but to join racially separate churches, given the eroding racial climate in both the church and the city of New Orleans. With whites turning them away at every door and the sacraments withheld despite canon law, the freedom from humiliation proved a compelling reason to retreat to a separate parish. Acceptance of separate Catholic churches reflected a larger pattern in which black Americans formed racially separate associations, from social to educational and professional, to provide opportunities otherwise unavailable and to protect themselves from the abuse and even physical danger of interracial contact. M. E. church members had reached the same conclusion, agreeing to a racially separate jurisdiction during the very same years that black Catholics poured into separate parishes in New Orleans. Both black Catholics and their M. E. counterparts remained fundamentally opposed to race distinctions. But the divisions in society, and now in religion, gave them few options. In separate churches, black Catholics found a ready welcome and participated in the life of the congregation as equal members. No longer would they have to sit in the back, wait until

Figure 7.2. First communion at Corpus Christi Church, June 2, 1918. Corpus Christi, a Creole parish in downtown New Orleans staffed by the Josephites, began in 1916. First communions and other important ceremonies were held outside until a new, larger sanctuary opened in 1920. Courtesy Arthur P. Bedou Photographs, Xavier University Archives and Special Collections, New Orleans.

whites had received the sacrament, or risk being turned away altogether. Nor would they be excluded from the ranks of altar boys, choirs, ushers, or parish societies. The 1922 request of the Colored Christian Doctrine Society of St. Louis Cathedral to transfer to the racially separate parish of St. Peter Claver signaled how widely accepted segregated parishes had become. The society had been a part of the cathedral for nearly a century and had long been hailed by black and white Catholics alike as a testament to the unique racial character of New Orleans Catholicism. By the 1920s, this historic organization preferred the safety of a separate church to its constant humiliation in a predominantly white congregation.[51]

A new wave of antagonism against Catholics of color pushed them to reconsider the advantages of separate churches. In 1915, uptown white residents submitted a petition to the city council opposing the use of the old Southern University building as a school "for Negro educational purposes." The Sisters of the Blessed Sacrament had hoped to purchase the uptown building to begin Xavier, the city's first black Catholic high school.

Although the council rejected the petition, the white neighbors' ability to complicate and delay the purchase of the building forced Drexel to think twice before finally agreeing to establish Xavier in that location. In the same neighborhood a few years later, whites began attending Mass at the newly constructed Blessed Sacrament church, "saying it is too good for the 'niggers.' " Black church members did not oppose worshiping with whites, who sometimes occupied as many as one-quarter of the church's seats. What annoyed them, as one parishioner explained to Archbishop Shaw, was that "on several occasions our white friends who attend the church that is especially set apart for the colored people, have objected to colored people sitting in the pews with them and have frequently moved from pew to pew to avoid getting next to us, the colored people." The inconsistency of the practice was galling, since at the black Blessed Sacrament church "the white people come and sit any place they wish, notwithstanding that we are screened in nearly all the white Catholic churches in the city." Downtown whites were no more tolerant. As the pastor of Corpus Christi parish searched for a location to open his parochial school in 1918, he discovered "that nobody wanted 'Father Kelly and his little niggers' in their buildings." Even the priests of a white congregation refused to rent an unused building. Kelly had to occupy two abandoned buildings and fix them up as much as his limited funds allowed. When the Josephites made arrangements in 1919 to purchase an old Presbyterian church to open Holy Redeemer parish, a committee of three whites had gone to the archbishop to express their "opposition to the colored having the place." Others expressed their opposition to the Josephite presence more directly. Holy Redeemer's priest was "the recipient of unwholesome fruit and eggs" in the parish's first year.[52]

As they faced increasing hostility, black Catholics recognized the material as well as spiritual advantages of belonging to separate churches. The archdiocese's reliance on the Josephites and the Sisters of the Blessed Sacrament to fund and staff churches for the city's black Catholics had its benefits. A clergy and sisterhood dedicated to service among the African-American community provided a refreshing contrast to a diocesan clergy who admitted "we do not know how to treat" black Catholics and a white laity that refused to support black missions. Black Catholics also recognized the advantages of not having to depend on the local hierarchy, given its past unwillingness to provide funds or clergy to aid black Catholic interests. The Sisters of the Blessed Sacrament, endowed with the resources of its wealthy founder, Katharine Drexel, provided a particularly promising source of support for future needs. Black Catholics further realized that in the church, as in society, African Americans were more likely to receive benefits from whites when they asked for them in the context of segregation, evidenced by Drexel's generous contributions toward churches and schools set apart exclusively for Catholics of color in New Orleans.[53]

Declining educational opportunities were among the clearest advantages pushing black Catholics toward separate parishes. The lack of integrated educational opportunities and alternatives softened resistance to separatism. Between 1906 and 1916, nine parishes in New Orleans closed their black parochial schools while each of these parishes continued to operate its white school uninterrupted. After 1916 only three mixed parishes operated parochial schools for African-American students, and only in one of those did the number of black students served exceed 20 percent of the number of white students.[54] Black families who remained in predominantly white parishes so that their children might attend the parochial schools endured ever-expanding reminders of their inferior status. For white parishioners, closing existing black parish schools served the dual purpose of encouraging black parishioners to leave the church while also conserving resources to improve the quality of the white parochial school.

Black and white interests converged in the parochial schools of separate parishes. For black Catholic families, the new schools filled the void left by limited educational opportunities in both the public and parochial schools. Only Protestant schools provided an alternative. Parents seeking a Catholic education for their children thus flocked to the schools associated with the new separate churches, and in many cases to the churches as well. Although the schools were segregated institutions, staffed by religious orders dedicated to working exclusively with African Americans, Catholic education in New Orleans had always been segregated. The schools of separate parishes also met the needs of the Catholic hierarchy in New Orleans. Ever since the Third Plenary Council in 1884, American Catholic officials had stressed the need for a parochial school in every parish. Archbishops Blenk and Shaw shared this concern and made the formation of black parochial schools the key to building separate churches. Recognizing the importance of education to African Americans, they first attracted children and families to the schools and then encouraged them to attend the separate churches associated with the schools. While common in black parishes throughout the United States, the pattern inverted the process in immigrant parishes, where the erection of a church nearly always preceded the establishment of a parochial school. For both parents and the hierarchy, black Catholic schools were an important step in stemming the attraction of Protestant schools and the possibility of conversion that accompanied them. The converging interests of Catholic leaders and black Catholic residents produced impressive results. At Corpus Christi, the school had nine hundred children in grades one through six only three years after its opening. Teachers had to turn away over half who wanted to attend, even with "two children sitting in one single seat." Corpus Christi soon became the largest Catholic school in New Orleans, black or white.[55]

The opening of Xavier High School in 1915 increased the attraction of black parochial schools and the churches with which they were associated. Xavier was the first black Catholic high school in New Orleans and was funded and staffed by the Sisters of the Blessed Sacrament for the benefit of black Catholics throughout the city. Parochial schools became an important and even necessary step to prepare students to enter the ninth grade at Xavier, since public schools did not offer black students instruction past the fifth grade. The timing of its opening proved especially propitious, occurring within days of the September 1915 hurricane that destroyed the Indigent Orphan School. Aspiring students swelled the ranks of parochial schools in hopes of attending the new high school. Xavier also eliminated a dilemma for black Catholic families, who had long been torn between the limits of public education and the dangers of sending their children to Protestant schools. The new school provided a meaningful alternative to the Methodist and Congregationalist schools that had been attracting and sometimes converting black students in search of a higher education. Not only did Xavier help preserve the faith, it even became a way to win converts to Catholicism. Nearly one-third of Xavier's students were non-Catholic, resulting in an average of forty conversions each year. The high school quickly filled to capacity, attracting many downtown students despite its uptown location. As students flocked to the new school from across the city, it furthered the mixing and growing sense of shared identity among the city's diverse black populations. In 1929, the school added a college, which remains the nation's only black Catholic university.[56]

Black Catholic loyalty paralleled that of black M. E. church members to their denomination. Like their M. E. counterparts, black Catholics found just enough evidence of concern for their welfare to believe their church offered the best hope for the race. With each expression of concern, most recently manifest in a rash of new schools, Catholics of color hoped their church was moving toward a fuller expression of the inclusiveness at the very root of Catholic identity. That breadth, they hoped, might yet transform the church, the nation, and eventually the world. In the words of one black Catholic activist, they would "cling to the banner of the Lord Jesus Christ," contesting for the integrity of the church by their ongoing presence, rather than compromising Christian integrity by deserting it.[57] Creoles in particular refused to abandon the Church standing at the center of their identity. Rejecting Catholicism would be tantamount to rejecting their Creole heritage. Few were willing to forsake an identity that many could trace back almost two centuries. Despite dramatic transformations in the city's social and religious organization, religious and racial identity were so inextricably wedded that to reject one was to reject the other. Catholicism had been central in recognizing and advocating the rights of free people of color. Their descendants, the Creoles of color, were unwilling to abandon Catholicism even when the church failed to uphold its universal ideal. Creoles would remind the church of its inclusive claims and through their ongoing participation hold it accountable to those standards. In order to retain and assert their identity, Creoles would remain Catholic, even if that meant doing so within separate parishes.

WHILE MANY ACCEPTED SEPARATE CHURCHES as a temporary compromise, others maintained their opposition to racial segregation in their churches. Critical voices continued even as most Catholics of color found their ways into separate churches, schools, and societies by 1920. When Archbishop Blenk denied the black priest John Plantevigne permission to lead the opening mission at St. Dominic's, area residents threatened to berate the prelate's hypocrisy in the public press. Black residents regularly sent protests to the archbishop asking to be included in regular territorial parishes when rumors of a separate parish arose. Even after the erection of six new parishes in five years, black Catholics continued to print articles critical of both the archbishops and of the Josephites for segregating a church that supposedly knew no boundaries. Even parishioners willing to accept separate churches criticized the church's refusal to train and assign black priests to congregations of black Catholics. Both Archbishop Shaw and the Josephite superior in Baltimore reported receiving newspaper clippings critical of their shared agenda of separate parishes. In 1920, Shaw admitted observing "a discontented and rebellious spirit which is gradually manifesting itself among even our colored Catholics." Both men brushed off the attacks as "unwarranted," and Shaw excused them as "the ravings of those misguided and conceited people whose bugaboo is social equality." The Josephite Superior reported "efforts made to harass the work" at the flourishing Corpus Christi ten years after its founding, including an inflammatory article published in a newspaper in Baltimore, where the Josephite headquarters were located.[58]

Even the Indigent Orphan School board, which had relinquished so much of its identity and authority, found in 1920 a last gasp of resistance to archdiocesan authority. Archbishop Shaw was annoyed that the reorganized school still did not conform to the parochial school model. Regular parochial schools stood under the authority of the parish priest and, by extension, the archbishop. The Indigent Orphan School, by contrast, remained under the supervision of an independent board even though it functioned as the parochial school for Holy Redeemer parish. The Sisters of the Blessed Sacrament who staffed and administered the school thus reported, in theory at least, to a lay board rather than the parish priest. That the board supervising these white women consisted entirely of black men no doubt compounded Shaw's anxiety. In the summer of 1920, the archbishop attempted to leverage the school's precarious financial situation to place the school under his supervision. He declined to release a three-hundred-dollar bequest to the school, claiming that the board existed improperly and that Widow Couvent had always intended the school to be under diocesan authority. Shaw offered to release the bequest and obtain additional funding if the board ceded control to him. The board rejected the archbishop's offer and voted unanimously "not to surrender their rights" because they "felt it a duty of their race." Shaw vowed to take no more interest in the school when presented with the board's decision. He kept his word. Two years later he had still not released the bequest.[59]

Black Catholics also protested separate parishes by continuing to worship in the churches to which they and their families had belonged, despite the designation of such churches as "white." Josephite priests expressed frustration that well into the 1920s some black Catholics refused to attend the separate parishes to which they supposedly belonged. Clergy at Holy Redeemer and St. Peter Claver reported that many of their potential parishioners "are still going to neighboring churches." At Holy Redeemer, the priest complained that nearly four years after its opening, "more go to St. Augustine Church and to the cathedral than to my church. They will continue to go there." For some, attending another church was largely a matter of convenience, since the eight separate churches in 1920 were insufficient to provide a local neighborhood congregation for many of the city's black Catholics. In other cases, people remained in the churches to which they had ancestral ties. Black Catholics had belonged to St. Augustine's from its erection in 1841, which they helped finance, and to the cathedral since the colonial era. Black Catholics in these congregations simply refused to heed the church's call for segregation. The pastor of Corpus Christi engaged in a dispute with the Benedictine priest of a nearby congregation over the right of that priest to minister to people who lived nearby yet, because of their skin color, technically fell within the parish limits of Corpus Christi. Many of those refusing to attend Corpus Christi had belonged to the now predominantly white church for thirty to forty years. Nor were these individual acts restricted to downtown parishes. Redemptorist priests uptown noted that several black Catholics regularly attended each of their churches in 1922. Parish reports indicate that black Catholics continued to seek the sacraments in nearly every one of the city's white churches, despite a citywide system of territorial black parishes. Marcus Christian, a black scholar of Louisiana history, reported as late as 1942 that African Americans frequently attended services at "white churches." By that point, white churches did not consider it a problem, "provided they take seats which are especially assigned them in the rear of white parishioners."[60]

Ambiguity in the relationship between black and white parishes enabled black Catholics to continue worshiping in white churches. Canon law prohibited bishops and clergy from requiring black Catholics to attend separate churches. Technically, the obligation to attend Mass could be fulfilled in any church, a fact that some black Catholics in New Orleans used to avoid separate parishes. These individual acts of resistance characterized the most common response to segregation, religious or secular, in the early-twentieth-century South. In most cases, organized mass protest and resistance was both unfeasible and too dangerous. But individual acts could be effective as well. Black Catholic attendance patterns created confusion as to who belonged to which parish. One priest taking a census of his parish realized that both the territorial parish and the separate parish were likely to count the area's black Catholics among their members. Even with a quarter-century history of separate parishes in New Orleans, the priest conceded that it was unclear "what are the relations to exist between myself and the colored Catholics, and between them and the other pastors whose churches are within the limits" of his separate parish.[61] Black Catholics foiled efforts to impose complete segregation in New Orleans when they exercised their freedom to move between black and white parishes. Like the Methodists who offered just enough resistance to forestall their denomination casting them into a separate jurisdiction or denomination, black Catholics injected an ambiguity into racial and religious identities that prevented the implementation of a fixed system of rigidly segregated churches.

Even members of segregated parishes could use that separation to resist their church's and their city's efforts to homogenize black identity. In New Orleans, as in other cities with multiple black churches, particular parishes became associated with different class or color identities. Black parishes in the city's downtown district preserved and even strengthened Creole distinctiveness, even though separate black churches emerged from a white rejection of such differences. Residential patterns dating to the early nineteenth century meant most African Americans lived uptown, while Creoles lived and worshiped in the historically French downtown districts. Several downtown parishes became centers for nurturing Creole identity simply by their geography. In particular, Corpus Christi, and several of the parishes to which it gave birth, became synonymous with Creole identity. Creole children could learn and affirm their distinct identity and cultural practices, while adults used parish affiliation to mark the bounds of that community. Membership in particular parishes became an emblem of Creole identity, whether or not whites acknowledged its significance. No group was more aware of these ongoing differences than uptown African Americans who frequently commented on the insular and aloof world of the downtown Creoles of color.[62] Insulating Creoles in separate parishes strengthened their sense of their identity against a segregation that ignored the unique role they had played in New Orleans's racial milieu. Religion remained central to the constant renegotiations of racial identity in New Orleans.

Catholicism in New Orleans was fundamentally divided along racial lines by 1920, examples of resistance notwithstanding. The pervasiveness of segregated parishes created a striking contrast with both antebellum and postbellum Catholicism, which lacked separate black churches altogether. Catholic churches formed a clear measure of how the recent segregation marked a distinct break with previous racial patterns. The separation only increased. Five more separate parishes opened in New Orleans, bringing the total to thirteen by 1949. The number of racially segregated societies and federations would increase as well, as New Orleans and the South grew more fixed in its practice of Jim Crow within the church and beyond. Similar to the Methodists who had resisted and then capitulated to racial segregation, Catholics in New Orleans turned to race as the central division within their denomination. Black and white Catholics, like their M. E. counterparts, stood more divided by race than united by any common religious affiliation, practice, or heritage. And it was not merely separation, but inferiority. While white Catholics worshiped under priests of their same race and sent their children to financially stable schools, black Catholics struggled under white teachers, priests, and prelates who were often unable to escape their own racial biases. By 1920, the rising tide of Jim Crow had so widened the distance between black and white that no claim to a common religious identity could bridge the gap.

Religion and Baseball in New Orleans

MARCH 10, 1917, "WAS A GREAT DAY FOR XAVIER," exulted John Clarke, a Josephite priest and chaplain of New Orleans's only black Catholic high school. Clarke's enthusiasm stemmed from an exciting victory for Xavier: "Our boys defeated in a grand game of baseball the team from New Orleans University." The day after the victory, Clarke wrote to share the good news with Katharine Drexel, the school's benefactor. With the win over the Congregationalist Straight University the previous week, the victory completed a sweep of the Protestant schools that was "the talk of the city (among the colored)." For the black community in New Orleans, the baseball games were social and communal events, not merely athletic contests. Clarke described to Drexel how "New Orleans University students and their many friends (perhaps 500 in all) were on dress parade." He assured Drexel that "the students from Xavier were not undone."[1]

Defeating the Methodist Episcopal New Orleans University was especially satisfying to the city's black Catholics. At the meeting of the M. E. Louisiana Annual Conference the preceding year, the president of New Orleans University "gave in striking way valuable lessons why New Orleans University should receive the united support of all our people, rather than [Xavier] University, a Roman Catholic institution, which was trying to proselyte our people into Catholicism." At New Orleans University's commencement ceremonies a few months later, the president further fanned the flames of rivalry when he declared, "Xavier was not to be considered at all when it came to Athletics." Xavier's victory suggested otherwise, raising the stature of the Catholic high school throughout the city's black community. "The success," Clarke rejoiced, "means a great deal more than a mere game." It also represented more than the community recognition for either school that so excited Clarke. The athletic contest embodied the very tension between marginalization and expectation that has consistently characterized the African-American religious experience.[2]

The rivalry between Xavier and New Orleans University belied an underlying unity among black members of the M. E. and Catholic churches in New Orleans. Both denominations had traveled a similar trajectory in the four decades since the end of Reconstruction. Black members of both churches had sustained a semblance of interracial churches for the first quarter-century after Emancipation, believing a common religious identity could overcome racial divisions and usher in a new age of racial harmony. Yet starting in the 1890s, both black Catholics and black M. E. church members found themselves increasingly marginalized and ostracized within their denominations. By the time they met on the baseball diamond in 1917, both traditions were segregated. Whether fans sat behind the bench of New Orleans University or Xavier, it was not the world the generation before had envisioned. Black Catholics would have ideally played against, or even with, white Catholics, just as black Methodists would have preferred interracial competitions. The contest between Xavier and New Orleans demonstrated how racial affinity had overcome religious differences, an inversion of earlier hopes that a common religious affiliation could transcend race. Abandoned by white coreligionists, these Catholic and Methodist schools constructed community along racial rather than religious lines. Their churches and their city left them little option.

The baseball game also revealed how changes in Crescent City churches paralleled those taking place in the city as a whole. In the early 1880s, New Orleans hosted contests between black and white baseball teams.[3] By the twentieth century, the Crescent City no longer permitted such encounters. White secular authorities in New Orleans would no more tolerate an interracial athletic event than would the city's white church members. As late as the 1870s, visitors to New Orleans had commented on its extensive racial mixing and relatively liberal racial structure. Throughout the 1880s, Crescent City residents sustained the hope that their city might be the first to vanquish the problems of race. A state that passed the most racially progressive constitution of the Reconstruction era, a city that had experimented with interracial public schools, and a society that had once tolerated, though not always condoned, interracial business and personal relationships, had become committed to a rigid and legally enforceable racial segregation that extended from public accommodations to the bedroom. By 1912, *Southwestern Christian Advocate* editor Robert Jones believed that "the racial relations in the City of New Orleans are perhaps more acute than in any city in the country."[4] The observations marked how dramatically race relations, in practice and not merely in law, had changed between 1880 and 1920.

What was true of New Orleans was true of the nation. This book's narrative of the shift from resistance to capitulation began with the particularity of New Orleans at the end of Reconstruction. This later-nineteenth-century secular and religious opposition to racial separation and inequality in the Crescent City was remarkable, though not unique. Nearly every region of the South had experimented with some degree of interracialism, whether in politics, labor, religion, or any other number of spheres. The regional and contextual distinctiveness of these struggles for racial equality is fundamental to understanding the character of late-nineteenth-century race relations, whether within the church or beyond. These particularities gave way to uniformity by 1920. Difference undoubtedly persisted. But the uniformity and national institutionalization of segregation in the early twentieth century was far more descriptive and striking than the nuances of regional variation. What was true for Methodists or Catholics in New Orleans was true in every denomination and region, not just the South. Separate churches and religious institutions linked black Christians throughout the United States. Black Creoles, for example, remained connected by their participation in separate black parishes throughout the nation, so much so that Creoles emigrating from New Orleans to places as diverse as Cleveland and Los Angeles played a central role in erecting separate black Catholic parishes in those cities. The baseball contest in New Orleans that had so excited the Catholic priest was striking not for its uniqueness but for its typicality.

The shared experiences of black Catholics and black Methodists therefore proved a larger and more dominant reality than any denominational differences and rivalries that appeared to distinguish the two teams on the baseball diamond. The game itself, a segregated event by the expectations of both religious and secular authorities, embodied the marginalization that all black residents experienced in every aspect of their lives, religion included. M. E. church members on one side and Catholics behind the other bench celebrated the victories of their respective teams and remained suspicious of the efforts of rivals schools to win them as converts. Yet the two schools faced each other because different religious affiliations made little difference in the quest for racial equality. African Americans had joined the M. E. and Catholic churches because neither denomination prescribed a particular racial identity, unlike membership in an African Methodist or Black Baptist denomination. But neither the M. E. Church nor the Catholic Church had managed to overcome racial discrimination within their own institutions, let alone transform racial dynamics in society at large. Church members discovered that they would always be known as black Catholics or black Methodists, even within biracial traditions. The inability of the teams to play with or against white members of their own denominations made this abundantly evident. Differences in religious affiliation disappeared before the larger forces of segregation, resulting in the common experience of alienation for Methodists and Catholics alike. While the meaning of racial identities had shifted over time, the inextricable intertwining of religion and race never wavered.

The M. E. and Catholic churches had moved from different starting points to their common embrace of racial segregation. Methodists worked from integrated regional and national jurisdictions, hoping that their influence would extend both upward into the episcopacy and downward into the already racially separate congregations. Catholics, in contrast, started with their uniquely mixed parishes in hopes of integrating the priesthood and hierarchy. But black members of each denomination found themselves fighting a losing battle to sustain what little they had, let alone expanding integration into new areas. They fought different battles but struggled in the same war. White Catholics and white Methodists also approached segregation from opposite sides of the same coin. On one side, Catholics rationalized separate churches as an effort to attract black members and only implicitly acknowledged their role in assuaging white members. On the other side, M. E. leaders advocated racial separation as necessary to succeed among white Southerners. Either way, the segregationists won, as the particularities of each approach spread to represent a uniformly applied religious segregation equal to any efforts in the social and political realms.

Yet churches had not been inconsequential in their struggles against the rising tide of Jim Crow. Black Catholics and black Methodists, and occasionally their white counterparts, had articulated a vision of an interracial church and society and had made concrete efforts to realize that vision. Their petitions and protests delayed the passage of anti-miscegenation legislation in Louisiana and streetcar segregation in New Orleans. In the final decades of the nineteenth century, the interracial Louisiana Annual Conference and interracial worship in Catholic churches countered white supremacists' claims that it was impossible for black and white to interact without incident or degradation to whites. Black commitment to integration in religious institutions also challenged white segregationists who charged that African Americans preferred separation. The ongoing presence of black Catholic or black M. E. church members complicated and countered these arguments of white supremacists. Each time whites pointed to separate African Methodist or Baptist churches as evidence of the black preference for segregation, black members of the M. E. and Catholic churches in New Orleans could offer their own institutions as evidence to the contrary. But the impact was only one of degree, not direction. Church members delayed segregation, but they could not stop it.

Institutionalizing racial segregation in the religious sphere was an important and, in many ways, culminating role in the hegemony of Jim Crow. Given the centrality of religion to southern identity, segregation's reach was not complete until it permeated religious institutions. As the nation's two largest biracial denominations, the M. E. and Catholic churches were a measure of how far religious institutions embraced Jim Crow. When white members and leaders made conscious choices that moved these denominations in the direction of segregation, they implied a moral—and perhaps divine—approval for the larger project of racially separating all of southern society. Here, the church influenced society. But the opposite influence was also crucial. The act of segregating religious institutions was largely a response to processes well under way in the secular order. Separating M. E. annual conferences and Crescent City Catholic parishes was often a decision to ensure that church practices conformed to those already taking place in the social, political, and economic realms. The cause-and-effect relationship between church and society flowed in both directions. Each justified the other. Either way, religion's role further institutionalized segregation, rather than overturning it. The centrality of religion to the southern social order was its very weakness: few whites considered the possibility that churches might take a stand in opposition to the prevailing paradigm. Segregation in church and segregation in society functioned like mirrors that infinitely reflected each other, creating a mutually reinforcing and ultimately indistinguishable pattern between them. Black church members' protests proved insufficient to break open an altogether new view.

In many ways, those watching and playing the baseball game between Xavier and New Orleans University had endured a story full of despair. The despair came as much from lost prospects along the way as from the story's final outcome. The most intriguing analysis of an athletic contest often focuses more on the possibilities that might have been than on the final score. The same holds true for religion and the rise of Jim Crow in New Orleans. Churches, and individuals within those churches, made conscious and deliberate decisions, with clear alternatives, that pushed their churches toward segregation. The M. E. Church chose to remove A.E.P. Albert as editor of the *Southwestern Christian Advocate* and effectively eliminate not only his voice but also the influence of the church from the fight against segregation. Francis Janssens pushed on with his well-intentioned but fatally misguided plan to erect a separate church for New Orleans's black Catholics, despite acknowledging overwhelming opposition from the people he sincerely wanted to benefit. James Blenk effectively ended the hope of a black priesthood for two generations when he rejected the possibility of black priests serving in his archdiocese, even though their presence would have dramatically expanded the number of black parishioners Blenk claimed to desire. The M. E. Church chose first to deny and then to restrict the election of black bishops. These and hundreds of other decisions marked lost moments when the churches consciously chose to go one direction rather than another, preferring conformity with existing patterns when they might have been a prophetic voice against the prevailing racial sentiment and in favor of the religious principles that they claimed to uphold. The methodical and deliberate steps leading to segregation in the religious order, no less than those in social or political spheres, highlight the extent to which Jim Crow represented a change from previous patterns. Its emergence was the product of a long, deliberate, and highly contested chain of decisions.

Yet in the African-American religious experience there were always moments of hope accompanying those of alienation. New Orleans conformed to this American tendency as well. What might appear to be the story of one loss after another on a slow march to defeat does not represent the way that African Americans experienced the story. No one event was the nail in the coffin of integration or hope, no matter how discouraging. For every big loss, there were little gains, from individual acts of white conciliation to formal restraint such as Janssens's insistence that all parishes remained opened to all people, or Jones's election as a general superintendent rather than a missionary bishop. Even the Xavier–New Orleans University baseball game in 1917 revealed the conciliatory place of the churches, despite their acceptance of segregation. Black Methodists and Catholics had preserved spaces where they could safely gather and engage in recreational and social, as well as spiritual, activities. Over a thousand people attended the game between Xavier and New Orleans University, marking it as a large-scale social event in the Crescent City. The two teams also represented the efforts to provide higher education to black church members at a time when the New Orleans public schools had not yet opened a high school for black residents. These and similar religious institutions trained the vast majority of black teachers, doctors, and lawyers, who were both responsible for and evidence of the remarkable educational and economic advancements African Americans had made in the sixty years since Emancipation. Churches still acknowledged the humanity of their black members, even as they failed to admit their equality.

Other developments in New Orleans suggested that the failures of particular churches to challenge racial discrimination did not signal the inability of religion to foster change. As the M. E. and Catholic churches retreated from their earlier rhetoric of inclusion and equality, new groups filled the gap and began building bridges between the city's black and white residents. Women from the Southern Methodist Church, a denomination once extreme in its commitment to racial segregation and exclusion, established ministries for and among the city's black women. These white women did not merely raise money but ventured into black neighborhoods and black homes to provide assistance and education. The racial interaction was intimate, even if paternalistic. Southern Methodist women were also on the forefront of national efforts such as the Commission on Interracial Cooperation.[5] On the one hand, these efforts demonstrated the ironic consequence that once firmly institutionalized, segregation sometimes facilitated previously intolerable racial interaction. On the other hand, the resulting interracial alliances created the cracks that would eventually bring down the wall of legalized segregation. Other religious traditions also made important contributions. Crescent City Jews, among them Ida Weis Friend and Rabbi Max Heller, initiated new interracial efforts in New Orleans, providing a prophetic religious voice where Christian churches had failed. Jews engaged in their work even without the evangelical interest that had motivated earlier Catholic and Methodist efforts among the city's black residents.[6] Popular religion also played a role, as whites admitted an interest in voodoo and visited black practitioners, often for entertainment but sometimes for aid as well.[7] In 1923, the Society of the Divine Word would begin training black candidates for the priesthood in Mississippi, and soon after, new national Catholic interracial organizations would emerge, such as the Federated Colored Catholics and the Catholic Interracial Council. That same decade, in a move Jones believed heralded a new day, an interracial coalition of local and national Protestant leaders facilitated the merger of the M. E. New Orleans and Congregationalist Straight Universities to create Dillard University.[8] Religion retained the possibility of bridging the city's racial divide.

The baseball contest between black Catholics and Methodists in New Orleans illuminated the place of black Christians throughout the United States in the early twentieth century. Out of those widespread shared experiences of alienation and oppression emerged a new wave of racial cooperation. In New Orleans, this unity echoed earlier efforts in the 1890s when black Methodists like A.E.P. Albert turned to fellow black residents to fight segregation, despite religious differences, or when the predominantly Catholic Citizens Committee recruited Protestant ministers to its cause. Once again in the twentieth century, even as church members remained loyal to their particular religious traditions and rivalries, new racial alliances arose that further collapsed previous distinctions. Community organizations such as the NAACP and the Urban League emerged from a consciousness of common experiences and shared needs across denominational lines. And churches continued as an important locus of organization.

In 1879, Octavia Albert, the wife of A.E.P. Albert, recorded the story of Charlotte Brooks, an M. E. church member and former slave living in southern Louisiana. Brooks poignantly articulated the hope and longing that sustained her generation:

> You see, my child, God will take care of his people, said Aunt Charlotte. He will hear us when we cry. . . . We are all free, but we can't stop praying; we must keep on; we ain't out of Egypt yet. We have been let loose, and now we are just marching on to a better land.[9]

Across subsequent generations, black Christians, whether Catholic or Protestant, continued to hold their churches accountable to the message of freedom and equality at the root of their Christian faith. Amid despair, there would again emerge reason to hope, a pattern with which African Americans were long familiar. Within the lifetime of many of the students witnessing Xavier's victory at the 1917 baseball game, a religiously based coalition would burst forth with new vigor in a Civil Rights movement thoroughly grounded in the churches. Religion had failed to transform society by 1920, but it would rise again to turn back the tide of Jim Crow and move African Americans ever closer to the elusive Promised Land.

Abbreviations

AANO	Archives of the Archdiocese of New Orleans, New Orleans, Louisiana
AMA	American Missionary Association
ARC	Amistad Research Center, Tulane University, New Orleans, Louisiana
BCM	Baudier Collection, Manuscripts, Archives of the Archdiocese of New Orleans, New Orleans, Louisiana
BCP	Baudier Collected Papers, Archives of the Archdiocese of New Orleans, New Orleans, Louisiana
DFC-CC	Desdunes Family Collection, "New Orleans *Crusader* Clippings," Xavier University Archives and Special Collections, New Orleans, Louisiana
DU	Archives and Special Collections, Will W. Alexander Library, Dillard University, New Orleans, Louisiana
GCAH	General Commission on Archives and History, United Methodist Church, Drew University, Madison, New Jersey
JFA	Josephite Fathers Archives, Baltimore, Maryland
JGC	*Journal of the General Conference of the Methodist Episcopal Church*
LSU	Special Collections, Hill Memorial Library, Louisiana State University, Baton Rouge, Louisiana
Memorandum for Guste	Roger Baudier, "Memorandum for Rev. Robert Guste: On White and Negro Relationships After War Between the States," August 22, 1956, Baudier Collection, Manuscripts, "White and Negro Relationships," 14-03-4-25, Archives of the Archdiocese of New Orleans, New Orleans, Louisiana
REJP	Robert E. Jones Papers, Amistad Research Center, New Orleans, Louisiana

SBS   Archives of the Sisters of the Blessed Sacrament, Bensalem, Pennsylvania

SQA-RCCM   "Series of Questions to be Answered by Applicants for Aid from the Commission for the Catholic Missions Among the Colored People and the Indians," in *Reports to the Commission for the Catholic Missions Among the Colored People and the Indians*, Josephite Fathers Archives, Baltimore, Maryland; particular years of the reports are noted parenthetically along with the corresponding catalogue number for locating the report within the Josephite Archives

SWCA   *Southwestern Christian Advocate*, New Orleans, Louisiana

UNO   Archives, Manuscripts and Special Collections, Earl K. Long Library, University of New Orleans, New Orleans, Louisiana

XUA   Xavier University Archives and Special Collections, Xavier University, New Orleans, Louisiana

Notes

Introduction

1. E. O. Haven, "No Separate Conferences for Whites," *SWCA*, July 3, 1873.

2. P.B.S. Pinchback, who had been lieutenant governor, served as governor from December 9, 1872, to January 13, 1873. Pinchback was completing the final weeks of the term of impeached Gov. Henry Warmoth. On Pinchback and other black leaders during Reconstruction, see Alice Dunbar-Nelson, "People of Color in Louisiana, Part II," *Journal of Negro History* 2 (January 1917): 75–76; David Rankin, "Origins of Black Leadership in New Orleans During Reconstruction," *Journal of Southern History* 40 (August 1974): 417–40; and Charles Vincent, *Black Legislators in Louisiana During Reconstruction* (Baton Rouge: Louisiana State University Press, 1976). On Reconstruction in Louisiana and the 1868 constitution, see W.E.B. Du Bois, *Black Reconstruction in America, 1860–1880* (1935; reprint, New York: Atheneum, 1993), 451–84; Eric Foner, *Reconstruction: America's Unfinished Revolution, 1863–1877* (New York: Harper and Row, 1988), 45–50, 63–66, 318–22; Joe Gray Taylor, *Louisiana Reconstructed, 1863–1877* (Baton Rouge: Louisiana State University Press, 1974), 151–55; Ted Tunnell, *Crucible of Reconstruction: War, Radicalism and Race in Louisiana, 1862–1877* (Baton Rouge: Louisiana State University Press, 1984), 111–35; Charles M. Vincent, "Black Constitution Makers: The Constitution of 1868," in Warren M. Billings and Edward F. Haas, eds., *In Search of Fundamental Law: Louisiana's Constitutions, 1812–1974,* (Lafayette, La.: Center for Louisiana Studies, University of Southwestern Louisiana, 1993), 69–80. On the black experience in New Orleans during Reconstruction, see John W. Blassingame, *Black New Orleans, 1860–1880* (Chicago: University of Chicago Press, 1973). On the desegregation of the public schools in New Orleans, see Donald E. Devore and Joseph Logsdon, *Crescent City Schools: Public Education in New Orleans, 1841–1991* (Lafayette, La.: Center for Louisiana Studies, University of Southwestern Louisiana, 1991), 40–81; Roger A. Fischer, *The Segregation Struggle in Louisiana, 1862–1877* (Urbana and Chicago: University of Illinois Press, 1974), 42–87; Louis R. Harlan, "Desegregation in New Orleans Public Schools During Reconstruction," *American Historical Review* 48 (April 1962): 663–75; Leon F. Litwack, *Trouble in Mind: Black Southerners in the Age of Jim Crow* (New York: Alfred A. Knopf, 1998), 102–3.

3. The white Democrats who regained control of Southern state and local governments at the end of Reconstruction were called "Redeemers," reflecting Southern whites' perception that Democrats had "redeemed" the South from the Republicans' domination during Reconstruction. But the "redemption" was far more than a matter of party politics. For many Southerners, it was also redemption from federal intervention, from Northern influence, and especially from African-American participation in the political process.

4. Edwin S. Gaustad and Philip L. Barlow, *New Historical Atlas of Religion in America* (New York: Oxford University Press, 2001), 157–58, 219–31; Joseph C.

Hartzell, "Methodism and the Negro in the United States," *Journal of Negro History* 8 (July 1923): 315.

5. "New Orleans and Our Southern Work," *SWCA*, March 31, 1881; Grant S. Shockley, ed., *Heritage and Hope: The African American Presence in United Methodism* (Nashville: Abingdon Press, 1991), 85–86; *Soards' New Orleans City Directory* vols. 1–46 (New Orleans: Soards' Directory Company, 1874–1920).

6. While New Orleans and Louisiana have been the subject of many recent focused and specific studies, older accounts remain useful overviews of the city's history. See, for example, Charles Gayarré, *History of Louisiana*, 4 vols., 4th ed. (New Orleans: F. F. Hanson & Bro., 1903); John Smith Kendall, *History of New Orleans*, 3 vols. (Chicago: Lewis Publishing Company, 1922); and Henry Rightor, ed., *Standard History of New Orleans, Louisiana* (Chicago: Lewis Publishing Company, 1900).

Other histories emphasizing the distinctive flavor of New Orleans include Grace King, *New Orleans: The Place and the People* (1895; reprint, New York: Negro Universities Press, 1968); Lyle Saxon, *Fabulous New Orleans* (New York: Century Company, 1928); Harold Sinclair, *The Port of New Orleans* (Garden City, N.Y.: Doubleday, Doran & Co., 1942); Edward Larocque Tinker, *Creole City: Its Past and Its People* (New York: Longmans, Green & Co., 1953); and a volume of essays celebrating New Orleans's 250th anniversary, Hodding Carter, ed., *The Past as Prelude: New Orleans (1718–1968)* (New Orleans: Tulane University, 1968).

On Creoles in New Orleans, and the changes affecting Creoles of color, see Agnes Arthé Anthony, "The Negro Creole Community in New Orleans, 1880–1920: An Oral History" (Ph.D. diss., University of California Irvine, 1978); Caryn Cossé Bell, *Revolution, Romanticism, and the Afro-Creole Protest Tradition in Louisiana, 1718–1868* (Baton Rouge: Louisiana State University Press, 1997); Rodolphe Lucien Desdunes, *Our People and Our History: A Tribute to the Creole People of Color in Memory of the Great Men They Have Given Us and of the Good Works They Have Accomplished*, originally published as *Nos Hommes et Notre Histoire* (1911), Dorothea Olga McCants, trans. and ed., (Baton Rouge: Louisiana State University Press, 1973); Virginia R. Domínguez, *White By Definition: Social Classification in Creole Louisiana* (New Brunswick, N. J.: Rutgers University Press, 1986); James H. Dormon, ed., *Creoles of Color of the Gulf South* (Knoxville: University of Tennessee Press, 1996); Alice Dunbar-Nelson, "People of Color in Louisiana, Part I," *Journal of Negro History* 1 (October 1916): 361–76; Alice Dunbar-Nelson, "People of Color in Louisiana, Part II," *Journal of Negro History* 2 (January 1917): 51–78; Adam Fairclough, *Race and Democracy: The Civil Rights Struggle in Louisiana, 1915–1972* (Athens: University of Georgia Press, 1995), 1–20; Arnold Hirsch and Joseph Logsdon, eds., *Creole New Orleans: Race and Americanization* (Baton Rouge: Louisiana State University Press, 1992); Paul F. Lachance, "The Formation of a Three-Caste Society: Evidence From Wills in Antebellum New Orleans," *Social Science History* 18:2 (1994): 211–42; and Charles B. Rousseve, *The Negro in Louisiana: Aspects of His History and His Literature* (New Orleans: Xavier University Press, 1937).

7. Joseph Logsdon and Caryn Cossé Bell, "The Americanization of Black New Orleans," in Hirsch and Logsdon, eds., *Creole New Orleans*, 201–61. Given the social construction of race, racial designations are problematic and inevitably imperfect. "Black" is the inclusive term I use to describe all people of color, including

both Creoles of color and African Americans, who were affected by the racial reconfigurations this book describes.

8. "Race Identity in New Orleans, *SWCA*, July 19, 1900.

9. Carl Degler, *Neither Black nor White: Slavery and Race Relations in Brazil and the United States* (New York: Macmillan, 1971), xi, 5–6, 185, 203–4, 244; George M. Fredrickson, *Racism: A Short History* (Princeton: Princeton University Press, 2003), 102; and Frank Tannebaum, *Slave and Citizen: The Negro in the Americas* (New York, Vintage Books, 1946), 3–4, 100–119.

10. Jane Dailey, *Before Jim Crow: The Politics of Race in Postemancipation Virginia* (Chapel Hill: University of North Carolina Press, 2000), 168; Reginald F. Hildebrand, *The Times Were Strange and Stirring: Methodist Preachers and the Crisis of Emancipation* (Durham, N.C.: Duke University Press, 1995), 114. The recognition that segregation in the 1890s was intentional and qualitatively different began with C. Vann Woodward, *The Strange Career of Jim Crow* (New York: Oxford University Press, 1955).

CHAPTER 1
INTERRACIAL METHODISM IN NEW ORLEANS

1. Gilbert Haven, "Greeting from Africa," *SWCA*, April 19, 1877. Haven had been elected a bishop in 1872 and was assigned to Atlanta and the South for his first episcopal term (1872–76), during which time he visited a variety of southern states, including Louisiana, to learn of their efforts on behalf of African Americans. On Haven's life and work, see William B. Gravely, *Gilbert Haven, Methodist Abolitionist: A Study in Race, Religion and Reform* (Nashville, Tenn.: Abingdon, 1973); and George Prentice, *The Life of Gilbert Haven: Bishop of the Methodist Episcopal Church* (New York: Phillips and Hunt, 1884).

2. Gilbert Haven, "Greeting from Africa," *SWCA*, April 19, 1877.

3. C. Vann Woodward argued for the promise of the 1880s, focusing on the centrality of the 1890s in the forceful institutionalization of Jim Crow. See Woodward, *Origins of the New South, 1877–1913* (Baton Rouge: Louisiana State University Press, 1951); and Woodward, *The Strange Career of Jim Crow*, 3rd ed., rev. (New York: Oxford University Press, 1974). Howard Rabinowitz countered that segregation was essentially complete by 1890, so that exclusion and segregation, not inclusion or integration, remained the only options left for African Americans. See Howard N. Rabinowitz, *Race Relations in the Urban South, 1865–1890* (New York: Oxford University Press, 1978). In Louisiana, the tendency toward integration in one small town and segregation in another is the focus of Geraldine McTigue, "Forms of Racial Interaction in Louisiana, 1860–1880" (Ph.D. diss., Yale University, 1975), while two other studies of Louisiana support Woodward's contention that race relations remained unsettled through the 1880s and into the 1890s: Henry C. Dethloff and Robert R. Jones, "Race Relations in Louisiana, 1877–98," *Louisiana History* 9 (Fall 1968): 301–24; and Dale A. Sommers, "Black and White in New Orleans: A Study in Urban Race Relations, 1865–1900," *Journal of Southern History* 40 (February 1974): 19–42.

4. On religious reorganization as an expression of freedom, see Leon F. Litwack, *Been in the Storm So Long: The Aftermath of Slavery* (New York: Vintage Books, 1979), 450–501; and Grant S. Shockley, ed., *Heritage and Hope: The African-American Presence in United Methodism* (Nashville: Abingdon Press, 1991), 19. On the Methodist options available to African Americans, and the distinctive appeal of each, see Reginald F. Hildebrand, *The Times Were Strange and Stirring: Methodist Preachers and the Crisis of Emancipation* (Durham, N.C.: Duke University Press, 1995); Joseph C. Hartzell, "Methodism and the Negro in the United States," *Journal of Negro History* 8 (July 1923): 301–15; Harry V. Richardson, *Dark Salvation: The Story of Methodism as It Developed Among Blacks in America* (Garden City, N.Y.: Doubleday, 1976).

5. Hunter Dickinson Farish, *The Circuit Rider Dismounts* (Richmond, Va.: Dietz Press, 1938), 172; Hildebrand, *Times Were Strange and Stirring*, xv, xvii, 86, 88, 90, 95, 100, 122; and Daniel W. Stowell, *Rebuilding Zion: The Religious Reconstruction of the South, 1863–1877* (New York: Oxford University Press, 1998), 70. On Congregationalist efforts in the South, see Joe M. Richardson, *Christian Reconstruction: The American Missionary Association and Southern Blacks, 1861–1890* (Athens: University of Georgia Press, 1986).

6. A. K. Davis, "The Birmingham Matter," *SWCA*, January 11, 1883.

7. Andrew E. Murray, *Presbyterians and the Negro: A History* (Philadelphia: Presbyterian Historical Society, 1966), 150, 152; Daniel Stowell, *Rebuilding Zion*, 87–88.

8. On violence as a way to enforce racial boundaries, see Leon F. Litwack, *Trouble in Mind: Black Southerners in the Age of Jim Crow* (New York: Alfred A. Knopf, 1998), 7–16.

9. *SWCA*, September 6, 1877; "An Unfraternal Record," *SWCA*, July 3, 1879; *SWCA*, February 1, 1877.

10. "Fraternity in the Southwest," *SWCA*, February 8, 1877; Rev. Miles Proctor, "Not After Titles," *SWCA*, July 8, 1880.

11. *SWCA*, November 21, 1878; "Ninth Session of the Louisiana Conference," *SWCA*, January 18, 1877; "Bishop Ames and the 'Seizure' of Southern Methodist Churches During the War," *SWCA*, July 17, 1879; "Our Property Dispute Settled," *SWCA*, August 30, 1877; E. N. Cobleigh, "Church Property Questions in the South," *Methodist Quarterly Review* 53 (1871): 614–41; Katharine L. Dvorak, *An African-American Exodus: The Segregation of the Southern Churches* (Brooklyn, N.Y.: Carlson Publishing, 1991), 99, 140, 158; William E. Montgomery, *Under Their Own Vine and Fig Tree: The African-American Church in the South, 1865–1900* (Baton Rouge: Louisiana State University Press, 1993), 87–96, 119–21; and Clarence E. Walker, *A Rock in a Weary Land: The African Methodist Episcopal Church During the Civil War and Reconstruction* (Baton Rouge: Louisiana State University Press, 1982), 74, 76, 84–85, 93–97, 105.

12. "A Useless Church," *SWCA*, September 20, 1883.

13. Those who limit discussions of denominational shifting to the Reconstruction era include Dvorak, *African-American Exodus*; Hildebrand, *Times Were Strange and Stirring*; Montgomery, *Under Their Own Vine and Fig Tree*; and Walker, *Rock in a Weary Land*.

14. *SWCA*, September 7, 1882; "A Useless Church," *SWCA*, September 20, 1883.

15. Stephen Priestly, "Stop and Think," *SWCA*, March 13, 1879; "A Useless Church," *SWCA*, September 20, 1883; D. W. Hays, "The Living Spirit of Caste," *SWCA*, August 10, 1882.

16. Gardiner H. Shattuck Jr., *Episcopalians and Race: Civil War to Civil Rights* (Lexington: University Press of Kentucky, 2000), 16–29; J. Morris Shumpert, "The Colored Bishop Question," *SWCA*, September 18, 1879; "New Orleans Preachers on a Bishop of African Descent," *SWCA*, August 7, 1879; A.E.P. Albert, "Shall We have a Colored Bishop," *SWCA*, December 18, 1879; Rev. T. C. Clendenning, "Why There?" *SWCA*, May 17, 1883.

17. A.E.P. Albert, "A Vindication of Our Colored Membership," *SWCA*, July 1, 1880; Marshall W. Taylor, "What I Know About a Color Line in the M. E. Church," *SWCA*, January 25, 1883; *SWCA*, January 22, 1885. Concerning the decision to remain in the M. E. Church rather than depart for an African Methodist denomination, C. Eric Lincoln notes that "in true freedom the option to stay is as viable as the option to leave. To stay with the Mother [M. E.] church was the expression of freedom and the challenge of responsibility the Black Remnant decided to pursue." Shockley, ed., *Heritage and Hope*, 19.

18. A. K. Davis, "The Birmingham Matter," *SWCA*, January 11, 1883; B. J. Donnell, "A Letter from a Prominent Colored Man," *SWCA*, April 5, 1882.

19. "Steadily Advancing," *SWCA*, February 7, 1878.

20. The presiding elder supervised all the ministers and churches in a geographic area. The Louisiana Conference, encompassing the entire state, was divided into first four and then five districts while Hartzell was a presiding elder, with each district containing between 15 and 25 churches.

21. See statements on circulation, for example, in *SWCA*, October 11, 1877, and *SWCA*, November 22, 1877; and Otto H. Olsen, *The Thin Disguise: Turning Point in Negro History, Plessy v. Ferguson, A Documentary Presentation* (New York: Humanities Press, 1967), 67. One of the first white M. E. missionaries to New Orleans after the Civil War, the Rev. John P. Newman, had founded and privately published the *New Orleans Advocate* from 1866 to 1869, which was the *SWCA*'s predecessor.

22. Reverend Joseph. C. Hartzell Papers, LSU; Joseph Crane Hartzell Papers, GCAH. On the life and work of Hartzell, especially in New Orleans, see Anne C. Loveland, "The 'Southern Work' of the Reverend Joseph C. Hartzell, Pastor of Ames Church in New Orleans, 1870–1873," *Louisiana History* 16 (Fall 1975): 391–407; and Barbara Myers Swartz, "The Lord's Carpetbagger: A Biography of Joseph Crane Hartzell" (Ph.D. diss., SUNY Stony Brook, 1972).

23. Untitled typescript (n.d.), Hartzell Papers, Box 5, GCAH; Loveland, "Rev. Joseph C. Hartzell," 395–97; J. C. Hartzell to Sister Pearson, June 30, 1870, and Mrs. L. S. Sadler to J. C. Hartzell, May 31, 1871, Hartzell Papers, Letters (1870–1871), LSU; "Woman's Work in the House Land: W.H.M.S. Annual Thank Offering Address," notes, January 20, 1907, Hartzell Papers, Box 1, GCAH; J. C. Hartzell to J. P. Newman, June 6, 1870, Hartzell Papers, Letters (1870–1871), LSU; "The Matter of Fraternity in Texas," *SWCA*, January 2, 1879; Hartzell, "The Educational Work of the Methodist Episcopal Church in the Southern States," *SWCA*, December 22, 1881.

24. Hartzell to Pearson, June 30, 1870, Hartzell Papers, Letters (1870–1871), LSU; untitled typescript, Hartzell Papers, Box 5, GCAH; Loveland, "Rev. Joseph C. Hartzell," 396, 406; Frank J. Wetta, " 'Bulldozing the Scalawags': Some Examples of the Persecution of Southern White Republicans in Louisiana During Reconstruction," *Louisiana History* 21 (Winter 1980): 43–58; Farish, *Circuit Rider*, 112–26; Ralph E. Morrow, *Northern Methodism and Reconstruction* (East Lansing: Michigan State University Press, 1956), 221–23.

25. "Encouraging," *SWCA*, May 3, 1877; shortly before Hartzell assumed his position at Ames, the church adopted segregated seating, which Hartzell did not immediately change. However, when Hartzell was editor of the *SWCA*, the issue was raised again, and this time Hartzell advocated on behalf of Ames's black members, who won their case. See Loveland, "Rev. Joseph C. Hartzell," 399; John Blassingame, *Black New Orleans, 1860–1880* (Chicago: University of Chicago Press, 1973), 199.

26. Untitled typescript, Hartzell Papers (n.d.), Box 5, GCAH; J. C. Hartzell to J. P. Newman, June 6, 1870, Hartzell Papers, Letters (1870–1871), LSU; speech at Founders Day, New Orleans University, March 22, 1927, Hartzell Papers, Box 3, GCAH; L. S. Sadler to Hartzell, May 31, 1871, Hartzell Papers, Letters (1870–1871), LSU; Hartzell, "The Educational Work of the Methodist Episcopal Church in the Southern States," *SWCA*, December 22, 1881; Hartzell to A. J. Kynett, March 21, 1870, Hartzell Papers, Letters (1870–1871), LSU; "The Picayune and the Exodus," *SWCA*, March 11, 1880.

27. Wilbur Thirkield to G. W. Cable, May 14, 1889, George W. Cable Papers, Manuscripts Collection 2, Manuscripts Department, Tulane University Archives, New Orleans, La.; Hildebrand, *Times Were Strange and Stirring*, 86–87, 102, 104, 109, 113, 115; Farish, *Circuit Rider*, 108, 112–13, 172; Morrow, *Northern Methodism*, 192–93; J.W.E. Bowen, duplicate of confidential letters written to Revs. E.W.S. Peck; A.E.P. Albert; C. P. Westbrook, April 10, 1884, Hartzell Papers, Box 2, GCAH.

28. D. Stevenson, "Our Work Among the Whites in the South—First Paper," (n.d.), newspaper clipping, Scrapbook No. 6 (Education), pp. 48–49, Hartzell Papers, Box 4, GCAH; Morrow, *Northern Methodism*, 97–98, 237–42; Daniel Stowell, *Rebuilding Zion* 27–28, 89, 133; Octavia Albert, *The House of Bondage, or, Charlotte Brooks and Other Slaves* (1890; reprint, New York: Oxford University Press, 1988), 135–37; Farish, *Circuit Rider*, 139; Murray, *Presbyterians and the Negro*, 171.

29. From 1864 to 1865, the M. E. Church held every Southern Methodist Church building in New Orleans, and ten of twelve in Nashville, under a war provision that authorized the War Department to turn over to northern denominations all churches not served by a "loyal minister." Within five years, the U.S. government returned New Orleans churches to their original owners, and two years later had also returned those in Nashville. Morrow, *Northern Methodism*, 33–40; Daniel Stowell, *Rebuilding Zion*, 30.

30. "A Good Work," *SWCA*, July 26, 1877; "Ames Church," *SWCA*, February 16, 1882.

31. "Bishop Turner and Dr. Taylor," *SWCA*, December 23, 1880; "A Useless Church," *SWCA*, September 20, 1883; Murray, *Presbyterians and the Negro*, 184–86.

32. L. M. Hagood, "Assimilation and Not Separation," *SWCA*, January 31, 1884; James W. Lee, "Letter From Illinois," *SWCA*, July 22, 1880; Marshall W. Taylor, "What I Know About a Color Line in the M. E. Church," *SWCA*, January 25, 1883.

33. Scholars of both segregation and American religion have generally overlooked the relationship between segregation in religious institutions and other forms of segregation. This tendency is based on the assumption that segregation in churches was completed by 1870, an assumption disproved by the ongoing battles between the M. E. Church and African Methodists over issues of racial separation. On one side, historians of segregation have largely ignored the role of religion in analyzing segregation, including Woodward, *Origins of the New South*; Woodward, *Strange Career of Jim Crow*; Rabinowitz, *Race Relations in the Urban South*; and Edward L. Ayers, *The Promise of the New South: Life After Reconstruction* (New York: Oxford University Press, 1993). On the other side, religious historians have likewise overlooked connections between segregation inside and outside of the church, including Dvorak, *African-American Exodus*; Montgomery, *Under Their Own Vine and Fig Tree*; David M. Reimers, *White Protestantism and the Negro* (New York: Oxford University Press, 1965); and Walker, *Rock in a Weary Land*.

34. F. C. Moore, "The Color Line and a Colored Bishop," *SWCA*, April 1, 1880; "A Bishop of African Descent," *SWCA*, July 31, 1879; *SWCA*, September 6, 1877; Marshall W. Taylor, "What I Know About a Color Line in the M. E. Church," *SWCA*, January 25, 1883.

35. "Bishop Merrill and 'Colored' Methodists," *SWCA*, July 29, 1880; "Break Up the Color Line in the Church as Well as the Nation," *SWCA*, August 16, 1888; Marshall W. Taylor, "What I Know About a Color Line in the M. E. Church," *SWCA*, January 25, 1883.

36. *Proceedings of the Southern Baptist Convention* (1888), cited in Reimers, *White Protestantism*, 30; L. M. Hagood, "Tanner's Apology for African Methodism," *SWCA*, August 12, 1886.

37. Marshall W. Taylor, "What I Know About a Color Line in the M. E. Church," *SWCA*, January 25, 1883; "Pernicious Doctrines of the American Colonization Society," *SWCA*, August 2, 1888. On the complex divisions within New Orleans's black community, see Arthé Agnes Anthony, "The Negro Creole Community in New Orleans, 1880–1920: An Oral History" (Ph.D. diss., University of California Irvine, 1978), 93–118.

38. J. C. Akers, "Letter from Crockett, Texas," *SWCA*, July 22, 1880; "A Useless Church," *SWCA*, September 20, 1883; P. G. Brown, "A Colored Bishop," *SWCA*, April 15, 1880.

39. Marshall W. Taylor, "What I Know About a Color Line in the M. E. Church," *SWCA*, January 25, 1883; F. C. Moore, "The Color Line and a Colored Bishop," *SWCA*, April 1, 1880; Jas. W. Lee, "Letter from Illinois," *SWCA*, July 22, 1880; *SWCA*, October 4, 1883; R. G. Gillum, "What Does African Methodism Mean?" *SWCA*, October 14, 1886; L. M. Hagood, "Tanner's Apology for African Methodism," *SWCA*, August 26, 1886; "Central Congregational Church [Atlanta], the First Twenty-Five Years," p. 14, typescript, Central Congregational United Church of Christ Records, 1860–1990, Box 10, ARC; I. G. Pollard, "Letter from Arkansas," *SWCA*, January 23, 1879.

40. "Fraternal Speeches," *SWCA*, January 16, 1879; *SWCA*, September 9, 1880.

41. Daniel Stowell, *Rebuilding Zion*, 81–82; Reimers, *White Protestantism*, 31.

42. African-American Christianity undoubtedly emerged as a distinctive experience and often unifying force for African Americans against the pressures of racial oppression; however, this tendency has been overemphasized at the expense of diversity and tensions within and between the denominations to which African Americans belonged. On the importance of acknowledging differences among black denominations, see Laurie F. Maffly-Kipp, "Denominationalism and the Black Church," in Robert Bruce Mullin and Russell E. Richey, eds., *Reimagining Denominationalism: Interpretative Essays* (New York: Oxford University Press, 1994), 58–73. See also William B. Gravely, "African Methodism and the Rise of Black Denominationalism," in Russell E. Richey and Kenneth E. Rowe, eds., *Rethinking Methodist History* (Nashville, Tenn.: Kingswood Books, 1985), 111–24. Hildebrand, *Times Were Strange and Stirring*, also acknowledges the importance of denominationalism through his examination of different conceptions of freedom among Methodist denominations.

43. I. G. Pollard, "Letter from Arkansas," *SWCA*, January 23, 1879.

44. Morrow, *Northern Methodism*, 248.

45. Murray, *Presbyterians and the Negro*, 166; "Fraternity—'What of the Night?' " *SWCA*, December 30, 1880; W. Harrison Daniel, "Virginia Baptists and the Negro, 1865–1902," *Virginia Magazine of History and Biography* 76 (1969): 340–41. On charges of Southern Methodist support of the Confederacy, see, for example, "That Southern Methodist Claim," *SWCA*, March 28, 1878. On Southern Methodist attitudes toward African Americans, see Eugene Portlette Southall, "The Attitude of the Methodist Episcopal Church, South Toward the Negro from 1844 to 1870," *Journal of Negro History* 16 (October 1931): 359–70. On Southern Methodist support of the Confederacy, see Lewis M. Purifoy, "The Southern Methodist Church and the Proslavery Argument," *Journal of Southern History* 23 (August 1966): 333, 341. For an overview of the Southern Methodist attitudes toward African Americans after Emancipation, see Farish, *Circuit Rider*, 209–33.

46. S. C. Lockett, "Shall We Have One Methodism in the South?" *SWCA*, October 2, 1879; *SWCA*, February 8, 1883; *SWCA*, May 18, 1882; *SWCA*, August 11, 1881.

47. "The Problem of Our African Population," *Methodist Quarterly Review* 66 (January 1884): 124; Rev. H. Webb, "Missionary Sermon," *SWCA*, March 3, 1881.

48. "The Louisiana Conference," *SWCA*, January 29, 1880. For an example of Southern hostility toward churches addressing political issues, see, for example, "The Gospel of Hate," *Daily Picayune*, April 9, 1877.

49. "The Problem of our African Population," *Methodist Quarterly Review* 66 (January 1884): 114; *SWCA*, November 22, 1883.

50. "Thank God and Take Courage," *SWCA*, February 15, 1877; J. D. Walsh, "The Methodist Episcopal Church in the South," *Methodist Review* 72 (January 1890): 36; Daniel Stowell, *Rebuilding Zion*, 172; "Pastoral Address of the General Conference," *SWCA*, June 17, 1880.

51. "The Problem of Our African Population," *Methodist Quarterly Review* 66 (January 1884): 120, 122; "Current Discussions: The Race Question," *Methodist Review* 72 (January 1890): 118.

52. Hiram Revels, quoted in William B. Gravely, "Hiram Revels Protests Racial Separation," *Methodist History* 8 (April 1970): 18–19; J. D. Walsh, "The Methodist Episcopal Church in the South" *Methodist Review* 70 (March 1888): 249; Morrow, *Northern Methodism*, 20–23.

53. Rev. H. Webb, "Missionary Sermon," *SWCA*, March 3, 1881; "A Bishop of African Descent," *SWCA*, July 31, 1879; "New Orleans Preachers on a Bishop of African Descent," *SWCA*, August 7, 1879.

54. Among the studies exploring ways that African Americans resisted discrimination and segregation are Ayers, *Promise of the New South*; William Cohen, *At Freedom's Edge: Black Mobility and the Southern White Quest for Racial Control, 1861–1915* (Baton Rouge: Louisiana State University Press, 1991); Glenda Elizabeth Gilmore, *Gender and Jim Crow: The Politics of White Supremacy in North Carolina, 1896–1920* (Chapel Hill: University of North Carolina Press, 1996); Evelyn Brooks Higginbotham, *Righteous Discontent: The Women's Movement in the Black Baptist Church, 1880–1920* (Cambridge, Mass.: Harvard University Press, 1993); and Litwack, *Trouble in Mind*.

55. J.W.E. Bowen to Hartzell, May 10, 1884, Hartzell Papers, Box 2, GCAH.

56. Reimers, *White Protestantism*, 21; Morrow, *Northern Methodism*, 181.

57. *Zion's Herald*, January 29, 1874, quoted in Morrow, *Northern Methodism*, 182.

CHAPTER 2
INSTITUTING INTERRACIAL METHODISM

1. "That Odious Municipal Order Revoked," *SWCA*, May 15, 1879; "That Odious Municipal Order," *SWCA*, May 8, 1879; Joseph Crane Hartzell, speech from Founders Day, New Orleans University, March 22, 1927, Joseph Crane Hartzell Papers, Box 3, GCAH. A similar attempt to restrict worship hours occurred in 1865. See Marcus B. Christian, *A Black History of Louisiana*, "Chp 20: The Negro Church in Louisiana," p. 16, unpublished manuscript, Marcus Christian Collection, Literary and Historical Manuscripts, Box 8, Folder 1, UNO.

2. Eric Arnesen, *Waterfront Workers of New Orleans: Race, Class, and Politics, 1863–1923* (New York: Oxford University Press, 1991); Edward L. Ayers, *The Promise of the New South: Life After Reconstruction* (New York: Oxford University Press, 1992); Jane Dailey *Before Jim Crow: The Politics of Race in Postemancipation Virginia* (Chapel Hill: University of North Carolina Press, 2000).

3. Technically, only clergy and churches belonged to the annual conferences. The M. E. Church did not hold annual conferences for lay church members until after the turn of the century. Frederick A. Norwood, *The Story of American Methodism: A History of the United Methodists and Their Relations* (Nashville: Abingdon, 1974), 140–41, 258. For a history of annual conferences in Methodist denominations that eventually became the United Methodist Church, see Albea Godbold, "Table of Methodist Annual Conferences (U.S.A.)," *Methodist History* 8 (October 1969): 25–64.

4. W. Scott Chin, *Wesley Methodist Church: 113 Years* (New Orleans, n.p., 1951), 13; Reginald F. Hildebrand, *The Times Were Strange and Stirring: Methodist Preachers and the Crisis of Emancipation* (Durham, N.C.: Duke University Press, 1995), 92;

First Street Methodist Church, United Methodist Church Collection, Box 4: Central Jurisdiction, Louisiana Conference "B" Churches, Folder 92, DU; *Journal of the Louisiana Annual Conference, Methodist Episcopal Church, thirteenth session, Held at Shreveport, January 26–30, 1881* (New Orleans: Willis A. Brainerd), 14; *Journal of the Louisiana Annual Conference, Methodist Episcopal Church, twelfth session, Held at New Orleans, January 21–25, 1880* (n.p.), 15; Daniel W. Shaw, *Should the Negroes of the Methodist Episcopal Church Be Set Apart in A Church by Themselves?* (New York: Eaton and Mains, 1912), 41; untitled typescript, Hartzell Papers, Box 5, GCAH; "Civil Rights in the Churches," *Louisianian*, April 25, 1874; William B. Gravely, *Gilbert Haven, Methodist Abolitionist: A Study in Race, Religion, and Reform, 1850–1880* (Nashville, Tenn.: Abingdon Press, 1973), 182; Ralph E. Morrow, *Northern Methodism and Reconstruction* (East Lansing: Michigan State University Press, 1956), 192–93.

5. Untitled typescript, Hartzell Papers, Box 5, GCAH.

6. *Journal of the Louisiana Annual Conference, Methodist Episcopal Church, twelfth session, Held at New Orleans, January 21–25, 1880* (n.p.), 15.

7. Joseph Hartzell, "The Question of the Color Line," *Louisianian*, March 20, 1875. Anne C. Loveland, "The 'Southern Work' of the Reverend Joseph C. Hartzell, Pastor of Ames Church in New Orleans, 1870–1873," *Louisiana History* 16 (Fall 1975): 399; John Blassingame, *Black New Orleans, 1860–1880* (Chicago: University of Chicago Press, 1973), 199; "Toward the Southland," clipping from *Zion's Herald*, Scrapbook M, Hartzell Papers, (unnumbered box), GCAH.

8. Trinity United Methodist Church, United Methodist Church Collection, Box 5: Central Jurisdiction, Louisiana Conference "B" Churches, Folder 141, DU; J. W. Hudson, "Simpson Chapel, M. E. Church, New Orleans, La.," *SWCA*, January 17, 1889.

9. Ivan A. Beals, *Our Racist Legacy: Will the Church Resolve the Conflict?* (Notre Dame, Ind.: Cross Cultural Publications, 1997), 142; Hildebrand, *Times Were Strange and Stirring*, 109; David M. Reimers, *White Protestantism and the Negro* (New York: Oxford University Press, 1965), 23, 34–35; Morrow, *Northern Methodism*, 186–87; Andrew E. Murray, *Presbyterians and the Negro: A History* (Philadelphia: Presbyterian Historical Society, 1966), 138, 168.

10. "The Louisiana Conference As Seen by a Southern Neighbor," excerpts from an article by Rev. Wimberly in the *New Orleans Christian Advocate*, reprinted in *SWCA*, March 14, 1889; H. Shelton Smith, *In His Image, But . . . Racism in Southern Religion, 1780–1910* (Durham, N.C.: Duke University Press, 1972), 229.

11. Russell E. Richey, *The Methodist Conference in America: A History* (Nashville, Tenn.: Abingdon Press, 1996); Morrow, *Northern Methodism*, 188–89.

12. Daniel W. Stowell, *Rebuilding Zion: The Religious Reconstruction of the South, 1863–1877* (New York: Oxford University Press, 1998), 138, 143–45; Gravely, *Gilbert Haven*, 246; Hildebrand, *Times Were Strange and Stirring*, 95, 110–16; Morrow, *Northern Methodism*, 127–28, 186–93; *JGC* (1876), 189, 206, 288, 329–31, 326. On opposition to the proposal, see also "A Square Issue," *SWCA*, November 22, 1883. The provision that a majority of both races agree was an amendment added to the proposal in an attempt to ensure that any division represented a mutual agreement by both races, making such divisions a choice of separation rather than segregation imposed by whites. For many, it was small consolation. In nearly every case,

according to Bishop Wilbur Thirkield, whites forced black members to vote for segregation. See Reimers, *White Protestantism*, 57. In contrast, Methodist historian Grant Shockley considers the formation of black annual conferences an important and necessary step for advancing the rights of black clergymen, since they could then ordain other black clergy and be certain that African Americans would have representation at the denomination's quadrennial General Conference. Grant S. Shockley, "The Methodist Episcopal Church: Promise and Peril, 1784–1939," in Shockley, ed., *Heritage and Hope*, 55.

13. A.E.P. Albert quoted in "The Color Line," *SWCA*, December 28, 1882. Hiram Revels, Letter to the Editor, *SWCA*, May 4, 1876, as reprinted in William B. Gravely, "Hiram Revels Protests Racial Separation in the Methodist Episcopal Church (1876)," *Methodist History* 8 (April 1970): 16–20.

14. For descriptions of segregation moving from the particular to the general, see Ayers, *Promise of the New South*; Michael Perman, *Struggle for Mastery: Disfranchisement in the South, 1888–1908* (Chapel Hill: University of North Carolina Press, 2001); Barbara Young Welke, *Recasting American Liberty: Gender, Race, Law, and the Railroad Revolution, 1865–1920* (Cambridge: Cambridge University Press, 2001); C. Vann Woodward, *The Strange Career of Jim Crow*, 3rd ed., rev. (New York: Oxford University Press, 1974).

15. John Newman, an early white M. E. Church missionary to New Orleans, had published a predecessor to the *SWCA* called the *New Orleans Advocate*, from 1866–1869.

16. *SWCA*, November 22, 1877. On the *SWCA*, see Morrow, *Northern Methodism*, 55–56, 192; Shockley, ed., *Heritage and Hope*, 85–86; Gravely, "Hiram Revels," 15.

17. *JGC* (1876), 304; "Meeting of the Book Committee," *SWCA*, March 1, 1877; Gravely, "Hiram Revels," 14; Shockley, ed., *Heritage and Hope*, 85–86; "A Good Endorsement," *SWCA*, June 20, 1878; *SWCA*, December 26, 1878; I. Garland Penn, *The Afro-American Press and Its Editors* (1891; reprint, New York: Arno Press, 1969), 226; Henry Nathaniel Oakes Jr., "The Struggle for Racial Equality in the Methodist Episcopal Church: The Career of Robert E. Jones, 1904–1944" (Ph.D. diss., University of Iowa, 1973), 45; Barbara Myers Swartz, "The Lord's Carpetbagger: A Biography of Joseph Crane Hartzell" (Ph.D. diss., SUNY Stony Brook, 1972), 444.

18. L. M. Hagood, "The Atlanta Advocate," *SWCA*, April 5, 1883. For a similar affirmation, see *Journal of the Louisiana Annual Conference, Methodist Episcopal Church, fifteenth session, Held at Alexandria, February 1–5, 1883* (New Orleans: Elliott & Sagendorph Printers, 1883), 141; Shockley, ed., *Heritage and Hope*, 85.

19. See, for example, Rev. M. D. Collins, "Dr. Collins' Observations in New Orleans," *SWCA*, February 2, 1888, and numerous advertisements throughout the 1880s, such as that in *SWCA*, September 14, 1882, for testimonies of the university's racially inclusive admissions policies.

20. New Orleans University Catalogues, 1874–1896 (vol. 1) and 1897–1911 (vol. 2), New Orleans University Collection, Box 1, DU; *Seventy Years of Service: New Orleans University*, published by the faculty (New Orleans, 1935); Jay S. Stowell, *Methodist Adventures in Negro Education* (New York and Cincinnati: Methodist Book Concern, 1922); "Historical Data Concerning Straight University," from

Beard's "Crusade of Brotherhood," (1909), typescript, AMA Archives, Addendum, Series A: Field Records; Subseries: Dillard University, Box 90, Folder 1, DU, ARC; "New Orleans Public Schools Named for Persons Connected with Central Church," Central Congregational United Church of Christ, Records, 1860–1990, Box 1, Folder 3, ARC.

21. Morrow, *Northern Methodism*,165; Hildebrand, *Times Were Strange and Stirring*, 117; Murray, *Presbyterians and the Negro*, 170–77; Joe M. Richardson, *Christian Reconstruction: The American Missionary Association and Southern Blacks, 1861–1890* (Athens, Ga.: University of Georgia Press, 1986), 123–40; Jay Stowell, *Methodist Adventures*.

22. "Straight University, 25th Annual Report (1871)," typescript, AMA Archives, Addendum, Series A: Field Records; Subseries: Dillard University, Box 90, Folder 1, ARC; Murray, *Presbyterians and the Negro*, 177; Frank S. Loescher, *The Protestant Church and the Negro: A Pattern of Segregation* (New York: Association Press, 1948), 90.

23. "Ninth Session of the Louisiana Conference," *SWCA*, January 18, 1877; New Orleans University Catalogues, 1874–96 (vol. 1), New Orleans University Collection, Box 1, DU; *Seventy Years of Service*; "The New Orleans University," *SWCA*, June 27, 1878; *SWCA*, October 27, 1887; "Sketches of Some of the Graduates of New Orleans University: A.E.P. Albert," *SWCA*, June 6, 1889.

24. Cynthia Duplessis, "Dillard University From Its Beginning to 1885," typescript, AMA Archives, Addendum, Series A: Field Records; Subseries: Dillard University, Box 102, Folder 6, ARC; *JGC* (1884), 365–66. On debates over separate schools, see J. D. Walsh, "The Methodist Episcopal Church in the South," *Methodist Review* 70 (March 1888): 245–65; Dwight W. Culver, *Negro Segregation in the Methodist Church* (New Haven: Yale University Press, 1953), 56–57; Morrow, *Northern Methodism*, 197, 200; *Louisianian*, June 11, 1881, clipping, Scrapbook 6 (Education), Hartzell Papers, Box 4, GCAH.

25. Gary W. McDonogh, *Black and Catholic in Savannah, Georgia* (Knoxville: University of Tennessee Press, 1993), 37; Reimers, *White Protestantism*, 64–65.

26. Cynthia Duplessis, "Dillard University From Its Beginning to 1885," typescript, AMA Archives, Addendum, Series A: Field Records; Subseries: Dillard University, Box 102, Folder 6, ARC.

27. Mrs. J. C. Hartzell to the Louisiana conference, January 22, 1880, United Methodist History Collection, Box 3, Folder 60, DU; Mrs. J. C. Hartzell, "Christian Work Among the Freedwomen of the South," *SWCA*, November 21, 1878; "Mrs. Jennie C. Hartzell," *SWCA*, January 10, 1889; Joseph C. Hartzell, "Woman's Work in the House Land: W.H.M.S. Annual Thank Offering Address," January 20, 1907, Hartzell Papers, Box 1, GCAH; *JGC* (1880), 166, 345; "Missionary Work Among the Freedwomen," *SWCA*, February 13, 1879; "Christian Work Among the Freedwomen," *SWCA*, December 11, 1879; "Christian Work Among the Freedwomen," *SWCA*, April 8, 1880. Similar columns appeared weekly in the *SWCA* throughout the 1880s, reporting the visits and accomplishments of the city's female home missionaries. See also "Report of Woman's Home Missionary Society," *JGC* (1888), 740; Ellen Coughlin Keeler, *The Balance Wheel: A Condensed History of the Woman's Home Missionary Society of the Methodist Episcopal Church, 1880–1920* (New York: Woman's Home Missionary Society, 1920).

28. Daniel Stowell, *Rebuilding Zion*, 140; Anne H. Pinn and Anthony B. Pinn, *Fortress Introduction to Black Church History* (Minneapolis: Fortress Press, 2002), 75, 78; "Christian Effort Among Freedwomen," *SWCA*, June 20, 1878; "Colored Baptists in New Orleans," *SWCA*, November 25, 1885; "Light in Dark Places," *Journal of Education*, reprinted in *SWCA*, August 11, 1881.

29. Josephine Cowgill, "Woman's Home Mission Work in Louisiana," *SWCA*, November 6, 1884; "The Women at Work," *SWCA*, January 15, 1885; Josephine Cowgill, "Woman's Home Missionary Work in Louisiana," *SWCA*, May 27, 1886. For a similar report recounting accomplishments in 1888, see *JGC* (1888), 740.

30. Mrs. M. L. Dale, "Women's Home Work," *SWCA*, November 27, 1884; Andrew C. Chichon, "Woman's Home Missionary Society," *SWCA*, November 21, 1889. Black women celebrated the racial inclusiveness of General Conference meetings as well. See Octavia Albert, *The House of Bondage, or, Charlotte Brooks and Other Slaves* (1890; reprint, New York: Oxford University Press, 1988), 148–55. For analysis of how women elsewhere and in other traditions engaged in racial interaction and experienced its limitations, see Glenda Elizabeth Gilmore, *Gender and Jim Crow: The Politics of White Supremacy in North Carolina, 1896–1920* (Chapel Hill: University of North Carolina Press, 1996); and Evelyn Brooks Higginbotham, *Righteous Discontent: The Women's Movement in the Black Baptist Church, 1860–1920* (Cambridge, Mass.: Harvard University Press, 1993).

31. Rev. L. B. Ford, "The General Conference and the South," *SWCA*, April 15, 1880. For an excellent overview of postbellum anti-Catholicism, see John T. McGreevy, *Catholicism and American Freedom: A History* (New York: W. W. Norton, 2003), 91–126. On the role and nature of anti-Catholicism and nativism, see Ray Allen Billington, *The Protestant Crusade, 1800–1860: A Study of the Origins of American Nativism* (1938; reprint, Gloucester, Mass.: P. Smith, 1963); David Brion Davis, "Some Themes of Counter-Subversion: An Analysis of Anti-Masonic, Anti-Catholic, and Anti-Mormon Literature," *Mississippi Valley Historical Review* 47 (September 1960): 205–24; David Brion Davis, "Some Ideological Functions of Prejudice in Antebellum America," *American Quarterly* 15 (Summer 1963): 115–125; Jenny Franchot, *Roads to Rome: The Antebellum Protestant Encounter with Catholicism* (Berkeley and Los Angeles: University of California Press, 1994). Although strongest in antebellum America, much anti-Catholic rhetoric persisted well into the late nineteenth and even twentieth century, especially with the surge of Catholic immigrants from southern and eastern Europe. See John Higham, *Strangers in the Land: Patterns of American Nativism, 1860–1925*, 2nd ed. (New Brunswick, N.J.: Rutgers University Press, 1988); and Les Wallace, *The Rhetoric of Anti-Catholicism: The American Protective Association, 1887–1911* (New York: Garland Publishers, 1990).

32. "Shall Our Public Schools Go?" *SWCA*, November 15, 1883. On relations between Methodists and Catholics, see Charles Yrigoyen Jr., "Methodists and Roman Catholics in 19th Century America," *Methodist History* 3 (April 1990): 172–86; J. M. McPherson to M. E. Strieby, May 22, 1877, AMA Archives, Louisiana, microfilm (reel 3, 1877–n.d.) Item 46716, ARC.

33. "The Papacy and Civil Power," *SWCA*, August 16, 1877. Methodists as a whole also charged that Roman Catholicism was a danger to America and its freedoms. See Yrigoyen, "Methodists and Roman Catholics," 182; "Rev. J. W. E. Bowen, Ph.D. on Race Topics," *SWCA*, January 12, 1888. On insider and outsider

dynamics in American religion, especially with regard to Catholics, see R. Laurence Moore, *Religious Outsiders and the Making of Americans* (New York: Oxford University Press, 1985), 48–71.

34. *SWCA*, January 10, 1884; *SWCA*, January 11, 1883.

35. "Preacher's Meeting," *SWCA*, November 30, 1893; Jas. T. Newman, "All Saints Day in New Orleans," *SWCA*, April 8, 1886; "The Rape of the Christian Sabbath," *SWCA*, December 28, 1893; "Is it Possible?" *SWCA*, April 25, 1895.

36. Rev. C. S. Smith, "Our Duty," *SWCA*, June 7, 1877; *SWCA*, July 17, 1890; "Romanism and the Freedmen," *SWCA*, March 7, 1889. Using Catholic equality as leverage against Protestant discrimination required a delicate balancing act, especially in predominantly Catholic New Orleans, where black Methodists did not want to cede Catholics too much credit. Accordingly, they also emphasized Catholic racial failings, especially the lack of a black priesthood, and evidence of the color line and segregation within the city's Catholic parishes. See "The Roman Church and the Negro," *SWCA*, July 16, 1891; "Silly," *SWCA*, August 13, 1891; "Rev. S. E. H. Morant and Caste Proscription," *SWCA*, October 1, 1891; *SWCA*, January 21, 1892.

37. "Minutes of the 32nd Annual Session of the Louisiana Baptist Convention," (Keachi Baptist Church, 1880), 18, Louisiana Collection, Jones Hall, Tulane University, New Orleans; W. Harrison Daniel, "Virginia Baptists and the Negro, 1865–1902," *Virginia Magazine of History and Biography* 76 (1969): 345; and Murray, *Presbyterians and the Negro*, 165.

38. "Roman Catholicism in Louisiana," *SWCA*, September 11, 1879; "Justifies Murder," *SWCA*, October 22, 1891; "Roman Catholic Opposition to Negro Suffrage," *SWCA*, January 30, 1890; *SWCA*, October 18, 1883.

39. Yrigoyen, "Methodists and Roman Catholics," 176–82.

40. On the immigrant quest to construct a white racial identity, see Noel Ignatiev, *How the Irish Became White* (New York: Routledge, 1995); and Matthew Frye Jacobson, *Whiteness of a Different Color: European Immigrants and the Alchemy of Race* (Cambridge, Mass.: Harvard University Press, 1998).

41. Dale A. Somers, *The Rise of Sports in New Orleans, 1850–1900* (Baton Rouge: Louisiana State University Press, 1972), 119–21, 142–44, 286–90.

42. "The Labor Organizations of New Orleans," *SWCA*, December 7, 1882; Arnesen, *Waterfront Workers*, 34, 91–118. For examples of M. E. statements about biracial labor cooperation as a model for churches, see "The Status of Negro Labor," *SWCA*, July 26, 1906, and "Together: A Plea for Sanity in Race Relations," *SWCA*, August 31, 1916.

43. "Religio-Political," *SWCA*, September 4, 1879; "The Louisiana Conference," *SWCA*, January 29, 1880. For a similar sentiment, see also "Gospel Leaven in Politics," *SWCA*, October 4, 1877. On the relationship between Methodism and southern politics, see William W. Sweet, "Methodist Church Influence in Southern Politics," *Mississippi Valley Historical Review* 1 (March 1915): 546–60

44. See, for example, *SWCA*, March 17, 1881; "Our Salutation," *SWCA*, February 16, 1882; "Religious Papers and Politics," *SWCA*, December 13, 1883; Marshall W. Taylor, "Salutatory," *SWCA*, June 5, 1884; *SWCA*, August 28, 1884; "Political Uprightness," *SWCA*, November 6, 1884; *SWCA*, January 23, 1890.

45. Swartz, "Lord's Carpetbagger," 385; Donald E. Devore and Joseph Logsdon, *Crescent City Schools: Public Education in New Orleans* (Lafayette: Center for Louisiana Studies, University of Southwestern Louisiana, 1991), 94, 354; Pierre Landry, "Autobiographical Sketch," typescript, Dunn-Landry Family Papers, Box 1, Folder 1, ARC; *SWCA*, January 2, 1879. In Mississippi, M. E. clergyman Hiram Revels had been the first African American to serve in the United States Senate (1870–71), while another M. E. cleric, A. K. Davis, had served as Mississippi's lieutenant governor. Gravely, "Hiram Revels," 13–14; A. K. Davis, "The Birmingham Matter," *SWCA*, January 11, 1883.

46. See, for example, *SWCA*, May 24, 1877; "A Real Awakening," *SWCA*, May 20, 1880; *SWCA*, May 18, 1882; *SWCA*, August 3, 1882; "How They Treat It," *SWCA*, August 10, 1882; "Political Assessments," *SWCA*, September 21, 1882; *SWCA*, January 7, 1892.

47. "A Stirring Appeal," *SWCA*, August 30, 1888; "The Labor Strikes," *SWCA*, May 6, 1880; "Strikes and Preachers," *SWCA*, May 20, 1880.

48. Untitled typescript (n.d.), Box 5, Hartzell Papers, GCAH; Loveland, "Rev. Joseph C. Hartzell," 395–96; Margery Laporte, "A Woman's Rejoicing," *SWCA*, December 23, 1880; "Political Review," *SWCA*, March 8, 1888; *SWCA*, November 22, 1888.

49. Dailey, *Before Jim Crow*.

50. "The Anti-Chinese Bill," *SWCA*, March 6, 1879; "Veto of Chinese Bill," *SWCA*, April 13, 1882. See also "The Chinese Question," *Louisianian*, March 8, 1877. On the Chinese Exclusion Bill, see Sucheng Chan, ed., *Entry Denied: Exclusion and the Chinese Community in America, 1882–1943* (Philadelphia: Temple University Press, 1991); Andrew Gyory, *Closing the Gate: Race, Politics, and the Chinese Exclusion Act* (Chapel Hill: University of North Carolina Press, 1998). For the diplomatic wrangling over the Chinese Exclusion Bill, see David L. Anderson, "The Diplomacy of Discrimination: Chinese Exclusion, 1876–1882," *California History* 57:1 (1978): 32–45. The political side of efforts to restrict Chinese immigration, closely linked to the diplomatic developments discussed in Anderson, is recounted in Shirley Hune, "Politics of Chinese Exclusion: Legislative Executive Conflict, 1876–1882," *Amerasia Journal* 9:1 (1982): 5–28.

51. "The Chinese Bill," *SWCA*, March 16, 1882; *SWCA*, March 23, 1882. On the relationship between debates about Chinese immigration and black civil rights, see Najia Aarim-Heriot, *Chinese Immigrants, African-Americans, and Racial Anxiety in the United States, 1848–82* (Urbana: University of Illinois Press, 2003), 140–55, 196–241.

52. *SWCA*, April 13, 1882.

53. *SWCA*, May 11, 1882.

54. Norwood, *Story of American Methodism*, 80, 233–34, 348–50, 397–98; Mark Edward Lender and James Kirby Martin, *Drinking in America: A History* (New York: Free Press, 1982), 93–109; William A. Link, *The Paradox of Southern Progressivism, 1880–1930* (Chapel Hill: University of North Carolina Press, 1992), 32–51.

55. *SWCA*, March 7, 1878; "The Murphy Temperance Reform," *SWCA*, May 9, 1878; J. H. McCarty, "*The Curse of Strong Drink*," *SWCA*, May 16, 1878; *SWCA*, May 30, 1878. On Albert, see A.E.P. Albert, "Independent Order of Good Templars," *SWCA*, January 30, 1879; "A Good Appointment to a Good Work," *SWCA*,

March 20, 1879; A.E.P. Albert, "Temperance Jots and Dots," *SWCA*, April 3, 1879; M.C.B. Mason, "Letter from Houma," *SWCA*, May 1, 1879; *SWCA*, August 14, 1879; A.E.P. Albert, "Good Templarism in Louisiana," *SWCA*, January 29, 1880; W. S. Hawthorne, "Temperance in Terrebonne," *SWCA*, July 14, 1881.

56. *SWCA*, June 10, 1886. On whites who blamed racial tensions on alcohol, see Link, *Paradox of Southern Progressivism*, 70–71.

57. *SWCA*, January 6, 1881; "Good," *SWCA*, January 27, 1881; *SWCA*, February 21, 1881; S. J. Cotton, "Letter from Dekalb," *SWCA*, April 14, 1881. On the work of the Southern Methodist Church in temperance, see Hunter Dickinson Farish, *The Circuit Rider Dismounts: A Social History of Southern Methodism, 1865–1900* (Richmond, Va.: Dietz Press, 1938), 305–24.

58. Gilmore, *Gender and Jim Crow*, 47–52.

59. *SWCA*, May 21, 1885.

60. *SWCA*, May 2, 1889; "State Convention Women's Christian Temperance Union," *SWCA*, May 9, 1889. On the acceptance of segregation in the WCTU in North Carolina, see Gilmore, *Gender and Jim Crow*, 45–59.

61. *SWCA*, September 11, 1890; "The Colored People and Moral Reforms," January 19, 1882; Link, *Paradox of Southern Progressivism*, 58–72.

CHAPTER 3
THE DECLINE OF INTERRACIAL METHODISM

1. "Albert, Aristides Elphonso Peter," *Who's Who in America*, vol. 4 (Chicago: A. N. Marquis, 1906–7), 18; "Albert, Aristides E. P.," *Appelton's Cyclopaedia of American Biography*, vol. 7, supplement (New York: D. Appleton and Co.), 4; "Rev. A.E.P. Albert, D. D." *SWCA*, June 6, 1889; "Dr. A.E.P. Albert Crosses the Bar," *SWCA*, September 15, 1910; "Rev. A.E.P. Albert," *New Orleans Times-Picayune*, September 7, 1910; Cynthia Duplessis, "Dillard University From Its Beginning to 1885," typescript, AMA Archives, Addendum, Series A: Field Records; Subseries: Dillard University, Box 102, Folder 6, ARC.

2. "Complimentory," *SWCA*, October 20, 1887; "Congratulation," *SWCA*, October 27, 1887; "Reception to Dr. Albert," *SWCA*, November 3, 1887; *JGC* (1888), 342.

3. G. E. Cunningham, "Methodism's Problem in the South—I," *SWCA*, January 31, 1889. As late as 1890, northern voices refused to capitulate to southern mores on the question of racial inclusion. See, for example, J. D. Walsh, "The Methodist Episcopal Church in the South" *Methodist Review* 70 (March 1888): 249, 263; and J. D. Walsh, "The Methodist Episcopal Church in the South," *Methodist Review* 72 (January 1890): 36. David M. Reimers, *White Protestantism and the Negro* (New York: Oxford University Press, 1965), 51–82, discusses the pragmatic over theological considerations that drove northern denominations to accept segregation.

4. A.E.P. Albert, "Echoes from the January 1 Emancipation Celebration," *SWCA*, January 9, 1890. On the use of Exodus imagery within African-American Christianity, see Albert J. Raboteau, *A Fire in the Bones: Reflections on African-American Religious History* (Boston: Beacon Press, 1995), 4, 12, 28–36; Theophus H.

Smith, *Conjuring Culture: Biblical Formations of Black America* (New York: Oxford University Press, 1994), 55–80, 100–6; and David W. Wills, "Exodus Piety: African American Religion in an Age of Immigration," in Jonathan D. Sarna, ed., *Minority Faiths and the American Protestant Mainstream* (Urbana: University of Illinois Press, 1998), 136–90.

5. Glenda Elizabeth Gilmore, *Gender and Jim Crow: The Politics of White Supremacy in North Carolina, 1896–1920* (Chapel Hill: University of North Carolina Press, 1996), 45–46, 55–56; Eric Arnesen, *Brotherhoods of Color: Black Railroad Workers and the Struggle for Equality* (Cambridge, Mass.: Harvard University Press, 2001); and C. Vann Woodward, *Origins of the New South, 1877–1913* (Baton Rouge: Louisiana State University Press, 1951), 229–31.

6. *JGC* (1888), 451; "Our Educational Work Among the White People of the South," *SWCA*, July 23, 1891; "A Glorious Record," *SWCA*, June 6, 1889; Grant S. Schockley, ed., *Heritage and Hope: The African-American Presence in United Methodism* (Nashville: Abingdon Press, 1991), 72, 81; Jay S. Stowell, *Methodist Adventures in Negro Education* (New York and Cincinnati: Methodist Book Concern, 1922), 25–29; Ralph E. Morrow, *Northern Methodism and Reconstruction* (East Lansing: Michigan State University Press, 1956), 200; Reimers, *White Protestantism*, 62.

7. *SWCA*, September 14, 1893; "Louisiana Conference Appointments," *SWCA*, February 9, 1893. On Hartzell's work in New Orleans, see Anne C. Loveland, "The 'Southern Work' of the Reverend Joseph C. Hartzell, Pastor of Ames Church in New Orleans, 1870–1873," *Louisiana History* 16 (Fall 1975): 391–407; and Barbara Myers Swartz, "The Lord's Carpetbagger: A Biography of Joseph Crane Hartzell" (Ph.D. diss., SUNY Stony Brook, 1972), 195–529.

8. "Thought Our Friends All Dead," *SWCA*, October 5, 1893; Swartz, "Lord's Carpetbagger," 529.

9. Reimers, *White Protestantism*, 53–54; Louis W. Hodges, "A Christian Analysis of Selected Contemporary Theories of Racial Prejudice" (Ph.D. diss., Duke University, 1960), 136; Jean Russell, *God's Lost Cause: A Study of the Church and the Racial Problem* (London: S.C.M. Press, 1968), 70, 79–83, 91–94. Ralph Luker, *The Social Gospel in Black and White: American Racial Reform, 1885–1912* (Chapel Hill: University of North Carolina Press, 1991), argues for the often overlooked concern for race in the Social Gospel movement, while also highlighting its predominantly conservative character. On race and the Social Gospel, see also Ronald C. White, *Liberty and Justice for All: Racial Reform and the Social Gospel (1877–1925)* (San Francisco: Harper and Row, 1990).

10. *JGC* (1876), 353; *JGC* (1880), 282; *JGC* (1888), 332, 481–84; *JGC* (1896), 225–26, 380, 439; *JGC* (1900), 421–22, 498; *JGC* (1904), 622.

11. "The Truth About Chattanooga," *SWCA*, August 1, 1895; "Christian Progress vs. Separation," *SWCA*, July 11, 1895; "An Explanation That Does Not Explain," *SWCA*, August 8, 1895; Lucille Hutton, "This Is a Grand Work: A History of Central Congregational Church (United Church of Christ) New Orleans, Louisiana, 1872–1977" (1977), p. 35, typescript, Central Congregational United Church of Christ, Records, 1860–1990, Boxes 9–10, ARC; Edward L. Ayers, *The Promise of the New South: Life After Reconstruction* (New York: Oxford University Press, 1993), 176; Reimers, *White Protestantism*, 44.

12. Leon F. Litwack, *Trouble in Mind: Black Southerners in the Age of Jim Crow* (New York: Alfred A. Knopf, 1998), 468, 476; Grace Elizabeth Hale, *Making Whiteness: The Culture of Segregation in the South, 1890–1940* (New York: Vintage, 1998), 168.

13. "Mob-Law," *SWCA*, August 1, 1889; J. D. Walsh, "The Methodist Episcopal Church in the South," *Methodist Review* 72 (January 1890): 36; "Race Question," *Methodist Review* 72 (January 1890): 116; Litwack, *Trouble in Mind*, 208; "The Curse of Slavery," *SWCA*, November 11, 1892; A.E.P. Albert, et al., "The Address to the People of the United States," *SWCA*, September 20, 1888; *SWCA*, January 10, 1889, *SWCA* October 10, 1889; "Political Review," *SWCA*, August 23, 1888. African Americans were not the only people to experience mob violence in New Orleans. In March 1891, a group of Italians in prison on charges of murdering the chief of police the previous October were murdered by a white mob, although several appeared headed for acquittal. As with lynchings of African Americans, the New Orleans Grand Jury failed to bring indictments against the lynchers. See Marco Rimanelli and Sheryl Lynn Postman, eds., *The 1891 New Orleans Lynching and U.S.-Italian Relations: A Look Back* (New York: Peter Lang, 1992). On the changes in race relations in Louisiana and New Orleans, see Henry C. Dethloff and Robert R. Jones, "Race Relations in Louisiana, 1877–1898," *Louisiana History* 9 (Fall 1968): 301–23; Paul A. Kunkel, "Modifications in Louisiana Legal Status Under Louisiana Constitutions, 1812–1957," *Journal of Negro History* 44 (January 1959): 16–20; Joseph Logsdon and Caryn Cossé Bell, "The Americanization of Black New Orleans," in Arnold R. Hirsch and Joseph Logsdon, eds., *Creole New Orleans: Race and Americanization* (Baton Rouge: Louisiana State University Press, 1992), 251–61; Dale A. Somers, "Black and White in New Orleans: A Study in Urban Race Relations, 1865–1900," *Journal of Southern History* 40 (February 1974): 19–42. For broader descriptions of events in this crucial period, the pioneering works remain Woodward, *Origins of the New South* and C. Vann Woodward, *The Strange Career of Jim Crow*, 3rd ed. (New York: Oxford University Press, 1974). Subsequent analyses emphasizing changing race relations include Ayers, *Promise of the New South*; John Hope Franklin, *From Slavery to Freedom: A History of Negro Americans*, 3rd ed. rev. (New York: Alfred A. Knopf, 1967), 324–43; Litwack, *Trouble in Mind*; and Joel Williamson, *The Crucible of Race: Black-White Relations in the American South Since Emancipation* (New York: Oxford University Press, 1984).

14. *SWCA*, October 24, 1889; Editorial Notes, *SWCA*, September 13, 1888; *SWCA*, May 24, 1888; Political Review, *SWCA*, August 2, 1888; *SWCA*, January 3, 1889; *SWCA*, February 14, 1889. For examples of armed resistance and self-defense elsewhere in the South, see Alwyn Barr, "The Black Militia of the New South: Texas as a Case Study," *Journal of Negro History* 63 (July 1978): 209–29; and Lee W. Formwalt, "The Origins of African-American Politics in Southwest Georgia: A Case Study of Black Political Organization During Presidential Reconstruction, 1865–1867," *Journal of Negro History* 77 (Autumn 1992): 211–22.

15. Ayers, *Promise of the New South*, 145; Litwack, *Trouble in Mind*, xiii, 151–63, 208, 230, 322–23; Hale, *Making Whiteness*, 50; Michael Perman, *Struggle for Mastery: Disfranchisement in the South, 1888–1908* (Chapel Hill: University of North Carolina Press, 2001), xi.

16. *SWCA*, September 20, 1888; Editorial Notes, *SWCA*, August 15, 1889; *SWCA*, October 18, 1888; Political Review, *SWCA*, October 27, 1888.

17. "Obstacles to Race Progress," *SWCA*, June 11, 1891; Woodward, *Origins of the New South*, 218–20; Perman, *Struggle for Mastery*, 230. On the hopes of the 1888 Republican victory, see *SWCA*, November 22, 1888; *SWCA*, March 21, 1889, and "Martyrs to Patriotism," *SWCA*, September 12, 1889. On the failures of the Harrison administration, see Political Review, *SWCA*, November 21, 1889; Political Review, *SWCA*, April 10, 1890; "National Aid to Education," *SWCA*, May 1, 1890; Political Review, *SWCA*, May 12, 1892; Vincent P. De Santis, "The Republican Party and the Southern Negro," *Journal of Negro History* 45 (April 1960): 71–87; Rayford W. Logan, *The Betrayal of the Negro: From Rutherford B. Hayes to Woodrow Wilson*, rev. ed. (New York: Collier Books, 1965), 62–87. On the social factors contributing to the reunion of the North and South, see Ayers, *Promise of the New South*, 310–38; and Nina Silber, *The Romance of Reunion: Northerners and the South, 1865–1900* (Chapel Hill: University of North Carolina Press, 1993).

18. "Political Review," *SWCA*, April 10, 1890; "National Aid to Education," *SWCA*, May 1, 1890.

19. "Political Review," *SWCA*, April 10, 1890; "National Aid to Education," *SWCA*, May 1, 1890; Editorial Notes, *SWCA*, January 23, 1890; Litwack, *Trouble in Mind*, 370–71.

20. Otto H. Olsen, *The Thin Disguise: Turning Point in Negro History, Plessy v. Ferguson, A Documentary Presentation* (New York: Humanities Press, 1967), 10, 58; William B. Gravely, "Hiram Revels Protests Racial Separation in the Methodist Episcopal Church (1876)" *Methodist History* 8 (April 1970): 14; Jane Dailey, *Before Jim Crow: The Politics of Race in Postemancipation Virginia* (Chapel Hill: University of North Carolina Press, 2000); Woodward, *Origins of the New South*, 235–63, 323; Gerald H. Gaither, *Blacks and the Populist Revolt: Ballots and Bigotry in the "New South"* (Tuscaloosa: University of Alabama Press, 1977); Gilmore, *Gender and Jim Crow*, 121–22, 267 (n. 35); Perman, *Struggle for Mastery*, 32, 119. The working-class character of Populism did not attract large numbers of the black leadership in New Orleans, but its gains in the northwest cotton parishes, and throughout much of the South, were impressive. On Populism in Louisiana, see William Ivy Hair, *Bourbonism and Agrarian Protest: Louisiana Politics, 1877–1900* (Baton Rouge: Louisiana State University Press, 1969).

21. "A Word of Warning," *SWCA*, November 2, 1893; "Rev. S.E.H. Morant and Caste Proscription," *SWCA*, October 1, 1891; Editorial Comments, *SWCA*, January 20, 1898; "Injustice Against Colored Church by Insurance Companies," *SWCA*, July 25, 1889. On attempts at segregation by businesses during Reconstruction, see John W. Blassingame, *Black New Orleans, 1860–1880* (Chicago: University of Chicago Press, 1973), 183–86.

22. *SWCA*, June 25, 1891. The G.A.R. behaved similarly in the North. See *SWCA*, April 11, 1889. Litwack, *Trouble in Mind*, 236; David Goldfield, *Region, Race, and Cities: Interpreting the Urban South* (Baton Rouge: Louisiana State University Press, 1997), 140; "Rev. S.E.H. Morant and Caste Proscription," *SWCA*, October 1, 1891.

23. "Justice Requires the Protection of Both," *SWCA*, July 3, 1902; Hale, *Making Whiteness*, 126–50; Litwack, *Trouble in Mind*, 241, Ayers, *Promise of the New*

South, 138–46; Barbara Young Welke, *Recasting American Liberty: Gender, Race, Law, and the Railroad Revolution, 1865–1920* (Cambridge: Cambridge University Press, 2001), 283–92.

24. "Dr. Albert Narrowly Escapes a Texas Jail," *SWCA*, December 17, 1891; *Cleveland Gazette*, December 19, 1891.

25. "Report of the Proceedings for the Annulment of Act 111 of 1890 by the Citizens Committee" (1897), pp. 1, 3, Charles B. Rousseve Collection, Box 1, Folder 13, ARC.

26. *SWCA*, January 3, 1889; "The Truth As It Is," *SWCA*, April 4, 1889; "City Church Notes," *SWCA*, September 19, 1889; "The Evangelical Alliance, on Recent Outrages Upon Colored People," *SWCA*, October 3, 1889; *SWCA*, December 5, 1889.

27. "A Great National Movement," *SWCA*, March 20, 1890; "American Citizens' Equal Rights Association," *SWCA*, March 13, 1890; *Crusader*, March 22, 1890, Rousseve Collection, Box 1, Folder 7, ARC; Logsdon and Bell, "Americanization of Black New Orleans," 257; "American Citizens' Equal Rights Association," *SWCA*, March 13, 1890; "A Great National Movement," *SWCA*, March 20, 1890; "A.C.E.R. Association," *SWCA*, May 29, 1890. Members of the committee organizing the protest were Albert, P.B.S. Pinchback, Ernest Lyon, and R. L. Desdunes. See also *SWCA*, June 5, 1890, *SWCA*, June 12, 1890, and a copy of the petition in *SWCA*, June 19, 1890; Joseph Logsdon with Lawrence Powell, "Rodolphe Lucien Desdunes: Forgotten Organizer of the *Plessy* Protest," in Samuel C. Hyde Jr., ed., *Sunbelt Revolution: The Historical Progression of the Civil Rights Struggle in the Gulf South, 1866–2000* (Gainesville: University of Florida Press, 2003), 53.

28. *SWCA*, April 9, 1891; *SWCA*, October 29, 1891; *SWCA*, November 19, 1891.

29. Charles B. Rousseve, *The Negro in Louisiana: Aspects of His History and His Literature* (New Orleans: Xavier University Press, 1937); Rodolphe Lucien Desdunes, *Our People and Our History*, Dorothea Olga McCants, trans. and ed. (Baton Rouge: Louisiana State University Press, 1973), 141; *Crusader*, June 22, 1895, DFC-CC, Box 1; "Report of the Proceedings for the Annulment of Act 111 of 1890 by the Citizens Committee" (1897), Rousseve Collection, Box 1, Folder 13, ARC.

30. Bishop W. F. Mallalieu, "A Cry to Human Hearts," *SWCA*, June 6, 1889; C. H. Payne, "Address at the Dedication of the Medical College of the New Orleans University," *SWCA*, February 18, 1892; Jay Stowell, *Methodist Adventures*, 61–62; Olsen, *Thin Disguise*, 10; *SWCA*, March 3, 1892; "New Orleans University Medical College," *SWCA*, March 9, 1893; New Orleans University Catalogues, vol. 1 (1874–1896) and vol. 2 (1897–1911), New Orleans University Collection, Box 1, DU. For examples of Albert and Martinet praising each other and their efforts, see *SWCA*, March 21, 1889; *SWCA*, March 26, 1891; "On the Same Platform," *SWCA*, April 9, 1891; *SWCA*, March 3, 1892; *SWCA*, Sept. 29, 1892.

31. George M. Fredrickson, *The Arrogance of Race: Historical Perspectives on Slavery, Racism, and Social Inequality* (Middletown, Conn.: Wesleyan University Press, 1988), 103; Mark Elliott, "Race, Color Blindness and the Democratic Public: Albion W. Tourgée's Radical Principles in Plessy v. Ferguson," *Journal of Southern History* 67 (May 2001): 287–330; Sidney Kaplan, "Albion W. Tourgée: Attorney for the Segregated," *Journal of Negro History* 49 (April 1964): 128–33; Theodore L. Gross, *Albion W. Tourgée* (New York: Twayne Publishers, 1963), 17; Otto H. Olsen,

Carpetbagger's Crusade: The Life of Albion Winegar Tourgée (Baltimore: Johns Hopkins University Press, 1965), 49, 283.

32. Louis A. Martinet to Albion Tourgée, July 4, 1892, Albion Winegar Tourgée Papers, Item 6377, Chautauqua County Historical Society, Westfield, N.Y.; Olsen, *Carpetbagger's Crusade*, 320–21; Fredrickson, *Arrogance of Race*, 94–106.

33. *SWCA*, August 28, 1890; *SWCA*, November 19, 1891; "The Separate Car Must Go," *SWCA*, March 3, 1892; *Journal of the Louisiana Annual Conference, Methodist Episcopal Church, twenty-fourth session, Held at New Orleans January 13–19, 1892* (Cincinnati: Western Methodist Book Concern Press, 1892), 185.

34. *SWCA*, May 29, 1890; "American Citizens' Equal Rights Association," *SWCA*, December 11, 1890; *SWCA*, June 18, 1891; "A Coach for Negroes," *SWCA*, July 11, 1889; *Journal of the Louisiana Annual Conference, Methodist Episcopal Church, twenty-fourth session, Held at New Orleans January 13–19, 1892* (Cincinnati: Western Methodist Book Concern Press, 1892), 259, 277–78; "Louisiana Conference," *SWCA*, January 29, 1891; "Louisiana Conference Notes," *SWCA*, January 28, 1892. On the popularity of railroad excursions during Reconstruction, see Blassingame, *Black New Orleans*, 144–45.

35. Welke, *Recasting American Liberty*, 273, 358–62; Litwack, *Trouble in Mind*, 242; Perman, *Struggle for Mastery*, 265; August Meier and Elliot Rudwick, "The Boycott Movement Against Jim Crow Streetcars in the South, 1900–1906," *Journal of American History* 55 (March 1969): 756–75.

36. Frank C. Blundon to Booker T. Washington, January 8, 1891, in Louis R. Harlan, ed., *The Booker T. Washington Papers*, vol. 3 (Urbana: University of Illinois Press, 1974), 119.

37. "Bishop Newman and Negro Leagues," *SWCA*, January 29, 1891; "Rev. A.E.P. Albert, D. D.," *SWCA*, June 6, 1889; "Pleas Against Class Legislation," *SWCA*, June 19, 1890.

38. *JGC* (1892), 294–95, 526; "Valedictory," *SWCA*, June 2, 1892; Logsdon and Bell, "Americanization of Black New Orleans," 257.

39. Litwack, *Trouble in Mind*, 429.

40. A.E.P. Albert, "Valedictory," *SWCA*, June 2, 1892; *Journal of the Louisiana Annual Conference* (1892), 254.

41. A.E.P. Albert, "Pastoral Explanation," *SWCA*, March 17, 1892; "Albert, Aristides Elphonso Peter," *Who's Who in America*, 18; "Albert, Aristides E. P.," *Appelton's Cyclopaedia of American Biography*, 4; "Rev. A.E.P. Albert, D. D." *SWCA*, June 6, 1889; "Dr. A.E.P. Albert Crosses the Bar," *SWCA*, September 15, 1910; "Rev. A.E.P. Albert," *New Orleans Times-Picayune*, September 7, 1910.

42. "Our New Editor," *SWCA*, June 2, 1892.

43. Louis Martinet to Albion Tourgée, July 9, 1892 [letter begun on July 4], Albion Winegar Tourgée Papers, Item No. 6377, Chautauqua County Historical Society, Westfield, N.Y.; Howard Henderson in the *St. Louis Christian Advocate*, as quoted in *SWCA*, June 2, 1892; *SWCA*, June 2, 1892.

44. "Race Pride, Enterprise and Unity," *SWCA*, March 7, 1895. Gilmore, *Gender and Jim Crow*, 62–63, discusses the ways African Americans hoped to preserve their "manhood rights" in the notion of the "Best Man," meaning conformity to white middle-class values and notions of manhood. On the project of uplift and its contested meanings within the black leadership class, as well as the often contradic-

tory messages it entailed, see Kevin K. Gaines, *Uplifting the Race: Black Leadership, Politics and Culture in the Twentieth Century* (Chapel Hill: University of North Carolina Press, 1996).

45. "More Lynching," *SWCA*, May 18, 1893; "Dead Ducks," *SWCA*, September 8, 1892; Rev. Edward L. Gilliam, "The Present Status of the Colored Man in the South," *SWCA*, November 24, 1892; Gaines, *Uplifting the Race*, 4, 31.

46. "A Safe Leader," *SWCA*, September 5, 1895; Reginald F. Hildebrand, *The Times Were Strange and Stirring: Methodist Preachers and the Crisis of Emancipation* (Durham, N.C.: Duke University Press, 1995), 101; Litwack, *Trouble in Mind*, 355.

47. "Another Epoch," *SWCA*, September 26, 1895; Ayers, *Promise of the New South*, 322–26; Woodward, *Origins of the New South*, 356–68.

48. *SWCA*, February 21, 1895; "Ex-Senator Ingalls on 'The Negro Question,' " *SWCA*, April 20, 1893; J. H. Leonard, "The Influence of Education on the Material Progress and Moral Development of the Negro Race," *Minutes of the 30th Annual Session of the Southern La. Baptist Association, 5th District (1907)* Homer, La., 20–21; Litwack, *Trouble in Mind*, 79–80, 355–56.

49. *SWCA*, July 24, 1890; "The Relation Sustained by the Christian Minister to Current Politics," *SWCA*, September 29, 1892.

50. *JGC* (1896), 443; "Farewell!" *SWCA*, May 28, 1896; "Rev. I. B. Scott," *SWCA*, May 28, 1896.

51. "An Unconstitutional Constitution," *SWCA*, March 31, 1898; Warren M. Billings and Edward F. Hass, *In Search of Fundamental Law: Louisiana's Constitutions, 1812–1974* (Lafayette: Center for Louisiana Studies at the University of Southwestern Louisiana, 1993), especially chaps. 6–8; Ayers, *Promise of the New South*, 298–99; Woodward, *Origins of the New South*, 333–34, 342–43.

52. *Biennial Report of the Secretary of State of the State of Louisiana to the General Assembly, 1896–1898* (Baton Rouge: The Advocate, official journal of the state of Louisiana, 1898), 26; *Report of the Secretary of State, 1900*, 26; *Report of the Secretary of State to his Excellency the Governor of Louisiana, May 1904* (Baton Rouge: The Advocate, official journal of the state of Louisiana, 1904), 51; Perman, *Struggle for Mastery*, 5–6, 124–26; Joy J. Jackson, *New Orleans in the Gilded Age: Politics and Urban Progress, 1880–1896* (Baton Rouge: Louisiana State University Press, 1969), 318; Somers, "Black and White in New Orleans," 21; "The Death-Rate Among Us," *SWCA*, July 2, 1896; Editorial, *SWCA*, October 9, 1902.

53. "Shall We Perpetuate the Color Line?" *SWCA*, May 26, 1892; "Louisiana Conference," *SWCA*, January 30, 1896; "Separate Conferences in the M.E. Church," *SWCA*, August 2, 1894; Dwight W. Culver, *Negro Segregation in the Methodist Church* (New Haven: Yale University Press, 1953), 54–55; Reimers, *White Protestantism*, 56.

54. Presbyterians, for example, formally segregated presbyteries in 1904 to facilitate work in the South as well as reunion with the Cumberland church. See Reimers, *White Protestantism*, 137; Andrew E. Murray, *Presbyterians and the Negro: A History* (Philadelphia: Presbyterian Historical Society, 1966), 160, 168.

55. *Minutes of the Annual Conferences of the Methodist Episcopal Church (1889)* (New York: T. Mason and G. Lane for the Methodist Episcopal Church, 1889), 207; "Louisiana Conference," *SWCA*, February 9, 1888; "Report of the Mission District, Louisiana Conference," *SWCA*, February 16, 1888.

56. The evolving conference structures are tracked in the *Minutes of the Annual Conferences of the Methodist Episcopal Church* for the following years: 1889–1893; 1896, 1901, 1904; *The Doctrines and Discipline of the Methodist Episcopal Church, 1896* (New York: Eaton and Mains, 1896), 224; *JGC* (1892), 415; *JGC* (1896), 189, 399; *JGC* (1904), 55. Grant S. Shockley, ed., *Heritage and Hope: The African American Presence in United Methodism* (Nashville: Abingdon Press, 1991), 59. The Gulf Mission Conference received permission from the 1900 General Conference to organize as an annual conference at any point during the next four years. See "Committee on Boundaries, Report No. 1," *JGC* (1900), 325, 491.

57. "Committee on Boundaries, Report No. 4: Boundaries of Conferences," *JGC* (1904), 444. The 1900 edition of *Doctrines and Discipline* was the first to designate Louisiana as a "colored" conference (p. 244). On the shift toward national control and decision making, see Russell E. Richey, *The Methodist Conference in America: A History* (Nashville: Abingdon Press, 1996), 145–67. When northern and southern Methodists united in 1939, Louisiana black churches became part of the racially separate Central Jurisdiction, while white congregations joined the regional jurisdiction. When the Central Jurisdiction was eliminated at the 1968 General Conference, Louisiana churches remained in racially distinct districts: Conference A for white churches and Conference B for black churches. In 1971, the two conferences merged to once again create a racially integrated Louisiana Annual Conference. See "The Order of Worship Celebrating the Merger: La. Annual Conference A, La. Annual Conference B," June 1, 1971, United Methodist Church Collection, Box 6, Folder 190, DU; Walter N. Vernon, *Becoming One People: A History of Louisiana Methodism* (History Task Group, Commission on Archives and History, Louisiana Conference, United Methodist Church, 1987), 293–96.

58. Editorial Comments, *SWCA*, July 25, 1895; "Race Hindrances Here," *SWCA*, April 26, 1900; "Race Identity in New Orleans," *SWCA*, July 19, 1900. For testimony of New Orleans's earlier racial liberalism, see, for example, "New Orleans and Our Southern Work," *SWCA*, March 31, 1881.

59. "Obstacles to Race Progress," *SWCA*, June 11, 1891; *SWCA*, August 11, 1892.

CHAPTER 4
RENEGOTIATING BLACK METHODIST IDENTITY

1. "Dark Days in New Orleans," *SWCA*, August 2, 1900; Paul A. Gilje, *Rioting in America* (Bloomington: Indiana University Press, 1996), 111; William Ivy Hair, *Carnival of Fury: Robert Charles and the New Orleans Race Riot of 1900* (Baton Rouge: Louisiana State University Press, 1976); Leon F. Litwack, *Trouble in Mind: Black Southerners in the Age of Jim Crow* (New York: Alfred A. Knopf, 1998), 405–10; Joel Williamson, *The Crucible of Race: Black-White Relations in the American South Since Emancipation* (New York: Oxford University Press, 1984), 201–9.

2. "The City School Reduced in Grace," *SWCA*, July 5, 1900; Donald E. Devore and Joseph Logsdon, *Crescent City Schools: Public Education in New Orleans, 1841–1991* (Lafayette: Center for Louisiana Studies, University of Southwestern Louisiana, 1991), 118–19. On the declining racial climate in New Orleans leading up to 1900, see Henry C. Dethloff and Robert R. Jones, "Race Relations in Louisiana,

1877–98," *Louisiana History* 9 (Fall 1968): 301–24; and Dale Somers, "Black and White in New Orleans: A Study in Urban Race Relations, 1865–1900," *Journal of Southern History* 40 (February 1974): 19–42.

3. "Race Identity in New Orleans," *SWCA*, July 19, 1900; *SWCA*, August 16, 1900. On rioting in Wilmington and Atlanta, see Gilje, *Rioting*, 109–10; Glenda Gilmore, *Gender and Jim Crow: Women and the Politics of White Supremacy in North Carolina, 1896–1920* (Chapel Hill: University of North Carolina Press, 1996), 105–8, 111–17; Nell Irvin Painter, *Standing at Armageddon: The United States, 1877–1919* (New York: W. W. Norton & Co., 1987), 217–22; Williamson, *Crucible of Race*, 195–201, 209–20.

4. "Dark Days in New Orleans," *SWCA*, August 2, 1900; "Some Lessons Learned From the Outbreak Last Week," *SWCA*, August 2, 1900; "Better than the United States Flag," *SWCA*, August 2, 1900; "Personal and General," *SWCA*, August 2, 1900; "The Boston Meeting," *SWCA*, August 9, 1900; Hair, *Carnival of Fury*, 154–55.

5. William E. Montgomery, *Under Their Own Vine and Fig Tree: The African-American Church in the South, 1865–1900* (Baton Rouge: Louisiana State University Press, 1993), 328–32, 334, 336–38; Kevin Gaines, *Uplifting the Race: Black Leadership, Politics, and Culture in the Twentieth Century* (Chapel Hill: University of North Carolina Press, 1996).

6. "Some Lessons Learned From the Outbreak Last Week," *SWCA*, August 2, 1900; "The Folly of Harboring a Criminal," *SWCA*, August 2, 1900. "Negro Baptists in Convention," *Times-Picayune*, September 15, 1900; numerous black residents, African American and especially Creole, denounced those who harbored Charles and did not object to their indictment and subsequent suffering. Hair, *Carnival of Fury*, 188; Litwack, *Trouble in Mind*, 408.

7. "Mardi Gras," *SWCA*, February 12, 1891; " 'Rag-Time' Church Music," *SWCA*, December 4, 1902; Alecia P. Long, *The Great Southern Babylon: Sex, Race, and Respectability in New Orleans, 1865–1920* (Baton Rouge: Louisiana State University Press, 2004) 191–224.

8. Henry Nathaniel Oakes Jr., "The Struggle for Racial Equality in the Methodist Episcopal Church: The Career of Robert E. Jones, 1904–1944" (Ph.D. diss., University of Iowa, 1973); Sister Mary Veronica Miceli, O.P., "Bishop Robert Elijah Jones: New Orleans Challenger of a New Day for the Negro in the Early Twentieth Century," unpublished paper, Box 6, Folder 13, REJP.

9. "The Negro's Great Burden," *SWCA*, September 17, 1908; "Good Citizenship Association," *SWCA*, November 8, 1906; "We Plead for a Suspension of Judgment," *SWCA*, October 4, 1906. Jones frequently protested white tendencies to homogenize African Americans based on the worst example. See, for example, "To What Extent Is Crime Increasing Among Negroes and What is the Remedy," *SWCA*, August 28, 1902; and "The North's Indifference," *SWCA*, February 8, 1906.

10. Grace Elizabeth Hale, *Making Whiteness: The Culture of Segregation in the South, 1890–1940* (New York: Vintage, 1998), 128–32; Litwack, *Trouble in Mind*, 101, 151–63, 241. On segregation as an intentional response to black threats to white class status, see John W. Cell, *The Highest Stage of White Supremacy: The Origins of Segregation in South Africa and the American South* (Cambridge: Cambridge University Press, 1982).

11. "The Negro's Great Burden," *SWCA*, September 17, 1908; "An Educator Undertakes a Dirty Job," *SWCA*, February 11, 1904; "Negro Women Assailed," *SWCA*, February 22, 1906.

12. "The American Tragedy," *SWCA*, January 4, 1912; "Congressman Williams on the Negro," *SWCA*, January 2, 1908; Pamela D. Arceneaux, "Guidebooks to Sin: The Blue Books of Storyville," *Louisiana History* 28 (Fall 1987): 397–405; Craig L. Foster, "Tarnished Angels: Prostitution in Storyville, New Orleans, 1900–1910," *Louisiana History* 31 (Fall 1990): 387–97; Long, *Great Southern Babylon*.

13. M. E. bishop William Talbot Handy Jr., interview with author, New Orleans, La., July 1997.

14. "It Is Up to New Orleans," *SWCA*, July 12, 1906; *SWCA*, November 6, 1906; "The Separate Cars in New Orleans," *SWCA*, January 20, 1910; "The New Orleans Street Cars," *SWCA*, September 29, 1910.

15. "Where Is the Difference," *SWCA*, January 16, 1908; *SWCA*, September 20, 1906; "The Heart of the Race Question," March 25, 1909, typescript for *SWCA*, Box 4, Folder 2, REJP.

16. "An Era in Methodist History Closes," July 15, 1960, newspaper clipping, Box 1, Folder 13, REJP.

17. Robert E. Jones, "Lecture I: Background," 18–19 Box 2, Folder 18, REJP; Jones, "The Democracy of Love," a sermon based on Mt. 19:19, n.d., 24–25, Box 5, REJP; and Jones, "Unification: A Review of Dr. Blake's Article on the Unification of American Methodism," February 15, 1917, typescript for *SWCA*, Box 4, Folder 11, REJP; "Race Relations in Christian Church Considered," *SWCA*, September 28, 1916; "Race Relations," *SWCA*, March 11, 1920.

18. J.W.E. Bowen, "The Negro's Case in Equity Stated by Himself: Has the Church an Adequate Educational Program for the Negro?" *SWCA*, January 29, 1920.

19. Russell E. Richey, *The Methodist Conference in America: A History* (Nashville: Abingdon Press, 1996), 145, 167, discusses the move toward the bureaucratization of fraternity, as the General Conference took over annual conferences' authority in determining who was in and who was out of the M. E. Church.

20. "Report of the Commission on Federation," *JGC* (1916), 1301–15, includes a review of the relationship between the M. E. Church and Southern Methodists since the Civil War. This summary, of course, reflects the M. E. perspective of its authors. The shift from fraternity to a concrete discussion of union occurred between the 1908 and 1912 General Conferences of the M. E. Church; see *JGC* (1912), 206, 741–43. On Jones's involvement in unification negotiations, see Oakes, "Struggle for Racial Equality," 130–226. On the centrality of race to the unification process, see Dwight W. Culver, *Negro Segregation in the Methodist Church* (New Haven: Yale University Press, 1953), 60–61; Morris Davis Jr., "Christian Unity and Civilized Races: The Methodist Joint Commission on Unification, 1916–1920" (Ph.D. diss., Drew University, 2003); and Richey, *Methodist Conference*, 176.

21. "Has the Church Lost Interest in the Negro?" *SWCA*, March 3, 1910; President McKinley cited in Michael Perman, *Struggle for Mastery: Disfranchisement in the South, 1888–1908* (Chapel Hill: University of North Carolina Press, 2001), 118; Woodrow Wilson, *War Messages*, 65th Cong., 1st sess., 1917, Senate Doc. No. 5, Serial No. 7264, 3–8; Dwight W. Culver, *Negro Segregation*, 60–67. For analysis of

the shifting emphasis of southern Civil War commemorations from southern to national interests, see Gaines M. Foster, *Ghosts of the Confederacy: Defeat, the Lost Cause, and the Emergence of the New South, 1865–1913* (New York: Oxford University Press, 1987) and Charles Regan Wilson, *Baptized in Blood: The Religion of the Lost Cause, 1865–1920* (Athens, Ga.: University of Georgia Press, 1980), 161–81. The Southern Methodist fraternal delegate to the M. E. Church at the 1900 General Conference made explicit the connections between political reunion and Methodist unification, pointing to a common history, celebrating recent cooperation in the war with Spain, and predicting a common destiny for a united church and nation in the new century. "Address of Rev. Dr. E. E. Hoss, of the Methodist Episcopal Church, South," *JGC* (1900), 547–554.

22. Rev. J. H. Reed, "The Negro, His Conditions Past and Present," *SWCA*, February 20, 1902; "Fraternity—'What of the Night?'" *SWCA*, December 30, 1880; "Pastoral Address of the General Conference," *SWCA*, June 17, 1880; *Zion's Herald*, January 28, 1920; R. E. Gillum, "The Organic Union of Methodism," *SWCA*, November 16, 1916.

23. "What they Are Saying About Unification," March 14, 1918, typescript for *SWCA*, Box 4, Folder 8, REJP; F. C. Monford to J. C. Hartzell, November 27, 1918, Joseph Crane Hartzell Papers, Box 2, GCAH.

24. Robert E. Jones, "The Problem: The Negro," in *A Working Conference on the Union of American Methodism* (New York and Cincinnati: Methodist Book Concern, 1916), 223; "A Little Plain Talk on Organic Union," *SWCA*, March 7, 1918; "The Meeting at Nashville," *SWCA*, October 8, 1914; "Zion's Herald Unmasked," *SWCA*, January 3, 1918; J.W.E. Bowen, "I Rise to Questions of High Privilege," *SWCA*, January 3, 1918; J.W.E. Bowen, "The Voice of the Negro in the Methodist Episcopal Church," *SWCA*, March 7, 1918.

25. "Shall Colored Methodism Unite?" *SWCA*, March 2, 1916; "A Little Plain Talk on Organic Union," *SWCA*, March 7, 1918; "Proceedings of the General Conference," *SWCA*, May 13, 1920; J. C. Hartzell, "Unification and Minorities," *Christian Advocate*, April 1, 1920; Richey, *Methodist Conference*, 178. For examples of the unification meetings in which Jones participated as a member of his denomination's committee, see *Proceedings of the Joint Commission on Unification of the Methodist Episcopal Church and the Methodist Episcopal Church, South, Held in Traverse City, Michigan* (Louisville: Mayes Printing Co., 1918); and *Proceedings of the Joint Commission on Unification of the Methodist Episcopal Church and the Methodist Episcopal Church, South, Held in Savannah, Georgia* (Louisville: Mayes Printing Co., 1918); for an extended analysis of all the unification meetings, the role of race, and Jones's participation, see Morris Davis, "Civilized Races."

26. *SWCA*, July 6, 1916.

27. "The Negro on Organic Union," *SWCA*, March 16, 1916; "The Negro and the Proposed Plan," *SWCA*, April 8, 1920; Robert E. Jones "Unification: A Review of Dr. Blake's Article on the Union of American Methodism," February 15, 1917, typescript for *SWCA*, Box 4, Folder 11, REJP; Jones, "The Problem: The Negro," 223–24.

28. R. E. Gillum, "The Organic Union of Methodism," *SWCA*, November 16, 1916; "A Little Plain Talk on Organic Union," *SWCA*, March 7, 1918; Robert E. Jones, "The Problem: The Negro," 225–26.

29. Cited in *Christian Advocate*, February 12, 1920; *JGC* (1920), 701–4; Frederick A. Norwood, *The Story of American Methodism*, (Nashville: Abingdon Press, 1974), 406–10, 413.

30. Isaiah B. Scott, "The Editor's Letter from Chicago," *SWCA*, May 24, 1900; Frank B. Smith, "History of the Movement for Negro Bishops in the Methodist Episcopal Church," *SWCA*, November 5, 1914; J.W.E. Bowen, "The Negro's Case in Equity Stated by Himself: III," *SWCA*, February 5, 1920; Culver, *Negro Segregation*, 55–56. For statements that "color is no bar to elective office" and encouragement of the election of a black bishop, see *JGC* (1872), 253; *JGC* (1876), 353; *JGC* (1880), 282; *JGC* (1888), 332; *JGC* (1896), 177–78, 225–26, 380; *JGC* (1900), 421–22.

31. *JGC* (1904), 179, 195, 207, 260–61, 266, 274, 324–49, 350, 410, 424–25, 428–29, 622, 624. "The Colored Bishop Question," *SWCA*, May 19, 1904; "Transferred to Africa," *SWCA*, June 2, 1904; "Our Goodbye Word," *SWCA*, June 2, 1904. Of the 748 delegates elected to the 1904 General Conference, the *SWCA* reported that 79 were black. See *SWCA*, April 28, 1904.

32. "An Election That Gives Hope," *SWCA*, June 9, 1904; "Jim Crow Episcopacy," *SWCA*, September 15, 1904. While other black bishops had served in Africa, these men had been elected in Africa and only by the predominantly African Liberia Annual Conference, whose decision the General Conference merely reaffirmed and consecrated.

33. "An Election That Gives Hope," *SWCA*, June 9, 1904; "Jim Crow Episcopacy," *SWCA*, September 15, 1904; *The Doctrines and Discipline of the Methodist Episcopal Church (1900)* (New York: Eaton and Mains, 1900), 106–7.

34. "A Segment of the King's Army," *SWCA*, March 4, 1915. An institutional expression of the growing cooperation with African Methodists in the twentieth century included the formation within the M. E. Church of a Commission on the Federation of Colored Churches to explore cooperation and questions of federation or union with colored Methodist churches. See *JGC* (1908), 342, 624; *JGC* (1912), 387, 505, 744–75; "Commission on Federation of Colored Churches," *SWCA*, January 21, 1915.

35. P. J. Maveety, "Negro Episcopacy, or Some Other Form of Leadership," *SWCA*, February 8, 1912; "Chapter Two (New Orleans Area)," *SWCA*, April 29, 1920; J.W.E. Bowen, "The Negro's Case in Equity Stated by Himself: IV. Does the Church Need Bishops of African Descent? How Many and Why?" *SWCA*, February 12, 1920. The previous emphasis on countering the charges of rivals had not totally dissipated. Agitators for a black bishop frequently appended to their arguments that they still encountered taunting by rivals and that they labored under a disadvantage in relation to the African Methodist denominations who touted their black bishops. As they had in the 1880s, advocates admitted that black bishops would most certainly lead to a rise in membership of African Americans. See, for example, G. H. Trever, "Further Words for Justice to the Negro," *SWCA*, April 9, 1908; "Working Under a Handicap," *SWCA*, February 15, 1912; "Representation of Our Colored Membership in the Episcopacy—The Why and How," *SWCA*, March 14, 1912; and J.W.E. Bowen, "The Negro's Case in Equity Stated by Himself: III," *SWCA*, February 5, 1920. See also resolutions to the General Conference, *JGC* (1900), 190.

36. Bishop John W. Hamilton to Robert E. Jones, February 14, 1916, Box 1, Folder 2, REJP. Bishop Thomas Neely made a similar statement in a 1915 book; see Oakes, "Struggle for Racial Equality," 144–45. Daniel W. Shaw, *Should the Negroes of the Methodist Episcopal Church Be Set Apart in a Church by Themselves?* (New York: Eaton and Mains, 1912), 38–39.

37. J.W.E. Bowen, *An Appeal for Negro Bishops, But No Separation* (New York: Eaton and Mains, 1912), 17–28; G. H. Trevor, "Will the Methodist Episcopal Church Be Just to the Negro?" *SWCA*, March 12, 1908; G. H. Trevor, "Further Words for Justice to the Negro," *SWCA*, April 9, 1908; "Our Attitude on the Amendments Again Stated," *SWCA*, November 14, 1912; J.W.E. Bowen, "The Negro's Case in Equity Stated by Himself: IV. Does the Church Need Bishops of African Descent? How Many and Why?" *SWCA*, February 12, 1920; "Report of the Committee Appointed To Look Into the Needs as to Episcopal Supervision and Conditions for Growth of our 325,000 Colored Members," *JGC* (1912), 773. See also I. Garland Penn's resolution at the 1900 General Conference, *JGC* (1900), 185.

38. "Election of Negro Bishops," *Christian Advocate*, May 27, 1920. Among the first such understandings was the agreement to authorize "African" ordinations but to limit them to deacons, not elders. See Richey, *Methodist Conference*, 56.

39. *JGC* (1904), 186, 407–8, 428–29. On white rejection of black bishops over white conferences, even in the North, see Shaw, *Should the Negroes*, 7–8, 17–18, 45–46; and David M. Reimers, *White Protestantism and the Negro* (New York: Oxford University Press, 1965), 73.

40. Rev. J.W.E. Bowen, "Bishops for Races and Languages and Tongues," *SWCA*, June 23, 1904; *JGC* (1904), 410.

41. Gardiner H. Shattuck Jr., *Episcopalians and Race: Civil War to Civil Rights* (Lexington: University Press of Kentucky, 2000), 21.

42. Ernest Lyon, "A Voice from the Jungle," *SWCA*, January 9, 1908; "The Meeting at Nashville," *SWCA*, October 8, 1914; "Colored Conferences Approve Amendment," *SWCA*, March 9, 1916; I. Garland Penn, "The Voice of a Negro on Area Supervision in the South, Bishops for Races and Unification of Methodisms," *SWCA*, March 9, 1916; *JGC* (1908), 1127, 1130.

43. The same 1907 Episcopal General Convention did approve a plan for suffragan bishops to serve African Americans within existing dioceses, although it would be ten years before any were elected to that position. Shattuck, *Episcopalians and Race*, 24–25.

44. The General Conference elected eight white men as general superintendents in 1904, 1908, and 1912, and elected seven in 1912. *JGC* (1904), 316, 424, 622–23; *JGC* (1908), 333, 455–56, 772–74; *JGC* (1912), 405, 532, 927–28; *JGC* (1916), 370, 878–80.

45. "Bishops for Races and Languages," *SWCA*, August 22, 1912; "The Meeting at Nashville," *SWCA*, October 8, 1914. For the voting at the 1912 General Conference, see *JGC* (1912), 507, 516, 535–36.

46. I. Garland Penn, "The Voice of a Negro on Area Supervision in the South, Bishops for Races and Unification of Methodisms," *SWCA*, March 9, 1916. For the voting in the Louisiana conference, see W. Scott Chinn, "Louisiana Annual Conference, Forty-Eighth Session," *SWCA*, February 17, 1916; and *JGC* (1916), 1466.

47. "Race Relations in the Church Considered," *SWCA*, September 28, 1916; *JGC* (1916), 1465–67; "Colored Conferences Approve Amendment," *SWCA*, March 9, 1916. Debates leading up to the 1916 votes also centered on whether the amendment actually received the two-thirds vote necessary at the 1912 General Conference in order to send it to the annual conferences for an up or down vote. The question centered on whether the two-thirds required by the constitution was of the total number of delegates at the General Conference or only two-thirds of those voting. *JGC* (1916), 511–12, 525–26.

48. *JGC* (1920), 320, 364–65, 455, 1408; Oakes, "Struggle for Racial Equality," 297–300; "Bishop Robert E. Jones," *SWCA*, June 10, 1920; "New Orleans Area Receives Bishop R. E. Jones," *SWCA*, August 5, 1920; *SWCA*, November 4, 1920. Shattuck, *Episcopalians and Race*, 24–25.

49. Norwood, *American Methodism*, 364; *JGC* (1912), 429, 529–31; *JGC* (1916), 430, 480–82; Oakes, "Struggle for Racial Equality," 288–93.

50. *JGC* (1920), 320, 455; "Eleventh Day," *Christian Advocate*, May 20, 1920; "Proceedings of the General Conference," *SWCA*, May 27, 1920; separate episcopal elections actually began at the preceding General Conference in 1916. Both Hartzell and Scott retired as missionary bishops to Africa, and, in an effort to maintain one member of each race in that episcopacy, the General Conference held two separate elections for missionary bishop to Africa, one for white candidates and one for black candidates. Highlighting the ongoing centrality of New Orleans to black leadership in the M. E. Church, the black victor, Alexander P. Camphor, was a New Orleans native and graduate of New Orleans University. *JGC* (1916), 370, 406, 475; "Missionary Bishop-Elect Camphor," *SWCA*, June 1, 1916.

51. "The Negro in the General Conference," *SWCA*, April 25, 1912; Robert E. Jones, "Lecture I: Background: The Claims of Christianity," 6, Box 2, Folder 8, REJP; J.W.E. Bowen, "The Negro's Case in Equity Stated by Himself," *SWCA*, February 5, 1920; H. Shelton Smith, *In His Image, But . . . Racism in Southern Religion, 1780–1910* (Durham: Duke University Press, 1972), 36–47.

52. "Zion's Herald Unmasked," *SWCA*, January 13, 1918; "Lessons Drawn from Labor Day," *SWCA*, September 8, 1904; "The Status of Negro Labor," *SWCA*, July 26, 1906; "Together: A Plea for Sanity in Race Relations," *SWCA*, August 31, 1916; "Zion's Herald Unmasked," *SWCA*, January 3, 1918; Buchanan v. Warley, 245 U.S. 60 (1917). On the events leading to the Supreme Court decision on residential segregation, see Roger Rice, "Residential Segregation by Law, 1910–1917," *Journal of Southern History* 34 (May 1968): 179–99.

53. "Is It Social Equality?" *SWCA*, April 11, 1918; "Breaking Over Race Lines," *SWCA*, July 27, 1916; "Zion's Herald Unmasked," *SWCA*, January 3, 1918; "The Negro and the Forthcoming General Conference," *SWCA*, April 22, 1920.

54. Grant Wacker, *Heaven Below: Early Pentecostals and American Culture* (Cambridge, Mass.: Harvard University Press, 2001), 103–5, 226–34; Cheryl Sanders, *Saints in Exile: The Holiness-Pentecostal Experience in African American Religion and Culture* (New York: Oxford University Press, 1996), 17–34; Anne H. Pinn and Anthony B. Pinn, *Fortress Introduction to Black Church History* (Minneapolis: Fortress Press, 2002), 102–24; Vinson Synan, *The Holiness-Pentecostal Movement in the United States* (Grand Rapids, Mich.: Eerdmans, 1971), 166–72, 179.

55. Cited in "Central Congregational Church [Atlanta]: The First Twenty-Five Years," p. 16, typescript in Central Congregational United Church of Christ, Records, 1860–1990, Box 10, ARC. Culver, *Negro Segregation*, 83–93; Morris Davis, "Civilized Races," 83–95; William B. Gravely, *Gilbert Haven, Methodist Abolitionist: A Study in Race, Religion and Reform* (Nashville: Abingdon, 1973), 188; Ralph E. Morrow, *Northern Methodism and Reconstruction* (East Lansing: Michigan State University Press, 1956), 194–95; Reimers, *White Protestantism*, 55, 82. Methodists were far from unique in suggesting expediency rather than theology drove racial separation. See Andrew E. Murray, *Presbyterians and the Negro: A History* (Philadelphia: Presbyterian Historical Society, 1966), 198; and Shattuck, *Episcopalians and Race*, 24–29.

56. Hunter Dickinson Farish, *The Circuit Rider Dismounts* (Richmond, Va.: Dietz Press, 1938), 7–8; Daniel W. Stowell, *Rebuilding Zion : The Religious Reconstruction of the South, 1863–1877* (New York: Oxford University Press, 1998), 42; Culver, *Negro Segregation*, 11–12, 16–18, Frank S. Loescher, *The Protestant Church and the Negro: A Pattern of Segregation* (New York: Association Press, 1948), 16, 28; Reimers, *White Protestantism*, 101.

57. George A. Grant, "Race Conflict," *Methodist Review* 92 (May 1910): 427.

58. *New Orleans Christian Advocate*, July 30, 1870, quoted in Farish, *Circuit Rider*, 219–20; W. Harrison Daniel, "Virginia Baptists and the Negro, 1865–1902," *Virginia Magazine of History and Biography* 76 (1969): 342, 357; Presbyterian quoted in Reimers, *White Protestantism*, 29. For a suggestive framework on the relationship between sex, segregation, and religion, see Donald Mathews, " 'Christianizing the South'—Sketching a Synthesis," in Harry S. Stout and D. G. Hart, eds., *New Directions in American Religious History* (New York: Oxford University Press, 1997), 91–97.

59. Lillian Smith, *Killers of the Dream* (1949, reprint; New York: W. W. Norton and Co., 1961), 28–29.

60. J.W.E. Bowen, "The Negro's Case in Equity Stated by Himself: Principles Stated and Organic Union," *SWCA*, January 15, 1920; J.W.E. Bowen, "The Negro's Case in Equity Stated by Himself: III. The Need of Bishops of African Descent," *SWCA*, February 5, 1920; Bowen, *An Appeal for Negro Bishops*, 81–88; "Representation of Our Colored Membership in the Episcopacy—the Why and How," *SWCA*, March 14, 1912; Ernest Lyon, "A Voice From the Jungle," *SWCA*, January 9, 1908; "The Mississippi Proposition," *SWCA*, January 20, 1916; "The Negro on Organic Union," *SWCA*, March 16, 1916; Rev. C. A. Tindley, "The Negro Exodus," *SWCA*, July 25, 1918; Robert E. Jones, "Christmas—A Christian Festival With a Forward Look," December 21, 1916, typescript for *SWCA*, Box 4, Folder 6, REJP; Jones, "The Problem: The Negro," 224; Jones, "Lecture III: Barriers to Progress," 12, Box 2, Folder 10, REJP; Oakes, "Struggle for Racial Equality," 179.

61. "Not Guilty," *SWCA*, December 8, 1910; Morris Davis, "Civilized Races," 32, 78; Gilmore, *Gender and Jim Crow*, 137–38,

62. Culver, *Negro Segregation*, 63; Jean Russell, *God's Lost Cause: A Study of the Church and the Racial Problem* (London: S.C.M. Press, 1968), 67–69.

63. "The Color Line in a World Movement," *SWCA*, June 9, 1910; "An Example to Others," February 5, 1914, typescript for *SWCA*, Box 4, Folder 4, REJP; "The Negro Congress," *SWCA*, July 12, 1906; "Enemies of the South," *SWCA*, September 15, 1904.

64. "Have We Failed?" *SWCA*, May 26, 1910; Robert E. Jones, "Unification: A Review of Dr. Blake's Article on the Unification of American Methodism," February 15, 1917, typescript for *SWCA*, Box 4, Folder 11, REJP. On the potential extinction of black Americans, according to conservative whites, see George M. Fredrickson, *The Black Image in the White Mind: The Debate on Afro-American Character and Destiny, 1817–1914* (Middletown, Conn.: Wesleyan University Press, 1971), 228–55; Williamson, *Crucible of Race*, 6, 111–39.

65. Robert E. Jones, "The Problem: The Negro," 223–24; "The Freedmen," *SWCA*, March 3, 1910.

66. Rev. J. C. Sherrill, "It Has Been Done," *SWCA*, July 1, 1920; Robert E. Jones, "The Problem: The Negro," 229.

67. Robert E. Jones, "The Problem: The Negro," 224, 227–28; "Can the General Conference Divide the Church?" *SWCA*, May 31, 1906; Jones, "We Can Improve Race Relations," 14, Box 2, Folder 6, REJP; Jones, "Lecture II: The Problems of Segregation," 8, Box 2, Folder 9, REJP.

68. Bowen, *An Appeal for Bishops*, 72, 75.

69. "The Negro's Case Briefly Stated," December 30, 1909, typescript for *SWCA*, Box 4, Folder 2, REJP; Isaiah B. Scott, "America or Africa, Which?" *SWCA*, April 3, 1902. For an analysis of the contested meaning of Africa for African Americans, and debates over immigration and the religious language employed, see David W. Wills, "Exodus Piety: African American Religion in an Age of Immigration," in Jonathan D. Sarna, ed., *Minority Faiths and the American Protestant Mainstream* (Urbana and Chicago: University of Illinois Press, 1998), 136–88.

70. "The Negro and Preparedness," *SWCA*, June 29, 1916; "It Takes Team Work to Win," *SWCA*, March 21, 1918; "The Negro's Loyalty," *SWCA*, June 27, 1918; "No German Propaganda," *SWCA*, July 11, 1918; Nell Irvin Painter, *Standing at Armageddon: The United States, 1877–1919* (New York: W. W. Norton and Co., 1987), 304, 331, 356.

71. P. J. Maveety, "America's Most Serious Problem: Twelve Million Negroes a Challenge to Christian Democracy," *Christian Advocate*, February 5, 1920; "The American Negro as a Political Factor," *SWCA*, October 20, 1910; Robert E. Jones, "Innocent Blood Cries Aloud," August 1, 1910, typescript for *SWCA*, Box 4, Folder 3, REJP; Jones, "Unification: A Review of Dr. Blake's Article on the Unification of American Methodism," February 15, 1917, typescript for *SWCA*, Box 4, Folder 11, REJP; Jones, "Lecture II: The Problems of Segregation," 5, 16, Box 2, Folder 9, REJP.

72. Robert E. Jones, "The Democracy of Love," 1920, 4–6, Box 5, REJP; Jones, "The Problem: The Negro," 230; Oakes, "Struggle for Racial Equality," 180.

73. Octavia Albert, *The House of Bondage, or, Charlotte Brooks and Other Slaves* (1890; reprint, New York: Oxford University Press, 1988), 146–47.

74. R. E. Jones, "Old Black Joe and Young Joseph," *Christian Advocate*, October 3, 1918; "God's Supreme Challenge to the Negro Race," *SWCA*, January 3, 1918. For an example of Martin Luther King Jr.'s understanding of redemptive suffering, see "Eulogy for the Martyred Children," (1963) in James M. Washington, ed., *A Testament of Hope: The Essential Writings and Speeches of Martin Luther King, Jr.* (San Francisco: Harper San Francisco, 1986), 221–23.

75. Rev. E. C. Morris, "New Year's Greetings to Negro Americans," *SWCA*, January 3, 1918; Litwack, *Trouble in Mind*, 11. Jones expressed a similar sentiment when he warned "there is one Supreme Being who is the Judge of all the earth and He will do right, and if the laws of the great American nation are not sufficient to chastise and to bring to justice these high handed murderers, then God will bring them into account." Robert E. Jones, "Innocent Blood Cries Aloud," August 11, 1910, typescript for *SWCA*, Box 4, Folder 3, REJP.

76. "God and Democracy," October 25, 1917, typescript for *SWCA*, Box 4, Folder 7, REJP; [Isaiah B. Scott] "Lawlessness of Our Time the School of Crime," *SWCA*, August 16, 1900; "A Prophecy of a New Day," *SWCA*, January 22, 1914.

77. Robert E. Jones, "The Problem: The Negro," 234. See also Jones's editorial, "Have We Failed?" *SWCA*, May 26, 1910.

78. W.E.B. Du Bois, *The Negro Church* (Atlanta: Atlanta University Press, 1903), 135; W. J. Arnold, "Suggestions to the Delegates to the Conference of the M. E. Church," *SWCA*, April 28, 1904; Address of the Bishops, *Christian Advocate*, May 20, 1920; John D. Epps, "Class Legislation Unchristian," *Christian Advocate*, April 4, 1918; "Preaching Inter-racial Peace," *Christian Advocate*, May 29, 1919; George A. Grant, "Race Conflict," *Methodist Review* 92 (May 1910): 420, 428, 434; "Unification," *Methodist Review* 101 (January 1918): 42; Reimers, *White Protestantism*, 75, 105; *JGC* (1920), 393.

79. "The Negro on Organic Union," *SWCA*, March 16, 1916; Robert E. Jones, "The Problem: The Negro," 234; G. H. Trevor, "Further Words for Justice to the Negro," *SWCA*, April 9, 1908; Rev. J. C. Sherrill, "It Has Been Done," *SWCA*, July 1, 1920; Robert E. Jones, "Lecture I: Background: The Claims of Christianity and Democracy," typescript marked "reading copy," 8–9, 29, Box 2, Folder 8, REJP.

CHAPTER 5
INTERRACIAL CATHOLICISM IN NEW ORLEANS

1. Hartzell's comments originally appeared in the *SWCA* and were reprinted in "Civil Rights in the Churches," *Louisianian*, April 25, 1874.

2. Edwin S. Gaustad and Philip L. Barlow, *New Historical Atlas of Religion in America* (New York: Oxford University Press, 2001), 51–52; John T. McGreevy, *Catholicism and American Freedom: A History* (New York: W. W. Norton, 2003), 91–105.

3. Jay P. Dolan, *The American Catholic Experience: A History From Colonial Times to the Present* (Notre Dame, Ind.: University of Notre Dame Press, 1992), 295–303, 367–68; James J. Hennesey, *American Catholics: A History of the Roman Catholic Community in the United States* (New York: Oxford University Press, 1981), 148–55, 173.

4. Hennesey, *American Catholics*, 32–33.

5. Racial liberalism has been a persistent theme in New Orleans and Louisiana historiography. Studies that argue for varying degrees of racial liberalism in the second half of the nineteenth century include Caryn Cossé Bell, *Revolution, Romanticism and the Afro-Creole Tradition in Louisiana, 1718–1868* (Baton Rouge: Louisiana State University Press, 1997), 1, 222–75; Henry C. Dethloff and Robert R. Jones,

"Race Relations in Louisiana, 1877–98," *Louisiana History* 9 (Fall 1968): 301–24, William Ivy Hair, *Carnival of Fury: Robert Charles and the New Orleans Race Riot of 1900* (Baton Rouge: Louisiana State University Press, 1976), 89; Joseph Logsdon and Caryn Cossé Bell, "The Americanization of Black New Orleans," in Arnold R. Hirsch and Joseph Logsdon, eds., *Creole New Orleans: Race and Americanization* (Baton Rouge: Louisiana State University Press, 1992), 216; Dale A. Somers, "Black and White in New Orleans: A Study in Urban Race Relations," *Journal of Southern History* 40 (February 1974): 19–42. Education has been one specific avenue for demonstrating racial liberalism. See Roger A. Fischer, *The Segregation Struggle in Louisiana, 1862–1877* (Urbana: University of Illinois Press, 1974); and Louis R. Harlan, "Desegregation in New Orleans Public Schools During Reconstruction," *American Historical Review* 47 (April 1962): 663–75. Labor history, especially of dockworkers in New Orleans, has become another fruitful field for exploring the ebb and flow of racial liberalism and reaction in New Orleans. See especially Eric Arnesen, *Waterfront Workers of New Orleans: Race, Class, and Politics, 1863–1923* (New York: Oxford University Press, 1991). John Blassingame, *Black New Orleans, 1860–1880* (Chicago: University of Chicago Press, 1973), offers a picture of the city's black community after the Civil War that reveals its potential and promise but avoids romanticizing what is only a relative liberalism and never loses sight of the very real limits facing even the city's wealthiest and most powerful black residents.

6. Earl C. Woods and Charles Nolan, eds., *Sacramental Records of the Roman Catholic Church of the Archdiocese of New Orleans*, 10 vols. (New Orleans: Archdiocese of New Orleans, 1987–95), covering the years 1718 to 1812, reveals multiple racial identities within parties seeking the sacraments in colonial New Orleans. Cardinal Herbert Vaughan, during a tour of New Orleans, commented on the liberality of French colonial law, including the recognition of slave marriages, as an important influence on black Catholic loyalty in Louisiana, even in the nineteenth century. Herbert Vaughan Diary, February 8, 1872, typescript, Mill Hill Fathers Papers, JFA. See also John Bernard Alberts, "Origins of Black Catholic Parishes in the Archdiocese of New Orleans, 1718–1920" (Ph.D. diss., Louisiana State University, 1998), 22–25, 47, 51–53; and Caryn Cossé Bell, *Revolution, Romanticism*, 12–15, 65–74. For an institutional overview of Louisiana Catholicism, see Roger Baudier, *The Catholic Church in Louisiana* (New Orleans: A. W. Hyatt stationery co., 1939). On the colonial experience of Africans in Louisiana, including the role of the Catholic Church, see Gwendolyn Midlo Hall, *Africans in Colonial Louisiana: The Development of Afro-Creole Culture in the Eighteenth Century* (Baton Rouge: Louisiana State University Press, 1992); and Kimberly S. Hanger, *Bounded Lives, Bounded Places: Free Black Society in Colonial New Orleans, 1769–1803* (Durham, N.C.: Duke University Press, 1997). For debates about the religious treatment of slaves in Anglo-American colonies, see Sylvia Frey and Betty Wood, *Come Shouting to Zion: African American Protestantism in the American South and British Caribbean to 1830* (Chapel Hill: University of North Carolina Press, 1998), 1–34; and Albert J. Raboteau, *Slave Religion: The "Invisible Institution" in the Antebellum South* (New York: Oxford University Press, 1977), 96–146.

7. Arthé Agnes Anthony, "The Negro Creole Community in New Orleans, 1880–1920: An Oral History" (Ph.D. diss., University of California, Irvine, 1978),

16; Bell, *Revolution, Romanticism*, 36–46, 65; Virginia Domínguez, *White by Definition: Social Classification in Creole Louisiana* (New Brunswick, N.J.: Rutgers University Press, 1986), 23; James H. Dorman, "Louisiana's 'Creoles of Color': Ethnicity, Marginality, and Identity," *Social Science Quarterly* 73 (September 1992): 616; Laura Foner, "The Free People of Color in Louisiana and St. Domingue," *Journal of Social History* 3 (Summer 1970): 409–10, 413–14; Hanger, *Bounded Lives*, 17–54, 109–10, 125–26, 134; Thomas N. Ingersoll, "Free Blacks in a Slave Society: New Orleans, 1718–1812," *William and Mary Quarterly* 48 (April 1991): 180–92; Paul F. La-Chance, "The Formation of a Three-Caste Society: Evidence from Wills in Antebellum New Orleans," *Social Science History* 18 (Summer 1994): 226–27, 231; Joan M. Martin, "*Plaçage* and the Louisiana *Gens de Couleur Libre*: How Race and Sex Defined the Lifestyles of Free Women of Color," in Sybil Kein, ed., *Creole: The History and Legacy of Louisiana's Free People of Color* (Baton Rouge: Louisiana State University Press, 2000), 60, 63–64; Alice Dunbar-Nelson, "People of Color in Louisiana," in Kein, ed., *Creole: History and Legacy*, 18; David C. Rankin, "The Forgotten People: Free People of Color in New Orleans, 1850–1870" (Ph.D. diss., Johns Hopkins University, 1976), 46. Domínguez, *White by Definition*, 23, 25, 116, claims 23.8 percent were free colored in 1803, while Hanger, *Bounded Lives*, 12, says free people of color constituted 33.5 percent of the city's population in 1805.

8. The African Methodist Episcopal Church v. City of New Orleans, quoted in Paul A. Kunkel, "Modifications in Louisiana Negro Status Under Louisiana Constitutions, 1812–1957," *Journal of Negro History* 44 (January 1959): 3–4; Charles B. Rousseve, *The Negro in Louisiana: Aspects of His History and His Literature* (New Orleans: Xavier University Press, 1937), 21; Domínguez, *White by Definition*, 25; David Goldfield, *Region, Race and Cities: Interpreting the Urban South* (Baton Rouge: Louisiana State University Press, 1997), 140.

9. Rousseve, *Negro in Louisiana*, 25, 39–40. On the relative liberalism of Latin Catholics, see Anthony, "Negro Creole," 16; Bell, *Revolution, Romanticism*, 11–12, 65, 70; LaChance, "Formation of a Three-Caste Society," 231; and Logsdon and Bell, "Americanization of Black New Orleans," 201–261.

10. On the centrality of Catholicism to Creole identity, see Anthony, "Negro Creole," 24, 26, 32, 48, 128; Bell, *Revolution, Romanticism*, 3; Rodolphe Lucien Desdunes, *Our People and Our History: A Tribute to the Creole People of Color in Memory of the Great Men They Have Given Us and of the Good Works They Have Accomplished*, originally published as *Nos Hommes et Notre Histoire* (1911), Dorothea Olga McCants, trans. and ed. (Baton Rouge: Louisiana State University Press, 1973), 109; Domínguez, *White by Definition*, 164, 205, 219–24; Dorman, "Louisiana's 'Creoles of Color,' " 616; Kein, ed., *Creole: History and Legacy*, xiv; Rankin, "Forgotten People," 125; Robert C. Reinders, "The Churches and the Negro in New Orleans, 1850–1860," *Phylon* 22 (Fall 1961): 242; Rousseve, *Negro in Louisiana*, 24; and Loren Schweninger, "Socioeconomic Dynamics Among the Gulf Creole Populations: The Antebellum and Civil War Years," in James Dorman, ed., *Creoles of Color of the Gulf South* (Knoxville: University of Tennessee Press, 1996), 57.

11. Canon Peter L. Benoit, Diary of a Trip to America, April 9, 1875, CB7–188, JFA. Similarly, at St. Augustine's, Creoles provided much of the funding and helped construct the church. See C. M. Chambon, pastor, "Saint Augustine Church: Year 1939," (New Orleans 1940), 6, Parish History Collection, AANO; Charles B. Rous-

seve, "The Negro in New Orleans," 5, typescript, Charles B. Rousseve Collection, Box 7, Folder 1, ARC; Alberts, "Origins of Black Parishes," 88; Reinders, "Churches and the Negro," 242–43; Baudier, *Catholic Church in Louisiana*, 365; and Rousseve, *Negro in Louisiana*, 41.

12. The sacramental records during the French period are inconsistent, but during the Spanish era, which also coincides with the emergence of a free population as a distinct group, the pattern of tripartite classification becomes more clear in the sacramental records. See Woods and Nolan, eds., *Sacramental Records*. Catholic priests occasionally performed an illegal ceremony between slave and free, just as they occasionally performed marriages between white and black, perhaps undermining the strict tripartite separation but at the same time suggesting a racial blindness that only strengthened the loyalty of black Catholics to the church. See Tracy Fessenden, "The Sisters of the Holy Family and the Veil of Race," *Religion and American Culture: A Journal of Interpretation* 10 (Summer 2000): 193.

13. Bell, *Revolution, Romanticism*, 243; Baudier, *Catholic Church in Louisiana*, 365; Reinders, "Churches and the Negro," 242–43; C. M. Chambon, pastor, "Saint Augustine Church: Year 1939," (New Orleans: 1940), 6, AANO; Charles R. Rousseve, "The Negro in New Orleans," 5, typescript, Rousseve Collection, Box 7, Folder 1, ARC; Lucille Hutton, "Notes on St. James' A.M.E. Church," manuscript, Lucille Hutton Papers, Box 12, Folder 12, ARC.

14. Caroline Senter, "Creole Poets on the Verge of a Nation," in Kein, ed., *Creole: History and Legacy*, 276–94. Desdunes, *Our People and Our History*, discusses the wide range of Creole accomplishments.

15. Joseph Logsdon with Lawrence Powell, "Rodolphe Lucien Desdunes: Forgotten Organizer of the *Plessy* Protest," in Samuel C. Hyde Jr., ed., *Sunbelt Revolution: The Historical Progression of the Civil Rights Struggle in the Gulf South, 1866–2000* (Gainesville: University of Florida Press, 2003), 49–50.

16. *Three Catholic Afro-American Congresses* (1893; reprint, New York: Arno Press, 1978), 150; "The Problem of our African Population," *Methodist Quarterly Review* 66 (January 1884): 112. Frank Tannebaum, *Slave and Citizen: The Negro in the Americas* (New York: Vintage Press, 1946), compares the racial systems in post-Emancipation societies in North and South America. See also Carl N. Degler, *Neither Black nor White: Slavery and Race Relations in Brazil and the United States* (New York: Macmillan, 1971); George M. Fredrickson, *Racism: A Short History* (Princeton: Princeton University Press, 2002), 102, 185 (n. 5); Peter Wade, *Blackness and Race Mixture: The Dynamics of Racial Identity in Colombia* (Baltimore: Johns Hopkins University Press, 1993); and the special issue on comparative racial constructions in the Americas, *Latin American Perspectives* 25 (May 1998).

17. Thomas Low Nichols, *Forty Years of American Life, 1821–1861* (New York: Stackpole Sons, 1937), 127–28; Blassingame, *Black New Orleans*, 16. On visitors' reactions to and comments on New Orleans as distinctive in the American context, see Timothy F. Reilly, "Heterodox New Orleans and the Protestant South, 1800–1861," *Louisiana Studies* (Fall 1973): 533–51. Alberts, "Origins of Black Parishes," 47, 66, and Bell, *Revolution, Romanticism*, 20–29, 37–38, 42–46, discuss the impact of Caribbean refugees on New Orleans. For descriptions of large numbers of black Catholics worshiping at both St. Rose of Lima and St. Ann's in the 1850s, see Roger

Baudier, *Centennial St. Rose of Lima Parish, New Orleans, La.* (1957), 13, 17, Parish History Collection, AANO.

18. Blassingame, *Black New Orleans*, 16–17; Mary Bernard Deggs, *No Cross, No Crown: Black Nuns in Nineteenth-Century New Orleans*, Virginia Meacham Gould and Charles E. Nolan, eds. (Bloomington: Indiana University Press, 2001), 92; Cyprian Davis, *The History of Black Catholics in the United States* (New York: Crossroads, 1990), 90; John T. Gillard, *The Catholic Church and the American Negro* (Baltimore: St. Joseph's Society Press, 1929), 28–29.

19. Cited in Bell, *Revolution, Romanticism*, 73; Baudier, *Catholic Church in Louisiana*, 365; C. M. Chambon, pastor, "Saint Augustine Church: Year 1939," (New Orleans 1940), 6, Parish History Collection, AANO; Charles B. Rousseve, "The Negro in New Orleans," 5, typescript, Rousseve Collection, Box 7, Folder 1, ARC; Alberts, "Origins of Black Parishes," 88; Reinders, "The Churches and the Negro," 242–43.

20. Desdunes, *Our People and Our History*, 97; Roger Baudier, "Development of Catholic Education," 5–6, Catholic Education in Louisiana, 14–035–25, BCM; Baudier, "Sisters of the Holy Family," typescript for *Catholic Action*, 5, Sisters of the Holy Family, 14–05–10–16, BCP; Baudier, "The Negro and Catholic Education," Catholic Education in Louisiana, 14–03–5–21, BCM; Baudier, "Archdiocese Has Had Four Orders for Colored Women," *Catholic Action of the South*, March 8, 1959; notes from Brother Benedict Westrick, F.S.C., "The History of Catholic Negro Education in the City of New Orleans, La. (1724–1950)," 124-T-35, JFA; Deggs, *No Cross*; Fessenden, "Veil of Race." On the Oblate Sisters, see Diane Batts Morrow, *Persons of Color and Religious at the Same Time: The Oblate Sisters of Providence, 1828–1860* (Chapel Hill: University of North Carolina Press, 2002).

21. Memorandum for Guste, 3; Dethloff and Jones, "Race Relations in Louisiana," 315.

22. Francis Janssens, SQA-RCCM (1892), 161-DY-3; "Jubilate Deo is the Centenary History of the Priests of the Congregation of the Mission, 1848–1949, St. Stephen Parish, New Orleans, Louisiana," (1949), 50, St. Stephen's Parish, N. O., History and Anniversary Books, AANO; and Parish Annual Reports (1884–1885) St. Alphonsus Parish, N. O., AANO; Roger Baudier, "The Negro and Catholic Education," 3, Catholic Education in Louisiana, 14–03–5–21, BCM; "The House of the Good Shepherd," New Orleans *Daily Picayune*, November 1, 1896.

23. "The Colored Catholics of New Orleans," *Colored Harvest* 1 (October 1892).

24. "The Catholic Church and the Colored People," *Catholic World* 37 (June 1883): 374.

25. Edwardo J. Misch, *The American Bishops and the Negro from the Civil War to the Third Plenary Council of Baltimore (1865–1884)* (Rome: Pontificia Universitas Gregoriana Facultas Historiae Ecclesiasticae, 1968), 27, 45.

26. Misch, *American Bishops*, 21, 42–48; Hennesey, *American Catholics*, 161–62; "Filling in the Background," *Josephite Newsletter* (November–December, 1966, January, 1967), typescript, Josephite Records, Box 1, XUA.

27. Hennesey, *American Catholics*, 161–62, 173; Cyprian Davis, *Black Catholics*, 119–20; Peter Guilday, *A History of the Councils of Baltimore* (1791–1884), (New York: Macmillan, 1932), 213, 220; *The Memorial Volume: A History of the Third Plenary Council of Baltimore. November 9–December 7, 1884* (Baltimore, Md.: Baltimore

Publishing Co., 1885), 43; Misch, *American Bishops*, 55; Edwardo J. Misch, "The American Bishops and the Negro from the Civil War to the Third Plenary Council of Baltimore (1865–1884)" (Ph.D. diss., Pontificia Universitas Gregoriana Facultas Historiae Ecclesiasticae, 1968), 264.

28. John Slattery, "Some Aspects of the Negro Problem," *Catholic World* 38 (Feb. 1884): 604; *Memorial Volume*, 225; Guilday, *A History of the Councils of Baltimore*, 241; Misch, "American Bishops," 498, 573; Misch, *American Bishops*, 55.

29. Francis Janssens to John Slattery, February 16, 1893, 7-D-11, JFA; Sr. Austin Carroll to Slattery, December 15, 1888, 4-B-14, JFA; Canon Peter L. Benoit, Diary of a Trip to America, April 9, 1875, CB7–187, JFA; George Wilson, S.S.J., "You Have Walked a Long Way," sermon preached at 125th anniversary Mass at St. Louis Cathedral, reprinted in *Divine Word Messenger* 45 (March–April, 1968), 37–42, copy, Sisters of the Holy Family Papers, ARC; William Barnaby Faherty and Madeline Barni Oliver, *The Religious Roots of Black Catholics of Saint Louis* (St. Louis, Mo.: St. Louis University Press, 1977), 7; Misch, "American Bishops," 336, 438, 441, 457, 471–72, 476, 510–15; Charles E. Nolan, *The Catholic Church in Mississippi (1865–1911)* (Lafayette, La.: Center for Louisiana Studies, University of Louisiana at Lafayette and the Catholic Diocese of Jackson, Jackson, Mississippi, 2002), 300; Archbishop Kenrick in St. Louis was especially vehement in his resistance to any special work on behalf of black Catholics. See Cyprian Davis, *Black Catholics*, 130.

30. Dorothy Ann Blatnica, *At the Altar of Their God: African American Catholics in Cleveland, 1922–1961* (New York: Garland, 1995), 10; Dolan, *American Catholic Experience*, 294; Avery Robert Dulles, *Models of the Church* (Garden City, N.Y.: Doubleday, 1974), 31–41; John Tracy Ellis, *American Catholicism* (Chicago: University of Chicago Press, 1956), 89, 94; Hennesey, *American Catholics*, 145–55, 193; Joseph T. Leonard, *Theology and Race Relations*, (Milwaukee: Bruce Publishing Co., 1963), 255; Misch, "American Bishops," 46–47; *Memorial Volume*, 113; Stephen J. Ochs, *Desegregating the Altar: The Josephites and the Struggle for Black Priests* (Baton Rouge: Louisiana State University Press, 1990), 18–19, 31. On the conservatism of Odin and Perche on racial issues that emerged from their understanding of the church, see McGreevy, *Catholicism and American Freedom*, 30, 39, 81.

31. "The Catholic Church and the Colored People," *Catholic World* 37 (June 1883): 379; *Memorial Volume*, 71–74; Nolan, *Catholic Church in Mississippi*, 298; Leonard, *Theology and Race*, 28–29; Misch, "American Bishops," 471; Cyprian Davis, *Black Catholics*, 127.

32. Petition to the Very Rev. Superior General Sorin of the Congregation of the Holy Cross, in Notre Dame, Ind., April 10, 1885, Sacred Heart of Jesus Parish, N. O., Correspondence, AANO; Louis Dutto, "The Negroes in Mississippi," *Catholic World* 46 (February 1888): 584; John W. Shaw to Barry Kane, April 4, 1922, Blessed Sacrament Parish, N. O., Correspondence, 1915–1928, AANO; Henry J. Koren, *The Serpent and the Dove: A History of the Congregation of the Holy Ghost in the United States 1745–1984* (Pittsburgh: Spiritus Press, 1985), 122–23, 164; Gary W. McDonogh, *Black and Catholic in Savannah, Georgia* (Knoxville: University of Tennessee Press, 1993), 156; Misch, "American Bishops," 385–86; Cyprian Davis, *Black Catholics*, 199, 205.

33. Nolan, *Catholic Church in Mississippi*, 311; Baudier, *Catholic Church in Louisiana*, 433; Baudier, "Development of Catholic Education," 5, Catholic Education in

Louisiana, 14–03–5–25, BCM; Baudier, "The Negro and Catholic Education," 2, Catholic Education in Louisiana, 14–03–5–21, BCM; Memorandum for Guste, 3–4; Francis Janssens to Katharine Drexel, January 14, 1892, Archbishop Janssens Letters to Mother M. Drexel, 1891–1892, Box 30, Folder 14, SBS; Misch, "American Bishops," 285, 445.

34. Canon Peter L. Benoit, Diary of a Trip to America, April 9, 1875, CB7–188, JFA; Alberts, "Origins of Black Parishes," 228–29. Each year when Janssens applied for funds from the Commission for the Catholic Missions Among the Colored People and Indians, he complained of the unwillingness of both black and white Catholics to provide financial support for black institutions. See Reports to the Commission for the Catholic Missions Among the Colored People and Indians (1889–1897), 161-DY-1 to 161-DY-9, JFA.

35. Francis Janssens, "The Negro Problem and the Catholic Church," *Catholic World* 44 (1887): 724; Janssens, SQA-RCCM (1890), 161-DY-2. See also Janssens to John Slattery, November 21, 1887, 7-D-1, JFA; Janssens to Slattery, February 4, 1889, 7-D-8, JFA; Memorandum for Guste, 4; Misch, "American Bishops," 434.

36. Bell, *Revolution, Romanticism*, 65–88; Memorandum for Guste, 2. Claude Maistre, pastor of St. Rose of Lima Church in New Orleans, opposed the Confederacy, ministered to Union troops, and refused to keep separate registers for the black members of his congregation. Maistre's actions led Archbishop Odin to place Maistre and his church under interdict, and so Maistre built a new schismatic church to uphold his racial views. Eventually, however, Maistre "repented" and was reinstated to the priesthood. Baudier, *Centennial St. Rose of Lima Parish, New Orleans, La.* (New Orleans, 1957), 20–28, Parish History Collection, AANO; Stephen J. Ochs, *A Black Patriot and a White Priest: André Cailloux and Claude Paschal Maistre in Civil War New Orleans* (Baton Rouge: Louisiana State University Press, 2000).

37. Archbishop Napoleon Joseph Perche, "Pastoral Letter of His Grace the Archbishop of New Orleans, Prescribing Prayers and Thanksgiving for the Happy End of Our Political Troubles," May 1, 1877, p. 2, Pastoral Letters, AANO; Memorandum for Guste, 2. On Perche and his pro-Southern views, see also Baudier, *Catholic Church in Louisiana*, 443–59; Baudier, "Archbishop of New Orleans," 3, Archbishop Janssens, 14–04–01–04, BCP. Methodists in New Orleans reacted angrily to Perche's support of the Redeemer governor (and by implication, the racial views) and his call for a day of thanksgiving in May 1877. See "The Archbishop and Governor Nicholls," *SWCA*, May 10, 1877.

38. Canon Peter L. Benoit, Diary of a Trip to America, February 2, 1875, CB6–45, and April 9, 1875, CB7–192, JFA. Baudier also traced a heightened tension between the races to the era of the Civil War ("The War Between the States") and Reconstruction ("carpetbag" rule). Baudier placed the blame for increased antagonism on white Northerners and "Negroes . . . [who] became arrogant and lorded it over the whites," not on the racial policies and politics of white Catholics. Memorandum for Guste, 2.

39. Deggs, *No Cross*, 91–92; Canon Peter L. Benoit, Diary of a Trip to America, April 9, 1875, CB7–186, JFA; Memorandum for Guste, 4; Baudier, *Catholic Church in Louisiana*, 420.

40. "Colored Catholics: Archbishop Janssens Discusses the Old St. Joseph's Church Project," newspaper clipping, Archdiocesan Scrapbook, 1893–1897, p. 68, AANO; Herbert Vaughan Diary, February 8, 1872, typescript, Mill Hill Fathers Papers, JFA; Roger Baudier, *Mater Dolorosa Church (1848–1948) Parish Centennial Booklet* (1948), 41, Parish History Collection, AANO; Roger Baudier, *Centennial St. Rose of Lima Parish, New Orleans, La.* (New Orleans, 1957), 20–21, 42, Parish History Collection, AANO; Mother Mary to Roger Baudier, July 17, 1948, Sisters of the Holy Family, 14–05–10–16, BCP; Francis Janssens to Edward Dyer, "Observations on Report: Colored Missions, Diocese of New Orleans, 1896," 4, 52-DY-30, JFA; Janssens, SQA-RCCM (1890), 161-DY-2; Parish Annual Reports, (1884–1885), St. Mary's Parish, N. O., AANO.

41. Canon Peter L. Benoit, Diary of a Trip to America, April 6, 1875, CB7–173, JFA; "Father Dorsey in Louisiana," *Colored Harvest* 3 (January 1903): 381.

42. Joseph Anciaux, "Concerning the Wretched Condition of Negro Catholics in America," 5–6, typescript, Joseph Anciaux File, JFA. On the struggle for black priests, see Cyprian Davis, *Black Catholics*, 145–62, 202–3; Albert J. Foley, *God's Men of Color: The Colored Catholic Priests of the United States, 1854–1954* (New York: Farrar, Straus & Co., 1955); Ochs, *Desegregating the Altar*; Gardiner H. Shattuck Jr., *Episcopalians and Race: Civil War to Civil Rights* (Lexington: University Press of Kentucky, 2000), 15.

43. Roger Baudier, *The Catholic Church in Carrollton* (New Orleans, 1948), 35, Parish History Collection, AANO; Joseph Anciaux, "Concerning the Wretched Condition of Negro Catholics in America," 5, typescript, Joseph Anciaux File, JFA; Baudier, "The Negro and Catholic Education," 2, Catholic Education in Louisiana, 14–03–5–21, BCM; Baudier, "Archdiocese Has Had Four Orders for Colored Women," *Catholic Action of the South*, March 8, 1959; Baudier, *Catholic Church in Louisiana*, 376, 397; Bell, *Revolution, Romanticism*, 128–29; Mary Francis Borgia, *Violets in the King's Garden* (New Orleans: Sisters of the Holy Family, 1976); Cyprian Davis, *Black Catholics*, 105–6; Deggs, *No Cross*; Joseph H. Fichter, "The White Church and the Black Sisters," *U.S. Catholic Historian* 12 (Winter 1994): 31–48; Fessenden, "Veil of Race." On the requirement to labor only among their own race, see Fessenden, "Veil of Race," 203; and Deggs, *No Cross*, 37. On Sisters of Our Lady of Lourdes, see also notes from Brother Benedict Westrick, F.S.C., 124-T-35, JFA. For explorations of expanding women's roles in the Protestant realm, in politics as well as religion, see Glenda Elizabeth Gilmore, *Gender and Jim Crow: The Politics of White Supremacy in North Carolina, 1896–1920* (Chapel Hill: University of North Carolina Press, 1996); and Evelyn Brooks Higginbotham, *Righteous Discontent: The Women's Movement in the Black Baptist Church, 1880–1920* (Cambridge, Mass.: Harvard University Press, 1993).

44. Alberts, "Origins of Black Parishes," 208; "The Rules of the Congregation," Chp II. Nos. 5, 10, Holy Family Sisters Collection, 5–30–19, AANO; Deggs, *No Cross*, 41; Fessenden, "Veil of Race," 187–88. The orders sat in the cathedral by the date of their founding, front to back. As one of the earliest orders in New Orleans, the Holy Family sisters were assigned a pew near the front of the cathedral. See Deggs, *No Cross*, 91, 214–15 (n. 44).

45. Francis Janssens to Mother Katharine, April 29, 1894, Archbishop Janssens Letters to Mother M. Drexel, 1894–1896, Box 30, Folder 16, SBS; Janssens,

SQA-RCCM (1889), 161-DY-1; Janssens to Mother Katharine, February 17, 1893, Archbishop Janssens Letters to Mother M. Drexel, 1893, Box 30, Folder 15, SBS; John Slattery to Janssens, November 12, 1896, Josephite Fathers, Correspondence prior to 1910, AANO.

46. John Slattery to Francis Janssens, November 12, 1896, Josephite Fathers, Correspondence prior to 1910, AANO; Joseph Anciaux, "Concerning the Wretched Condition of Negro Catholics in America," 4–6, typescript, Joseph Anciaux File, JFA; Janssens, SQA-RCCM (1894), 161-DY-6.

47. Baudier, *Catholic Church in Louisiana*, 105, 183; Emily Clark, "By All the Conduct of Their Lives: A Laywoman's Confraternity in New Orleans, 1730–1744," *William and Mary Quarterly* 54 (October 1997): 778; Blassingame, *Black New Orleans*, 11; Donald E. Devore and Joseph Logsdon, *Crescent City Schools: Public Education in New Orleans* (Lafayette, La.: Center for Louisiana Studies, 1991), 41–42.

48. Devore and Logsdon, *Crescent City Schools*, 65–81; Fischer, *Segregation Struggle*, 42–60, 110–32; and Harlan, "Desegregation in New Orleans Public Schools."

49. Canon Peter L. Benoit, Diary of a Trip to America, April 7, 1875, CB7–178, JFA; Dolan, *American Catholic Experience*, 290–91.

50. Enrollment figures derived from totaling the numbers of black parochial school students in the parish annual reports for all parishes examined (1888–1893), AANO; Roger Baudier, "Church Pioneered in Negro Education in the Deep South," *The Claverite* (May-June, 1954), 5–7, clipping, Rousseve Collection, Box 4, Folder 5, ARC. On the rise of separate black Catholic schools in New Orleans in this period and subsequent decades, see John B. Alberts, "Black Catholic Schools: The Josephite Parishes of New Orleans During the Jim Crow Era," *U.S. Catholic Historian* 12 (Winter 1994): 77–98.

51. Francis Janssens to Katharine Drexel, August 8, 1893, Archbishop Janssens Letters to Mother M. Drexel, 1893, Box 30, Folder 15, SBS.

52. Roger Baudier, "The Story of St. Louis School of Holy Redeemer Parish, New Orleans, La.," (1956), White and Negro Relationships, 14–03–4–25, BCM; *History of the Catholic Indigent Orphan Institute, Dauphine and Touro Streets, Destroyed by the Hurricane, September 1915, Rebuilt in 1916* (New Orleans: Board of Directors of the Catholic Indigent Orphan Institute, 1916), copy, Widow Couvent's School Collection, AANO; Lawrence A. Young, "History and Origin of the Marie C. Couvent School at 2021 Pauger St.," pamphlet, Widow Couvent's School Collection, AANO; Bell, *Revolution, Romanticism*, 122–26; Desdunes, *Our People and Our History*, 21–22, 104–6; Rousseve, *Negro in Louisiana*, 43–44, 73.

53. Francis Janssens, SQA-RCCM (1896), 161-DY-5; Nolan, *Catholic Church in Mississippi*, 295; Misch, "American Bishops," 391, 395, 430, 487.

54. *Three Afro-American Congresses*, 153, 158; Slattery, "Some Aspects of the Negro Problem," 604–5; Leonard, *Theology and Race Relations*, 285; *Many Rains Ago: A Historical and Theological Reflection on the Role of the Episcopate in the Evangelization of African American Catholics* (Washington, D.C.: Secretariat for Black Catholics, National Conference of Catholic Bishops, 1990), 39–43; Ochs, *Desegregating the Altar*, 68, 71, 85; William Audley Osborne, *The Segregated Covenant: Race Relations and American Catholics* (New York: Herder and Herder, 1967), 25.

55. Canon Peter L. Benoit, Diary of a Trip to America, April 6, 1875, CB7–172, JFA.

CHAPTER 6
THE DECLINE OF INTERRACIAL CATHOLICISM

1. John Bernard Alberts, "Origins of Black Catholic Parishes in the Archdiocese of New Orleans, 1718–1920" (Ph.D. diss., Louisiana State University, 1998), 192–272; Annemarie Kasteel, *Francis Janssens, 1843–1897: A Dutch-American Prelate* (Lafayette: Center for Louisiana Studies, University of Southwestern Louisiana, 1992), 275–324; Dolores Egger Labbé, *Jim Crow Comes to Church: The Establishment of Segregated Catholic Parishes in South Louisiana* (Lafayette, La.: University of Southwestern Louisiana, 1971); Douglas J. Slawson, "Segregated Catholicism: The Origins of Saint Katherine's Parish, New Orleans," *Vincentian Heritage* 17 (Fall 1996): 141–84.
2. Cyprian Davis, *The History of Black Catholics in the United States* (New York: Crossroads, 1990), 130–31, 185–86; John T. Gillard, *The Catholic Church and the American Negro* (Baltimore: St. Joseph's Society Press, 1929), 38; Henry J. Koren, *The Serpent and the Dove: A History of the Congregation of the Holy Ghost in the United States 1745–1984* (Pittsburgh: Spiritus Press, 1985), 161; Gary W. McDonogh, *Black and Catholic in Savannah, Georgia* (Knoxville: University of Tennessee Press, 1993), 147; Edwardo J. Misch, *The American Bishops and the Negro from the Civil War to the Third Plenary Council of Baltimore (1865–1884)* (Rome: Pontificia Universitas Gregoriana Facultas Historiae Ecclesiasticae, 1968), 37, 40, 66; Edwardo J. Misch, "The American Bishops and the Negro from the Civil War to the Third Plenary Council of Baltimore (1865–1884)" (Ph.D. diss., Pontificia Universitas Gregoriana Facultas Historiae Ecclesiasticae, 1968), 365–67, 391, 470, 502, 563; Stephen J. Ochs, *Desegregating the Altar: The Josephites and the Struggle for Black Priests* (Baton Rouge: Louisiana State University Press, 1990), 62, 75–76; *Three Catholic Afro-American Congresses*, (1893; reprint, New York: Arno Press, 1978), 54.
3. Diary of Archbishop Janssens, Archbishop of New Orleans (1888–1897), AANO; Roger Baudier, *The Catholic Church in Louisiana* (New Orleans: A. W. Hyatt stationery co. 1939), 473; Kasteel, *Janssens*, 1, 12, 17, 19, 26, 28, 32–33, 51, 81, 131–42, 177.
4. R. L. Desdunes, "The Use of Language," *Crusader*, n.d., Item Nos. 1/12/1 to 1/12/5, DFC-CC; "Explains His Position and Says He Will Return to His Post This Week," newspaper clipping, Archdiocesan Scrapbook, 1893–1897, p. 147, AANO; *Crusader*, Item Nos. 1/7/11 and 1/7/5, DFC-CC; Louis A. Martinet to Albion Tourgée, July 4, 1892, Albion Winegar Tourgée Papers, Item No. 6377, Chautauqua County Historical Society, Westfield, NY. I am grateful to Diana Williams who first directed my attention to this collection and provided me a copy of her personal transcription of the relevant portion of this letter. For Black Methodist Episcopal support of Janssens, see, for example, "Political Review," *SWCA*, July 7, 1892; "The Jim Crow Law," *SWCA* January 19, 1893.
5. Francis Janssens, SQA-RCCM (1895), 161-DY-8; "A Church Devoted to Colored Catholics," *Daily Picayune*, May 20, 1895; Janssens to Catherine Drescel [sic], March 14, 1891, Archbishop Janssens Letters to Mother M. Drexel, 1891–1892, Box 30, Folder 14, SBS; "Colored Catholics: Archbishop Janssens Discusses the Old St. Joseph's Church Project," newspaper clipping, Archdiocesan Scrap-

book, 1893–1897, p. 68, AANO; James Cardinal Gibbons, et al., *Mission Work Among the Negroes and Indians* (Baltimore: Foley Bros., 1893), 6.

6. Diary of Archbishop Janssens, Archbishop of New Orleans, AANO; Francis Janssens to Mother Katherine, June 6, 1891, January 9, 1892, January 14, 1892, and September 13, 1892, Archbishop Janssens Letters to Mother M. Drexel, 1891–1892, Box 30, Folder 14, SBS; Janssens to Edward Dyer, "Observations on Report: Colored Missions, Diocese of New Orleans, 1896" 52-DY-30, JFA; Rev. J. Bogaerts, V.G., "Golden Jubilee of the Sisters of the Holy Family" (1892), clipping, Holy Family Sisters Collection, Records, 1892–1987, ARC; Roger Baudier, *Centennial St. Rose of Lima Parish* (1957), 33, Parish History Collection, AANO; Baudier, "The Story of St. Louis School of Holy Redeemer Parish, New Orleans, La." (1956), 12–13, White and Negro Relationships, 14–03–4–25, BCM; and Baudier, Memorandum for Guste, 4–5.

7. Mary Bernard Deggs, *No Cross, No Crown: Black Nuns in Nineteenth-Century New Orleans*, Virginia Meacham Gould and Charles E. Nolan, eds. (Bloomington: Indiana University Press, 2001), 91; Francis Janssens, SQA-RCCM (1890), 161-DY-2; Roger Baudier, "Church Work Among Negroes," Catholic Education in Louisiana (Research Notes), 14–03–5–21, BCM. Janssens first publicly floated his proposal for a black priesthood and vocations in "The Negro Problem and the Catholic Church," *Catholic World* 44 (March 1887): 721–26; Kasteel, *Janssens*, 139–42, 145, 150–51; Ochs, *Desegregating the Altar*, 68.

8. Francis Janssens to Katherine Drexel, August 8, 1893, Archbishop Janssens Letters to Mother M. Drexel, 1893, Box 30, Folder 15, SBS; Janssens, SQA-RCCM (1889), 161-DY-1; Janssens to Very Rev. Thos. Smith, S. General, C.M., August 16, 1893, Archbishop Janssens Letters to Mother M. Drexel, 1893, Box 30, Folder 15, SBS. For Janssens's estimates on the number of black Catholics in Louisiana, and subsequent losses, see his comments in SQA-RCCM (1889–1897), 161-DY-1 to 161-DY-9; Janssens to Edward Dyer, "Observations on Report: Colored Missions, Diocese of New Orleans, 1896, 52-DY-30, JFA. Janssens was bound to be frustrated with his efforts, since later investigations suggest that unreliable statistics led him to overestimate the number of black Catholics in the archdiocese. Janssens therefore created unattainable goals for the numbers he could return to the church. See James G. Dauphine, *A Question of Inheritance: Religion, Education, and Louisiana's Cultural Boundary, 1880–1940* (Lafayette, La.: Center for Louisiana Studies, University of Southwestern Louisiana, 1993), 34–36; Gillard, *The Catholic Church*, 48, 63–64, 258–59; John T. Gillard, *Colored Catholics in the United States* (Baltimore, Md.: Josephite Press, 1941), 88–95, 97; Labbé, *Jim Crow Comes to Church*, 31–33.

9. "St. Katherine's Church: The Old St. Joseph's Puts on a New Dress and Changes Its Name," newspaper clipping, Archdiocesan Scrapbook, 1893–1897, p. 80, AANO; Herbert Vaughan Diary, February 8, 1872, typescript, Mill Hill Fathers Papers, JFA; Canon Peter L. Benoit, Diary of a Trip to America, April 9, 1875, CB7–188, JFA; "The Colored Catholics of New Orleans," *Colored Harvest* 1 (October 1892); Memorandum for Guste, 3; Baudier, *Catholic Church in Louisiana*, 365, 459; Joseph Logsdon and Caryn Cossé Bell, "The Americanization of Black New Orleans," in Arnold R. Hirsch and Joseph Logsdon, eds., *Creole New Orleans: Race and Americanization* (Baton Rouge: Louisiana State University Press, 1992), 234.

10. Francis Janssens, SQA-RCCM (1894), 161-DY-6; Janssens to Mother Katharine, November 11, 1893, Archbishop Janssens Letters to Mother M. Drexel, 1893, Box 30, Folder 15, SBS; Janssens to Edward Dyer, "Observations on Report: Colored Missions, Diocese of New Orleans, 1896," 4, 52-DY-30, JFA; "St. Katherine's Church: The Old St. Joseph's Puts on a New Dress and Changes its Name" and "New Catholic Church," newspaper clippings, Archdiocesan Scrapbook, 1893–1897, pp. 80, 81, AANO.

11. Mother Mary to Roger Baudier, July 17, 1948, Sisters of the Holy Family, 14–05–10–16, BCP.

12. Francis Janssens, SQA-RCCM (1895), 161-DY-8; Joseph Anciaux, "Concerning the Wretched Condition of Negro Catholics in America," 6, typescript, Joseph Anciaux File, JFA; Pierre LeBeau, "Immaculate Conception Church, Palmetto P.O., Louisiana," *Colored Harvest* 2 (October 1898); Memorandum for Guste, 3.

13. Joseph Anciaux, "Concerning the Wretched Condition of the Negro in America," 4–5, typescript, Joseph Anciaux File, JFA; "Our Lady of the Sacred Heart," typescript, Josephite Records, Box 3, XUA; "Diamond Jubilee: Our Lady of the Sacred Heart Parish, 1871–1946, St. Boniface Parish 1871–1917" (1946), 23, Parish History Collection, AANO; Paul Schaeuble to James Blenk, June 23, 1916, St. Boniface Parish, N. O., Correspondence, AANO; letter from St. Joseph's Abbey, St. Benedict, La., n.d., St. Boniface Parish, N. O., Correspondence, AANO; "St. Katherine's Church: The Old St. Joseph's Puts on a New Dress and Changes its Name" and "New Catholic Church," newspaper clippings, Archdiocesan Scrapbook, 1893–1897, pp. 80–81, AANO; Francis Janssens to Edward Dyer, "Observations on Report: Colored Missions, Diocese of New Orleans, 1896," 4, 52-DY-30, JFA; Baudier, *Catholic Church in Louisiana*, 452.

14. *Mission Work Among the Negroes and Indians* (1894) and *Mission Work Among the Negroes and Indians* (1895), clippings, Scrapbook of Publications: Mission Work Among the Negroes and Indians, pp. 10, 14, AANO; Francis Jannsens, SQA-RCCM (1889), 161-DY-1, (1891), 161-DY-4; and (1895), 161-DY-8, JFA; "Colored Catholics: Archbishop Janssens Discusses the Old St. Joseph's Church Project," clipping, Archdiocesan Scrapbook, 1893–1897, p. 68, AANO.

15. "Louisiana," *American Missionary Magazine* 17 (May 1873), clipping, Central Congregational United Church of Christ Records, 1860–1990, Box 10, ARC; J. M. McPherson to M. E. Strieby, February 4, 1878, AMA Archives, Louisiana, microfilm (reel 3), Item No. 46851, ARC; "Leaders and Stewards Minutes and Collections, 1900–1902," May 30, 1902, Wesley M. E. Church, New Orleans, Records (1864–1951), ARC; Francis Janssens to Edward Dyer, "Observations on Report: Colored Missions, Diocese of New Orleans, 1896," pp. 3–4, 52-DY-29 to 52-DY-30, JFA; Janssens to Katharine Drexel, November 11, 1893, Archbishop Janssens' Letters to Mother M. Drexel, 1893, Box 30, Folder 15, SBS; William Barnaby Faherty and Madeline Barni Oliver, *The Religious Roots of Black Catholics of Saint Louis* (St. Louis, Mo.: St. Louis University Press, 1977), 35; Misch, "American Bishops," 455; Ochs, *Desegregating the Altar*, 63, 100, 108.

16. Francis Janssens, SQA-RCCM (1894), 161-DY-6; Janssens to Katharine Drexel, July 4, 1891, Archbishop Janssens' Letters to Mother M. Drexel, 1891–1892, Box 30, Folder 14, SBS; Janssens to Edward Dyer, "Observations on Report: Colored Missions, Diocese of New Orleans, 1896," pp. 3–4, 52-DY-29 to 52-DY-

30, JFA; "Straight University, New Orleans," n.d. [ca. 1908], AMA Archives, Addendum, Series A: Field Records; Subseries: Dillard University, Box 92, Folder 1, ARC; "Straight University, 25th Annual Report (1871)," typescript, AMA Archives, Addendum, Series A: Field Records; Subseries: Dillard University, Box 90, Folder 1, ARC; Roger Baudier, *Centennial, St. Rose of Lima Parish, New Orleans, La.*, 33–35, Parish History Collection, AANO; Dauphine, *A Question of Inheritance*, 53.

17. Francis Janssens to Katharine Drexel, March 4, 1892, Archbishop Janssens' Letters to Mother M. Drexel, 1891–1892, Box 30, Folder 14, SBS; Francis Nugent to Drexel, January 23, 1895, Fr. Nugent, C. M., Letters to Mother M. Drexel, Box 40, Folder 23, SBS; Gillard, *The Catholic Church*, 151, 268–71; Gillard, *Colored Catholics*, 42.

18. Ireland quoted in Sr. Sharon M. Howell, C.S.J., " 'The Consecrated Blizzard of the Northwest': Archbishop John Ireland and His Relationship with the Black Catholic Community," in *Many Rains Ago: A Historical and Theological Reflection of the Episcopate in the Evangelization of African American Catholics* (Secretariat for Black Catholics, National Conference of Bishops, 1990), 40. Cyprian Davis, *Black Catholics*, 131–32; John T. Gillard, *The Catholic Church and the American Negro* (Baltimore: St. Joseph's Society Press, 1929), 37; Koren, *The Serpent and the Dove*, 122–23, 184; McDonogh, *Black and Catholic in Savannah*, 152; Misch, "American Bishops," 386. For a discussion of Catholic approaches to slavery, see John T. McGreevy, *Catholicism and American Freedom: A History* (New York: W. W. Norton, 2003), 43–67.

19. Francis Janssens to Katharine Drexel, April 29, 1894, Archbishop Janssens Letters to Mother M. Drexel, 1894–1896, Box 30, Folder 16, SBS; Francis Janssens, SQA-RCCM (1889), 161-DY-1; "Colored Catholics: Archbishop Janssens Discusses the Old St. Joseph's Church Project," newspaper clipping, Archdiocesan Scrapbook, 1893–1897, p. 68, AANO; Diary of Archbishop Janssens, Archbishop of New Orleans, July 16, 1895, AANO; Janssens to Very Rev. Thos. Smith, August 16, 1893, Archbishop Janssens Letters to Mother M. Drexel, 1893, Box 30, Folder 15, SBS.

20. Francis Janssens, SQA-RCCM (1895), 161-DY-8; (1889), 161-DY-1; and (1891), 161-DY-4; Diary of Archbishop Janssens, Archbishop of New Orleans, August 23, 1892, AANO; "Colored Catholics: Archbishop Janssens Discusses the Old St. Joseph's Church Project," newspaper clipping, Archdiocesan Scrapbook, 1893–1897, p. 68, AANO; Charles E. Nolan, *The Catholic Church in Mississippi (1865–1911)* (Lafayette, La.: Center for Louisiana Studies, University of Louisiana at Lafayette and the Catholic Diocese of Jackson, Jackson, Mississippi, 2002), 315.

21. Francis Janssens to Katharine Drexel, February 13, 1894, and November 17, 1894, Archbishop Janssens Letters to Mother M. Drexel, 1894–1896, Box 30, Folder 16, SBS.

22. Consuela Marie Duffy, *Katharine Drexel: A Biography* (Philadelphia: The Peter Reilly Company, 1965); Patricia Lynch, *Sharing Our Bread for Service* (Bensalem, Pa.: Sisters of the Blessed Sacrament, 1998). The name of the church was originally spelled with an "a" (Katharine) in honor of Drexel and her patron saint but was so often misspelled with an "e" that it eventually adopted that spelling.

23. Bishop Heslin of Natchez, for example, told a priest wanting to establish a separate church that the priest could only proceed if he secured the funds himself, since the diocese would not contribute any. Nolan, *Catholic Church in Mississippi*, 311.

24. "Colored Catholics: Archbishop Janssens Discusses the Old St. Joseph's Church Project," newspaper clipping, Archdiocesan Scrapbook, 1893–1897, p. 68, AANO; Francis Janssens to Francis Nugent, January 9, 1894, Archbishop Janssens Letters to Mother M. Drexel, 1894–1896, Box 30, Folder 16, SBS; "St. Katherine's Church," "A Church Devoted to Colored Catholics," and "New Catholic Church," newspaper clippings, Archdiocesan Scrapbook, 1893–1897, p. 81, AANO; Janssens to the Very Rev. Thos. Smith, August 16, 1893, and Janssens to Katharine Drexel, November 11, 1893, both in Archbishop Janssens Letters to Mother M. Drexel, 1893, Box 30, Folder 15, SBS; Francis Janssens, SQA-RCCM (1894), 161-DY-6.

25. On the domination of American-style politics in this era, see Joy Jackson, *New Orleans in the Gilded Age: Politics and Urban Progress, 1880–1896* (Baton Rouge: Louisiana State University Press, 1969). For an overview of politics in Louisiana as a whole during this period, see William Ivy Hair, *Bourbonism and Agrarian Protest: Louisiana Politics, 1877–1900* (Baton Rouge: Louisiana State University Press, 1969). For a discussion of Americanization in racial terms in New Orleans, see Bell and Logsdon, "The Americanization of Black New Orleans."

26. Jay P. Dolan, *The American Catholic Experience: A History From Colonial Times to the Present* (Notre Dame, Ind.: University of Notre Dame Press, 1992), 294, 304–17; Avery Robert Dulles, *Models of the Church* (Garden City, N.Y.: Doubleday, 1974), 31–41; Gerald P. Fogarty, *The Vatican and the American Hierarchy From 1870 to 1965* (Stuttgart: Anton Hiersemann, 1982), 10, 35; Charles R. Morris, *American Catholic: The Saints and Sinners Who Built America's Most Powerful Church* (New York: Times Books, 1997), 81–112; Ochs, *Desegregating the Altar*, 73–76, 101; Thomas T. McAvoy, *Great Crisis in American Catholic History, 1885–1900* (Chicago: Henry Regnery, 1957); the relationship between Liberalism and American Catholicism stands at the center of McGreevy, *Catholicism and American Freedom*.

27. James Cardinal Gibbons, et al., *Mission Work Among the Negroes and Indians (1896)* (Baltimore, Md.: Foley Bros, 1896), 15, pamphlet, Scrapbook of Publications, AANO; Francis Janssens to Katharine Drexel, May 21, 1895, August 19, 1895, and January 26, 1897; Archbishop Janssens' Letters to Mother M. Drexel, 1894–1896, Box 30, Folder 16, SBS; Janssens to Edward Dyer, April 24, 1897, 52-DY-33, JFA; Janssens SQA-RCCM (1895), 161-DY-8; Alberts, "Origins of Black Parishes," 267.

28. Kasteel, *Janssens*, 301–24; Labbé, *Jim Crow Comes to Church*, 42–62; Slawson, "Segregated Catholicism"; and Alberts, "Origins of Black Parishes," 192–271.

29. "Report of the Proceedings for the Annulment of Act 111 of 1890 by the Citizens Committee," (1897), Charles B. Rousseve Collection, Box 1, Folder 13, ARC; Bell, *Revolution, Romanticism*, 1–2, 24, 38, 41–44, 46–51, 64; Joseph Logsdon with Lawrence Powell, "Rodolphe Lucien Desdunes: Forgotten Organizer of the *Plessy* Protest," in Samuel C. Hyde Jr., ed., *Sunbelt Revolution: The Historical Progression of the Civil Rights Struggle in the Gulf South, 1866–2000* (Gainesville: University of Florida Press, 2003), 43, 56.

30. Rodolphe Lucien Desdunes, *Our People and Our History*, Dorothea Olga McCants, trans. and ed. (Baton Rouge: Louisiana State University Press, 1973), 21–22, 107; Roger Baudier, "The Story of St. Louis School of Holy Redeemer Parish," 4–6, 12, White and Negro Relationships, 14–03–4–25, BCM.

284 • Notes to Chapter Six

31. "Report of the Proceedings for the Annulment of Act 111 of 1890 by the Citizens Committee," (1897), Rousseve Collection, Box 1, Folder 13, ARC; Charles A. Lofgren, *The Plessy Case: A Legal-Historical Interpretation* (New York: Oxford University Press, 1987); Otto H. Olsen, *The Thin Disguise: Turning Point in Negro History*, Plessy v. Ferguson, *A Documentary Presentation (1864–1896)* (New York: Humanities Press, 1967).

32. Edward L. Ayers, *The Promise of the New South: Life After Reconstruction* (New York: Oxford University Press, 1993), 140–42; Barbara Young Welke, *Recasting American Liberty: Gender, Race, Law, and the Railroad Revolution, 1865–1920* (Cambridge: Cambridge University Press, 2001), 296–97, 300–2, 353, 358.

33. Louis Martinet to Albion Tourgée, July 4, 1892, Albion Winegar Tourgée Papers, Item 6377, Chautauqua County Historical Society, Westfield, NY; Francis Janssens, SQA-RCCM (1891), 161-DY-4; and (1892), 161-DY-3. See also Janssens to Katharine Drexel, February 13, 1894, April 29, 1894, and November 11, 1894, Archbishop Janssens Letters to Mother M. Drexel, 1894–1896, Box 30, Folder 16, SBS.

34. Nolan, *Catholic Church in Mississippi*, 311.

35. *Three Afro-American Congresses*, 109–10.

36. *Three Afro-American Congresses*, 12; David Spalding, "The Negro Catholic Congresses, 1889–1894," *Catholic Historical Review* 55 (October 1969): 337–57; Cyprian Davis, *Black Catholics*, 163–96; Ochs, *Desegregating the Altar*, 77–78, 88–89. The proceedings mention two delegates from Louisiana at the first congress, one at the second, and none by the third. See *Three Afro-American Congresses*, 22–23, 93, 132.

37. "The Meaning of Creole," *Catholic Morning Star*, August 4, 1894; Charles Gayarré, *The Creoles of history and the Creoles of romance. A lecture delivered in the hall of the Tulane University, New Orleans, by Hon. Charles Gayarré, on the 25th of April, 1885* (New Orleans: C. E. Hopkins, 1885). An 1880 census report on New Orleans, for example, noted that "while there are French, Spanish, and even, for convenience, 'colored' Creoles, there are no English, Scotch, Irish, Western, or 'Yankee' Creoles, these all being included under the distinctive term 'Americans.'" George E. Waring, *Social Statistics of Cities: History and Present Condition of New Orleans, Louisiana, and Report on the City of Austin, Texas* (Washington, D.C.: Department of Census, 1888), 10. The meaning of "Creole" was, and remains, a highly contested and polemicized terrain. On the meaning and development of the definition of "Creole," see Arthé Agnes Anthony, "The Negro Creole Community in New Orleans, 1880–1920: An Oral History" (Ph.D. diss., University of California, Irvine, 1978), 24–25; *Colored Harvest* 9 (October 1920): 7; Virginia Domínguez, *White by Definition: Social Classification in Creole Louisiana* (New Brunswick, N.J.: Rutgers University Press, 1986), 100–1, 106, 110, 114–30; Gwendolyn Midlo Hall, *Africans in Colonial Louisiana: The Development of Afro-Creole Culture in the Eighteenth Century* (Baton Rouge: Louisiana State University Press, 1992), 157–59; Charles B. Rousseve, *The Negro in Louisiana: Aspects of His History and His Literature* (New Orleans: Xavier University Press, 1937), 23; and Joseph G. Tregle Jr., "Creoles and Americans," in Hirsch and Logsdon, eds., *Creole New Orleans*, 131–85, who offers a particularly insightful analysis of the changing and contested meanings of "Creole" and the racial myths than have accompanied and informed it.

38. Rodolphe L. Desdunes, *A Few Words to Dr. DuBois with Malice Toward None* (New Orleans, 1907), copy, Desdunes Family Collection, XUA. On Desdunes and Creole separateness, see Logsdon and Powell, "Rodolpe Lucien Desdunes." For a similar sentiment, see Louis A. Martinet to Albion Tourgée, July 4, 1892, Albion Winegar Tourgée papers, Item No. 6377, Chautauqua County Historical Society, Westfield, NY.

39. Desdunes, "Our Constituents," *Crusader*, September 2, 1895, cited in Lester Sullivan, "The Unknown Rodolphe Desdunes: Writings in the New Orleans *Crusader*," *Xavier Review* 10 (Spring 1990): 13.

40. E.W.S. Hammond, "For Colored People," *SWCA*, June 6, 1895; *Three Afro-American Congresses*; Logsdon and Powell, "Rodolphe Lucien Desdunes," 53–54, 56.

41. C. Richards et al, "Petition against Jim Crow Church," January 3, 1894, Negro Church, Protest against Building Colored Missions, 1888–1894, AANO; Alberts, "Origins of Black Parishes," 239–42.

42. R. L. Desdunes, *Daily Crusader*, Item No. 1/24/5, DFC-CC; "A Separate Church," *Crusader*, n.d., clipping, Rousseve Collection, ARC; Logsdon and Powell, "Rodolphe Lucien Desdunes," 61 (n. 41).

43. Thomas Smith to Francis Nugent, July 8, 1894, Thomas J. Smith, C. M., Letters to Mother M. Drexel, Box 51, Folder 16, SBS; R. L. Desdunes, "Mother Katherine Drexel," *Crusader*, March 6, 1895, Item No. 1/24/8, DFC-CC.

44. R. L. Desdunes, "Mother Katherine Drexel and the Color Line," *Crusader*, February 28, 1895, Item No. 1/24/1, DFC-CC; Francis Janssens, SQA-RCCM (1895), 161-DY-8; Alice Ruth Moore, "Louisiana," *Women's Era* 2 (June 1895); "Colored Catholics: Archbishop Janssens Discusses the Old St. Joseph's Church Project," "St. Katherine's Church: The Old St. Joseph's Puts on a New Dress and Changes its Name," "A Church Devoted to Colored Catholics," and "New Catholic Church," newspaper clippings, Archdiocesan Scrapbook, 1893–1897, pp. 68, 80, 81, AANO; Roger Baudier, "Church Work Among Negroes," Catholic Education in Louisiana, 14–03–5–21, BCM.

45. Francis Janssens, SQA-RCCM (1894), 161-DY-6; R. L. Desdunes, "Mother Katherine Drexel and the Color Line," *Crusader*, February 28, 1895, Item No. 1/24/1, DFC-CC; Francis Janssens to Katharine Drexel, November 11, 1893, Archbishop Janssens Letters to Mother M. Drexel, 1893, Box 3, Folder 15, SBS; Alberts, "Origins of Black Parishes," 239.

46. Alice Ruth Moore, "Louisiana," 5; R. L. Desdunes, "Mother Katherine Drexel," *Crusader*, March 6, 1895, Item No. 1/24/8, and R. L. Desdunes, no title, *Crusader*, no date, Item No. 1/24/5, both in DFC-CC; Marcus B. Christian, *A Black History of Louisiana, 1904–1942*, "Chp. 20: The Negro Church in Louisiana," p. 4, Marcus Christian Collection, Literary and Historical Manuscripts, Box 8, Folder 1, UNO; Rousseve, *The Negro in Louisiana*, 139.

47. R. L. Desdunes, "Mother Katherine Drexel," *Crusader*, March 6, 1895, Item No. 1/24/6, and "Mother Katherine Drexel and the Color Line," *Crusader*, February 28, 1895, Item No. 1/24/1, DFC-CC; "A Separate Church," *Crusader*, n.d., and Y.Y.Y., "Prejudice in Catholic Churches," *Crusader*, June 2, 1891, clippings, Rousseve Collection, Box 1, ARC; Cyprian Davis, *Black Catholics*, 195–96.

48. McDonogh, *Black and Catholic in Savannah*, 102–6, 148. 155; Nolan, *Catholic Church in Mississippi*, 311; Cyprian Davis, *Black Catholics*, 185–86; John Muffler,

"This Far by Faith: A History of St. Augustine's, the Mother Church of Black Catholics in the Nation's Capital" (Ed.D. diss., Columbia University, 1989); Koren, *The Serpent and the Dove*, 158; Diary, Diocese of Jackson, Miss., March 23, 1893, copy in files of African-American Religion: A Documentary History Project, Amherst College, Amherst, Mass.; *Three Afro-American Congresses*, 99, 148.

49. Diary, Diocese of Jackson, Miss., March 23, 1893, copy in files of African-American Religion: A Documentary History Project, Amherst College, Amherst, Mass.; Ochs, *Desegregating the Altar*, 38; Misch, "American Bishops," 447. The three who wrote to Janssens had been involved in an earlier unsuccessful effort to raise funds for a separate black Catholic church in 1884. They had located a Jesuit priest to staff their new church but, ironically, ran into resistance from their current parish priest and had to cease their efforts. See Francis Janssens to John Slattery, September 22, 1888, 7-D-6, JFA; Alberts, "Origins of Black Parishes," 195; and Misch, "American Bishops," 447.

50. "St. Katherine's Church: The Old St. Joseph's Puts on a New Dress and Changes its Name," newspaper clipping, Archdiocesan Scrapbook, 1893–1897, p. 80, AANO; Moore, "Louisiana"; "A Separate Church," *Crusader*, n.d., and "Citizen's Committee," *Crusader*, February 14, 1895, clippings, Rousseve Collection, Box 1, ARC; Marcus B. Christian, *A Black History of Louisiana, 1904–1942*, Chp. 20: "The Negro Church in Louisiana," p. 4, Marcus Christian Collection, Literary and Historical Manuscripts, Box 8, Folder 1, UNO; Alberts, "Origins of Black Parishes," 229–30, 239, 248.

51. Arthur Esteves, president; N. E. Mansion, acting secretary, "Citizen's Committee," *Crusader*, February 4, 1895, Rousseve Collection, Box 1, ARC; R. L. Desdunes, "Mother Katherine Drexel," March 6, 1895, Item No. 1/24/6–7, DFC-CC.

52. Francis Janssens to Francis Nugent, January 9, 1894, Archbishop Janssens Letters to Mother M. Drexel, 1894–1896, Box 30, Folder 16, SBS; Nugent to Wm. Rudolph Smith, Esq., July 12, 1894, Fr. Nugent, C. M., Letters to Mother M. Drexel, Box 40, Folder 22, SBS.

53. Adele Wakefield, "A Baleful Tendency," *Crusader*, June 1, 1895, Rousseve Collection, Box 1, ARC; Parish Annual Reports (1895–1920), St. Katherine Parish, N. O., AANO; Alberts, "Origins of Black Parishes," 266; Sick Calls Registers, June 6, 1902–July 28, 1911, St. Joseph's Roman Catholic Church Records, UNO; Roger Baudier, *Golden Jubilee, Church of St. Katherine of Sienna, 1895–1945* (New Orleans, 1945), 4, Parish History Collection, AANO.

54. Pierre Lebeau to John Slattery, June 27, 1900, 18-T-9, JFA; Fogarty, *Vatican and American Hierarchy*, 52–55, 181, 189–90. Chapelle erected only one parish in New Orleans during his entire tenure, suggesting that work among whites suffered as well. Baudier, *Catholic Church in Louisiana*, 493, 495–96.

55. Consuela Marie Duffy, *Katharine Drexel: A Biography* (Philadelphia: Peter Reilly Company, 1965), 314; Parish Annual Reports (1896–1918), St. Katherine Parish, N. O., AANO; Diary of Archbishop Janssens, Archbishop of New Orleans, July 16, 1895, AANO; Labbé, *Jim Crow Comes to Church*, 56–57. On Janssens's negotiations with the Assumptionists, see Kasteel, *Janssens*, 313–24.

56. Roger Baudier, "Catholic Education in Louisiana," (Research Notes), 14–03–5–21, BCM; Parish Annual Reports for all parishes examined, (1897–1905), AANO; Alberts, "Origins of Black Parishes," 275–76; even Baudier conceded that

"Archbishop Chapelle did little or nothing" on behalf of black Catholics. Memorandum for Guste, 6. SQA-RCCM (1889–1905), 161-DY-1 to 161-DY-14.

CHAPTER 7
RENEGOTIATING BLACK CATHOLIC IDENTITY

1. Pierre LeBeau to Justin McCarthy, March 12, 1909, 28-N-19, JFA; Joseph Verrett, S.S.J., interview with author, Baltimore, Md., August 27, 1998; "St. Joan of Arc, New Orleans, Louisiana," Josephite Records Box 2, III-031, XUA; Roger Baudier, *The Catholic Church in Louisiana* (New Orleans, 1939), 516, 559; Roger Baudier, *Mater Dolorosa Church (1848–1948): Parish Centennial Booklet* (New Orleans, 1948), 47–48, Parish History Collection, AANO; Stephen J. Ochs, *Desegregating the Altar: The Josephites and the Struggle for Black Priests* (Baton Rouge: Louisiana State University Press, 1990), 166–67, 169–71. St. Dominic's was renamed St. Joan of Arc in 1923.
2. Parish Annual Reports (1910–1927), St. Joan of Arc Parish, N. O., AANO; "The New Mission in New Orleans Louisiana," *Colored Harvest* 5 (June 1909): 197–98; "Father Lebeau's Year Among Negroes," *Colored Harvest* 6 (June 1910): 42–43.
3. Donald E. Devore and Joseph Logsdon, *Crescent City Schools: Public Education in New Orleans* (Lafayette, La.: Center for Louisiana Studies, University of Southwestern Louisiana, 1991), 118–19, 182–89.
4. Pierre Lebeau to Justin McCarthy, March 12, 1909, 28-N-19, JFA. St. Joseph's Church, near the segregated St. Katherine's, used the proximity of a "colored Church" as reason to limit black Catholics to the last two rows of pews. See J. J. Albert to McCarthy, April, 1909, 28-K-3, JFA. Albert also commented on segregated seating in Our Lady of Lourdes, where the priest had hung a sign "for colored only" over a few of the rear seats. Albert to McCarthy, April 5, 1909, 28-K-2, JFA. Joseph Anciaux, "Concerning the Wretched Condition of Negro Catholics in America," 4, typescript, Joseph Anciaux File, JFA; Memorandum for Guste, 3.
5. Henry C. Dethloff and Robert R. Jones, "Race Relations in Louisiana, 1877–98," *Louisiana History* 9 (Fall 1968): 301–24; Paul A. Kunkel, "Modifications in Louisiana Negro Legal Status Under Louisiana Constitutions, 1812–1957," *Journal of Negro History* 38 (April 1953): 174–95; Germaine A. Reed, "Race Legislation in Louisiana, 1864–1920," *Louisiana History* 6 (Fall 1965): 379–92; Dale A. Somers, "Black and White in New Orleans: A Study in Urban Race Relations, 1865–1900," *Journal of Southern History* 40 (February 1974):19–42. On the Robert Charles Riot, see William Ivy Hair, *Carnival of Fury: Robert Charles and the New Orleans Race Riot of 1900* (Baton Rouge: Louisiana State University Press, 1976); Leon F. Litwack, *Trouble in Mind: Black Southerners in the Age of Jim Crow* (New York: Alfred A. Knopf, 1998), 405–10; and Joel Williamson, *The Crucible of Race: Black-White Relations in the American South Since Emancipation* (New York: Oxford University Press, 1984), 201–209. On North-South reunion and military celebrations that both remembered and healed the divisions of the Civil War, see Gaines M. Foster, *Ghosts of the Confederacy: Defeat, the Lost Cause, and the Emergence of the New South, 1865–1913* (New York: Oxford University Press, 1987); and Charles Reagan Wilson,

Baptized in Blood: The Religion of the Lost Cause, 1865–1920 (Athens, Ga.: University of Georgia Press, 1980), 18–36.

6. John Bernard Alberts, "Origins of Black Catholic Parishes in the Archdiocese of New Orleans, 1718–1920" (Ph.D. diss., Louisiana State University, 1998), 287–88, 313–14; Baudier, *Catholic Church in Louisiana*, 507; Mary Bernadine Hill, "The Influence of James Hubert Blenk on Catholic Education in the Archdiocese of New Orleans, 1885–1917," (M.A. thesis, Louisiana State University, 1964), 51.

7. Baudier, *Catholic Church in Louisiana*, 525.

8. James Blenk to Katharine Drexel, June 29, 1915, Archbishop Blenk Letters to Mother M. Drexel, 1915–1917, Box 4, Folder 7; and Blenk to Drexel, March 25, 1909, Archbishop Blenk Letters to Mother M. Drexel, 1909, Box 4, Folder 6, SBS.

9. James Blenk to Katharine Drexel, March 25, 1909, Archbishop Blenk Letters to Mother M. Drexel, 1909, Box 4, Folder 6, SBS; Pierre Lebeau to Justin McCarthy, May 13, 1909, 28-N-21, JFA. Roger Baudier was among those who emphasized the role and importance of St. Katherine's. See for example his text for the fiftieth-anniversary souvenir booklet for St. Katherine's Parish, *Golden Jubilee, Church of St. Katherine of Sienna* (1945), Parish History Collection, AANO, as well as the introductory comments by W. F. Darling, the church's pastor, in the same booklet, in which he calls St. Katherine's "the mother church of the eleven negro parishes in New Orleans."

10. Pierre Lebeau to Justin McCarthy, January 5, 1909, 28-N-14, JFA; *Holy Redeemer Church 1860–1960* (New Orleans, 1960), Parish History Collection, AANO; Peter Hogan, "Holy Redeemer, New Orleans, Louisiana," typescript, Josephite Records, Box 2, III-134, XUA.

11. Rev. Barbier to Pierre Lebeau, April 13, 1915, 32-R-11b, JFA; Lebeau to Katharine Drexel, February 2, 1914, Rev. P. O. Lebeau S.S.J., Letters to Mother M. Drexel, 1911–1915, Box 33, Folder 31, SBS. In the case of St. Ann's, which became St. Peter Claver, the priest had consulted multiple missionary orders to create a bidding war to generate the highest possible price for his buildings. "St. Peter Claver, New Orleans, Louisiana," Josephite Records, Box 2, III-138, XUA; *The History of St. Peter Claver Parish, Founded October 3, 1920, New Orleans, Louisiana* (n.d.), 1, Parish History Collection, AANO; Louis Pastorelli to John Shaw, August 31, 1918; Pastorelli to Shaw, November 1, 1919; Shaw to Pastorelli, November 5, 1919; Pastorelli to Shaw December 21, 1919; Shaw to Pastorelli, December 25, 1919; Pastorelli to Shaw, December 31, 1919; Pastorelli to Shaw, January 3, 1920; all in Josephite Fathers, Correspondence, 1911–1919 (c), AANO; Baudier, *Catholic Church in Louisiana*, 529; Alberts, "Origins of Black Parishes," 359.

12. "Holy Redeemer Mission, New Orleans," *Colored Harvest* 9 (June 1920): 5; Pierre Lebeau to Justin McCarthy, May 31, 1909, 28-N-21, JFA; Lebeau to McCarthy, November 3, 1909, 29-D-17, JFA; and J. J. Albert to McCarthy, March 29, 1909, 28-K-1, JFA; *Josephite Harvest* 78 (Fall, 1976): 18; Joseph Lally to Louis Pastorelli, October 29, 1923, 41-K-16, JFA. As late as 1920, pastors at St. Dominic expressed concern and frustration at the location of the church relative to the population they served. See Parish Annual Report (1921), St. Joan of Arc Parish, N. O., AANO; Joseph Wareing to Pastorelli, May 9, 1921, 39-V-11, JFA; and J. A. St. Laurent to Pastorelli, May 13, 1920, St. Laurent Correspondence, JFA; interview

with Mrs. Edna St. Cyr Williams by Sr. Mary Reginald, Oblate of Providence and Sr. Roberta Smith, S.B.S., n.d., typescript, JFA.

13. "The Negro Vow Taken By Priests St. Joseph's Society of the Sacred Heart," *Colored Harvest* 4 (March 1904): 473; Pierre Lebeau to John Slattery, August 28, 1898, 18-S-16, JFA; and Slattery to Joseph Anciaux, February 19, 1900, 11-D-18, JFA. The Josephites arose from the Mill Hill Foreign Missionary Society, an order based in Mill Hill, England. The Josephites became an independent American-based order in 1893. *The Josephites: A Century of Evangelization in the African American Community* (Baltimore, Md.: The Josephites, 1993), 20, 22; Ochs, *Desegregating the Altar*, 83. Ochs's study, while primarily an examination of the quest for black priests, focuses on that struggle within the Josephite community and thus also constitutes the best history of the Josephite order. Cyprian Davis, *The History of Black Catholics in the United States* (New York: Crossroads, 1990), 199–200.

14. On Katharine Drexel and the Sisters of the Blessed Sacrament, see Consuela Marie Duffy, *Katharine Drexel: A Biography* (Philadelphia: Peter Reilly Company, 1965); Patricia Lynch, *Sharing Our Bread for Service* (Bensalem: Sisters of the Blessed Sacrament, 1998).

15. Samuel Kelly to Justin McCarthy, April 12, 1909, 28-N-2, JFA; John T. Gillard, *The Catholic Church and the American Negro* (Baltimore, Md.: St. Joseph's Society Press, 1929), 217.

16. Albert S. Foley, S.J., *God's Men of Color: The Colored Catholic Priests of the United States, 1854–1954* (New York: Farrar, Straus & Co., 1955), 81–94; Ochs, *Desegregating the Altar*, 164–174. Ochs lists another Creole of color, Adrian Esnard, who was ordained in 1905 as the eighth black American to become a priest. While Esnard was from New Orleans, he was never a priest in the United States. He attended seminary and was ordained in Europe and became a missionary in Africa. Therefore, he was not a priest in the United States as were the seven before him, and Plantevigne, who followed him. See Foley, *God's Men*, 63–71.

17. John Plantevigne to James Blenk, March 23, 1909, and Blenk to Plantevigne, March 31, 1909, both in Josephite Fathers, Correspondence prior to 1910, AANO. Foley, *God's Men*, 87, claims that Blenk acted at the behest of Josephite Pierre Lebeau, pastor of St. Dominic's, in insisting Plantevigne not come to New Orleans for the mission. However, Lebeau, in a letter to his Superior, expressed his regret that Plantevigne could not come, placing the blame on the archbishop's objection. Pierre Lebeau to Justin McCarthy, March 20, 1909, 28-N-20, JFA.

18. John Plantevigne to James Blenk, March 23, 1909, and Plantevigne to Blenk, April 13, 1909, both in Josephite Fathers, Correspondence prior to 1910, AANO; John J. Albert to Justin McCarthy, March 29, 1909, 28-K-1, JFA; Plantevigne to McCarthy, April 1, 1909, 27-R-1, JFA; Albert to McCarthy, March 29, 1909, 28-K-1, JFA.

19. John J. Albert to Justin McCarthy, March 29, 1909, 28-K-1, JFA; and Samuel Kelly to McCarthy, April 12, 1909, 28-N-2, JFA.

20. John Plantevigne to James Blenk, April 13, 1909, Josephite Fathers, Correspondence prior to 1910, AANO; Foley, *God's Men*, 91; Ochs, *Desegregating the Altar*, 174; Lucille Hutton, "This is a Grand Work: A History of Central Congregational Church (United Church of Christ) New Orleans, Louisiana, 1872–1977,"

(1977), p. 58, Central Congregational United Church of Christ, Records, 1860–1990, Box 10, ARC.

21. John Shaw to Louis Pastorelli, April 12, 1920, 69-S-30, JFA; and J. A. St. Laurent to Pastorelli, September 15, 1920, St. Laurent Correspondence, JFA; Cyprian Davis, *Black Catholics*, 233–34; Gary W. McDonogh, *Black and Catholic in Savannah, Georgia* (Knoxville: University of Tennessee Press, 1993), 220; Ochs, *Desegregating the Altar*, 162–63, 175.

22. Louis Pastorelli to John Shaw, November 2, 1920, St. Peter Claver Parish, N. O., Correspondence, 1920–1936, AANO; Pastorelli to Shaw, December 31, 1919, Josephite Fathers, Correspondence, 1911–1919 (c), AANO.

23. James Blenk to Katharine Drexel, March 25, 1909, Archbishop Blenk Letters to Mother M. Drexel, 1909, Box 4, Folder 6, SBS; John Shaw to Louis Pastorelli, April 12, 1920, 69-S-30, JFA; Blenk to Drexel, June 29, 1915, Archbishop Blenk Letters to Mother M. Drexel, 1915–1917, Box 4, Folder 7, SBS; John A. Clarke, S.S.J., "Memorandum: Concerning the Erection of a Church in the Vicinity of the Southern University," Josephite Fathers, Miscellaneous Documents, 1897–1920, AANO.

24. Avery Robert Dulles, *Models of the Church* (Garden City, N.Y.: Doubleday, 1974), 31–42, 153.

25. J. A. St. Laurent to Louis Pastorelli, May 22, 1920, and October 21, 1920, both in St. Laurent Correspondence, JFA; and Joseph Lally to Pastorelli, January 26, 1920, 38-K-24, JFA.

26. Alberts, "Origins of Black Parishes," 312, 354. For examples of the efforts to create a territorial black parish system in New Orleans, see "Limits of the Parishes for Colored People," n.d., St. Joan of Arc Parish, N. O., Correspondence, 1916–1934, AANO; Rev. S. J. Kelly, handwritten note on boundaries, n.d., Corpus Christi Parish, N. O., Correspondence, 1916–1931, AANO; James Blenk to Thomas Finny, C.M. (telegram), September 21, 1916, Corpus Christi Parish, N. O., Correspondence, 1916–1931, AANO; "A Decree," September 16, 1915, Blessed Sacrament Parish, N.O., Historical Documents, 1915–1919, AANO; "A Decree," September 21, 1915, Holy Ghost Fathers, Historical and Religious Documents, AANO; map, n.d., in Holy Ghost Parish, N. O., Correspondence, 1915–1925, AANO; "Decree for Boundaries of New Parish," December 24, 1919, Holy Redeemer Parish, N. O., Historical Documents, 1869–1922, AANO; St. Laurent to Pastorelli, November 8, 1920, St. Laurent Correspondence, JFA.

27. Jay P. Dolan, *The American Catholic Experience: A History From Colonial Times to the Present* (Notre Dame: University of Notre Dame Press, 1992), 335; John Tracy Ellis, *American Catholicism* (Chicago: University of Chicago Press, 1956), 89, 94; Joseph T. Leonard, *Theology and Race Relations* (Milwaukee: Bruce Publishing Co., 1963), 287; Ochs, *Desegregating the Altar*, 18–9, 31.

28. James Blenk to Katharine Drexel, March 25, 1909, Archbishop Blenk Letters to Mother M. Drexel, 1909, Box 4, Folder 6, SBS; Ochs, *Desegregating the Altar*, 137, 175, 179.

29. Dulles, *Models of the Church*, 35. Although the assertion referred primarily to differences between clergy and laity, it was easily transferred to other differences as well. This was especially true once the priesthood was closed to blacks, which created an intersection between lay-clergy and black-white differences.

30. Gillard, *The Catholic Church*, 69, 71, 76–88; Cyprian Davis, *Black Catholics*, 197; Dulles, *Models of the Church*, 41. In 1958, after balking by southern bishops and insistence by Pope Pius XII, the bishops of the United States released their first statement placing segregation in a religious framework: "Discrimination and the Christian Conscience." Among the first twentieth-century American Catholic theologians to recognize the moral dimensions of segregation was Francis J. Gilligan, *The Morality of the Color Line: An Examination of the Right and Wrong of the Discriminations Against the Negro in the United States* (1928; reprint, New York: Negro University Press, 1969), ix, 47, 59, 175–209. See also John LaFarge, *The Catholic Viewpoint on Race Relations* (Garden City, N.Y.: Hanover House, 1956), 19, 186–92; Leonard, *Theology and Race Relations*, 9, 29, 259–61, 282; John T. McGreevy, *Catholicism and American Freedom: A History* (New York: W. W. Norton, 2003), 208–11; John T. McGreevy, *Parish Boundaries: The Catholic Encounter with Race in the Twentieth-Century Urban North* (Chicago: University of Chicago Press, 1995), 90–91; Ochs, *Desegregating the Altar*, 222, 228.

31. Gillard, *The Catholic Church*, 73; Ochs, *Desegregating the Altar*, 181; James Blenk to Katharine Drexel, March 25, 1909, Archbishop Blenk Letters to Mother M. Drexel, 1909, Box 4, Folder 6, SBS (emphasis mine); Dulles, *Models of the Church*, 38.

32. Ochs, *Desegregating the Altar*, 124, 133, 173, 241.

33. John Shaw to Louis Pastorelli, April 12, 1920, 69-S-30, JFA; Alberts, "Origins of Black Parishes," 372.

34. "The Meaning of 'Creole'," *Catholic Morning Star*, August 4, 1894; Alecia P. Long, *The Great Southern Babylon: Sex, Race, and Respectability in New Orleans, 1865–1920* (Baton Rouge: Louisiana University State Press, 2004), 209, 212, 216; Virginia R. Domínguez, *White by Definition: Social Classification in Creole Louisiana* (New Brunswick, N.J.: Rutgers University Press, 1986), 28–32, 93–94; Alice Dunbar-Nelson, "People of Color in Louisiana, Part I," *Journal of Negro History* 1 (October 1916): 366–67; "What is a Colored Creole," *Colored Harvest* 9 (October, 1920); Arthé Anthony, "The Negro Creole Community in New Orleans, 1880–1920: An Oral History" (Ph.D. diss., University of California Irvine, 1978); Joseph G. Tregle Jr., "Creoles and Americans," in Arnold R. Hirsch and Joseph Logsdon, eds., *Creole New Orleans: Race and Americanization* (Baton Rouge: Louisiana State University Press, 1992), 131–85.

35. Rodolphe Lucien Desdunes, *A Few Words to Dr. Du Bois: "With Malice Toward None"* (New Orleans, 1907), 11, copy, Desdunes Family Collection, XUA. Alberts, "Origins of Black Parishes," 139. On the collapse from a tripartite to biracial classification and its impact on Creoles, see Joseph Logsdon and Caryn Cossé Bell, "The Americanization of Black New Orleans, 1850–1900," in Hirsch and Logsdon, eds., *Creole New Orleans*, 201–261.

36. James Blenk to Katharine Drexel, March 25, 1909, Archbishop Blenk Letters to Mother M. Drexel, 1909, Box 4, Folder 6, SBS; Pierre Lebeau to Justin McCarthy, April 12, 1912, 29-D-40, JFA; Samuel Kelly to Katharine Drexel, May 28, 1917, Fr. Samuel Kelly, S.S.J. Letters to Mother M. Drexel, Box 32, Folder 13, SBS; "French and English," *Catholic Morning Star*, September 28, 1895; *Catholic Morning Star*, April 2, 1898; Roger Baudier, *Centennial St. Rose of Lima Parish* (New Orleans, 1957), 17, 48, Parish History Collection, AANO; Alberts, "Origins of

Black Parishes," 294, 343–45. The predominantly Creole Holy Family sisters had begun the transition to English as early as the 1890s, despite very strong connections to and heritage in the city's Francophone culture.

37. Alberts, "Origins of Black Parishes," 282–90; George E. Cunningham, "The Italian, a Hindrance to White Solidarity in Louisiana, 1890–1898," *Journal of Negro History* 10 (January 1965): 22–36; Noel Ignatiev, *How the Irish became White* (New York: Routledge, 1995); McDonogh, *Black and Catholic in Savannah*, 45. For wider considerations of the relation of ethnicity to race, and especially the homogenization of whiteness, see Richard D. Alba, *Ethnic Identity: The Transformation of White America* (New Haven: Yale University Press, 1990); Matthew Frey Jacobson, *Whiteness of a Different Color: European Immigrants and the Alchemy of Race* (Cambridge, Mass.: Harvard University Press, 1998).

38. Alberts "Origins of Black Parishes," 332. Alberts's dissertation is primarily about this process of creating territorial parishes to conform to the 1918 Vatican decree on regular parishes. On the push for territorial parishes and its implication for race and separate churches, see especially 316–21. On separate racial churches and the declining place of national churches, see Lizabeth Cohen, *Making a New Deal: Industrial Workers in Chicago, 1919–1939* (New York: Cambridge University Press, 1990), 55, 83–94; John T. Gillard, *Colored Catholics in the United States* (Baltimore, Md.: The Josephite Press, 1941), 115; McGreevy, *Parish Boundaries*, 9–13, 29–38.

39. McDonogh, *Black and Catholic in Savannah*, 306.

40. In reality, there were far fewer black than white Catholic churches. As a result, many black parishioners, unlike whites, had to travel great distances to reach their "territorial" parishes, since black congregations were assigned existing buildings rather than new facilities appropriately centered within the territories and communities they served. Josephite priests often complained of this problem of location. For examples of such complaints, see Pierre Lebeau to Justin McCarthy, May 13, 1909, 28-N-21, JFA; Joseph Waering to Louis Pastorelli, May 19, 1921, 39-V-11, JFA; and *Colored Harvest* 7 (June 1920): 5. The maps and correspondence that illustrate the emerging separate territorial system for the city's black Catholics began with St. Dominic's in 1909 and continued with the opening of each new separate black parish in New Orleans. See, for example, "Limits of the Parishes for Colored People," n.d., St. Joan of Arc Parish, N. O., Correspondence, 1916–1934, AANO; "A Decree," September 16, 1915, Blessed Sacrament Parish, N. O., Historical Documents, 1915–1919, AANO; "A Decree," September 21, 1915, Holy Ghost Fathers, Historical and Religious Documents, AANO; map, n.d., in Holy Ghost Parish, N. O., Correspondence, 1915–1925, AANO; Rev. S. J. Kelly, hand-written note on boundaries, n.d., Corpus Christi Parish, N. O., Correspondence, 1916–1931, AANO; James Blenk to Thomas Finny, C. M. (telegram), September 21, 1916, Corpus Christi Parish, N. O., Correspondence, 1916–1931, AANO; "Decree for Boundaries of New Parish," December 24, 1919, Holy Redeemer Parish, N. O., Historical Documents, 1869–1922, AANO; J. A. St. Laurent to Pastorelli, November 8, 1920, St. Laurent Correspondence, JFA.

41. "Archbishops Meet," *Colored Harvest* (January 1907): 2; Cyprian Davis, *Black Catholics*, 195–207; Dolan, *American Catholic Experience*, 319, 355; Henry J. Koren, *The Serpent and the Dove: A History of the Congregation of the Holy Ghost in the United*

States 1745–1984 (Pittsburgh: Spiritus Press, 1985), 185; LaFarge, *Catholic View-point*, 55; Ochs, *Desegregating the Altar*, 140–42.

42. Dorothy Ann Blatnica, *At the Altar of Their God: African American Catholics in Cleveland, 1922–1961* (New York: Garland, 1995), 40, 55–56, 66–67; Dolan, *American Catholic Experience*, 365–66; William Barnaby Faherty and Madeline Barni Oliver, *The Religious Roots of Black Catholics of Saint Louis* (St. Louis: St. Louis University Press, 1977), 8; Gillard, *The Catholic Church*, 46, 48, 58, 60.

43. "Colored Catholics Plan Confederation of Societies," May 23, [no year], press release, 32-H-234, JFA; Joseph Lally to A. J. Bruening, n.d., Josephite Fathers, Correspondence, 1920–1932, AANO; "Colored Federation," *Colored Harvest* 8 (January 1917): 11; "The Federation of Catholic Societies for the Colored People of the Gulf States," *Catholic Morning Star*, September 1, 1917; "Federation of Colored Catholic Societies of the Gulf States," *Catholic Morning Star*, September 22, 1917. On "black churches" and "white churches," see for example, Pierre Lebeau to Justin McCarthy, May 13, 1909, 28-N-21, JFA; and Fr. Anselm to John Shaw, December 32, 1921, Josephite Fathers, Correspondence, 1920–1932, AANO.

44. Pierre Lebeau to Katharine Drexel, November 21, 1911, Rev. P. O. Lebeau S.S.J. Letters to Mother M. Drexel, 1911–1915, Box 33, Folder 31, SBS; J. J. Albert to Justin McCarthy, April 5, 1909, 28-K-2, JFA; and Albert to McCarthy, April 1909, 28-K-3, JFA.

45. Alberts, "Origins of Black Parishes," 362; interview with Mrs. Edna St. Cyr Williams by Sr. Mary Reginald, Oblate of Providence and Sr. Roberta Smith, S.B.S., p. 5, typescript, JFA; Faherty and Oliver, *Religious Roots*, 33; John Albert to Justin McCarthy, April, 1909, 28-K-3, JFA. For the decline in baptisms, see Parish Annual Reports for all parishes examined (1895–1920), AANO; Alberts, "Origins of Black Parishes," 339.

46. Loren Schweninger, "Antebellum Free Persons of Color in Postbellum Louisiana," *Louisiana History* 30 (Fall 1989): 345–64. Light-skinned leaders in Savannah, for example, experienced a similar decline in wealth and status. See McDonogh, *Black and Catholic in Savannah*, 48. On Tureaud and changing leadership, see Arnold Hirsch, "Simply a Matter of Black and White," in Hirsch and Logsdon, eds., *Creole New Orleans*, 263–70. Hirsch characterizes the period between the Plessy case and the new generation exemplified by Tureaud as one dominated by patronage and a system of personal rather than communal relationships and organized resistance.

47. "History of the Catholic Indigent Orphan Institute, Dauphine and Touro Streets, Destroyed by the Hurricane September 1915, Rebuilt in 1916," (Board of Directors, 1916), Widow Couvent's School Collection, AANO; [Louis Charbonnet], "Report to Board of Directors," Record Books, Catholic Institute for Indigent Orphans (1915–1920), Widow Couvent's School Collection, AANO, November 9, 1916; and Lawrence A. Young, "History and Origin of the Marie C. Couvent School at 2021 Pauger St.," Widow Couvent's School Collection, AANO; "The Lafon Will," 1894, clipping, Archdiocesan Scrapbook, 1893–1897, AANO; Roger Baudier, "The Story of St. Louis School of Holy Redeemer Parish, New Orleans, La.," 5, 8–9, 12–13, typescript, White and Negro Relationships, 14-03-4-25, BCM; "Memo de School for Indigent Colored Children of N.O., La.," Holy Redeemer Parish, N. O., Historical Documents, 1869–1922, AANO; "Petition of Most Rev. Francis Xavier Leray to Civil District Court in the Case of the 'Society

for the Instruction of Indigent Orphans,' " n.d., Holy Redeemer Parish, N. O., St. Louis School, Historical Documents (Baudier Research Notes), AANO; Sr. M. Georgiana Rockwell, S.B.S., "Vision-Reality: Madame Couvent l'Institution Catholique des Orphelins Indigents Mother M. Katharine Drexel-St. Louis School, New Orleans," 6–7, manuscript, Charles B. Rousseve Collection, Box 4, Folder 6, ARC; Rodolphe Lucien Desdunes, *Our People and Our History: A Tribute to the Creole People of Color in Memory of the Great Men They Have Given Us and of the Good Works They Have Accomplished*, originally published as *Nos Hommes et Notre Histoire* (1911), Dorothea Olga McCants, trans. and ed. (Baton Rouge: Louisiana State University Press, 1973), 21–22, 101–8; Charles B. Rousseve, *The Negro in Louisiana: Aspects of His History and His Literature* (New Orleans: Xavier University Press, 1937), 43–44.

48. *Record Books, Catholic Institute for Indigent Orphans (1915–20)*, 41, 44, 86, 115–20, Widow Couvent's School Collection, AANO; [Louis Charbonnet] "Report to Board of Directors," November 9, 1916, *Record Books, Catholic Institute for Indigent Orphans (1915–20)*, Widow Couvent's School Collection, AANO; Sr. M. Georgiana Rockwell, S.B.S., "Vision-Reality: Madame Couvent l'Institution Catholique des Orphelins Indigents Mother M. Katharine Drexel-St. Louis School, New Orleans," 9, Rousseve Collection, Box 4, Folder 6, ARC; Roger Baudier, "The Story of St. Louis School of Holy Redeemer Parish, New Orleans, La.," 14, White and Negro Relationships, 14–03–4–25, BCM.

49. *Record Books, Catholic Institute for Indigent Orphans (1915–20)*, 93, 115–16, 124–25, 129–30, Widow Couvent's School Collection, AANO; Sr. M. Georgiana Rockwell, S.B.S., "Vision-Reality: Madame Couvent l'Institution Catholique des Orphelins Indigents Mother M. Katharine Drexel-St. Louis School, New Orleans," 10, 16, Rousseve Collection, Box 4, Folder 6, ARC; Roger Baudier, "The Story of St. Louis School of Holy Redeemer Parish, New Orleans, La.," 14–15, 17, White and Negro Relationships, 14–03–4–25, BCM. Over the next generation the school came under the regular control of the parish and its pastor, and became known as the St. Louis School of Holy Redeemer parish.

50. John J. McWilliams to John Shaw, May 22, 1919, Vincentian Fathers (Lazarists), Correspondence, 1897–1932, AANO; Pierre Lebeau to Justin McCarthy, May 13, 1909, 28-N-21, JFA; Parish Annual Reports for all parishes examined, (1893–1920), AANO; "Corpus Christi, New Orleans, Louisiana," p. 2, Josephite Records, Box 2, III-013, XUA; "Dedication in New Orleans," *Colored Harvest* 5 (January 1920): 5–7.

51. John Shaw to J. A. St. Laurent, March 18, 1922, copy, St. Peter Claver Parish, N. O., Correspondence, 1920–1936, AANO.

52. Katharine Drexel to James Blenk, May 16, 1915, Sisters of the Blessed Sacrament, Correspondence, 1898–1917 (a), AANO; Joseph Lally to Louis Pastorelli, February 19, 1919, 36-L-1, JFA; A. J. Bell to John Shaw, September 17, 1920, Blessed Sacrament Parish, N. O., Correspondence, 1915–1918, AANO; Samuel Kelly to Katharine Drexel, December 31, 1918, Fr. Samuel Kelly, S.S.J. Letters to Mother M. Drexel, Box 32, Folder 13, SBS; Lally to Pastorelli, June 20, 1920, 38-K-36, JFA; James Blenk to Katharine Drexel, Archbishop Blenk Letters to Mother M. Drexel, 1915–1917, Box 4, Folder 7, SBS; John Clarke to Justin McCarthy, June 12, 1915, 32-H-5, JFA; Samuel Kelly to Katharine Drexel, February 5, 1919, Fr.

Samuel Kelly, S.S.J. Letters to Mother M. Drexel, Box 32, Folder 13, SBS; Lynch, *Sharing Our Bread*, 204–7.

53. John J. Albert to Justin McCarthy, April 5, 1909, 28-K-2, JFA; Cyprian Davis, *Black Catholics*, 205; Hirsch, "Simply a Matter of Black and White," 267–68.

54. Parish Annual Reports for all parishes examined (1906–1920), AANO; Roger Baudier, "Catholic Schools by Parish, 1888–1918," Catholic Education in Louisiana, 14–03–5–16, BCP.

55. Joseph Lally to Louis Pastorelli, December 12, 1919, 37-K-17, JFA; Samuel Kelly to Katharine Drexel, January 9, 1920, Fr. Samuel Kelly S.S.J., Letters to Mother M. Drexel, Box 32, Folder 14, SBS; M. M. Agatha Ryan, S.B.S., "Proposed Sketch for Catholic History," n.d., 2–3, Xavier Prep, St. Francis Xavier Convent Annals, Foundation to 1967, SBS; Leo Gassler to Justin McCarthy, September 10, 1914, Josephite Fathers, Correspondence, 1911–1919 (a), AANO; Blatnica, *At the Altar*, 57; Dolan, *American Catholic Experience*, 290–91; Gillard, *The Catholic Church*, 42; Hill, "Influence of James Hubert Blenk," 84; Leonard, *Theology and Race Relations*, 284; McDonogh, *Black and Catholic in Savannah*, 50, 96, 106, 142.

56. "Blessed Sacrament, New Orleans, Louisiana," Josephite Records, Box, 3, III-009, XUA; Roger Baudier, "Development of Catholic Education," 16, Catholic Education in Louisiana, 14–03–5–21, BCM; and Baudier, "Golden Jubilee: The Sisters of the Blessed Sacrament," 10, typescript, St. Katharine, N. O., 14–04–04–26, BCP; "Xavier University Goes Forward with Good Speed," n.d., clipping, Josephite Records, Box 4, XUA; interview with Mrs. Edna St. Cyr Williams by Sr. Mary Reginald, Oblate of Providence and Sr. Roberta Smith, S.B.S., n.d., typescript, JFA.

57. Ochs, *Desegregating the Altar*, 230.

58. John Shaw to Louis Pastorelli, April 12, 1920, 69-S-30, JFA; Shaw to Pastorelli, May 2, 1920, 69-S-31, JFA; Pastorelli to Shaw, May 8, 1920, Josephite Fathers, Correspondence, 1920–1932, AANO; Pastorelli to Shaw, August 6, 1926, 69-S-85, JFA; John J. Albert to Justin McCarthy, March 29, 1909, 28-K-1, JFA; and John Plantevigne to McCarthy, April 1, 1909, 27-R-1, JFA; Alberts, "Origins of Black Parishes," 336.

59. Catholic Society for the Instruction of Indigent Orphans to John Shaw, August 8, 1920, and "Report of Special Meeting," July 29, 1920, *Record Books, Catholic Institute for Indigent Orphans (1915–1920)*, Widow Couvent's School Collection, AANO; Shaw to B. A. Rousseve, April 27, 1922, Holy Redeemer Parish, N. O., Historical Documents, 1869–1922, AANO; Shaw to Sister Mary Camilla, July 21, 1932, Archbishop Shaw Letters to Mother M. Drexel, Box 50, Folder 9, SBS; Roger Baudier, "The Story of St. Louis School of Holy Redeemer Parish, New Orleans, La.," 17, White and Negro Relationships, 14–03–4–25, BCM.

60. J. A. St. Laurent to Katharine Drexel, [1922?], Fr. J. A. St. Laurent, S.S.J., Letters to Mother M. Drexel, Box 49, Folder 13, SBS; Joseph Lally to Louis Pastorelli, October 29, 1923, 41-K-16, JFA; Marcus B. Christian, "A Black History of Louisiana: Churches, 1904–1942," pp. 4–5, typescript, Marcus B. Christian Papers, Literary and Historical Manuscripts, Box 10, Folder 1, UNO; Joseph Lally to Louis Pastorelli, January 26, 1920, 38-K-34, JFA; Fr. Anselm, O.S.B., to John Shaw, December 21, 1921 Josephite Fathers Correspondence, 1920–1932, AANO; Samuel Kelly to Shaw, December 21, 1921, Josephite Fathers, Correspondence, 1920–

1932, AANO; John Shaw to Harry Kane, April 4, 1922, Blessed Sacrament Parish, N. O., Correspondence, 1915–1928, AANO; Parish Annual Reports for all parishes examined (1920–1925), AANO. When St. Peter Claver opened three years earlier, not far from St. Augustine, the priests of the two congregations had an understanding that black parishioners would be free to choose between the two churches and neither forced into St. Peter Claver nor out of St. Augustine's. See St. Laurent to Pastorelli, November 8, 1920, St. Laurent Correspondence, JFA.

61. Joseph Lally to John Shaw, December 4, 1919, Holy Redeemer Parish, N. O., Correspondence, 1919–1936, AANO; Lally to A. J. Bruening, [1919], Josephite Fathers, Correspondence, 1920–1932, AANO.

62. Joseph Verrett, S.S.J., interview with the author, Baltimore, Md., August 27, 1998; interview with Mrs. Edna St. Cyr Williams by Sr. Mary Reginald, Oblate of Providence and Sr. Roberta Smith, S.B.S., n.d., typescript, JFA; "What is a Colored Creole?" *Colored Harvest* 9 (October 1920): 7; Anthony, "Negro Creole Community," 139–62; Domínguez, *White by Definition*, 224; Aline St. Julien, *Colored Creole: Color Conflict and Confusion in New Orleans* (New Orleans: n.p., 1977); McDonogh, *Black and Catholic in Savannah*, 87–89, 143.

EPILOGUE
RELIGION AND BASEBALL IN NEW ORLEANS

1. John Clarke to Katharine Drexel, March 11, 1917, Fr. John Clarke S.S.J., Letters to Mother M. Drexel, 1917, Box 14, Folder 22, SBS.

2. *Journal of the Louisiana Annual Conference of the Methodist Episcopal Church, forty-eighth session, Held at First Street Methodist Episcopal Church New Orleans, La., January 26–31, 1916*, 19, Louisiana Collection, Jones Hall, Tulane University, New Orleans, La.; John Clarke to Katherine Drexel, March 11, 1917, Fr. John Clarke S.S.J., Letters to Mother M. Drexel, 1917, Box 14, Folder 22, SBS; Albert J. Raboteau, *A Fire in the Bones: Reflections on African-American Religious History* (Boston: Beacon Press, 1995), 37–56.

3. Edward L. Ayers, *The Promise of the New South: Life After Reconstruction* (New York: Oxford University Press, 1992), 312; Henry C. Dethloff and Robert R. Jones, "Race Relations in Louisiana, 1877–98," *Louisiana History* 9 (Fall 1968): 312; Dale A. Somers, *The Rise of Sports in New Orleans, 1850–1900* (Baton Rouge: Louisiana State University Press, 1972), 119–21.

4. *SWCA*, June 20, 1912.

5. Alice Knotts, "Race Relations in the 1920s: A Challenge to Southern Methodist Women," *Methodist History* 26 (July 1988): 199–212; Alice Knotts, "Southern Methodist Women and Interracial Relations in the 1930s," *Methodist History* 27 (July 1989): 230–40; John Patrick McDowell, *The Social Gospel in the South: The Women's Home Mission Movement in the Methodist Episcopal Church, South, 1886–1939* (Baton Rouge: Louisiana State University Press, 1982); David M. Reimers, *White Protestantism and the Negro* (New York: Oxford University Press, 1965), 88–90. Secular women's organizations did not actively advocate on behalf of black women's rights until the middle of the twentieth century. See Pamela Tyler, *Silk*

Stockings and Ballot Boxes: Women and Politics in New Orleans, 1920–1950 (Athens, Ga.: University of Georgia Press, 1996).

6. "Ida Weis Friend," in Paula Hyman and Deborah Dash Moore, eds., *Jewish Women in America: An Historical Encyclopedia* (New York: Routledge, 1997); Bobbie Malone, *Rabbi Max Heller: Reformer, Zionist, Southerner, 1860–1929* (Tuscaloosa: University of Alabama Press, 1997). Max Heller, for example, gave a speech at Central Congregation in 1911 entitled, "Manliness Under Prejudice." See "Notable Events in history of Central Congregational Church Commencing with the Year 1907," Central Congregational United Church of Christ, Records, 1860–1990, Box 9, ARC.

7. Barbara Rosendale Duggal, "Marie Laveau: The Voodoo Queen Repossessed," in Sybil Kein, ed., *Creole: The History and Legacy of Louisiana's Free People of Color* (Baton Rouge: Louisiana State University Press, 2000), 157–78; Ron Bodin, *Voodoo: Past and Present* (Lafayette, La.: Center for Louisiana Studies, University of Southwestern Louisiana, 1990); Blake Touchstone, "Voodoo in New Orleans," *Louisiana History* 13 (Fall 1972): 371–86; Lyle Saxon, *Fabulous New Orleans* (New York: Century Co., 1928), 3–69, 243, 309–22. Of course, numerous racialized options also remained a response to the tepid opportunities in biracial traditions. African Methodist and Black Baptists churches continued to flourish throughout the era. New African-American religious alternatives also emerged, though, in keeping with New Orleans's distinctive history, they sometimes developed along unique lines. Most notable in New Orleans were the Spiritual churches. See Claude F. Jacobs and Andrew J. Kaslow, *The Spiritual Churches in New Orleans: Origins, Beliefs, and Rituals of an African-American Religion* (Knoxville: University of Tennessee Press, 1991).

8. Cyprian Davis, *The History of Black Catholics in the United States* (New York: Crossroads, 1990), 220, 224–28, 234; Stephen J. Ochs, *Desegregating the Altar: The Josephites and the Struggle for Black Priests* (Baton Rouge: Louisiana State University Press, 1990), 5, 279; Robert E. Jones to Edwin R. Embree, March 29, 1929, in AMA Archives, Addendum, Series A: Field Records; Subseries: Dillard University, Box 88, ARC.

9. Octavia V. R. Albert, *The House of Bondage* (1890; reprint, New York: Oxford University Press, 1988), 47.

Index

Abbot v. Hicks, 179

African Americans: and anti-Catholicism, 57–61, 251n.31; and Christianity, 31–32, 130–31, 246n.42; commitment to democracy, 133, 134; commitment to racial equality, 8–9, 39–40; and distinct liturgies in the Catholic Church, 214–15; loyalty to the M. E. Church, 130–35; and the notion of the "Best Man," 259–60n.44; and philanthropy, 109–10; racial leadership among in the nineteenth century, 96–97; and religious affiliations, 33–34; supposed sexual aggressiveness of, 83, 107; voting patterns of, 81–83

African Methodist Episcopal (A.M.E.) Church, 15, 27, 47, 117, 140, 188; criticism of by the M. E. church for racial exclusivism, 28–31; criticism of the M. E. church for racial integration, 19–20. *See also* African Methodist Episcopal (A.M.E.) Church, in New Orleans

African Methodist Episcopal (A.M.E.) Church, in New Orleans, 28, 31

African Methodist Episcopal Zion (A.M.E. Zion) Church, 15, 18, 28, 47

Albert, A.E.P., 50–51, 66, 69, 71–74, 80–81, 84–85, 96, 97, 99–100, 104, 108–9, 117, 184, 235; and the Citizens Committee, 85–92; criticism of, 91–92; as editor of the *Southwestern Christian Advocate*, 72–73, 92–93, 94; 182, 233 education of, 71–72; and involvement in *Plessy v. Ferguson*, 85; political activism of, 81; racial advocacy of, 90–92. *See also* American Citizens' Equal Rights Association (ACERA)

Albert, Octavia, 235

Aliquote, Marie-Jeanne, 155

Allen, Richard, 47

American Catholic Tribune, 181, 182

American Citizens' Equal Rights Association (ACERA), 86–87, 89, 91, 92

American Missionary Association, 54, 147

Ames M. E. Church (Ames Chapel), 21, 23, 24, 26, 45, 56, 64, 67, 76, 98

Arthur, Chester A., 65, 66

Asbury, Francis, 131

Assemblies of God, 125

Atlanta, 4, 15, 24, 25, 32, 49, 101, 107

Baptists, 4, 33, 35, 43, 52, 104; and racial uplift policies, 95–96; and women missionaries, 55

baseball, in New Orleans, 40, 61, 164, 229–35, 259n.37

Baudier, Roger, 144, 286–87n.56, 288n.9

Benoit, Peter, 153, 169

Birth of a Nation, 129

Bishops for Races and Languages amendment, 118–20, 121

Blenk, James H., 193, 195–99, 202–3, 204, 225, 289n.17; Southern perspective on race, 210–11, 216

Blessed Sacrament Church, 206

Boston University, 53

Brazil, 8, 142

Brooks, Charlotte, 235

Brown v. Board of Education, 88

Cable, George Washington, 183

Camphor, Alexander P., 267n.50

Catholic Board for Mission Work Among the Colored People, 215–16

Catholic Indigent Orphan Institute, 158–59, 167, 179, 189, 218–19, 225; destruction of by hurricane, 219–20, 224; name change to the St. Louis School, 219–20

Catholic Interracial Council, 235

Catholic World, The, 176

Catholicism/Catholics. *See* Roman Catholic Church; Roman Catholic Church, in New Orleans

Chapelle, Louis Placide, 190–92, 286–87n.56; as archbishop, 194, 286n.54

Charles, Robert, 101, 107

Charles riots. *See* race riots, Charles riots

Chinese immigration laws, 65; African-American opposition to, 65–66

Christian, Marcus, 226

Christian Recorder, 30, 51

Christian Sabbath Union, 85